The British Aes

From Shaftesbury to Wittgenstein

The British Aesthetic Tradition: From Shaftesbury to Wittgenstein is the first single volume to offer readers a comprehensive and systematic history of aesthetics in Britain and the United States from its inception in the early eighteenth century to major developments in the late twentieth century. The book consists of an introduction and eight chapters, divided into three parts. The first part, The Age of Taste, covers the eighteenth-century approaches of internal sense theorists, imagination theorists, and associationists. The second, The Age of Romanticism, takes readers from debates over the picturesque through British Romanticism to late Victorian criticism. The third, The Age of Analysis, covers early twentieth-century theories of Formalism and Expressionism, concluding with Wittgenstein and a number of views inspired by his thought.

Timothy M. Costelloe is Associate Professor of Philosophy at the College of William & Mary. In 2003 and 2006 he was a Humboldt Fellow at Maximilians-Universität München, Germany. He is author of *Aesthetics and Morals in the Philosophy of David Hume* (2007) and editor of *The Sublime: From Antiquity to the Present* (Cambridge, 2012), and his work has appeared in a variety of edited collections and scholarly journals.

For Freyja, Oscar, Adam, Toby, and Daphne

The British Aesthetic Tradition

From Shaftesbury to Wittgenstein

TIMOTHY M. COSTELLOE

College of William & Mary

CAMBRIDGE UNIVERSITY PRESS
Cambridge, New York, Melbourne, Madrid, Cape Town,
Singapore, São Paulo, Delhi, Mexico City

Cambridge University Press
32 Avenue of the Americas, New York, NY 10013-2473, USA

www.cambridge.org
Information on this title: www.cambridge.org/9780521734486

First published 2013

Printed in the United States of America

A catalog record for this publication is available from the British Library.

Library of Congress Cataloging in Publication data
Costelloe, Timothy M.
The British aesthetic tradition : from Shaftesbury to Wittgenstein /
Timothy M. Costelloe.
p. cm.
Includes bibliographical references and index.
ISBN 978-0-521-51830-7 (hardback) – ISBN 978-0-521-73448-6 (paperback)
1. Aesthetics, British – History.   2. Aesthetics, American – History.   I. Title.
BH221.G7C67   2013
111′.850941–dc23   2012021360

ISBN 978-0-521-51830-7 Hardback
ISBN 978-0-521-73448-6 Paperback

Contents

Illustrations

Acknowledgments

My thanks goes, first and foremost, to Beatrice Rehl, Publishing Director, Humanities and Social Sciences, at Cambridge University Press, who first approached me with the idea of writing this book. I am grateful for the confidence she showed in my abilities to complete the project in a satisfactory and timely manner, and for her enthusiastic support and guidance throughout. During the early stages I received useful feedback from David Fate Norton and four anonymous reviewers of the original proposal, and, in the latter stages, from Paul Guyer, who read the completed manuscript in its entirety and made a number of suggestions that proved invaluable when undertaking the final round of revisions. I have benefited enormously over the years from Professor Guyer's knowledge about and insight into the discipline, and I look forward to the appearance of his three-volume *A History of Aesthetics*, which is forthcoming from Cambridge. Initial research for *The British Aesthetic Tradition* was undertaken while I was a visiting scholar at Northwestern University in 2008–9, and I am grateful to the chair and faculty members of its philosophy department for their hospitality, and to the College of William & Mary for release from usual teaching and administrative duties during my sabbatical. I have Rachel Zuckert to thank for the invitation to spend the year at Northwestern and for the opportunity it provided for us to read together and discuss many of the issues and texts that subsequently formed the backbone of the book. I have learned a good deal from her. I am grateful to Adam Potkay for his generous comments and gentle guidance in my reading and understanding of the British Romantics, and to the students in my aesthetics classes at William & Mary – especially those in the Advanced Seminar on Eighteenth-Century British Aesthetics that I taught in the spring of 2008 – in whose presence I rehearsed material and who kept me, more or less, on the straight and narrow. Needless to say, I alone am responsible for the final product and any waywardness it might contain. Elements of Chapters 1 and 2 formed the basis for "Imagination and Internal Sense: The Sublime in Shaftesbury, Reid, Addison, and Reynolds," Chapter 4 in *The Sublime: From Antiquity to the Present*, ed. Timothy M. Costelloe (Cambridge: Cambridge University Press, 2012), 50–63.

Preface

In a *nota bene* to the introduction of his *Elements of Criticism*, Henry Home, Lord Kames, informs readers of his decision to omit the definite article from the title in order to avoid the impression that he ever intended to exhaust his subject, as if it were possible to enumerate *all* the elements of criticism rather than offer a representative selection from a very large sample: because the "author is far from imagining that he has completed the list," Kames writes, "a more humble title is proper, such as may express any number of parts less than the whole" (*Elements* 1.19). The title of the present study – *The British Aesthetic Tradition* – would not survive grammatically without a definite article, but, in the spirit of Kames, its retention should not be read as a claim to have written a definitive or exhaustive study. Some readers will object to the choice of figures and themes included, as others will wonder at those omitted, or find reason to criticize the relative space devoted to each and what is claimed of and for the content of their work. The gracious reader might bear in mind, however, that, by one estimate, the number of publications on aesthetics in the eighteenth century alone ran to some five thousand, and one dare not even speculate on how many fold that has risen with the passage of time, developments in publishing, and the growth of an academic industry. Besides, a history of thought is less a mirror of reality than a representation of its subject matter, crafted in good faith, accurate and honest as it goes, but refracted in the narrative it develops: something must always be left out and surely, as Hume remarks of the *Iliad*, the reader does not want to know every time Achilles ties his shoelaces.

Although the present study has no pretensions to be definitive, its design is not arbitrary nor its perspective partial. The book aims to give the reader a coherent and unified view of the tradition of British "philosophical aesthetics," and the criterion for selection is simply that the thinker in question has made an original or noteworthy contribution to it. Some figures, arguably, could be removed and others added, but rather like the moments of consciousness in Hegel's *Phenomenology*, it is hard to imagine that revisions of this sort would make a substantive difference to the body of the whole. The book is not intended, moreover, to read as a history of literature or any of the fine arts, nor is it principally about the philosophy or critical appreciation of them, although inevitably each is touched on in due course and as occasion demands. The study concentrates fundamentally on theoretical contributions that have been made from the beginning of the eighteenth century through the latter part of the twentieth to understanding the phenomena that all these disciplines presuppose, namely, the nature and origin of aesthetic value and the various issues that arise from reflecting on it. The book, I hope, sails close to its theme and steers a course that will inform, engage, and entertain; this is certainly the spirit in which it was written and if even a little of that contagion spreads to those who read it, then the labor has been worthwhile.

T. M. C.
Williamsburg, VA

Introduction

A Brief History of "Aesthetics"

Today the term *aesthetics* refers to an identifiable subdiscipline of philosophy concerned with the nature and expression of beauty and the fine arts. The discipline covers a broad spectrum of issues, problems, and approaches, but students and practitioners generally agree that its origins can be traced unequivocally to eighteenth-century British philosophers working predominantly, though not exclusively, in England and Scotland. Many of these writers were based in and around the old universities of Edinburgh, Glasgow, and Aberdeen, where (with the exception of David Hume who was denied a position twice on account of his religious views) they held chairs in philosophy and related disciplines; these thinkers were the intellectual force at the heart of what has come to be known as the Scottish Enlightenment. Other eighteenth-century writers, such as Anthony Ashley Cooper, third earl of Shaftesbury, Joseph Addison, and Edmund Burke, were involved in politics or cut central figures in the polite society of English letters, or, like William Hogarth and Sir Joshua Reynolds, were practicing artists. The earliest works in the tradition are Shaftesbury's *Characteristicks of Men, Manners Opinions, Times* (1711), and Addison's essays on the "Pleasures of the Imagination" in *The Spectator* (1712), with Francis Hutcheson's *Inquiry into the Original of our Ideas of Beauty and Virtue* (1725) often cited as the first systematic and self-conscious attempt to address questions that came to define a new area of philosophical inquiry, which, by the beginning of the twentieth century crystallized into the discipline complete, in its modern form, with all the attendant paraphernalia of academic respectability.

Although the intellectual roots of modern aesthetics are buried deep in British soil, the term *aesthetics* is of distinctly German stock. Its linguistic heritage lies in the Greek nominal αισθητικός (*aisthetikos*), sensitive or sentient, derived in turn from the verb αισθάνησθαι (*aisthanesthai*), meaning to perceive, feel, or sense. Famously, Immanuel Kant used the term for that part of his *Kritik der reinen Vernunft* (*Critique of Pure Reason*) (1781/1787) concerned with the principles of "a priori sensibility" given in the "pure" intuitions of space and time.[1] In doing so he was following the lead of the precocious twenty-one-year-old Alexander Gottlieb Baumgarten (1714–62), who had already traded on the Greek in his master's thesis, *Meditationes philosophicae de nonullis ad poema pertenentibus* (*Philosophical meditations on some requirements of the poem*) (1735), coining the phrase *episteme aisthetike* both to designate knowledge based on sense perception and name the faculty that makes it possible. In his lectures from 1742 onward – the basis for the two-volume *Aesthetica* (1750 and 1758) – Baumgarten subsequently extended the term to designate a "science of sensual cognition" more generally.[2] By the middle of the eighteenth century, the term felt quite at home in the beer cellars and lecture halls of Germany, a state of affairs confirmed in 1781 by Kant, who, though rejecting as "abortive" Baumgarten's attempt "to bring the critical treatment of the beautiful under rational principles," at once acknowledges that the "Germans are the only people who currently make use of the word 'aesthetic' in order to signify what others call the critique of taste" (CPR A21/B35–6n).

Making the short journey across the Channel to visit those "others" was to enter a different world. In England and Scotland, "aesthetics" did not become common currency until well into the nineteenth century, and was long disparaged as bastard offspring of the German brain – Kant's in particular – with much handwringing for decades at the lack of an acceptable English alternative. British writers had been discussing for decades matters to which their Teutonic kin came somewhat later, but used "taste" – as Kant pointed out – for the affective faculty and the species of knowledge derived from it, and assigned the term *criticism* to the inquiry that attempted to elucidate its principles. *Aesthetics* is absent from Samuel Johnson's *A Dictionary of the English Language* (1755), and in 1798 William Taylor could still regard it coolly as part of the "dialect peculiar to Professor Kant."[3] Things developed apace over the next two decades, however, and by 1821 at least this element of the peculiar dialect had made sufficient inroads that Samuel Taylor Coleridge lamented the lack of a "more familiar word than æsthetic, for works of taste and criticism";[4]

---

[1] See Immanuel Kant, *Kritik der reinen Vernunft*, in *Kant's gesammelte Schriften*, Königlichen Preussichen (later Deutcshen) Akademie der Wissenschaften, 29 vols. (Berlin: Reimer [later Walter de Gruyter], 1900–) (KGS), vols. 3/4; *Critique of Pure Reason*, trans. Paul Guyer and Alan E. Wood (Cambridge: Cambridge University Press, 1999), A19–22/B33–36 (CPR).

[2] See Kai Hammermeister, *The German Aesthetic Tradition* (Cambridge: Cambridge University Press, 2002), 3ff., and Paul Guyer, "The Origins of Modern Aesthetics: 1711–35," in *The Blackwell Guide to Aesthetics*, ed. Peter Kivy (Oxford: Blackwell, 2004), reprinted in Paul Guyer, *Values of Beauty: Historical Essays in Aesthetics* (Cambridge: Cambridge University Press, 2005), 3–36.

[3] William Taylor, *Monthly Review* 25, 585, quoted in *Oxford English Dictionary*: "In the dialect peculiar to Professor Kant, his *receptivity* for *aesthetic* gratification [is] not delicate." According to the entry in *Le Trésor de la Lange français*, "ésthetique" has a similar history with the earliest references being to Baumgarten and Kant.

[4] *The Collected Works of Samuel Taylor Coleridge*, 16 vols. (Princeton, NJ: Princeton University Press, 1983), *Shorter Works and Fragments* II, ed. H. J. Jackson and J. R. de J. Jackson, 11:938.

that Coleridge should be expressing the sentiment is ironic, to say the least, given that he was almost single-handedly responsible for introducing Kant and German Idealist philosophy into Britain. This irony notwithstanding, by 1846 John Ruskin could report in *Modern Painters* II that "aesthetic" was "commonly employed" with reference to impressions of beauty, and in the 1883 edition of the work he inserted the word *now* before *commonly* and added that "It [aesthetic] was, of course, never so used by good or scholarly English writers, nor ever could be."[5] This was a piece of wishful thinking and willful reconstruction on Ruskin's part, a fact attested by Sir William Hamilton's grudging but clear acknowledgment in his *Lectures on Metaphysics* (1859) that the term was by then entrenched and immovable. "It is now nearly a century," Hamilton reports,

since Baumgarten ... first applied the term Æsthetic to the doctrine which we vaguely and periphrastically denominate the Philosophy of Taste, the theory of the Fine Arts, the Science of the Beautiful and Sublime, &c., – and this term is now in general acceptation, not only in Germany, but throughout the other countries of Europe.

Hamilton could not resist adding that the "term Apolaustic" – meaning "devoted to enjoyment" – "would have been a more appropriate designation,"[6] but his plea fell on deaf ears and by the time Walter Pater published *Studies in the History of the Renaissance* in 1873, and George Santayana gave the first course explicitly titled "Aesthetics" at Harvard University in the early years of the same decade, there was no longer any question that the term had arrived and was here to stay. Rather than complaining about its presence, philosophers now made the term welcome and concentrated their efforts on explaining what the concept and the discipline founded in its name might amount to.

Whether one focuses on the term or concept, however, it is clear that the first part of the eighteenth century saw the birth of a new and distinct discipline, which one might appropriately call "philosophical aesthetics" to distinguish it from its related but recognizably different kin. For there is an "aesthetics" before aesthetics, if by that one means philosophical reflection on beauty and the arts, and as any decent anthology will attest, the likes of Plato, Aristotle, Longinus, Plotinus, Augustine, and Aquinas all have more or less interesting things to say about aesthetic value, human creativity, and what we now call the "arts," itself a relatively new invention.[7] In addition to the

---

5 John Ruskin, *Modern Painters* II (1846), *The Complete Works of John Ruskin (Library Edition)*, ed. E. T. Cook and Alexander Wedderburn, 39 vols. (London: George Allen, 1903–12), 4:42.

6 Sir William Hamilton, *Lectures on Metaphysics* I (1859), *Works of Sir William Hamilton*, ed. H. L. Mansel and John Veitch, 7 vols. (London: William Blackwood and Sons, 1828–1960), 3:124.

7 See P. O. Kristeller, "The Modern System of the Arts: A Study in the History of Aesthetics Part I," and "The Modern System of the Arts: A Study in the History of Aesthetics Part I," *Journal of the History of Ideas* 12, 4 (1951): 496–527 and 13, 1 (1952): 17–46, respectively. R. G. Collingwood had made much the same point, albeit it in less detail, in *The Principles of Art* (Oxford: Clarendon Press, 1938), 5–7.

philosophical literature, there is also a tradition of the "art treatise" – including Roger de Piles's *L'Abrégé de la Vie des Peintures* (1699) (*The Art of Painting and the Lives and Characters of the Most Eminent Painters*, 1706) and Jonathan Richardson's *Essay on the Theory of Painting* (1715) – and, closer to concerns of the nascent discipline, that of "literary criticism," the systematic inquiry into and informed judgment about writing or discourse according to rules or principles governing (primarily) works of literature. This tradition has its roots in Aristotle's *Rhetoric* and Longinus's *Peri Hupsous* (*On the Sublime*), and found its most self-conscious expression in late-seventeenth-century Europe, associated in particular with French writers Pierre Corneille (1606–84), Jean-Baptiste Racine (1639–99), Jean-Baptiste l'Abbé Dubos (1670–1742), and Nicolas Boileau-Despréaux (1636–1711); these figures also had their now less-famous counterparts in England, in the shape of John Sheffield, first Duke of Buckingham (1647–1721), Wentworth Dillon, fourth Earl of Roscommon (1630–1685), and the better-known John Dennis (1657–1734) whose *The Advancement and Reformation of Modern Poetry* (1701) and *The Grounds of Criticism in Poetry* (1704) are often read as broaching issues – notably the concept of the sublime – that were taken up soon after by Shaftesbury and Addison. The tradition of criticism blended seamlessly with its younger rival and even retained some independence in the shape of Hume and the "literary" essay, and Henry Home, Lord Kames, who, as if to make the point, decisively titled his main work on the subject *Elements of Criticism*.

Whatever shared moments or points of intersection it enjoys with these intellectual traditions, however, philosophical aesthetics remains singular and, as the suggestions of various commentators have shown, a little prodding quickly reveals some distinguishing marks of its birth. These include, as Paul Guyer has enumerated them,[8] a new conception of subjectivity and the individual (Peter de Bolla and Luc Ferry), a concern with "genius" (M. H. Abrams), the rise of new aesthetic categories of the sublime (Samuel Holt Monk) and the picturesque (Christopher Hussey), and the beginning of modern ideology (Terry Eagleton).[9] One might also add George Dickie's contention that the period marks a shift in emphasis from "objective notions of beauty to the subjective notion of taste"; Ronald Paulson's observation that aesthetics was an

[8] See Guyer, "The Origins of Modern Aesthetics," 4–5.
[9] The works in question are Peter de Bolla, *The Education of the Eye: Painting, Landscape, and Architecture in Eighteenth-Century Britain* (Stanford, CA: Stanford University Press, 2003), and introduction to *The Sublime. A Reader in Eighteenth-Century Aesthetic Theory*, ed. Andrew Ashfield and Peter de Bolla (Cambridge: Cambridge University Press, 1996), 1–16; Luc Ferry, *Homo Aestheticus: The Invention of Taste in the Democratic Age*, trans. Robert de Loaizia (Chicago: Chicago University Press, 1993); M. H. Abrams, *The Mirror and the Lamp: Romantic Theory and the Critical Tradition* (Oxford: Oxford University Press, 1953); Samuel Holt Monk, *The Sublime: A Study of Critical Theories in Eighteenth-Century England* (New York: Modern Language Association of America, 1935); Christopher Hussey, *The Picturesque: Studies in a Point of View* (London: Putnam, 1927; repr., Hamden, CT: Archon, 1967); and Terry Eagleton, *The Ideology of the Aesthetic* (Oxford: Blackwell, 1990).

"empiricist philosophy based on the sense rather than reason or faith"; James Engell's contention that the Enlightenment created the idea of the "creative imagination"; and Guyer's own suggestion that the "central idea" of aesthetics was the "freedom of the imagination."[10] There is no doubt some or even a good deal of truth to each of these proposals, but the aim of the present study at least is not to endorse one in particular or reduce any other period of the discipline's progress to some theoretical slogan or handy historical tag. The aesthetic tradition stands proudly and independently apart, sovereign over its own domain rather than an afterthought to metaphysics and epistemology or in service to religious dogmatism, artistic instruction, or literary style. The pudding and its proof, as we shall see in the chapters that follow, are very much in the eating.

DESIGN OF THE BOOK

Before readers dig in, however, they are owed at least a brief account of the rationale behind the book's title and its organization. First, it will be immediately obvious to any reader that not every writer considered in what follows is British; the majority of them do fall under that epithet, but there are exceptions, especially as one follows the narrative into the twentieth century where philosophy in general and aesthetics in particular becomes thoroughly professionalized and moves, at least in part, to the institutionalized setting of American higher education. The "British" in the title of the book, it should be emphasized, is not intended to claim national affiliation for a body of work or denote the citizenship of its practitioners; it is meant instead to convey the continuity of a *tradition* of philosophical reflection that transcends the narrower and artificial category of state or nation. Because this tradition originates in Britain at the beginning of the eighteenth century and remains largely on that soil for the next two centuries and beyond, *The British Aesthetic Tradition* is simply the most appropriate and accurate title among the available alternatives.

Second, although many would agree, I hazard, that the work of writers considered in this book forms the historical backbone that supports what is now called aesthetics, it is by no means the only element that gives the discipline shape. This might be obscured in focusing on the British aesthetic tradition, and some might interpret it as willful dismissal of the discipline's wider origin, namely, the international context in which stretches of its history moves, and

---

[10] See George Dickie, *The Century of Taste: The Philosophical Odyssey of Taste in the Eighteenth Century* (Oxford: Oxford University Press, 1996), 3; Ronald Paulson, editor's introduction to *William Hogarth, The Analysis of Beauty* (New Haven, CT: Yale University Press, 1997), xix; James Engell, *The Creative Imagination: Enlightenment to Romanticism* (Cambridge, MA: Harvard University Press, 1981), ch. 1; and Guyer, "The Origins of Modern Aesthetics." This latter thesis is elaborated (along with much else) in Paul Guyer, *A History of Aesthetics*, 3 vols. (Cambridge: Cambridge University Press, forthcoming).

the complex reciprocal influences at play between Britain and the Continent: the importance of Dubos for eighteenth-century British writers, for example; the effect of the Scottish Enlightenment on Kant and later German philosophy; and the impact of Benedetto Croce on English philosophy during the early decades of the twentieth century. The plan, aim, and focus of the book do prevent exploring such wider terrain, and dictate that these and other matters be acknowledged rather than explored, the reader being provided with background sufficient only for the purposes of the developing narrative, signposts to vistas unseen from the path along which the reader is led. This might be seen legitimately as a downside to the present study, but one might also emphasize the positive result: the rewards of sharper focus are rich because, as we shall see in what follows, the somewhat narrower perspective taken discourages distraction and facilitates detailed scrutiny of the flora and fauna at hand to reveal the internal coherence and continuity of a tradition that might be lost to a more promiscuous and less discerning eye.

Third, turning to matters of organization, it is now commonplace to consider the eighteenth century as the "Age of Taste," and I follow that convention in characterizing writers considered in Part I of the book, although I break with some earlier scholarship – notably Walter J. Hipple's *The Beautiful, The Sublime, & The Picturesque in Eighteenth-Century British Aesthetic Theory*, a justly classic study to which any student of aesthetics owes a debt – by dividing the discussion thematically, rather than chronologically, into "internal sense theorists," "imagination theorists," and "associationist theories."[11] As with arrangement of material, this choice has its drawbacks. It threatens, for one, to distort variations of emphasis among thinkers into principled differences of doctrine, and risks underplaying the degree to which eighteenth-century writers were engaged in a common project with almost every contributor to the Age of Taste ranging across the full spectrum of contemporary concerns. This intellectual eclecticism on the part of the writers leads, inevitably, to methodological questions over how precisely to categorize them, and some do refuse obstinately to fall in line easily or unambiguously under one banner or the other. Alexander Gerard and Archibald Alison – association theorists – have a good deal to say about the imagination, for instance, and Hume, perhaps the most difficult case, adopts at least in part Hutcheson's model of internal sense but shares more philosophically with those who focus on the imagination. The other downside of the chosen division is managing the anachronism that follows from introducing certain thinkers before considering earlier work on which they relied: Thomas Reid, for example, writes in the 1760s but as an internal sense theorist appears in the narrative (Chapter 1) before Addison

---

[11] I am indebted to James Shelley for this general way of organizing the discussion. See his entry on "British Aesthetics in the Eighteenth Century" in the *Stanford Encyclopedia of Philosophy*, ed. Edward N. Zalta, plato.stanford.edu/entries/aesthetics-18th-british (2006; rev. 2010), accessed May 15, 2007.

(Chapter 2), an imagination theorist, who makes his influential contribution near the beginning of the century.

It might be noted in response to these potential problems that, as Hipple expresses it succinctly at the end of his own study, there is "no tendency for multiplicity to reduce to unity in the British speculations of the eighteenth century, and in consequence no simple historical progression from adequacy to completeness, from error to truth."[12] This is surely an accurate assessment, for although eighteenth-century writers often draw on work accomplished by their predecessors and contemporaries – albeit selectively and often without acknowledgment – they tend to treat their subject matter on its own terms and are not conscious of themselves as parties to a common effort moving toward a collectively realizable goal. With this in mind, it becomes less crucial to consider the eighteenth-century tradition as a plot moving to a dénouement than it is to present each contribution for its own sake and intrinsic value, while also trying to convey connections, indicate anticipations, and recall echoes where possible and appropriate. Cases of both ambiguous categorization and egregious anachronism are rarer than one might expect, and, on balance, the drawbacks of organizing the discussion thematically are far outweighed by the great advantage of being able to highlight for the reader both the main philosophical movements of the century and how the work of different philosophers cohere around them.

Anybody writing a history of the British aesthetic tradition runs into something of an impasse when the Age of Taste comes to end, rather abruptly as conventional wisdom has it, with Dugald Stewart's *Philosophical Essays* of 1810. After that date, "philosophical aesthetics" in a strict sense moves across the Channel, where it finds place as the purview of the big hitters and system builders of German Idealism. In Britain, and this is a fact overlooked or underappreciated by students of the discipline, the advances are made more obliquely, but no less profoundly, in the prose writings of poets and critics of Victorian England, defined by the sensibility of what we now call "Romanticism": this denotes a tenor of thought and best describes the arc of the tradition as traced in Part II of the book from William Wordsworth through John Keats (Chapter 5) to the criticism of William Hazlitt, John Ruskin, John Stuart Mill, and Walter Pater (Chapter 6). The bridge, moreover, from the Age of Taste to the Age of Romanticism is both more solid and traversable than might at first sight appear: it emerges in the debates over the "picturesque" (Chapter 5) that begin in earnest with the writings of William Gilpin in the latter part of the eighteenth century, joined, as the eighteenth century wanes and turns, by the often loud and sometimes eccentric voices of Uvedale Price, Richard Payne Knight, and Humphrey Repton in a complex babble of

---

[12] Walter J. Hipple Jr., *The Beautiful, The Sublime, & The Picturesque in Eighteenth-Century British Aesthetic Theory* (Carbondale: Southern Illinois University Press, 1957), 284.

philosophy, art, and the practice of "landscape gardening." These figures might be unfamiliar to many contemporary aestheticians, but it is through them, by way of the prose works of Wordsworth, that the discipline discovers its course, desultory and uncharted as it might be, from its origins in Hutcheson and his contemporaries, to the more recognizable figures at the end of the nineteenth century in whose hands it moves into the "Age of Analysis," the most appropriate title for Part III of the study.

Analysis is a contested term, but like *taste* and *Romanticism* it captures the philosophical spirit of an age. The narrative here begins with "theories of expression" (Chapter 7), a phrase that gathers collectively the contributions of George Santayana, Roger Fry, Clive Bell, John Dewey, and R. G. Collingwood, the latter, with a philosophical and biographical foot in either century, standing as a transitional figure between Romanticism and the analytic turn made decisively in mid-century under the influence of Ludwig Wittgenstein and the burgeoning field of philosophy of language. Wittgenstein's aesthetics (Chapter 8) bear marks of the discipline's eighteenth-century origins – one cannot escape "taste" and "appreciation" whatever one's methodological predilection – but at once signals the arrival of a brave new world, where from the 1950s onward aesthetics confronts "problems" and creates "views," and the debates that emerge take on a gloss of technical detail largely absent from earlier eras.

The aesthetics of the period from the mid-twentieth century onward is also distinguished by its exponential growth, expanding to occupy the space provided by the modern academy, which gives the discipline a shape, molded by the institutional forces of the university replete with its professional structures and assembly of research and publication. The two principal journals of the discipline by themselves account for many hundreds of articles – the *Journal of Aesthetics and Art Criticism* was established in 1942, and the *British Journal of Aesthetics* in 1960 – and if one adds to that number other relevant venues in philosophy and the humanities along with the steady stream of monographs, edited collections, guidebooks, handbooks, dictionaries, and encyclopedias, one has a mountain of material that few have either time, inclination, or energy to climb. A separate volume might be a suitable occasion for attempting at least a partial assault, but to conclude this history of aesthetics in such a way would be foolhardy and terminate at best in a literature review that would bloat the whole and blur the lines that have given the narrative definition. To avoid this eventuality, *The British Aesthetic Tradition* runs its course and concludes, as it must somewhere, by indicating three directions the discipline has taken "after Wittgenstein" and that point forward to contemporary work in the field. The volume thus ends, though the British aesthetic tradition marches on, and does so, whether players are aware of it or not, in time to a tune learned long ago and committed to a collective memory of which current practice is surely the product, summation, and living body. At least a part of that, it is hoped, has been captured and conveyed in the pages that follow.

PART I

THE AGE OF TASTE

I

Internal Sense Theorists

We begin our history of the British aesthetic tradition with a group of eighteenth-century British writers who, though not coincident in time, share a similar philosophical predilection for approaching aesthetic matters through the idea of "internal sense." The idea of imagination and association is not entirely absent from their writings, as that of internal sense can be found in those to be considered in later chapters (Hume and Kames being obvious cases in point). As we shall see in what follows, however, these thinkers are united by the conviction that aesthetic value is to be explained ultimately through a sense of taste that, analogously or literally, shares crucial features with its external counterparts, especially, as writers emphasize throughout, that of sight. On this view, objects possess or exhibit certain qualities that elicit, directly or indirectly and in more or less complicated ways, a certain response on the part of the subject; that is only possible, these theorists conjecture, if some distinct organ or capacity is present and correctly adapted to receive and be affected by the qualities in question.

ANTHONY ASHLEY COOPER, THIRD EARL OF SHAFTESBURY

The first internal sense theorist of the tradition – Anthony Ashley Cooper, third Earl Shaftesbury (1671–1713) – is also, fittingly, the philosopher whose work is usually regarded as its founding text. "The Moralists, A Philosophical Rhapsody" is one of a series of lengthy essays Shaftesbury composed between 1705 and 1710 and published together in three volumes as *Characteristicks of Men, Manners, Opinions, Times* in 1711;[1] with the exception of John Locke's *Second Treatise of Civil Government* (1690), it was destined to become the

---

[1] Anthony Ashley Cooper, third Earl of Shaftesbury, *Characteristicks of Men, Manners, Opinions, Times*, 3 vols. (Indianapolis, IN: Liberty Fund, 2001 [1711]). "The Moralists" is contained in vol. 2, 103–247 (M). All references are to volume and page number.

most reprinted English-language book in the eighteenth century. Shaftesbury was educated under the direction of Locke (whose patron was the first earl, Shaftesbury's grandfather), but he came to take issue with central doctrines of his former tutor,[2] and although Lockean language pervades the *Characteristicks*, it is largely a gloss on a philosophical canvas indebted to the rationalist lineage of neo-Platonism with its origins in the thought of the third-century philosopher Plotinus. Shaftesbury's aesthetics is reminiscent, in particular, of *Ennead* I.6 "On Beauty," in which Plotinus (echoing Plato of the *Symposium*) argues that the beauty of physical objects is but a "trace" of some higher reality to which the philosophical mind ascends.[3] In Shaftesbury's own time, this school of thought was alive and well largely through the influence of the late-seventeenth-century group of philosophers known as the Cambridge Platonists, and Shaftesbury was responsible for publishing the posthumous edition of the *Select Sermons* of Benjamin Whichcote (1609–83), generally considered the founding father of the movement.[4]

This debt is reflected not only in the realist view Shaftesbury develops, but also in the form of Socratic dialogue through which he presents it. "The Moralists" is structured around the character of Philocles relating to his friend Palemon a past conversation with Theocles, who emerges as the effective mouthpiece for Shaftesbury's own philosophical position. Unlike Hume's *Dialogues Concerning Natural Religion*, this tactic is not intended as a subterfuge to complicate or obscure the author's position, but as a means of expression Shaftesbury employs deliberately for reasons of both literary style and dramatic effect to carry his philosophical message. As in many of Plato's writings, the indirect dialogue style of "The Moralists" is intended to distance the reader from the content of the work, giving emphasis to Shaftesbury's conviction that ultimately reason, rather than feeling, is the source of beauty and the means by which the philosopher (and reader) grasp its source and come to experience it most fully. Shaftesbury also presents his interlocutors in various scenes of pastoral life, conversing at their ease over the course of two days spent walking, dining, and riding on a coach, echoing the ancient ideal of philosophy as a discursive practice developing naturally over a span of time that is both of the world and out of it. Philosophy should not, as in the tradition of the scholastic schools, be confined to the artifice of monkish cell or academic cloister, but should be integrated into a civil discourse that is part and parcel of

---

[2] For a recent treatment of some of these disagreements, see Daniel Carey, *Locke, Shaftesbury, and Hutcheson: Contesting Diversity in the Enlightenment and Beyond* (Cambridge: Cambridge University Press, 2006).

[3] See *Ennead* I.6, "On Beauty," in *Plotinus*, Greek text with English translation by A. H. Armstrong, 7 vols. (Cambridge, MA: Harvard University Press; Loeb Classical Library, 1968–88), vol. 1, *Porphyry on Plotinus, Ennead I*.

[4] Benjamin Whichcote, *Select Sermons*, with a preface by Anthony Ashley Cooper, Third Earl of Shaftesbury (London: Awnsham and Churchill, 1698).

earthly life. Philosophy is a rarefied time out of mind, Shaftesbury maintains, an initiation into the secrets of existence, but at once part of the human condition to which the educated, inquiring – and, one must admit – socially privileged mind is naturally led.

The bucolic setting also allows Shaftesbury to depict wild untamed "Nature" (juxtaposed to the artifice of the gardener) as a dramatis personae in the argument that unfolds, hinting at the relationship he plans to tease out between human beings and the natural world and, in the final dénouement, to identify the ordering principle of the universe as the Divine Mind, which is synonymous with it. If philosophers contemplate Nature – the expression of the settled order of the universe – they both locate a source of philosophical insight – a naturalized version of Socrates's *daimon* – and contemplate the original, source, or pattern for all things beyond the partial and derivative appearances given through perception, manifest in the products of human art or represented as the idealized view of the human body. Nature is a source of inspiration, a channel to an altered state – a rhapsody as the title of the essay expresses it – a religious or philosophical conversion that the character of Philocles undergoes. This is not, as it is for other eighteenth-century philosophers, a cause for embarrassment, but in Shaftesbury's view the *sine qua non* of philosophical inquiry. Nature is divine and its contemplation the occasion for revelation, a mystical union with God through which one attains the ultimate insight that the whole is one, harmonious, and ordered by universal genius: God is Nature, in Shaftesbury's view, and Nature a kind of machine infused with and animated by the Divine Mind, immanent and alive and, reminiscent of the pantheism in the *Ethics* of Baruch Spinoza, a single substance expressed through an infinity of modes and grasped through the attributes of thought and extension.[5]

Shaftesbury is well aware of the irony contained in this picture of the philosopher as a created being, limited by imperfection and the constraints of a discursive mind, confronting the mysteries of the eternal and infinite: the conclusions at the end of philosophical inquiry can only be drawn when the cool dictates of reason are overcome by flights of fancy and a heated imagination. Theocles is a man at war with himself, a rational investigator tinged by a madness that carries him away in fits of enthusiasm and ecstasies of poetic expression from which he struggles to withdraw and return, embarrassed and apologetic. Shaftesbury thus dramatizes the profound paradox of his view, namely, that philosophy is like a painting that represents and distorts nature in the very act of stripping away the veil of appearance that hides its real form: Shaftesbury can only move beyond the world by way of the very appearances he seeks to unveil. As Philocles describes it at one point, philosophy is

5 See Baruch Spinoza, *Ethics*, in *The Complete Works*, ed. Michael L. Morgan, trans. Samuel Shirley (Indianapolis, IN: Hackett, 2002), Part 1, "Of God."

a "magical glass" (M 202) that imposes a conceptual scheme on nature and by representing and distorting it breaks the "Uniformity, and destroy[s] that admirable Simplicity of Order, from whence the ONE infinite and perfect Principle is known" (M 189).

As we shall see, this tension between nature and art, reality and appearance, presentation and representation finds voice in various ways throughout the eighteenth century. It is a tension that cannot be resolved, although it can be relaxed by weighing one side over the other, something Shaftesbury achieves by subsuming the copy under some higher original. In this vein, he criticizes various schools of thought that dogmatically adopt a compromise position and settle for a partial view of the whole that disdains the presence of design and trusts everything to blind chance. Thus the skeptic, he charges, simply gives up on the idea of ever knowing the original; the atomist or Epicurean willingly accepts the world as emerging out of chaos; and the materialist resorts to the blind forces of matter in motion. Shaftesbury brushes aside such weak philosophical spirits and, removing in turn the obvious and immediate sources of beauty, rises above appearance to the form of beauty itself.

What, then, prevents philosophy from creating a mere copy, even if one achieves rhapsodic insight into the source of beauty beyond sensuous experience? Shaftesbury's philosopher might be compared to the initiate at the outset of René Descartes's *Meditations on First Philosophy* who sets out to discover the Archimedean point on which to balance the edifice of human knowledge; there is an intellectual journey to be undertaken in the course of which philosophy shows itself capable of discovering truths that are not available to ordinary cognition.[6] He begins, like Descartes's meditator, by rejecting the most obvious source of beauty in immediate feeling and sense. Nothing can be of value, Shaftesbury observes, except what is constant and thus a real source of pleasure, and this cannot be won through the senses or what one simply feels to be pleasurable. Pleasure and pain are inconstant, convertible, and mixed: what seems good, beautiful, and true is often the very opposite, namely, what is ill, mere amusement, and opinion; feeling can occasion as much pain as it does pleasure, and some take pleasure in objects that others find painful. We might be tempted to find a fixed and constant point in ourselves, Shaftesbury observes, but even here good is chimerical and has its origin in some higher principle: in the case of the good, virtue has its source in the love of mankind, a complex, universal virtue beyond the object deemed worthy of love, and in the case of beauty, a statue from ancient Rome pleases because it stands for and refers to the people of Rome, a principle that transcends the physical object. Indeed, Shaftesbury concludes, it is not the pleasure or the immediate

---

[6] See René Descartes, *Meditations on First Philosophy*, in *The Philosophical Writings of Descartes*, vol. 2, trans. John Cottingham, Robert Stoothoff, and Dugald Murdoch (Cambridge: Cambridge University Press, 1984).

object that produces value, but what makes a pleasure valuable, and that lies in beauty itself.

Shaftesbury supports this view by developing two theses. He argues first that there is some principle above and beyond the immediate object of perception, namely, the order of Nature, displayed in the relation of parts that combine and cooperate to form a perfect whole. In an image that evokes Plato's Allegory of Cave,[7] Shaftesbury urges that contemplating Nature enables the mind to move increasingly higher from the base elements and minerals that compose the lowest regions of the earth, through its surface into the region of plants and animal bodies, and at a final level from which each particular system, apparently complete in itself, is revealed as having place only within the whole. "Now in this which we call the UNIVERSE," Shaftesbury writes,

whatever the Perfection may be of any *particular Systems*; or whatever *single Parts* may have Proportion, Unity, of Form within themselves; yet if they are not united all in general, in ONE *System*, but are, in respect of one another, as the driven Sands, or Clouds, or breaking Waves; then there being no Coherence in *the Whole*, there can be infer'd no Order, no Proportion, and consequently no Project or *Design*. But if none of these are independent, but all apparently united, then there is the WHOLE *a system* compleat, according to one *simple, consistent*, and *uniform* DESIGN. (M 162)

Having recognized the unity, design, and perfection of each part, Shaftesbury reasons, one cannot but acknowledge the order and perfection of the whole to which they contribute and are subservient. To deny this would be as obtuse as recognizing some detail in a painting and then refusing to acknowledge it as only an element of the complete canvas. The detail alone might well be beautiful, but its beauty depends upon and receives its full meaning as a part of the whole in which it has place; properly speaking, the whole is beautiful and the part is of value only to the extent that it participates in it. Moreover, the whole is the source of beauty because it makes the particular valuable. Being content with the beauty of the part is to remain at the level of appearance, akin to thinking the Roman statue is itself beautiful when beauty is contained in and conferred by the higher principle to which it refers, namely, the Roman people.

How then, we might ask, does the limited, imperfect mind have access to this region of transcendent being? Shaftesbury answers this question by identifying a feature "imprinted on our Minds" or "closely interwoven with out Souls," which he calls the "Idea or Sense of *Order* and *Proportion*" through which we grasp the "Force of *Numbers*, and those powerful *Arts* founded on their Management and Use" (M 160). By means of this internal sense, we are able

---

[7] See Plato, *The Republic*, in *Plato: Complete Works*, ed. John M. Cooper (Indianapolis, IN: Hackett, 1997), Book VII, 514a–20a.

to decipher harmony from discord, cadency from convulsion, orderly motion from its accidental counterpart, and design from randomness. This is not, however, a feeling that comes from "Sense *alone*," he emphasizes, which, as we have seen, terminates in a lower form of apparent beauty, but is an expression of our reason through which we "contemplate" Nature and receive a higher kind of "rational enjoyment" (M 221). Beauty is not sensed as a feature of the experienced world, but apprehended as a mystery of the universe.

Shaftesbury, however, has yet to explain precisely in what this ordering principle consists; answering this question forms his second thesis, which concerns identity and explaining why an object endures as one and the same through the diversity of its appearances. The aesthetic value of a beautiful coin, to take Shaftesbury's example, lies not in its matter or substance – its metallic compound – but in the cause that gives it form and thus makes it the thing it is. The coin is beautiful in virtue of the workmanship displayed in the engraving and that imposes a particular form on the material. "For that which is beautify'd, is beautiful," as Shaftesbury expresses the idea, "only by the accession of something beautifying: and by the recess or withdrawing of the same, it ceases to be beautiful" (M 226). The source of the beauty – the ordering principle – is the power that imposes this form – the artist who created it – without which it would cease to have the feature that confers aesthetic value. The same thought (clearly Lockean in origin) applies to the identity of living beings, such as plants, trees, and animal bodies, although in this case we cannot explain the "*Oneness* or *Sameness*" of a mighty oak, say, in terms of human art working on inanimate matter, nor can we account for their continued existence by reference to that matter, which undergoes alteration while the object remains the same. In this case, Shaftesbury urges, the causal principle consists in the "*Sympathizing of Parts*" or their "*plain Concurrence in one common End*" that provide for its "*Support, Nourishment, and Propagation*" (M 195–6). "By virtue of this," he urges, "our Tree is a real *Tree*; lives, flourishes, and is still *One and the same*; even when by Vegetation and change of Substance, not one Particle in it remains *the same*" (196). Further, when we consider personal identity – what explains "how you, Philocles, are *You*," as Shaftesbury puts it in the voice of Theocles, "and I'm *My-self*" (M 196) – things become more complicated, because there is no real substance or matter to which the term refers apart from the affections, passion, appetites, and imaginations that we experience as belonging to the same being: that formal identity, which, to use Locke's expression, is a "Forensic Term appropriating Actions and their Merit," the idea of "*one and the same being*" who can be held responsible for past and present actions, praised for virtue, and punished for vice (M 197).[8] This identity, too, must have an ordering principle, Shaftesbury insists, which

---

[8] John Locke, *An Essay Concerning Human Understanding*, ed. Peter H. Nidditch (Oxford: Oxford University Press, 1975 [1689]), 2.27.26 (*Essay*).

in this case is supplied by "*general* Mind" to which each "*particular-one* must have a relation" (M 201). We cannot, without absurdity, deny the unity of an individual any more than we can refuse to acknowledge the order and identity of Nature. If we accept the latter we at once discover the principle that both orders any individual and shows that the whole is animated by Universal Mind.

At this point, Shaftesbury has proposed and argued for the two theses mentioned previously, one concerning the ordering principle of Nature, the other concerning the effect of that principle in identity. As he writes, expressing both conclusions at once, "*the Beautiful, the Fair, the Comely*, were never in the *Matter*, but in the *Art* and *Design*; never in the *body* it-self, but in the *Form* or *forming Power* ...'Tis *Mind* alone which forms. All which is void of *Mind* is horrid: and Matter formless is *Deformity it-self*" (M 226). On this basis, Shaftesbury then proposes "*Three* Degrees or Orders of Beauty," which express the idea of an ordering principle beyond appearances that explains the identity of all things ultimately in the ordering principle of the Divine Mind. As we progress from one to the other through contemplating Nature, we move increasingly upward toward the true origin of beauty. The first is the beauty of "*the dead forms* ... which bear a Fashion, and are form'd whether by Man, or nature; but have no forming Power, no Action, or Intelligence" (M 227); at this level we find works of the plastic arts and craft, like the minting of coins, which require some cause in order to come into existence; the beauty of such objects lies in the form appreciated and not the object, which contains no forming power. The second degree of beauty is comprised of grasping that power to which the dead forms refer, what Shaftesbury calls "*the Forming Forms*; that is, which have Intelligence, Action, and Operation." Here we find the power of human mind that gives dead forms the shapes they have, "such as the Palaces, the Coins, the Brazen or the Marble Figures of Men" (M 227). At this level, as Shaftesbury points out, there is a "double beauty," because we both see the dead form that is formed and grasp it as the effect of something higher, "*Mind* itself." The third and highest Order of Beauty, finally, encompasses and absorbs both of these, for at this level we arrive at the principle that explains the mind of man, that "which forms not only such as we call mere Forms, but even *the Forms that form*" (M 227–8), that is, the source of the power of human mind to give identity to what is dead. This, Shaftesbury concludes, is the "Principle, Source, and Fountain of all Beauty" (M 228) into which all lower forms resolve. When we contemplate Nature and arrive at his level, we necessarily include the other two and, in a moment of insight, grasp the world from the view of eternity.

Shaftesbury's Sublime

One way to understand the culmination of the argument in "The Moralists" is in terms of the sublime, a concept destined to loom large as the tradition develops, but which receives its first tentative philosophical treatment in Shaftesbury.[9] The only other writer with any claim to have addressed it before him is Dennis, for whom sublimity is less an aesthetic category in its own right than a corollary to his treatment of religion. That being said, Shaftesbury's own approach still bears the stamp of Augustan criticism and the tradition of Longinus, and when he does use the term *sublime* – which is seldom – it is with reference to the ecstatic effect of studied literary style on an audience irresistibly astounded or passionately compelled.[10] Shaftesbury follows Longinus's emphasis on authorial intent to produce these effects through rhetorical technique, and on the immediate, untutored nature of the emotions aroused, although he does so critically, seeing it as an early and conceptually primitive mode of writing. For Shaftesbury the term denotes one among "several Styles and Manners of Discourse or Writing" that also includes "the *Miraculous* [and] the *Pompous*," distinguished from them by the particular emotion of "astonishment" it excites; "of all other Passions," he adds, it is "the easiest rais'd in raw and unexperienc'd Mankind" (1.149). In this style of "Poetry, and study'd Prose," Shaftesbury continues, "the *astonishing* Part, or what commonly passes for *Sublime*, is form'd by the variety of Figures, the multiplicity of Metaphors, and by quitting as much as possible the natural and easy way of Expression, for that which is most unlike to Humanity, or ordinary Use" (1.150). For this reason one often finds the sublime style employed by the "earliest Poets" and their love of metaphor – what Locke had already bemoaned as the ascendancy of "figurative speeches" over "*natural* and *simple*" expression (*Essay*, 3.10.34) – a state of affairs Shaftesbury finds remedied only by the genius of Homer who extracted and retained what was "decent" in these "spurious" forebears by turning his "thoughts towards the real Beauty of Composition, the Unity of Design, the Truth of Characters, and the just Imitation of Nature in each particular" (1.150; see also 1.160).[11]

It would be a mistake to confine Shaftesbury's treatment of sublimity to the context of Longinian criticism, however, and while his aesthetics clearly focuses on beauty, it at once articulates the concept on which later writers focus. It is thus useful to distinguish clearly between the Longinian sublime or sublime style to describe a mode of written or spoken discourse, and the aesthetic sublime or sublimity, which isolates a particular kind of ecstatic experience or state involving feelings of elevation, transcendence, awe, fear, and

---

[9] For a comprehensive treatment of the concept, including its history and various manifestations, see editor's introduction in *The Sublime: From Antiquity to the Present*, ed. Timothy M. Costelloe (Cambridge: Cambridge University Press, 2012).

[10] For an overview and assessment of Longinus's view, see Malcolm Heath, "Longinus and the Ancient Sublime," in Costelloe, *The Sublime*, and for the rise and fall of Longinus in the early modern period, see Monk, *The Sublime*, ch. 1, and Hipple, *The Beautiful, The Sublime, & The Picturesque*, 16–17.

[11] Shaftesbury also describes friendship as a "sublime heroick passion" (M 135), and uses the term as a verb ("to sublime") in its other sense of "change into a vapor" (see M 167).

shock, excited by being in the presence of something greater than oneself. As we shall see, many subsequent writers in the tradition speak of the aesthetic sublime as "great" or "grand" and reserve "sublime" for the tradition of Longinus. In Shaftesbury, this distinction is implicit – still submerged in the concept of beauty – but active nonetheless and emergent in his view that all aesthetic value has its ultimate source in a metaphysical principle, the discovery of which is inseparable from the experience that the contemplative mind undergoes in ascending through the three orders of beauty.

In "The Moralists," the nascent philosophical sense of sublime is manifest in Shaftesbury's appeal to ekstasis or "rhapsody," the state experienced – or at least articulated – by Theocles, and tied to the attitude of "disinterestedness," an idea that also receives its first formulation in Shaftesbury long before Edmund Burke made it a condition of the sublime, Kant identified it as the *sine qua non* of aesthetic judgment, or the English psychologist Edward Bullough (1880–1934) applied it to the idea of "psychical distance" in the appreciation of art.[12] In Shaftesbury's presentation, disinterestedness involves three fundamental characteristics. First, beauty is the function of rational contemplation, which means that it arises not (as Kant later expresses the same thought) in the form of gratification or liking given through the senses, but is apprehended in a moment of insight; when this happens beauty strikes adventitiously or against our will. Second, aesthetic experience is independent of practical everyday concerns in which we are involved, and transcends any particular artistic tradition that gives beauty a recognizable and customary form. Third, the rational pleasure of a beautiful object is absolutely incompatible with its possession. I might enjoy the land I own or the fruit of the tree in my orchard, as Shaftesbury points out by way of example, but the contemplation of Nature provides the occasion for beauty to arise; this is destroyed when a custodial relationship to the object is established. For Shaftesbury, these features show that there is a difference between a mere appearance or indirect representation of beauty at the level of interest and the direct presentation of beauty through the original, the order and design of which appears regardless of practical concerns, personal involvement, or feelings of gratification. Only when these drop away can the ordering principle in which aesthetic value originates be apprehended and experienced in a moment of sublime insight.

By way of conclusion we might note that, as the century develops, Shaftesbury's aesthetics appears increasingly as an oddity, a nod back to a tradition, which, with the exception of certain elements that surface in the work of

---

[12] See Immanuel Kant, *Kritik der Urteilskraft*, KGS 5:203–11 (CJ), and Edward Bullough, "Psychical Distance," *British Journal of Psychology* 5 (1912): 87–117. For an appreciation of Shaftesbury's contribution, see Jerome Stolnitz, "On the Significance of Lord Shaftesbury in Modern Aesthetic Theory," *Philosophical Quarterly* 11, 43 (1961): 97–113, and "On the Origins of 'Aesthetic Disinterestedness,'" *Journal of Aesthetics and Art Criticism* 20, 2 (1961): 131–44.

Reid, Joshua Reynolds, Archibald Alison, and the late Romantics,[13] was largely rejected by his eighteenth-century successors in favor of empiricism, the force of which turned them decisively away from pantheism and the quasimystical implications of the One and Universal Mind. Only a few years later, in Book I of the *Treatise*, Hume declares Shaftesbury's appeal to a sympathy of parts as the "uniting principle of the universe" to be a philosophical fiction, an obtuse theory the appeal of which stands in need of explanation by a more sound and experimental investigation of the principles of human nature (T 1.4.6.6n50). Hume's observation notwithstanding, Shaftesbury's approach involves a number of elements that, while they are taken up and absorbed in the work of his successors, should be seen as original contributions and founding themes of philosophical aesthetics.

First, Shaftesbury can be credited not only with the first systematic presentation and use of "disinterestedness," but also of equating aesthetic value more generally with a particular kind of experience that involves being affected in a distinct way by the presence of objects with certain qualities; the result are those states we call beauty and sublimity. Second, Shaftesbury emphasizes the view, Platonic in origin, that beauty is absolute and real. This presages a debate on which every major writer in the Age of Taste felt obliged to express some opinion, namely, whether, and if so in what sense, there is a standard of beauty independent of and to which our judgments must conform, or whether all beauty is relative, a product of time and place; this is a debate to which Shaftesbury contributes, albeit obliquely, when he distinguishes the appearance of beauty from its form, reflected in the fact that we tacitly accept the existence of standards in our judgments of value.

Third, while Shaftesbury in this manner comes down on the side of a real standard, he at once gives voice to the idea that beauty also has an origin in our judgments, and holds that we are fitted in some way to receive and be affected by it, although the pleasure is of a distinctly rational sort. In much of the eighteenth century this idea of "fit" turns on sentiments rather than reason, but Shaftesbury is the first to articulate clearly the thought that aesthetic value has a foundation in human nature, without which we could not speak of beauty or sublimity at all. The very notion of an internal sense suggests immediately a basic counterpart to sight, hearing, touch, and gustatory taste, the external senses through which the world impinges on the subject independent of volition. There is, moreover, an ambiguity in this use of "sense," raised and addressed explicitly by later writers, for although beauty, like colors, sounds, objects touched, and food tasted, should strike us immediately, aesthetic taste involves not only receptivity, but also active discernment so that time and effort are required in order to feel (or, in Shaftesbury's idiom, apprehend) the beauty in question. For this reason, the idea of the connoisseur, critic, or "true judge"

---

[13] Reid I consider in the current chapter; Reynolds, Alison, and the Romantics in chs. 2, 3, and 5, respectively.

looms large in those who take up and develop this idea. Finally, while again a familiar Platonic theme, Shaftesbury can be seen as setting the stage for what becomes the routine comparison between aesthetic value and moral value. For Shaftsbury, aesthetic value is without question comparable to moral value, and although others do not follow him and resolve both ultimately into the single principle of order manifest in the form of the Divine Mind, the equation of these two orders of value is a largely unquestioned assumption for those who follow. This is pronounced in nobody more than Francis Hutcheson and it is to his *Inquiry* we now turn.

FRANCIS HUTCHESON

Given that Shaftesbury articulates and establishes a number of themes that form the weave through which much of eighteenth-century aesthetics runs, we should not be surprised to find points of comparison between his thinking and the aesthetics of Francis Hutcheson (1694–1746), who spent his career teaching at the private school he founded in Dublin and later as Chair of Moral Philosophy at Glasgow. On the title page of the first edition of *An Inquiry into the Original of Our Ideas of Beauty and Virtue in Two Treatises Inquiry* (1725), Hutcheson characterizes his work as an explanation and defense of "the principles of the late Earl of Shaftesbury."[14] Although Hutcheson acknowledges a debt to his forebear – initially at least, because the subtitle is omitted in later editions – in practice his approach owes little to neo-Platonism and a great deal to Locke and, one assumes, Joseph Addison, who had already broached aesthetic matters in a similar, if less systematic way; his series of essays in *The Spectator* on "Pleasures of the Imagination" includes a distinction between Primary and Secondary Pleasures that tracks very closely Hutcheson's Original and Comparative Beauty.[15]

If Shaftesbury's "principles" do guide Hutcheson's thought, they are refracted so completely through the lens of empiricism as to be hardly recognizable. In Hutcheson's hands, Shaftesbury's principle of order and harmony is transformed into "uniformity amidst variety"; the idea of an internal sense

---

[14] See the textual note in Francis Hutcheson, *An Inquiry into the Original of Our Ideas of Beauty and Virtue in Two Treatises*, 2nd ed. (Indianapolis, IN: Liberty Fund, 2004 [1726]), 199n1. All references, following Hutcheson's division, are to treatise, section, and paragraph number. Hutcheson also conceives the *Inquiry* as a response to the "Author of the *Fable of the Bees*," Bernard Mandeville, who argued, as the subtitle of his infamous work makes clear, that vice is a necessary condition for general economic prosperity. See Bernard Mandeville, *The Fable of the Bees or Private Vices, Publick Benefits*, 2 vols. (Indianapolis, IN: Liberty Fund, 1988 [1732; 1st ed. 1714]).

[15] I consider Addison's essays in ch. 2. It is worth noting at this juncture, however, that writing toward the end of the century (*Essays on the Nature and Principles of Taste* [1790]), Archibald Alison identifies his philosophy with what he characterizes as the "Platonic School" of *inter alia* Shaftesbury, Hutcheson, and Reid. See ch. 3.

becomes a literal counterpart to the external senses; the metaphysical idea of the Divine Mind takes the attenuated form of a final cause based on design; and disinterestedness is detached from any quasimystical associations and, in conjunction with Locke's indirect realism and the distinction between primary and secondary qualities, appears as the doctrine that ideas of beauty simply strike immediately and independently of knowledge or advantage. Unlike Shaftesbury, Hutcheson is comfortable with the plain lessons of experience, which he regards happily as the way we perceive qualities possessed by objects that affect a mind fitted by nature and cultivation to receive them; it is no longer a parade of mere appearances behind which stands some ultimate, transcendent reality, into which the inquiring mind must penetrate. Beauty is explicable instead as a function of the relation between an individual and the world, and Hutcheson has no use either for obscure metaphysical principles or rhapsodic states of philosophical enthusiasm.

Hutcheson's more earthly empiricism and debt to Locke from which it derives is evident in the terminology and definitions adumbrated at the outset of the *Inquiry*. "Sensations," Hutcheson says, are to be understood as ideas raised in a passive mind by the presence of external objects that act upon our bodies, and "senses" refer to the various powers of receiving these perceptions in the form of simple ideas, upon which the mind acts through its powers of compounding, comparing, enlarging, diminishing, and abstracting, to create complex ones. "Pleasure and pain," further, are feelings raised immediately "and without any knowledge of the Cause" (I.I.VI), although, in a nod to Shaftesbury's idea of disinterestedness, Hutcheson adds that a "rational Pleasure" might arise from such knowledge as might joy or aversion from the perceived advantage or good or evil; these are quite distinct, however, and independent of the "sensible" pleasure that comes adventitiously from perceptions of sense (I.I.VI). With this terminology in place, "The Word Beauty," Hutcheson then proposes, "is taken for the *Idea rais'd in us*, and a Sense of Beauty for our *Powers of receiving this Idea*" (I.I.IX, emphasis added) where the capacity to do so is what we "commonly call a fine Genius or Taste" (I.I.X). There are, moreover, two kinds of beauty, distinguishable through the source of the pleasure involved, namely, "uniformity in the Object itself" or "Resemblance to some Original" (I.I.XVIIn). The first kind is appropriately called "Original or Absolute," because it arises "when we perceive Objects without any comparison to any thing external," and the second kind is "Comparative or Relative," because its foundation is in objects that imitate or resemble something else. The aim of the first Treatise of the *Inquiry*, then, Hutcheson announces, is to illustrate these two kinds of beauty and "to discover what is the immediate Occasion of these pleasant Ideas, or what real Quality in the Objects ordinarily excites them" (I.I.IX).[16]

---

[16] The aim of the Treatise II of the *Inquiry*, the details of which lie beyond our current concerns, is to discover the origin of morals as a parallel to the explanation of the origin of beauty.

One can see straightaway the central role of "sense" and an "Internal Sense" in Hutcheson's approach; in the *Illustrations on the Moral Sense* published three years after the *Inquiry*, Hutcheson counts external sense and the sense of beauty as only two among "several Senses" that include "Publick Sense," a "Sense of Honour," and "other Perceptions distinct from all these Classes,"[17] an enumeration that threatens to rob or at least denude "sense" of its explanatory power. Hutcheson shows little concern for this eventuality, but is more interested in exploiting the term literally to emphasize the equivalence between internal and external senses, a notable departure from Shaftesbury, who employs it in a vague and largely metaphorical way to denote our exclusively internal appreciation of proportion and harmony all forms of which resolve into the Divine Mind. Hutcheson even suggests that the terms *internal* and *external* can be used interchangeably. It "is of no consequence," he writes,

whether we call these Ideas of Beauty and Harmony, Perceptions or the External Senses of Seeing and Hearing, or not. I should rather chuse [*sic*] to call our Powers of perceiving these ideas, an Internal Sense were it only for the Convenience of distinguishing them from other Sensations of Seeing and Hearing, which men may have without Perception of Beauty and Harmony. (I.I.X)

The important difference to bear in mind when comparing internal and external sense is that the perception of beauty involves some internal or mental element, and can function on occasions when the external senses play no role: beauty is to be found in mathematical and logical theorems, universal truths, general causes, and even principles of action, and in these instances the idea of beauty is "pretty different" (I.III.I) than in cases in which we actually perceive the qualities of the object in question.

Hutcheson's main point, however, is that, like ideas that have their origin in the external sense of sight and hearing, the internal idea of beauty is excited immediately and adventitiously, prior to and independent of volition, and distinct from the rational pleasure associated with advantage, knowledge, possession, and property (I.VII.I). Beauty also arises regardless of any theoretical knowledge of its origin, whether or not the spectator has reflected on and discovered its "general Foundation" (I.II.XIV). Internal sense, moreover, is a necessary condition of aesthetic experience, without which we could never receive the idea in question. "Had we no such Sense of Beauty and Harmony," Hutcheson insists, "Houses, Gardens, Dress, Equipage, might have been recommended to us as convenient, fruitful, warm, easy; but never as beautiful: ... And no Custom, Education, or Example could ever give us Perceptions

---

[17] Francis Hutcheson, *An Essay on the Nature and Conduct of the Passions and Affections, with Illustrations on the Moral Sense* (Indianapolis, IN: Liberty Fund, 2002 [1728]), I.I.I. (IMS followed by treatise, section, and paragraph). Under the last of these, Hutcheson includes decency, dignity, and the suitableness to human nature of certain actions and circumstances, and their opposites in the form of indecency, meanness, and unworthiness.

distinct from those of the Senses which we had the use of before, or recommend Objects under another Conception than grateful to them" (I.I.XVI).

Equally clear from Hutcheson's discussion of sense, powers, and the like, is the degree to which he adopts the Lockean distinction between primary and secondary qualities; beauty is a variety of the latter because it "properly denotes the Perception of the Mind" (I.I.XVII) rather than corresponding to any quality in the object. "All beauty is relative to the Sense of some Mind perceiving it" (I.III.I), Hutcheson insists, and although it may be "excited" by the object, an object could not be beautiful at all without a mind to receive the idea and a subject with the capacity to feel pleasure. For this reason, Hutcheson cannot, in the final analysis, be considered a realist;[18] unlike Shaftesbury, he holds that beauty is not some feature of the world or in objects per se – there is no beauty or deformity *in itself* – but it amounts to a dispositional property formed through the interaction between objects, with their primary qualities, and a mind with a sense fitted to receive the idea and feel pleasure or pain from it. Even when we develop our taste or genius, it brings us no closer to some quality called beauty, but refines our capacity to receive the idea in question. It follows from this that if human beings had another kind of sense, they would find different things beautiful, and, by extension, lacking any internal sense at all, the world would be void of beauty altogether. Hutcheson takes the fact that we find ourselves in a world populated with objects structured to affect the kind of sense we actually have, to be a contingent though happy situation and evidence for the existence of Providence or some designing mind that we may call God.

Uniformity Amidst Variety

What, then, on this view, explains why the idea of beauty arises or which feature of objects occasions it? The answer to this question lies in Hutcheson's central principle of uniformity (or unity) amidst variety (or number) or, expressed mathematically, the "compound Ratio of Uniformity and Variety: so that where the Uniformity of Body is equal, the Beauty is as the Variety; and where the Variety is equal, the Beauty is as the Uniformity" (I.II.III). In the case of absolute beauty, Hutcheson sees this principle operating in three different areas. First, in shapes (or what he calls "figures"), the degree of beauty is proportional to the variety of sides amidst the uniformity displayed; squares, triangles, and pentagons contain equal uniformity (equal sides of three, four, and five, respectively), but beauty increases with the number (variety) of sides in question. Where there is equal variety, by contrast, as in the case of triangles all of which have three sides, beauty is proportional to the uniformity of the

---

[18] Cf. Peter Kivy, *The Seventh Sense: Francis Hutcheson and Eighteenth-Century British Aesthetics*, 2nd ed. (Oxford: Oxford University Press, 2003 [1976]).

sides; an equilateral triangle is more beautiful than an isosceles, and the latter more than a scalenum. Second, the natural world is beautiful due to the "vast Uniformity amidst an almost infinite Variety" that it displays (I.II.V). The planets, for example, are uniformly spherical and their orbits elliptical, but there is variety in the different forms they take. The seasons follow a temporal order and yet spring, summer, autumn, and winter are quite different, and the uniform green of the earth is "diversify'd with various Degrees of Light and Shade, according to the different Situations of the Parts of its Surface, in Mountains, Valleys, Hills, and open Plains" (I.II.VI). Among plants, vegetables, animals, and birds there is a seemingly endless variety of species, but a discernible uniformity in propagation, growth, mechanical structure, and proportion; turning our gaze to the parts that compose them – leaves, colors, limbs, and feathers – we cannot help be struck by the variety within each feature, so great, Hutcheson observes, as to "surpass our Imagination!" (I.II.VII).

Third, and finally, Hutcheson proposes the same explanation for the beauty of theorems, axioms, or "universal Truths," including philosophical ones. Unlike shapes or objects of the natural world, these are independent of external sense, but we find them beautiful according to the same principle. Hutcheson understands a theorem as an "Agreement, or Unity of an Infinity of Objects" (I.II.III) so that within the single universal truth (its uniformity) is included a "Multitude of particular Truths" (its variety) (I.III.II). "Thus, for instance," he writes,

the 47th Proposition of the first Book of Euclid's *Elements* contains an infinite Multitude of Truths, concerning the infinite possible Sizes of right-angled Triangles, as you make the Area greater or less; and in each of these Sizes you may find an infinite Multitude of dissimilar Triangles, as you vary the Proportion of the Base to the Perpendicular; all which Infinites of Infinities agree in the general Theorem. (I.III.II)

Where the unity is precise, that is, where the principle or "canon" expressed by the theorem and applied to the particulars is "distinct and determinate," the beauty is always proportionally greater; when the relation in question is vague and indefinite, by contrast, the beauty is diminished. We thus find some beauty and take pleasure in the theorem that shows a cylinder to be greater than the sphere it inscribes, but far more in one that expresses a constant ratio between solids or shows the area of a triangle to be a proportional relation between base and height; in these latter cases we have perfect unity expressed in the variety of forms the triangle can take. Similarly, there is want of beauty and satisfaction in the proposition that "*Every Whole is greater than its Part*" because agreement is "only in a vague, undetermin'd Conception of Whole and Part" (I.III.IV). Hutcheson admits that beauty is also proportional to the difficulty of the proposition and the degree to which effort is required to discover the truth in question; pleasure and perceived beauty accompany the surprise or novelty that comes at the conclusion of a demonstration or some other process of thought, and in contrast to

Euclid's proof concerning the infinite possible sizes of right-angled triangles, that "*Equilateral Triangles are Equiangular*" is so familiar as to be obvious and almost intuitive. Hutcheson insists, however, that such elements only heighten beauty, but do not explain it; they presuppose that beauty arises originally from uniformity amidst variety.

It is also worth noting in this context how Hutcheson observes that "Love of Uniformity" explains why philosophers and natural scientists are drawn so often to reduce their inquiries to a "favourite Principle" or single proposition from which they take "innumerable Effects" to follow. Hutcheson clearly thinks that this tendency can have explanatory power – Newton's appeal to gravitational force, or the deduction of moral duties from the principle of original rights – but he warns how quickly it passes from being useful or enlightening into becoming absurdity and "silly Affectation": in this category he places Descartes's *cogito ergo sum*, G. W. Leibniz's use of the principle of sufficient reason, and Samuel Puffendorf's claim to deduce the duties of men to God from a "single principle of Sociableness to the whole Race of Mankind" (I.III.V). In these cases, philosophers (from whose number Hutcheson, one assumes, exempts himself and his own principle) are seduced by the beauty of knowledge into creating "Contortions of common Sense" that terminate in a kind of "Fantastick Beauty" (II.III.V). Perhaps the internal sense is oversensitive and the pleasures of contemplation too easily enjoyed in these cases, but in Hutcheson's view it is to be explained in the same way: through the principle of uniformity amidst variety, and the capacity of human beings to have the idea of beauty raised in them.

Hutcheson's second category of beauty is relative (or comparative) beauty, an extension (as we shall see) of Addison's treatment of poetry and representation in *The Spectator*. Relative beauty is an application of "uniformity amidst variety" to the case of artistic production where there is a "unity" between an original and its resembling copy, which the mind discovers through comparison, an activity that is itself a source of pleasure. Hutcheson is careful to clarify the two ways in which he uses the term *relative*. "All Beauty is relative to the Sense of some Mind perceiving it," he emphasizes, "but what we call relative is that which is apprehended in any Object, commonly consider'd as an Imitation of some Original: And this Beauty is founded on a Conformity, or kind of Unity between the Original and the Copy" (I.III.I). "Relative beauty" is not intended as another expression of the dispositional view of beauty, but as a way of identifying a distinct idea of beauty that arises from imitation and the act of comparing one thing to another, something we do naturally and from which we derive considerable pleasure. So great is our inclination in this regard, Hutcheson observes, that we find ourselves committing what has come to be termed the "pathetic" or "naturalistic fallacy" of attributing emotional states to inanimate objects: bodily gestures are taken as signs of mental disposition, a storm becomes a symbol of wrath, a drooping tree in the rain stands for sadness, and a withered flower the "Death of a blooming Hero" (I.III.IV).

Hutcheson aims to explain the beauty of artifacts that either imitate a natural object or conform to some accepted standard or rule that governs artistic practice. "Thus a Statuary, Painter, or Poet," he writes by way of example, "may please us with Hercules, if his Piece retains that Grandeur, and those marks of strength, and Courage, which we imagine in that Hero" (I.IV.I).[19]

Hutcheson's description of relative beauty makes it clear that the degree of beauty depends on the accuracy of the copy made of some original. Artists are obliged to refer to and represent the original as closely as possible because failing to do so would reduce the aesthetic value of their work. This is most obvious in cases in which artists preserve the imperfection of real life in order to inspire "lively ideas" required to engage an audience. Successful artists capture the grandeur, strength, and courage of Hercules in their depiction, for example. Likewise, an author should give a "just Representation of Manners or Characters as they are in Nature" and ensure that the "Actions and Sentiments be suited to the Characters of the Persons to whom they are ascrib'd in Epick and Dramatick Poetry" (I.IV.II) if the imagination is to be warmed and the reader moved; perfectly virtuous characters, however, will render the representation abstract and, divorced from our experience of human beings, leave the imagination cold and the audience distant from the action.

Hutcheson complicates this picture, however, by also suggesting that a "just Representation" does not require that there be any beauty in the original, the beauty of the copy being in some degree independent of it. For the "Deformitys of old Age in a Picture," he remarks, "the rudest Rocks or Mountains in a Landskip, if well represented shall have abundant Beauty, tho perhaps not so great as if the Original were absolutely beautiful, and as well represented" (I.IV.I). As a result, Hutcheson commits himself to the view that the source of the imitation does not lie primarily in the original, but in the creative activity of the artist who manipulates or plays with it for aesthetic effect. The imitation is not simply a reproduction or presentation of the original, but a representation of it that "depart[s] from the Rules of Original Beauty" (I.IV.VI) in a way that perfects and improves upon it. "It is not necessary that there be *any* beauty in the Original," Hutcheson observes, "the Imitation of absolute beauty may indeed make a more lovely Piece, and yet an exact Imitation shall still be beautiful, tho' the Original were intirely void of it" (I.IV.I, emphasis added). Beautiful gardens, for instance, abandon the strict regularity of parterres, vistas, and parallel walks for irregularity and lack of proportion; a sculptor will choose a less beautiful shape such as a cylinder or regular square for its base

---

[19] Hutcheson points out that the beauty of art can also be original insofar as we are struck by uniformity amidst variety. A building or garden exhibits a "Unity of Proportion among its Parts, and of each Part to the Whole," but this unity is expressed in diverse ways: in Classical and Chinese architecture, for example, or English as opposed to French landscaping (I.III. VIII). He clearly considers relative beauty, however, to be the primary kind of beauty relevant to art.

over the absolutely more beautiful form of pyramid or obelisk because the former better suits the intention of conveying the honor accorded the celebrated subject of the monument. For the same reason an imperfect pillar with a taper at the middle or toward the bottom will be used as a design for columns because this conveys to the eye a sense of stability that would be lost if the shape were uniform.[20] Literary tropes such as simile, metaphor, and analogy are also beautiful for this reason, Hutcheson urges, where the poet inspires us to imagine a resemblance between the depiction and the thing depicted. Artists are obliged to embellish and transform the original for the sake of raising the idea of beauty and pleasure in the audience.

The Standard of Taste

One interesting result of the position developed in the *Inquiry* is its implications for understanding the standard of taste, an issue for which Hutcheson (rather than Shaftesbury) effectively sets the stage across which every writer on aesthetics throughout the eighteenth century parades one view or another. From the side of relative beauty, Hutcheson is obliged to hold that the standard inheres in an original that provides the rules in terms of which the copy can be "fixed." The degree to which the copy successfully imitates and reproduces the original increases or diminishes the work of art and constitutes a clear criterion for deciding whether a work of art is beautiful or not and for ranking it alongside others that surpass or fall short of it. The same is not true, however, for representations that depart from the original, notably in those nonimitative arts such as music, architecture, and gardening where beauty is independent altogether of any correspondence between original and copy. These arts please – in conformity with Hutcheson's central principle – due to the unity and proportion among the parts and of the parts to the whole, but for this very reason they leave room for an indefinite diversity in the particular forms beauty can take over time and across place. As Hutcheson points out, Chinese and Persian architecture may differ radically from the style of the Greek and Roman, but they all share an emphasis on proportion and resemblance among elements in each building. In all cases, "that Proportion which is observ'd in the rest of the Building, is displeasing to every Eye, and destroys or diminishes at least the Beauty of the Whole" (I.III.VIII). For Hutcheson, then, there is a standard insofar as objects possess qualities of proportion, uniformity, and variety that occasions the idea of beauty in a being so structured to receive it; the form this beauty takes, however, that is, the expression of absolute beauty

---

[20] This idea of artistic intention can be extended – in a clear echo of Shaftesbury – to the "Author of Nature," where, Hutcheson thinks, we infer reason and design in the cause from the effects, Nature herself, as if the whole were a complex machine indicative of a designing intelligence.

or the way the principle of unity amidst variety is manifest, depends ultimately on the contingencies of a particular culture.

By way of analogy with the external senses, we might think of a person who is deaf or blind; this does not change the nature of the world, but it prevents the person from experiencing it as fully as they otherwise might. Thus, as a matter of fact, beauty is real in being founded on uniformity amidst variety, but certain tastes – for Gothic architecture above the Romanesque, for example – can be dismissed as imperfect or bad. Human nature is structured such that the same qualities should give rise to the same idea, but it is in their judgments that people err as a result of certain intervening causes: "accidental Ideas" produce "fantastick Aversions" to swine, snakes, and insects even though these are "really beautiful enough" (I.VI.IV; see IMS I.IV.IV), and sometimes individuals are led astray by their disposition or passions, including the powerful desire for recognition and eminence even when they lack the requisite talent (IMS I.IV.II). In the final analysis, Hutcheson concludes, beauty and the sense of beauty are universal, but actual tastes are not, and for this reason it is misleading to speak of a "standard of taste" at all.

As a corollary to this conclusion, Hutcheson also holds that there is no actual ugliness or deformity in the world, only a lack of perceived beauty due to some inconvenience or fault of internal sense. For this reason, connoisseurship looms large, the practice of improving, educating, or cultivating one's taste, necessary if the internal sense is to work properly and at its full potential. "Education and Custom may influence our internal Senses," Hutcheson writes, "... by enlarging the Capacity of our Minds to retain and compare the parts of complex Compositions; And then if the finest Objects are presented to us, we grow conscious of a Pleasure far superior to what common Performances excite." As Hutcheson also adds, "all this presupposes our Sense of Beauty to be natural" (I.VII.III), for without the feature of uniformity amidst variety in objects and the capacity to be affected by it, beauty as an idea raised in us would never exist. We might note in closing that Hutcheson's view of a standard or lack thereof is perfectly consistent with his interest in and focus on the internal sense of the subject rather than on features of the object: because he denies that we can speak of beauty independent of some perceiving mind, it would make no sense for him to discover an independent standard somehow in or of the world itself.

THOMAS REID

Thomas Reid (1719–96) occupied a professorship at King's College, Aberdeen, before being called to succeed Adam Smith as Professor of Moral Philosophy at Glasgow. He is best known for *An Inquiry into the Human Mind on the Principles of Common Sense* (1764) and as founder of the school of thought named for the "principles" the work adumbrates. This work contains no reference to aesthetics at all, and although Reid apparently delivered lectures on the subject,[21] only some twenty years later did he publish "On Taste," the last essay of *Essays on the Intellectual Powers of Man* (1785), in which he applies his "principles of common sense" to the beautiful and sublime. There is a distance of some sixty years between Hutcheson's *Inquiry* and Reid's *Essays*, but in the main – and despite obvious differences between the two approaches – a fundamental feature around which both revolve is the idea of an internal sense, a feature that puts Reid more naturally in the company of Shaftesbury and Hutcheson than in that of either imagination theorists or associationists. The categorization is appropriate despite the fact that Reid counts Hutcheson among the "modern Philosophers" (III.584.11) who have flouted the "dictates of common sense" (III.584.16–17) and reduced the material world to a "phænomenon only" that "has no existence but in the mind" (III.584.5–6). This does not prevent Alison (as already noted) from seeing a kindred philosophical spirit manifest in Reid's doctrine that beauty and sublimity are properly understood as the expression of mind, although this connection does not touch Reid's status as an internal sense theorist.

Two aspects of Reid's approach should be emphasized at the outset, both of which frame his contribution to aesthetics. First, he rejects the tendency he discerns in Shaftesbury, Hutcheson, and other writers who follow them, to reduce aesthetic experience to "fewer principles than the nature of the things will permit,"[22] which results, in Reid's estimation at least, in many writers having focused on "some particular kinds of beauty, while they overlooked others" (I.575.14–16). "Beauty," after all, is used of a great variety of objects that are more different than they are similar – *inter alia*, poems, palaces, music, a "fine woman," animals, the body and mind of men, and God (I.575.5–8) – and this speaks persuasively against the temptation, born of a "love of simplicity," to reduce it to some univocal source in Universal Mind (Shaftesbury) or uniformity amidst variety (Hutcheson).

Second, and more fundamentally, as already indicated, Reid undertakes a tireless campaign against the doctrine of primary and secondary qualities, inaugurated by the Ancients, refined in Descartes and Locke, and brought to perfection by Hume. Reid acknowledges that aesthetic experience requires some affective capacity – "it is impossible to perceive the beauty of an object, without perceiving the object, or at least conceiving it," he remarks – but "Modern philosophers," he contends, have been led astray by the fact that the sensation *and* the quality have the same name – "taste" – which has led them

---

[21] These lectures survive as a manuscript dated 1774, although not in Reid's hand, and add little to what is contained in the later published work. See *Thomas Reid's Lectures on the Fine Arts: Transcribed from the Original Manuscript with an Introduction and Notes*, ed. Peter Kivy (The Hague: Martinus Nijhoff, 1973).

[22] Thomas Reid, *Essays on the Intellectual Powers of Man* (University Park: Pennsylvania State University Press, 2002 [1785]), I.575.14–15. All references are to chapter, page, and line numbers of this edition.

to place both in the mind. This contradicts our common practice and our natural language in which we distinguish clearly between the "agreeable sensation we feel, and the quality in the object that occasions it" (1.573.27–8), the former really being the effect or "sign" of the latter, which is a distinct cause of the thing "signified" (I.573.33–5). The apparent similarity and the confusion to which it gives rise is the reason, Reid observes, that "Dr. Hutcheson called the senses of beauty and harmony reflex or secondary senses; because the beauty cannot be perceived unless the object be perceived by some other power of the mind" (I.578.22–5). The term is applied only metaphorically to denote a power of mind, he emphasizes, due to the analogy it bears to the "taste of the palate." This has "led men, in all ages ... to give the name of external sense to this power of discerning what is beautiful with pleasure, and what is ugly and faulty of its kind with disgust" (I.573.20–3).[23] This is a mistake, and making it does not provide warrant to denude the object of aesthetic value and assign it instead to some idea of the mind.

Thus, in contrast to Hutcheson and others in the Lockean tradition, although very much in the spirit of Shaftesbury, Reid insists that the commonsense distinction between sign and signified must be reflected in any philosophical approach to aesthetics and on this basis he develops a variety of direct realism. "Beauty or deformity in an object," as he writes, "results from its nature or structure. To perceive the beauty therefore, we must perceive the nature or structure from which it results. In this the internal sense differs from the external. Our external senses may discover qualities which do not depend upon any antecedent perception" (I.578.15–19). Thus, "When I hear an air in music that pleases me," he remarks, by way of example,

I say, it is fine, it is excellent. This excellence is not in me; it is in the music. But the pleasure it gives is not in the music; it is in me. Perhaps I cannot say what it is in the tune that pleases my ear, as I cannot say what it is in a sapid body that pleases my palate; but there is a quality in the sapid body which pleases my palate, and I call it a delicious taste; and there is a quality in the tune that pleases my taste, and I call it a fine or an excellent air. (I.574.2–9)

Like Hutcheson and the "moderns" he derides, Reid still defines taste as the power of the mind to discern beauty, but he understands it as an "*intellectual* power," and, in a way reminiscent of the Kantian contrast between the

---

[23] Given this distinction between sign and signified, some have seen in Reid the beginning of an "expressivist" theory of art, which finds a clearer voice in Alison and, more famously, in the aesthetics of Leo Tolstoy, Benedetto Croce, and R. G. Collingwood. For, as we grasp the beauty of nature as an expression of creation, so an object of art expresses the emotion or intention of the artist, which is given material form perceived by the spectator in any given work. See ch.7, and for an appreciation of Reid as an originator of expressivism in aesthetics, see Peter Kivy, "Reid's Philosophy of Art," in *The Cambridge Companion to Thomas Reid*, ed. Terence Cuneo and René van Woudenberg (Cambridge: Cambridge University Press, 2004), 267–88.

agreeable and a "judgment of taste," he distinguishes the perception of the quality that gives rise to a sensation from a judgment – "an affirmation or denial of one thing concerning another" (I.577.15–16) – that yields knowledge of something real and thus a belief or opinion that there is a quality in the object perceived. On Reid's view, "I feel pain" is an utterance that describes a sensation without the existence of an object, whereas "I see a tree" is a judgment involving an object that is independent of the observer. When it comes to aesthetics, then, "when I say that VIRGIL's Georgics is a beautiful poem," Reid maintains, I report not on "myself and my feelings" but am committed to the fact "that there is something in the power, and not in me, which I call beauty" (I.577.23–9). To deny this, Reid insists, is to deny that object *is* in fact beautiful, a contravention of the "necessary rules of construction" and principles of common sense that beauty is a real quality that causes agreeable sensation through the perception of a quality.

What then, for Reid, constitutes the "real quality" in question? Before answering this question, we should note first how Reid is willing to admit that sometimes the quality is unknown or "occult," although this is not to deny that the quality exists, only to acknowledge ignorance of its nature. Reid also refers to beauty as a "secondary perception," but this should not be confused with Locke's secondary *quality*; it means instead that beauty requires perception of an object through the external senses in which the quality resides, a claim in no way incompatible with Reid's insistence that beauty is more than an idea in the mind of the spectator. Reid claims that the real quality in question is an attribute adapted to please a good taste because it contains "excellence" or "perfection." Things "fit" for the nourishment of bodies, for example, are the most excellent of their kind, and this gives rise to the sensation of agreeableness. A depraved taste, conversely, is when we have a relish for something that has no nutritional value (eating dirt or ashes), and this can be explained, in the spirit of Hutcheson, through bad habits, arbitrary association, and the negative effects of education.

What is true of gustatory taste is also true of aesthetic taste and on this basis (adopting explicitly the triad that, as we shall see, Addison had coined some seventy years earlier), Reid distinguishes "three objects of taste" (II.579.5–7). The first is novelty, which he conceives as a "relation which the thing has to the knowledge of the person" (II.579.34–5) because something is only novel in reference to something not already known. It is a "real relation," however, rather than simply an agreeable sensation in the mind, with its foundation in the curiosity or love of the new that gives pleasure and involves a "stretch of the imagination." Reid understands this as the cause of unending desire and hope that, "by the appointment of Nature," spurs us on to the end of happiness. For this reason, novelty alone gives only entertainment (of the sort experienced by animals and children) and some additional element is required, that it be a "sign" of rank, worth, or usefulness, if it is to give true and "rational pleasure" (II.581.31–9).

The second object of taste is grandeur, or sublimity. Although writing in the latter part of the century, Reid retains the distinction – implicit in Shaftesbury and explicit in Addison – between sublime style and sublimity. He refers to the former as the "sublime in description" (III.586.1) and associates it with Longinus and literary composition (III.585.26–8), but calls the latter "grand," "truly grand," the "true sublime," or on one occasion simply "sublime" (III.591.5). The sublime in this sense – that is, sublimity – cannot arise from composition alone, he urges, but requires "grandeur in the subject" (III.586.11–12). Reid also holds that, strictly speaking, the grand (or what we can also simply call the sublime) applies only to qualities of mind and not to inanimate or material objects of sense; at the very least, he insists, there should be a "different name" for each to reflect that they are "very different in their nature, and produce very different emotions in the mind of the spectator" (III.591.16–17). Only people or depictions of people (historical or fictional) can be sublime because they alone possess "intellectual" qualities; inanimate objects, by contrast, are nominally sublime, the title being conferred on them because they "are the effects or signs" of "something intellectual," or "bear some relation or analogy" to it (III.588.24–6). When objects are called sublime, it is a metaphorical use of the term from connecting in imagination, and often unwittingly, otherwise different objects that are analogous, contrasting, resembling, or otherwise related; we thus extend the concept by ascribing qualities to "the one what properly belongs to the other" (III.589.1–2). Reid finds in this imaginative *transmutio* the origin of poetic language, and an explanation why sublimity is routinely connected with magnitude or terror;[24] qualities of mind are assigned to those of body (sweet, austere, simple, and duplicitous), and inanimate objects dignified with human qualities they obviously do not possess (the "raging" sea or "murmuring" rivulet).

With these observations in mind, it becomes clear why Reid distinguishes the emotion that constitutes the experience of the sublime from what "grandeur in an object *is*" (III.582.29–30, emphasis added). The emotion aroused by grand objects is not pleasure (as in novelty) or agreeableness (as in beauty), but "awful, solemn, and serious" (III.582.12), which – in a perfect description of the rhapsodic state of Shaftesbury's Theocles – "disposes to seriousness, elevates the mind above its usual state, to a kind of enthusiasm, and inspires magnanimity, and a contempt of what is mean" (III.582.25–7). It comes, moreover, in degrees, but finds highest expression in that "most grand" of objects, the Supreme Being, whose defining characteristics of eternity, immensity, power, justice, rectitude, and wisdom raise "devotion; a serious recollected temper

---

[24] Reid suggests that the "similarity between dread and terror" also explains Burke's equation in *A Philosophical Enquiry into the Sublime and Beautiful* of the sublime with what is terrible: both emotions are grave and solemn, Reid observes, but only admiration involves the "enthusiasm" requisite for sublimity. See III.590.30ff., and ch. 2 of the present study.

which inspires magnanimity, and disposes to the most heroic acts of virtue" (III.582.20–3).

While this describes the emotion raised by contemplating grand objects, grandeur is actually a "degree of excellence, in one kind or another, as merits our admiration" (III.582.31–2). It is admired, moreover, because it is "intrinsically valuable and excellent" (III.582.37) and is so "from its own constitution, and not from ours" (III.584.21). This "real intrinsic excellence" – as we saw earlier – refers primarily to qualities of mind and, secondarily, by transference, to inanimate objects: power, knowledge, wisdom, virtue, and magnanimity are attributes of mind or excellences that are admired, and when they exist to an "uncommon degree" (III.582.35–6) raise in the spectator the awful, solemn, serious emotion that constitutes sublime experience. Thus, "true grandeur," as Reid defines it, "is such a degree of excellence as is fit to raise an enthusiastical admiration" (III.591.6–7). This accounts not only for the sublimity of God and biblical descriptions of his works, but also for the emotions that attend reflection on historical and literary figures: the great souls of Cato and Seneca, for example, noble, superior, and magnanimous in the face of terrible misfortune; the characters, actions, and events of the *Iliad*; the virtues of Aristides, Socrates, and Marcus Aurelius, and those poets, philosophers, lawgivers, and orators whose "extraordinary talents and genius" fill us with admiration and awe. Reid insists that in all these cases sublimity is found in qualities of mind: either in the "grand thoughts" of the author (such as Homer) who conceived the characters, or, when the work is considered independent of the writer, in the qualities of the characters depicted (Hector and Achilles) (III.587.22ff.). Thus, as in the case of an object to which we attach the epithet due to some point of similarity, only by mistake do we call some deed sublime: the person is intrinsically excellent and raises admiration while the action is the effect (or sign) of that cause (or signified), and sublime by extension only. It is for this reason that Reid concludes his treatment of grandeur with an apt metaphor of light and life: grandeur is "discerned in objects of sense only by reflection, as the light we perceive in the moon and planets is truly the light of the sun; and that those who look for grandeur in mere matter, seek the living among the dead" (III.591.9–12).

The third object of taste is beauty. As we have seen, Reid rejects the idea that there is a quality common to all beauties, but he does maintain that there is a "common relation to us, or something else, which leads us to give them the same name" (IV.592.3–4). The quality in the object is a real excellence that produces the sensation of agreeableness coupled with the belief (from a judgment) that the object has the excellence in question. This excellence consists of what Reid calls a love or liking (or in the case of persons, benevolence), and the more we discover this excellence, the more beautiful the object appears. Reid then distinguishes two "senses of beauty." The first is "instinctive beauty" in which objects (such as the plumage of birds, the wings of butterflies, and the colors and forms of flowers or shells) "strike us at once, and appear beautiful at first sight, without any reflection" although we cannot say why (IV.596.10–11), and the second is "rational beauty," in which the quality in the object is conceived distinctly and on that account "may be specified": a mechanic, for example, finds a machine beautiful because he can "give a reason for his judgment, and point out the particular perfections in the object on which it is grounded" (IV.598.28–30).

In addition to senses of beauty, Reid also contrasts two kinds of "beauty itself," both of which can be traced ultimately to a real excellence, but differ in the way that excellence is perceived. "Original" beauty, as the term suggests, arises from the direct effect of the quality or, in Reid's metaphor, because "objects shine by their own light." "Derived" beauty, however, shines by a light that is "borrowed and reflected," because the original quality (the cause, end, or agent in the signified) is transferred to some other object (the effect, means, agent, or sign) (IV.599.3–6). As Reid points out, this is what happens when we speak of the sublimity of the *Iliad* (effect), when it is actually the conception of the author expressed in the work that is sublime. In a similar way, good breeding is not originally in the person of whom it is said, but is the expression, sign, or "picture" of certain qualities of mind – the real excellence that is intrinsically amiable and beautiful and the "natural objects of love and kind affection" – which are reflected in objects of sense and perceived behavior.

Reid's realist approach to aesthetics leads him, as one might expect, to a decisive stand on the question of a standard of taste. In an important respect, he departs from Hutcheson's emphasis on the universality of sense and bears comparison to Hume's famous treatment of the subject in "Of the Standard of Taste" (considered in Chapter 2), to which it is, like other contributions to the same subject in the latter part of the century (notably those of Burke and Gerard), indebted. Both Hume and Reid insist that there is a standard that everybody accepts, while acknowledging and explaining the diversity of judgments that depart from it. Unlike Hume, however, Reid appeals not to the test of time for evidence of real beauty, but to the intrinsic quality of object or work of art, and is prepared to dismiss variety simply as corrupt taste (rather than diagnose it, like Hume, as a contradiction into which people unwittingly fall). As we have seen, Reid denies that there is any single quality that all objects said to be beautiful possess, for which reason he regards it as both futile and simplistic to reduce all beauty and thus taste to a single explanatory principle. At the same time, he insists that there is a standard of taste, and thus a basis for improving judgment, precisely because any beautiful object – whatever the quality in question might be – always involves a real, that is, intrinsic excellence. Those with a "discerning eye" (I.575.22) perceive this excellence, and in so doing conform to the standard "in nature" and have a "just and rational" taste; this contrasts with those who lack the same and display a taste "depraved and corrupted." Reid acknowledges that tastes vary between people and across cultures due to acquaintance, custom, fancy, and (in an echo of Hutcheson) "casual associations" (I.576.11–17). Africans, he notes, esteem thick lips and a flat nose, while people of other nations put great value on "ears that hang over their shoulders" or on paint or grease adorning their faces. Similarly (according to Reid's anthropological sources at least), the Eskimos enjoy a "draught of whale-oil," Canadians can "feast upon a dog," and a "Kamschatkadale lives upon putrid fish" or the bark of trees (576.18–24). In the final analysis – and no doubt the reason Reid finds these examples so instructive – such tendencies are analogous to eating dirt or ashes, that is, they are tastes that depart from the excellence found "in nature" where the "standard of true beauty" lies.

2

Imagination Theorists

The writers who comprise the category of imagination theorists form what is the most extensive and eclectic group of the eighteenth century, their number spanning the period from Addison's graceful and seminal essays for *The Spectator* (1712), to Reynolds's *Discourses on Art*, delivered over the course of some thirty years, concluding in 1790 and published in their entirety in 1797, three years shy of the new century. In the interim, one finds Hume's disparate observations on beauty and taste, including his influential treatments of a standard and the curious nature of tragic emotions; Hogarth's singular and unduly neglected *The Analysis of Beauty*; and undoubtedly the most influential work of the entire eighteenth-century tradition, Burke's *A Philosophical Enquiry into the Origin of Our Ideas of the Sublime and Beautiful*, published in 1757 and destined to make waves so powerful that their effects are felt still, moving like ripples through the waters of contemporary aesthetics. Eclectic these contributors might be – literary gentleman, accomplished artists, philosophers of first rank – but they are united as a body by the emphasis each gives to imagination and its role as facilitator of artistic creativity and enabler of aesthetic receptivity. As noted in the introduction, only Hume might be snubbed as a possible interloper, as he flirts on the one side with Hutcheson's "internal sense" and anatomizes the principles of association on the other. As we shall see in due course, however, neither of these plays a prominent role in his aesthetics, and it is the faculty of imagination and its representative power that Hume finds most intriguing and defines his contribution to the tradition.

JOSEPH ADDISON

In the June 19, 1712, issue of *The Spectator*, Joseph Addison (1672–1719) announced his intention to enter on "an Essay *on the Pleasures of the Imagination*, which though it shall consider that Subject at large, will perhaps suggest to the reader what it is that gives a Beauty to many Passages of the finest Writers both in Prose and Verse." It will prove "an Undertaking," he promises, "... entirely new."[1] The claim to complete originality is an exaggeration; Shaftesbury's three-volume *Characteristicks* had appeared the previous year (1711), and much of the subject matter Addison considers had been given voice already in the well-established tradition of literary criticism stretching from Horace through modern French, Italian, and English writers of which Addison was surely aware. Even the title – "Pleasures of the Imagination" – though a phrase certainly popularized by Addison, was already in use.[2] Moreover, Addison had previously written papers for *The Spectator* on similar and related issues, most notably the series published between January and May 1712 devoted to the "Divine Genius" of John Milton, in which he touches many themes treated in the later essays on imagination.

That the essays on the "Pleasures of the Imagination" are not "entirely new," however, should not detract from their significance. Addison is writing in the tradition of neo-Augustan criticism, reflected in his focus on "Prose and Verse," but he is the first to look beyond it as well, signaled by his reference to the "Subject at large." Unlike Dennis, whose main concerns were criticism and religion, for Addison aesthetic matters take center stage; poetry and prose are illustrative of his philosophical inquiry rather than ends in themselves. It remains true that most, although by no means all, of the elements Addison treats in the essays are voiced in one way or another by his predecessors and contemporaries, and that compared to the portentous treatments to be found in the inquiries and treatises of his successors, *The Spectator* essays are neither systematic nor penetrating. This was never Addison's intention, however, and if Shaftesbury's *Characteristicks* heralds the birth of philosophical aesthetics, and Hutcheson's *Inquiry* is its inaugural systematic treatise, then Addison's essays stand as the sustained treatment of ideas and concepts that in one way or another dominate the new discipline up to and beyond the publication of Burke's *Enquiry* in mid-century. This is something the modern reader is apt to overlook, finding in the essays much that has grown familiar and subject to more detailed and sustained treatment in the hands of others.

With the phrase the "Pleasures of the Imagination," Addison conveys the idea – familiar from Locke and prominent later in Hutcheson – that aesthetic value arises through the interplay of an object with certain primary qualities,

---

[1] *The Spectator*, no. 409 (June 19, 1712), in *The Spectator*, ed. Donald F. Bond, 5 vols. (Oxford: Clarendon Press, 1965), 3:530–1. "The Pleasures of the Imagination" comprises eleven essays published between June 21 and July 3, 1712, in Bond, 535–82. Unless otherwise indicated, all references are to the pagination in this volume of Bond's edition followed by the original essay number.

[2] In his editorial notes to *The Spectator* (pp. 536 and 538), Bond notes that the phrase had been used by Sir William Temple in his *Observations upon the United Provinces of the Netherlands* (1687), and appears in a letter written by Lady Mary Pierrepont of July 21, 1709. Mark Akenside (1721–70) adopted the title later for his didactic poem, which drew on Addison's ideas in particular. See *The Pleasures of the Imagination*, in *The Poetical Works of Mark Akenside*, ed. Robin Dix (Cranbury, NJ: Associated University Presses, 1996).

and a faculty – the imagination – so constituted to receive those qualities and capable of being affected by them to give rise to a particular feeling we call pleasure; pleasure is the occasion for saying of the object that it has certain aesthetic qualities and attributing them to it. Pleasures arise, as Addison puts it, "from visible Objects, either when we have them actually in our view, or when we call up their Ideas in our Minds by Paintings, Statues, descriptions, or any the like Occasion" (3:536–7, no. 411). Pleasures are of "two kinds," depending on their origin. "Primary Pleasures" arise from the "actual view and survey of outward Objects" (3:540, no. 412); we perceive real objects that are "Great" (i.e., sublime), "Uncommon" (novel), or "Beautiful," ideas of which strike the imagination immediately and produce pleasure.[3] "Secondary Pleasures," by contrast, come not from the qualities of objects, but originate in the "Action of the Mind" called *comparison*, a spontaneous mechanism of imagination rather than an act of understanding. In this case, we have the idea of an object, either a real one recalled by memory or a fictional one invented by the imagination, which we compare with the idea received from some other object that represents it, a "Statue, Picture, Description, or Sound" (3:559–60, no. 416). In both cases, Addison maintains – whether from an actual view or through comparison – pleasure is immediate and independent of cognition.

Although Addison is clearly indebted to Locke for the general outlines of this view, he introduces modifications of his own. First, he embraces Locke's distinction between primary and secondary qualities, but unlike Locke he applies it specifically to explaining aesthetic value. To speak of an object as great, uncommon, or beautiful is not to identify features of the object, but to predicate qualities of it on the basis of a feeling that is produced in the observer. There is a fit or causal relationship between primary qualities that are in the object and secondary ones that are in us, so that the secondary quality arises as a function of the relation between the object and a mind with the capacity to be affected by it.

It should be emphasized in this context that Addison's primary and secondary qualities do not correspond to primary and secondary pleasures because all pleasures, primary and secondary, are secondary qualities.[4] Nor does the primary/secondary distinction coincide with Addison's categories of "nature" and "art." We might be tempted to think this is the case because the latter involves the representation of an original in a copy, where the comparison between them is the source of pleasure; art might then be equated with secondary pleasures leaving primary pleasures to flow from nature. This is not Addison's view, however, because primary pleasures arise from viewing *objects*, whether natural or contrived, whereas secondary pleasures involve comparison, an act of

---

3 While individually the three elements had long been in currency, there is no precise source for the triad as such, which appears to be original to Addison. See Bond's editorial comment in *The Spectator*, 540n2.

4 See in this context Hipple, *The Beautiful, The Sublime, & The Picturesque*, 20ff.

mind that is independent of objects as such. For this reason, Addison pays particular attention to the case of grandeur in architecture, the prime example of how the imagination can be stretched. This takes place either by the sheer size or extravagance of the edifice (the Hanging Gardens of Babylon) or the power of religious buildings (the Tower of Babel) to imprint awfulness and reverence on the mind, or from their manner independent of size, as in life-size statues and the Greek Parthenon, which have more grandeur than an enormous Gothic cathedral. Of central importance here, Addison emphasizes, is the use of concave and convex designs and the "greater air" such figures carry (3:556, no. 415): for pillars round (rather than square) and roofs vaulted (rather than angular) allow the eye to take in as much as possible, giving the impression of height and extent above and beyond physical shape, as in the Hagia Sophia in Istanbul, where the inside of the dome is greater than one might expect from an outward view of the building. In principle at least, there is no reason why the same cannot be applied to other arts, though Addison does not do so himself; in painting, for example, one might consider how the manner of depiction produces an effect not restricted to the size of the canvas: Peter Paul Rubens's *The Dying Seneca* is surely sublime in Addison's sense, but achieves this status independent of the similarity it bears to any original.

The second modification Addison makes to Locke concerns the latter's concept of mind without which the doctrine of qualities would make little sense. Addison adopts Locke's two "Fountains of Knowledge," namely, the senses that supply the understanding with ideas of external objects, and that same faculty "employ'd about the ideas it has got" to produce ideas of the operations of our own minds. In Addison's version, however, the imagination is the ascendant faculty and plays the same role in aesthetic experience as does the understanding in Locke's account of knowledge as that "Power to repeat, compare, and unite them [Ideas] even to an almost infinite Variety, and so can make at Pleasure new complex Ideas" (*Essay* 2.2.2). Addison's imagination is no longer the weak bystander spurned for its tendency to error and illusion, but a full-fledged player, a faculty, albeit limited, with the power to create new ideas and endowed with the sensitivity to feel pleasure. Like Locke's understanding, it receives and stores ideas, but has the power to alter and compound those ideas "into all varieties of Picture and Vision" that are "most agreeable" to it (3:537, no. 411). Addison acknowledges that there are pleasures to be had through the understanding as well – more refined and preferable to those of the imagination because they increase knowledge and improve the intellectual – but these pleasures require a "Bent of Thought" (3:539, no. 411), which enervates and threatens one's peace of mind, and supplies pleasures different in kind from those attained more readily through the imagination. Pleasures of the understanding are wrestled from the deep, disturb the animal spirits, and bring grief and melancholia; those of the imagination, by contrast, are easy, obvious, and gentle, and bring clarity and brightness that disperse the demons of serious thought. Who would court the disease of the learned by contemplating the darkness of eternity and infinity when they could be delighting in such "splen-did illustrious objects, as Histories, Fables, and Contemplations of Nature" (3:539, no. 411)?

As this latter point makes clear, what appeals to Addison in particular is the way the imagination involves a kind of *seeing*, and to such a degree is he taken with the analogy, that imagination and sight are essentially of a piece. Addison observes that, of the external senses, sight is the origin of the "largest Variety of Ideas" because free of the constraints involved in touch, smell, and hear-ing; in particular, sight overcomes distance and is not easily tired or satiated. It is a "more delicate and diffusive kind of Touch," he writes, "that spreads it self over an infinite Multitude of Bodies, comprehends the largest Figures, and brings into our reach some of the most remote Parts of the Universe" (3:536, no. 411). In a comparable way, the imagination involves a *mental* seeing; it is the eye by which the mind roams the world and discovers in material objects of art and nature, as well as ideal objects of history and fable, an endless source of untold pleasure. Like the physical eye, the imagination moves outward and is pleased in proportion to the liberty it enjoys to expand and – in notable contrast to Shaftesbury's disinterestedness – possesses and make objects its own. The imagination does not move downward – it has no interest in pene-trating to ultimate reality – but spreads itself in a way that changes the view, as a new source or quality of light leads one to see the physical world in a dif-ferent way. As Addison writes through a metaphor that expresses this idea, an individual in whom the imagination is active "looks upon the World, as it were, in another Light, and discovers in it a Multitude of Charms" and makes a "kind of Property in everything he sees" (3:538, no. 411). This identification of physical with mental seeing means pleasures of the imagination arise imme-diately and adventitiously. "It is but opening the Eye, and the Scene enters," he writes. "Colours paint themselves on the Fancy, with very little Attention of Thought or Application of the Mind in the Beholder." On the contrary, "We are struck," he adds, "we know not how, with the Symmetry of any thing we see, and immediately assent to the Beauty of an Object, without enquiring into the particular Causes and Occasions of it" (3:538, 411). This is true not only of pri-mary pleasures where objects are actually present, but of secondary pleasures as well where gratification arises from the act of comparing ideas of absent or fictitious objects with their representations. In both cases, Addison suggests, pleasures arise without the aid of understanding and independently of our will. We cannot but see physical objects when we open our eyes, and cannot but feel the pleasure that comes when the imagination is charmed, delighted, refreshed, invigorated, or otherwise transported.

The Great, Uncommon, and Beautiful

With this modified but distinctly Lockean view of the relation between mind and world, we can appreciate better Addison's triad of "Great, Uncommon, and Beautiful," each element of which, when apparent in a given object, gives rise to an emotion or emotions that strike the imagination and constitute those feelings that Addison categorizes as primary pleasures. First, objects are great or have grandeur, in Addison's terminology, not in view of their magnitude or size, but in terms of "Largeness of a Whole View, considered as one entire Piece" (3:540, no. 412). Addison chooses the term *great* rather than *sublime* in this context although he uses the latter elsewhere – in his discussions of Milton's *Paradise Lost*, for example – where it is intended to invoke the Longinian tradition and its focus on the use of language, literary imagery, and tropes to produce an emotional state. When Addison speaks of greatness in "Pleasures of the Imagination," however, he explicitly distinguishes it from this Longinian tradition, and marks a shift from associating the sublime exclusively with style to isolating it as an aesthetic response and category in its own right. In this respect, Addison ushers in an important distinction: "To write on the sublime style is to write on rhetoric," as Monk puts it succinctly, "to write on sublimity is to write on aesthetic."[5] Hutcheson and Hume hardly mention the sublime, and when they do so it is in the Longinian sense (sublime style) rather than in Addison's sense of greatness (sublimity as an aesthetic response). As the century progresses, the phenomenon Addison calls "greatness" is increasingly designated by the term *sublime*, and although Longinus remained a central figure in literary circles at least to mid-century, his influence on philosophical speculation dims: when the subject receives its fullest and most famous treatments in Burke and Kant, Longinus and the Longinian sublime are but faint echoes.

By great – or what we can now without risk of ambiguity call sublime – Addison attempts to convey the experience of some phenomenon striking as a whole, totality, or single entity that fills and surpasses the capacity of the imagination to contain. "Such are the prospects of an open Champian Country," Addison writes at the head of a list of examples that become common coin in subsequent philosophical discussion,

a vast uncultivated Desart, of huge Heaps of Mountains, high Rocks and Precipices, or a wide Expanse of Waters, where we are not struck with the Novelty or Beauty of the Sight, but with that rude kind of Magnificence which appears on many of these stupendous works of Nature. (3:540, no. 412)

We might expect to feel pain – terror, horror, or panic – in the face of such overwhelming phenomena, but Addison emphasizes that at such moments we actually experience a sense of calm and clarity. This happens because when the imagination expands or is stretched, our emotional response is astonishment or amazement rather than fear. It is the experience of trying to take in something barely comprehensible, even if, paradoxically, in the form of an object that transcends possible experience. Addison articulates the feeling of

[5] See Monk, *The Sublime*, 12.

exultation and sense of the freedom that comes when barriers collapse and limits are transgressed. "Our imagination loves to be filled with an Object," he observes, "or to graspe at any thing that is too big for its Capacity. We are flung into a pleasing Astonishment at such unbounded Views, and feel a delightful Stillness and Amazement in the Soul at the Apprehension of them" (3:540, no. 412). If the pleasure of great objects comes from the expansion of the imagination, pain, correspondingly, arises from the feeling of desolation that comes with the contraction of the same faculty and the corresponding sense that one's liberty has been checked and freedom stifled. "The mind of Man naturally hates every thing that looks like a Restraint upon it," Addison remarks, "and is apt to fancy it self under a sort of Confinement, when the Sight is pent up in a narrow Compass, and shortened on every side by the Neighbourhood of Walls or Mountains" (3:540–1, no. 412).

If great objects please through expanding the imagination and the feeling of astonishment and freedom it produces, the other categories of primary pleasures – the novel and beautiful – produce calmer passions that refresh and sooth the imagination, respectively. A new object is a sort of tonic to the world-weary, like the effect of a long drink on a hot summer afternoon; it "gratifies the Curiosity" and elicits "agreeable Surprise" (3:541, no. 412), lifting the imagination from its stupor and relieving it from what familiarity has rendered obvious and unremarkable: it is a bubbling spring to a dreary winter landscape, the motion of rivers or waterfalls to a languorous lake. In novelty we find at every moment a new scene that relieves the monotony of what is fixed and unchanging. It "bestows charms on a Monster," Addison observes, "and makes even the Imperfections of Nature please us" (3:541, no. 412), and when combined with the beautiful or sublime it is part of a "double Entertainment" (3:542, no. 412).

Beauty, by contrast, calms and uplifts: Addison associates it with tranquility – it "immediately diffuses a secret Satisfaction and Complacency" – as well as the more expansive feelings of "inward Joy," cheerfulness, and delight. Beauty can thus combine easily with the other elements of the triad, giving a "Finishing to anything that is Great or Uncommon" (3:542, no. 412). It has the power to do this, moreover, because of all the primary pleasures beauty is the most direct and, in Addison's Lockean idiom, the secondary quality that arises most immediately from the fit between the structure of the object and the capacity of human beings to be struck without "previous Consideration" and "at first sight." Beauty renders one's entire life more pleasant as if one were living in a romantic novel:

In short, our Souls are at present delightfully lost and bewildered in a pleasing Delusion, and we walk about like the Enchanted Hero of a Romance, who sees beautiful Castles, Woods and Meadows; and at the same time hears the warbling of Birds, and the purling of Streams; but upon the finishing of some secret Spell, the fantastick Scene breaks up, and the disconsolate Knight finds himself on a barren heath, or in a solitary Desart. (3:546–7, no. 413)

Given Addison's equation of imagination and sight, it is not surprising to find him propose that wild vistas are a source of greater beauty than those of art, which only puts embellishments on "something more bold and masterly in the rough careless Strokes of Nature" (3:549, no. 414). Wide fields are thus a source of greater delight than the controlled garden or the palace, where the imagination feels reigned-in and constrained.

Secondary Pleasures and Poetry

Unlike the primary pleasures arising from the sublime, uncommon, and beautiful, their secondary counterparts originate from comparing ideas of an original object with those from some representation of it in the form of a statue, painting, or description. Addison emphasizes that we need not have seen the actual object depicted, it being sufficient to have experienced objects that are analogous. Because beauty arises from similitude between original and copy (as Hutcheson emphasized later in his category of relative beauty), beauty tends to be greater in those arts that produce representations most like the object and in doing so reproduce accurately the primary qualities of the original. Thus sculpture (or "statuary") most closely resembles the subject because it works in three dimensions; painting follows, because it represents three dimensions on a flat surface; and finally comes "description" in literature or music, both of which are "wholly void" of any resemblances (3:559, no. 416), although Addison accepts that great composers might in general terms depict scenes such as the hurry of battle or the melancholy of death and burial. Art, however, (as Addison conceives it at least) lacks the vastness and immensity of nature and is inferior to her on that account, although there is a mutual relationship between them. Nature is pleasing to the degree that it resembles art due to the agreeableness of objects to the eye and the similitude of other objects, and through comparison we see that variety and regularity are the effect of design and increase the beauty of objects. Art, however, is more beautiful to the degree that it resembles nature and the pattern in it.

Most of Addison's artistic references are to literature, although, as noted at the outset, he does so for purposes of illustration rather than as an end and subject matter in itself. He thus emphasizes the representational force of language, expressed later (albeit ambiguously) by Hutcheson and, as we shall see, fully developed by Hume, whose view of poetry and the poet is clearly indebted to Addison.[6] First, in comparison to the fine arts of sculpture and painting, Addison claims that language, despite being a faint copy of the original, often has a greater effect than other arts due to the specific kind of representations it involves and the effect these have on the imagination. Well-chosen words in a description produce a more lively idea of an object than arises from simply

---

[6] Addison, we might note, also appeals to final causes in the same way as Hutcheson does later in the *Inquiry*. See 3:542–6, nos. 412–13.

seeing it. "The Reader finds a Scene drawn in stronger Colours, and painted more to the Life in his Imagination, by the help of Words," he writes, "than by actual Survey of the Scene which they describe" (3:560, no. 416). Imagination can produce new ideas of objects that are more beautiful than objects found in nature. "[F]or by this Faculty [of imagination]," he insists, "a Man in a Dungeon is capable of entertaining himself with Scenes and Landskips more beautiful than any that can be found in the whole Compass of Nature" (3:537, no. 411). To recall an earlier part of the discussion, the physical eye is restrained by what it sees; the eye of imagination can depart from reality and what can be painted in words is limited only by the creative power of the imagination itself.

Second, a poet represents nature in such a way that idealizes and improves it, and thus "seems to get the better of Nature" (3:560, no. 416). The role of the poet is "to humour the Imagination" and satisfy the desire of the human mind to find perfection in a defective world. Unlike the physical eye, which rests content with what it sees, the imagination can correct nature by representing it without blemish. We thus find the poet "mending and perfecting Nature where he describes a Reality, and by adding greater beauties than are put together in Nature, where he describes a Fiction" (3:569, no. 418). This is possible because like the imagination, the poet is at liberty to combine ideas and produce fictions that depart from reality. This does not mean that the poet can flout rules of criticism – even nymphs and spirits must make sense when they speak – but the genius of the poet lies in manipulating the world and displaying the "Talent of affecting the Imagination" (3:578, no. 421) with ideas that, although their referents are fictional, warm, and please the reader. "Thus we see how many ways Poetry addresses it self to the Imagination, as it has not only the whole Circle of Nature for its Province, but makes new Worlds of its own" (3:573, no. 419).

Third, due to the effect of representation, poetry transforms what is disagreeable and a source of pain into something that is agreeable and a source of pleasure. It does so by creating an "apt Description," one that uses "suitable Expressions" to create an image of the object that is compared with ideas of the original. We are thus pleased with a description that transforms the pain that would ordinarily arise from something "Little, Common or Deformed" into a source of pleasure; even a dunghill (destined to become a favorite example for the rest of the century) can in this way be made acceptable by the imagination (3:567, no. 418). If objects are already great, uncommon, or beautiful, by contrast, the pleasure is increased: pleasure arises not only from the apt description but also from the original as well. Addison thinks pleasure increases when a description manages to move the passions of the viewer; a painting that captures the resemblance of the sitter is sure to please, but the satisfaction intensifies if that face is beautiful and more so if it carries an air of melancholy and sorrow, which affects a viewer more deeply than physical beauty alone. Among the various arts, Addison urges, literature has the greatest power to move an audience because it arouses the most violent passions, which, paradoxically, produce the greatest pleasure: the more the spectators

are moved by the pain of the subject depicted, the greater is the aesthetic pleasure they take in the artistic representation. Thus, as Addison points out, in
John Dryden's "Fairie way of Writing," readers willingly subject themselves to
the presence of strange fictional beings who "raise a pleasing kind of Horrour
in the Mind of the Reader" (3:570, no. 419), and, most dramatically, in the form
of tragedy, pleasure increases with the terror and pity the work inspires.[7]

The Paradox of Tragedy

With this latter point, Addison raises and responds to an issue that becomes
something of a preoccupation for writers through the end of the eighteenth
century, namely, the so-called paradox of tragedy or how to explain why
scenes that would induce pain, disgust, or horror when witnessed in real life
are a source of pleasure when confronted in artistic – and, specifically, literary – works. The debate over this phenomenon has its origins in Aristotle, who
speaks in the *Poetics* of the "tragic pleasure of pity and fear" that the poet aims
to "produce by a work imitation."[8] Addison articulates the same problem in
the following terms:

one would wonder how it comes to pass, that such Passions [Terror and Pity] as
are very unpleasant at all other times, are very agreeable when excited by proper
Descriptions. It is not strange, that we should take Delight in such Passages as are
apt to produce Hope, Joy, Admiration, Love, or the like Emotions in us, because
they never rise in the Mind without an inward Pleasure which attends them. But
how comes it to pass, that we should take delight in being terrified or dejected by a
Description, when we find so much Uneasiness in the Fear or Grief which we receive
from any Occasion? (3:567–8, no. 418)

Aristotle's official response is to emphasize the psychological mechanism of
catharsis, the process of purification through purging the emotions aroused in
a tragedy.[9] Some have argued, however, from evidence in the *Poetics* and the
Rhetoric, that his real solution lies in the concept of *mimesis* or imitation, the
human love of which the tragedian exploits to represent scenes in such a way
that arouses pleasure. Addison follows neither Aristotelian solution, but looks
instead to the power of reflection, through which the viewer becomes conscious of being removed from the events and scenes, and is thus able to remain
unaffected by the emotions that would ordinarily attend them.

---

[7] Addison also observes (3:540, no. 412) that an object might be so loathsome that it overbears
the pleasure from greatness, novelty, or beauty, but there will still be some delight mixed in
from one of these three sources.
[8] Aristotle, *Poetics*, in *The Complete Works of Aristotle*, ed. Jonathan Barnes, 2 vols. (Princeton,
NJ: Princeton University Press, 1984), 2:1453b12–13.
[9] The precise meaning Aristotle attaches to the term *catharsis* has been the subject of some
debate. For an overview, see Stephen Halliwell, *The Poetics of Aristotle: Translation and
Commentary* (Chapel Hill: University of North Carolina Press, 1985), appendix 5.

Despite Addison's earlier emphasis on the possessive character of imagination, there is clearly more than an echo of Shaftesbury's disinterestedness in this solution because he takes aesthetic value to arise at least in part from rational contemplation independent of practical concerns and the proprietary relation to what is depicted that they contain. In Addison's version, the pleasure in question arises not from the description of what is terrible directly – that would point either to a masochistic pleasure in our own pain or a sadistic pleasure in the pain of others – but from the self-conscious realization of our own safety. As Addison puts it, the pleasure of the literary description comes "from the Reflection we make on our selves at the time of reading it. When we look on such hideous Objects," he continues,

we are not a little pleased to think we are in no Danger of them. We consider them at the same time, as Dreadful and Harmless; so that the more frightful Appearance they make, the greater is the Pleasure we receive from the Sense of our own Safety. In short, we look upon the Terrors of a Description, with the same Curiosity and Satisfaction that we survey a dead Monster. (3:568, no. 418)

The same is true of the pleasure we receive from recalling memories of dangers past, or viewing a precipice from a safe distance. A singular feature of a literary depiction – or a historical one, which Addison also mentions in this connection – is its tendency automatically to distance readers from events, and provide the space necessary for them to turn toward themselves. Some balance must be struck in this respect: if we are too removed from events the passions of terror and pity could not arise, but if we are too close we are left no "leisure to reflect on our selves." Without a literary depiction to mediate the event, however – that is, when we are actually in the presence of a man under torture – "Our thoughts are so intent upon the Sufferer, that we cannot turn them upon our own Happiness" (3:569, no. 418). An element of *Schadenfreude* creeps into Addison's train of thought here, for beneath the grief we might genuinely feel at the "Torments, Wounds, Deaths, and like dismal Accidents" that afflict other people, he suspects that our real pleasure flows "from the secret Comparison which we make between our selves and the Person who suffers" (3:568, no. 418). Consciousness of our own safety leads us to an increased appreciation for our own good fortune, and blends into a feeling of relief and gratitude that others are suffering rather than ourselves.

Taste

Closely related to the representative and transformational power of language, Addison emphasizes the capacity to be affected by the scenes it creates, an idea he captures in the concept of taste, *"that Faculty of the Soul, which discerns the Beauties of an Author with Pleasure, and the Imperfections with Dislike"* (3:528, no. 409). Addison inherits the term from the tradition of criticism, but his use is original and must be considered the basis for the eighteenth-century aesthetic tradition that follows. First, Addison refers to taste as a "faculty," not on a par with reason, understanding, or even imagination, but as a general ability, capacity, or aptitude. As he points out, the idea of "Mental Taste" relevant to making judgments about the perfections and faults of literature is derived metaphorically from "Sensitive Taste." One implies the other because both involve making judgments about the qualities of the object in question: not only can people possessed of a fine palate with respect to tea – as Addison reports by way of example – distinguish different varieties even when they are mixed together in a single brew, but they can also articulate the general and specific qualities that unite and divide them. Similarly, a "man of fine Taste in Writing will discern, after the same manner," Addison observes, "not only the general beauties and Imperfections of an Author, but discover the several Ways of thinking and expressing himself, which diversify him from all other Authors," and trace the "Thought and Language" he uses to those others from whom he borrowed (3:528, no. 409).

Second, as in sensitive taste, there are degrees of refinement that particular judges can attain, and the "Man of Polite Imagination is let into a great many Pleasures that the Vulgar are not capable of receiving" (3:538, no. 411).[10] As Addison presents it, taste is an inherently ambiguous faculty, both natural and acquired. On the one hand, it "must in some degree be born with us," Addison writes, and like all capacities it varies among individuals and depends on their tendencies and disposition; an individual with a natural sensitivity to acidity would make a poor judge in matters of tea. Addison even recommends a procedure for testing whether one has it: read ancient and contemporary writers who have stood the test of time, and if one is not "delighted" by them but finds in their works a "Coldness and Indifference," then one can conclude that the faculty is lacking (3:529, no. 409). At the same time, Addison describes taste as a potential that can be actualized through practice, a thoroughly democratic idea even if it is effectively muted by the fact that a relatively small, affluent, and civilized section of society has the means and wherewithal to devote time and effort to its refinement. It is very difficult to lay down rules for acquiring taste, but there are "several Methods for Cultivating and Improving it" (3:529, no. 409), he suggests, such as becoming acquainted with the works of great writers, conversing with others for exposure to opinions other than our own, and becoming familiar with writings of good critics who have already acquired a high level of taste.

Since the structure of the human mind is universal such that taste can be acquired, it seems to follow that, with the appropriate exposure and cultivation, the same objects should elicit a similar aesthetic response in the majority of people. From this arises the question that, as we have seen already in Hutcheson and Reid, worries almost every writer in the eighteenth century from Addison onward: if judgments of taste vary so widely, in what sense can one speak of a

---

[10] For an informative discussion of this issue, see de Bolla, *The Education of the Eye*, ch. 1.

standard of taste, and if it does exist, where is it to be found? Addison raises this question in the context of poetry: why is one reader moved by a certain passage and another left cold and indifferent by the very same, or why does one judge fix on a representation to capture the original where another finds no likeness at all? Addison refers to this as a "different Taste," which, given his definition of that faculty, means degrees in the ability to discern the beauties or imperfections of an object and to feel the accompanying pleasure and pain. The variation must arise, he says, "either from the Perfection of Imagination in one more than in another, or from the different Ideas that several Readers affix to the same Words" (3:561, no. 416). That is to say, the beauties of the object in question are there to be discovered, but a judgment of it can be right or wrong. It is the task of the observer to develop his taste: to know which words and combinations of words properly express the ideas in question; which expressions in a language represent the object in the most advantageous light; and to have sufficient discrimination to receive and retain the ideas raised. Without this refined judgment it might be possible to grasp the general terms of a description, as one of weak sight can make out the general outlines of an object, but to discern the beauties of an object requires paying attention to detail and becoming a critic or "true judge," an idea that finds its most famous and enduring expression in the work of David Hume, to whom we now turn.

DAVID HUME

Of all the contributions made by eighteenth-century writers, that of David Hume (1711–76) is perhaps the most difficult to assess.[11] When he published the first two books of *A Treatise of Human Nature* in 1739 – "Of the Understanding" and "Of the Passions" – it came with a promise in the advertisement that were the work to "meet with success," it would be followed and completed with an "examination of Morals, Politics, and Criticism." The first of these was largely written already and appeared at the end of 1740 as Book 3 – "Of Morals" – but by that point Hume was sufficiently discouraged by the reception of his work and lack of success (sales were low and reviews mixed) that he abandoned the treatise form and the two final books were never composed. Hume opted instead for inquiry, dialogue, and essay, more palatable and accessible ways to cast his ideas for an increasingly wider and more educated audience.

---

[11] References to Hume's works are given as follows: *A Treatise of Human Nature*, ed. David Fate Norton and Mary Norton (Oxford: Oxford University Press, 2001) (T); *Enquiry Concerning the Principles of Morals*, ed. Tom Beauchamp (Oxford: Oxford University Press, 1998) (EPM); *Essays: Moral, Political, and Literary*, ed. Eugene F. Miller (Indianapolis, IN: Liberty Fund, 1985) (E); and *The History of England, From the Invasion of Julius Caesar to the Revolution in 1688*, with the author's last corrections and improvements, 6 vols. (Indianapolis, IN: Liberty Fund, 1983). References to the *Treatise* are to book, part, section, and paragraph; to the *Enquiries* to section and paragraph; and to the *Essays* and *History* to the page numbers of the editions cited.

Although the proposed book on politics never materialized, Hume addressed many essays to political themes, and devoted significant parts of Book 3 of the *Treatise* and the *Enquiry Concerning the Principles of Morals* to central questions in political philosophy. The same cannot be said for his proposed work on "criticism." Hume does address aesthetic issues *en passant* in parts of the *Treatise* and second *Enquiry*, and ventures into criticism at various points of the *History of England*; he also devotes specific essays, most notably "Of Tragedy" and "Of the Standard of Taste," to the same, and these are important contributions to the eighteenth-century literature and worthy of consideration. (Hume also has an important essay on the rise of the arts and sciences, but this falls properly under the sociology of art rather than aesthetic theory proper.) These remain short and focused treatments of particular topics, and nowhere does Hume offer any systematic or sustained presentation of his views, and as a result "Hume's aesthetics" is drawn from an amalgam of parts and passages scattered through his corpus. Despite this fact, Hume still makes significant contributions to the tradition (reflected in the extensive literature it has generated), especially in his contribution to debates over a "standard of taste," in his solution to the "paradox of tragedy," and in his emphasis on the role of representation, which effectively clears up the ambiguity in Hutcheson's discussion of "just representation."[12]

Hume's Aesthetics

Before considering these three areas, it is worth noting the main tenets of Hume's aesthetics more generally, all of which can be traced largely to Addison and Hutcheson.[13] First, Hume follows Locke's empiricism and takes aesthetic value to arise from the relationship between the individual and an object

[12] It is worth noting that Hume does not make any theoretical contribution to understanding the nature and scope of the sublime; he rarely even uses the term and when he does it is firmly with reference to Longinus (whom he mentions specifically) and elevated feeling (see EPM 7.4–9). Cf. the discussion of Hume's "moral sublime" in Karen Valihora, *Austen's Oughts: Judgment Aftert Locke and Shaftesbury* (Newark: University of Delaware Press, 2010), ch. 2. For a review of the extant secondary literature in the field more generally (through 2004 at least), see Timothy M. Costelloe, "Hume's Aesthetics: The Literature and Directions for Future Research," *Hume Studies* 30, 1 (2004): 87–126. Extended treatments of Hume's aesthetics and its relation to other parts of his philosophy are to be found in Dabney Townsend, *Hume's Aesthetic Theory: Taste and Sentiment* (New York: Routledge, 2001), and Timothy M. Costelloe, *Aesthetics and Morals in the Philosophy of David Hume* (New York: Routledge, 2007). See also Dickie, *The Century of Taste*, esp. ch. 6, who argues that Hume's "theory of taste is a far superior" (142) to that of Hutcheson, Gerard, Alison, and Kant, the other four figures he discusses.

[13] Cf. Peter Jones, *Hume's Sentiments* (Edinburgh: Edinburgh University Press, 1982), who argues the case for seeing Dubos as the principle influence on Hume's thinking. On Hume's attachment to Hutcheson's notion of "internal sense," see Simon Blackburn, "Hume on the Mezzanine Level," *Hume Studies* 19, 2 (1993): 273–88.

viewed; beauty is a secondary quality in the form of a sentiment or feeling of the subject. "Though it be certain," Hume writes in "Of the Standard of Taste," "that beauty and deformity, more than sweet and bitter, are not qualities in objects, but belong entirely to the sentiment, internal or external; it must be allowed, that there are certain qualities in objects, which are fitted by nature to produce those particular feelings" (E 235).[14] As Hume makes clear in the *Treatise*, beauty is a specific kind of sentiment, a "passion," a secondary or reflective impression that arises from some bodily sensation or from the idea of that sensation and produces pleasure. It is, moreover, a "calm" rather than "violent" passion, although Hume points out that the division is inexact because the effects of poetry and music can "rise to the greatest height" and produce "raptures" almost as violent the sentiments occasioned by love or hatred (T 2.1.1.3).

Second, Hume assumes that human beings are constituted in such a way that there is a natural fit – a "match" or "natural aptness" as commentators have called it[15] – between the aesthetic object and the subject who, by virtue of a natural receptivity, is capable of being affected in a certain manner. "Beauty is such an order and construction of parts," as Hume writes in the *Treatise*, "as either by the *primary constitution* of our nature, by *custom*, or by *caprice*, is fitted to give a pleasure and satisfaction to the soul" (T 2.1.8.2; see also EPM 5.38 and E 63–5). So "*beauty* of all kinds gives us a peculiar delight and satisfaction; as *deformity* produces pain" (T 2.1.8.1). These sentiments arise either from objects that are immediately agreeable or from the utility or fitness of parts that combine to further some end. Thus, a well-cultivated field appeals to us more than "briars and brambles" (EPM 2.9), and a "machine, a piece of furniture, a vestment, a house well contrived for use and conveniency, is so far beautiful, and is contemplated with pleasure and approbation" (EPM 2.10).[16]

Third, and finally, Hume emphasizes that the mere presence of beautiful objects and the capacity of human beings to be affected by them do not translate automatically into appropriate sentiments and correct judgments.

---

[14] See also T 2.1.8.6; EMP Appx. 1.13–14; and E 165. On this point, and for discussion of Hume's departure from Locke, see Peter Kivy, "Hume's Neighbour's Wife: An Essay on the Evolution of Hume's Aesthetics," *British Journal of Aesthetics* 23, 3 (1983): 195–208, and Dickie, *The Century of Taste*, 123–4. Cf. Theodore A. Gracyk, "Rethinking Hume's Standard of Taste," *Journal of Aesthetics and Art Criticism* 52, 2 (1994): 169–82.

[15] See, for example, Peter Railton, "Aesthetic Value, Moral Value, and Naturalism," in *Aesthetics and Ethics: Essays at the Intersection*, ed. Jerrold Levinson (Cambridge: Cambridge University Press, 1998), 67 and 93, and Nick Zangwill, "Hume, Taste, and Teleology," *Philosophical Papers* 23, 1 (1994): 1–18.

[16] On the parallel between Hume's treatment of moral aesthetic judgments, see William H. Halberstadt, "A Problem in Hume's Aesthetics," *Journal of Aesthetics and Art Criticism* 30, 2 (1971): 209–11. Cf. T 2.1.8 where Hume also explains the beauty of the body in terms of pride, a passion that arises when one's own accomplishments and attributes (i.e., self) are the object of reflection.

There is a natural basis for being affected by objects and experiencing them as beautiful, but the extent of the satisfaction depends upon the degree to which spectators have cultivated their taste and can be affected by the work in question (E 4–5). Ongoing critical reflection on one's judgments is required to educate the sentiments and achieve a "delicacy of taste." For only a mind that is "susceptible to those finer sensations" is in a position to "give praise to what deserves it" (EPM App. 1.16; see T 3.1.2.4). "When you present a poem or a picture to a man possessed of this talent," Hume writes, "the delicacy of his feeling makes him be sensibly touched with every part of it; nor are the masterly strokes perceived with more exquisite relish and satisfaction, than the negligencies or absurdities with disgust and uneasiness" (E 4). Perfection in such delicacy is "impossible to be attained," and those who come close to it are rare, but achieving even a modicum of good taste promises great satisfaction, and Hume thinks it is something for which we can and should strive over the course of a lifetime.

The Search for a Standard

Hume's "Of the Standard of Taste" holds an important place in the history of aesthetics, belied by its short length and rather haphazard origins: it comprises only some twenty pages in the now standard edition of the *Essays*, and was composed not as a position piece to express his views but as a replacement for two controversial essays – "On Suicide" and "On the Immortality of the Soul" – withdrawn after their first publication; if not for these peculiar circumstances the piece might never have been written at all.[17] Despite these facts, the essay has inspired a literature the size of which is rivaled only by the bewildering number of competing interpretations.[18] This degree of attention reflects more generally the dearth of Hume's writings on aesthetics and the place he occupies in the pantheon of great philosophers, and it should be borne in mind that although the essay's influence on contemporaries and successors is undeniable, it is only one contribution to a debate with other significant voices.

The central question Hume addresses in "Of the Standard of Taste" is how to explain the fact that, although beauty and the principles governing it are universal, there is great diversity through time and across place in the actual judgments people make. Addison, to recall the earlier discussion, argues that a standard arises from the universality of taste, and variety is explicable by judgments that can be right or wrong. Hutcheson, by contrast, argues that that beauty (founded on uniformity amidst variety) and the sense to appreciate it are both universal, while tastes vary, a fact explicable by the effects of culture,

---

[17] See Letter 465 in *The Letters of David Hume*, ed. J. Y. T. Greig, 2 vols. (Oxford: Clarendon Press, 1932), 2: 252–4; and Ernest Campbell Mossner, *The Life of David Hume*, 2nd ed. (Oxford: Clarendon Press, 1980 [1954]), 319–35.

[18] For an overview, see Costelloe, "Hume's Aesthetics."

prejudice, association, and education. For both, some beauties are still higher than others – the Romanesque really is more beautiful than the Gothic – but this just indicates that some tastes are more developed than others and those who possess them are better able to appreciate beauty because they are relatively free from the influences that hinder the proper function of their internal sense. Hume retains Hutcheson's Lockean view that beauty is not a quality of objects, but insists with Addison that the uniform features of human nature make beauty universal; he also appeals to the importance of cultivating or achieving "delicacy" of taste to appreciate the qualities in the object by which everybody should be universally affected. Rather than settling on various factors that interfere with the proper working of an internal sense, however, Hume focuses on "reconciling" the subjective character of aesthetic judgments (beauty, to recall, is a calm passion that arises as a sentiment in an individual) and the fact that they are governed by criteria to which any reasonable person should and does assent. Like Addison, then, and unlike Hutcheson, Hume argues that there is a universal standard of taste (not only a universal sense and principle of beauty), but that it is persistently overlooked in the course of people making actual judgments about beautiful objects.

Hume argues for this view by pointing out that aesthetic life is governed by two competing tendencies, which, expressed formally, constitute two contradictory principles of "common sense." On the one hand, he observes, our ordinary language implies a general standard, and the philosophical mind naturally seeks this out. After all, the "same Homer, who pleased at ATHENS and ROME two thousand years ago, is still admired at PARIS and at LONDON. All the changes of climate, government, religion, and language, have not been able to obscure his glory" (E 233). A man denying the greatness of such literature – putting Ogilby over Milton or Bunyan over Addison, to use another of Hume's examples – is to contravene standards that everyone accepts, and would be "no less an extravagance, than if he had maintained a mole-hill to be as high as TENERIFE, or a pond as extensive as the ocean" (E 230–1). Thus, Hume concludes, we can infer the existence of "general rules" that govern the appropriateness of aesthetic judgments and reveal the existence of a standard. On the other hand, given that beauty is a sentiment that arises in the subject, there is a natural tendency for human beings to take diversity at face value; the sheer variety of tastes provides evidence that judgments about the beautiful can be reduced to individual liking. This also seems to follow from the fact that beauty is a secondary quality, and as the same object may be both sweet and bitter depending on the "disposition of the organs," so we might reasonably conclude that "each mind perceives a different beauty" (E 230), and "passing into a proverb," Hume says, it "seems to have attained the sanction of common sense" (E 230): if *de gustibus non est disputandum* – in matters of taste there is no dispute – then the conclusion that there is a standard appears to be false. As Hume presents it, then, the question of a standard of taste revolves around taking these two propositions or "species of common sense" – one affirming and the other denying the existence of a standard – and finding "a rule, by which the various sentiments of men may be reconciled; at least, a decision, afforded, confirming one sentiment, and condemning another" (E 229).

Having accepted that the aim of the essay is to reconcile the opposition between sentiments and standards, however, the difficulty lies in understanding exactly how Hume achieves this reconciliation and what he means when he speaks of a "standard of taste." Answering these questions is complicated by the fact that Hume initially characterizes his search for a standard in terms of a "rule" or "rules of art," but apparently discover it in the rare character of the "true judge": "Strong sense, united to delicate sentiment, improved by practice, perfected by comparison, and cleared of all prejudice, can alone entitle critics to this valuable character; and the joint verdict of such, wherever they are to be found, is the true standard of taste and beauty" (E 241). Not surprisingly, a good deal of the literature attempts, in various ways, to reconcile or at least explain Hume's "two standards of taste."[19] One way to solve this problem and make sense of Hume's argument is to think of the two species of common sense as forming what Kant later terms an "antinomy," a pair of contradictory but equally unassailable propositions that arise from the demands made by reason that the understanding discover unconditioned conditions for phenomena beyond experience. Drawing on his discussion in the *Critique of Pure Reason*, in the *Critique of the Power of Judgment*, Kant generates an "Antinomy of Taste" by juxtaposing two commonly held assumptions or "commonplaces" (*Gemeinorte*) about taste: on one side, the assumption that "*everyone has his own taste*" and, on the other, the view that "*one can quarrel about taste* (though one cannot dispute about it)." The Antinomy then consists of a thesis stating that an aesthetic judgment has subjective validity (that it is not based on concepts) and an antithesis that it has universal validity (that it is based on concepts) (CJ, 5:338). Kant solves the dilemma by showing that the contradictory maxims take the same term in different but compatible ways. The conflict then arises because the determinate and indeterminate senses of "concept" become confused in the "commonplaces" about taste, and recognition of this fact transforms the contradiction into a dialectical illusion in which both principles "may both be true" (CJ, 5:341). It is true that everyone has their own taste and there is no dispute insofar as the claims involved express *subjective liking*; it is also true that there is a standard about which one can quarrel insofar as the claims involved are *objective demands* to universal agreement and assent. Only the latter, Kant urges, are properly termed "aesthetic judgments."

19 See Jeffrey Wieand, "Hume's Two Standards of Taste," *Philosophical Quarterly* 34, 135 (1984): 129–42. Cf. James Shelley, "Hume's Double Standard of Taste," *Journal of Aesthetics and Art Criticism* 52, 4 (1994): 437–45, and the subsequent exchange: Jeffrey Wieand, "Hume's True Judges," and James Shelley, "Rule and Verdict," *Journal of Aesthetics and Art Criticism* 53, 3 (1995): 318–19 and 319–20, respectively. For a more detailed expression of the interpretation that follows, see Costelloe, *Aesthetics and Morals in the Philosophy of David Hume*, ch. 3.

In a comparable way, Hume's argument in "Of the Standard of Taste" proceeds by juxtaposing the two "species of common sense" and showing them both to be true. On the one side, the assumption that in matters of taste there is no dispute (a standard does not exist) is true in reference to subjective claims about what people like, and in such cases, as we often say, people simply "agree to disagree." On the other side, the assumption that there is a rule to which people appeal (a standard does exist) is also true if we recognize that in such cases people are making objective claims with which others are expected to agree. Hume thus "solves" the contradiction by showing that, although beauty is both a function of an individual sentiment, there is also a standard governing judgments of taste. This is what Hume means by "reconciliation," namely, a philosophical solution that explains how a standard can both exist and be routinely denied. The practical solution to the problem is for people to develop and refine their delicacy of taste, although this is only a partial correction to the tendency for human beings to hold contradictory views about the same phenomena. This is simply a feature of human beings that cannot be undone: even when clarified in the way Hume (and Kant) propose, people continue to be seduced, albeit unwittingly, by the antinomical tendencies of human reason and recognize the existence of a standard that they routinely overlook.

The Paradox of Tragedy

As with "Of the Standard of Taste," Hume's "Of Tragedy" has generated a large (though not as extensive) literature, which also tends to ignore that, although the essay is influential, it is one contribution to a debate joined by a number of eighteenth-century writers. As we have seen, Addison raised the "paradox of tragedy" already in 1711, and his treatment presupposed in turn both Aristotle's *Poetics* and more recent French criticism on the subject. Writers in this latter tradition form Hume's own point of departure (explicitly at least), and he does not mention Addison at all. Hume characterizes the paradox in the following way:

> The whole art of the poet is employed, in rouzing and supporting the compassion and indignation, the anxiety and resentment of his audience. They are pleased in proportion as they are afflicted, and never are so happy as when they employ tears, sobs, and cries to give vent to their sorrow, and relieve the heart, swoln [*sic*] with the tenderest sympathy and compassion. (E 217)

There is nothing perplexing for Hume in the observation that literature arouses sympathy and compassion, but he finds something puzzling in the fact "that the same object of distress, which pleases in a tragedy, were it really set before us, would give the most unfeigned uneasiness" (E 218). It is thus "an unaccountable pleasure," as he puts it, "which the spectators of a well-written tragedy receive from sorrow, terror, anxiety, and other passions, that are in themselves disagreeable and uneasy" (E 216). Hume frames his discussion by way of solutions offered by two French writers, both of which, he argues, fail: Dubos had argued that because anything is better than languor, the pleasure of tragedy can be explained by an audience's willingness to be misled and have their high passions excited, and Bernard de Fontenelle had proposed that we can enjoy sorrow as long as it is softened by circumstances, which come to pass in the theater where the audience knows that, at bottom, all is artifice with no real suffering involved. The former solution is inadequate, Hume counters, because it ignores the fact that those same passions are also disagreeable when experienced outside the context of a literary depiction, and the latter (Hume cites Cicero as his source) because it assumes (without explanation) that we must first be convinced of the reality of the scene in order to enter into and be moved by it.

Drawing, one assumes, on Aristotle's discussion of tragedy in terms of imitation (though not catharsis), Hume proposes instead that "from that very eloquence, with which the melancholy scene is represented ... the whole impulse of those [melancholy] passions is converted into pleasure, and swells the delight which the eloquence raises in us" (E 219–20); some have dubbed this his "Principle of Conversion" or "Conversion Hypothesis."[20] There has been much debate over the form and content both of what Hume means by this principle and how he applies it to the case of tragedy, as well as various proposals – and much criticism – of whether it really solves the problem raised. Many have charged that the principle fails to account for the relevant facts of aesthetic experience, and at least one commentator has suggested that in the final analysis Hume is not really discussing tragedy at all.[21]

Hume's characterization of tragedy in terms of conversion brings to mind his use of the same term in his discussion of sympathy in the *Treatise*. Hume describes conversion as the process whereby the idea of a passion or emotion is enlivened and achieves a force and vivacity so that it is "converted into an impression." This conversion takes place in our own person when we recall or imagine an occasion that produced or could produce a given impression – anger, for example – which, although fainter than the original, reaches the status of a new impression and constitutes a *new* feeling of anger. Like all impressions in Hume's system, it can then be copied to form a new idea, itself capable of conversion into another impression. We then become angry, not by witnessing an event or seeing an object, but through the process of raising an idea – "converting" it – into an impression. Sympathy, Hume then urges, is the name we give to the same process when it takes place with respect to *others* rather than ourselves. When

---

[20] See Margaret Paton, "Hume on Tragedy," *British Journal of Aesthetics* 13, 2 (1973): 121, and Mark Packer, "Dissolving the Paradox of Tragedy," *Journal of Aesthetics and Art Criticism* 47, 3 (1989): 212.

[21] See Alex Neill, "Yanal and Others on Hume and Tragedy," *Journal of Aesthetics and Art Criticism* 50, 2 (1992): 152, and "Hume's Singular Phænomenon," *British Journal of Aesthetics* 39, 2 (1999): 112–25.

I sympathize with somebody, "my mind," Hume writes, "immediately passes from these effects to their causes, and forms such a lively idea of the passions, as is presently converted into the passion itself" (T 3.3.3.7). In this case "an idea of a sentiment or passion, may ... be so enliven'd as to become the very sentiment or passion," and through this "we enter so deep into the opinions and affections of others, whenever we discover them" (T 2.1.11.7).

The important difference between converting an idea into an impression in our own person and entering into the sentiments of others – the relevant case when it comes to tragedy – is that the idea, which forms the object of the conversion, has its origin not in our own recollection of anger or in some imagined cause of it, but in an impression originally in *somebody else*, that is, in *their* feeling of anger. "'Tis indeed evident," Hume writes,

> that when we sympathize with the passions and sentiments of others, these movements appear at first in *our* mind as mere ideas, and are conceiv'd to belong to another person, as we conceive any other matter of fact. 'Tis also evident, that the ideas of the affections of others are converted into the very impressions they represent, and that the passions arise in conformity to the images we form of them. (T 2.1.11.8)

Hume's appeal to the same concept in his discussion of tragedy is clearly relevant because it explains *what*, in that case, the phenomenon of conversion amounts to: we feel the passion portrayed in the drama because the sentiment in the characters becomes an idea in spectators and is then enlivened to the point where it is converted into and appears as a new impression in them. It does not, however, explain what is really at issue in the case of tragedy, namely, that we feel *pleasure* in a passion that would otherwise cause pain or, to express it differently, we take pleasure *in* another's pain, and that is the whole "problem" Hume is trying to solve. This part of the problem, Hume explains in terms of aesthetic representation.

One way to understand this point is to recognize that Hume is confronting, if not clearly distinguishing, two distinct issues, namely, the *psychological mechanism of conversion* – the account of conversion found in the *Treatise* – that explains how one emotion replaces another, and the *literary depiction* of the emotion through which "the melancholy scene is *represented*" (E 219, emphasis added) and, in Hume's view, forms the necessary cause for the effect of conversion to come about. The conversion thus takes place when the melancholic passions are redirected by the sentiments of beauty that arise from poetic representation. "The latter [sentiments of beauty], being the predominant emotion," Hume writes, "seize the whole mind, and convert the former into themselves, at least tincture them so strongly as totally to alter their nature" (E 220). We do not take pleasure *in* another's pain, then, but pleasure in the beauty of the representation. There are limits to this process, so that when we are too close to scenes so "bloody and atrocious" that the horror roused "will not soften into pleasure" (E 224); such is the scene of self-mutilation, Hume notes, in playwright Nicholas Rowe's *Ambitious Stepmother* (1699). With the exception of such graphic violence, however, poetic representations of otherwise painful emotion contain less force and vivacity than the original and transform reality into fiction – "convert" it – giving rise to sentiments of beauty and the pleasure that attends them.

Hume's "Just Representation"

This way of understanding "On Tragedy" at once points toward Hume's third contribution to the aesthetic tradition, which can be understood as a systematic application of Addison's remarks on the imagination and his notion of an "apt Representation," and in a way that effectively disambiguates Hutcheson's notion of "just Representation" discussed in Chapter 1. It is worth noting in this context that Hume's approach to these matters – including his view of imagination – appears to have had an effect on his friend and contemporary, Adam Smith, who broached the matter in the unfinished and posthumously published "Of the Nature of that Imitation which takes place in what are called The Imitative Arts," composed in or around 1777.[22] Smith rejects "exact" or "servile imitation" as the "most unpardonable blemish" in the imitative works of painting, sculpture, and (with qualification) music and dance (I.2.176), emphasizing instead how the "*disparity* between the imitating and the imitated object is the foundation of the beauty of imitation. It is because one object does not naturally resemble the other, that we are so much pleased with it, when by art it is made to do so" (I.14.183, emphasis added).[23] The pleasure amounts to a "wonder at seeing an object of one kind represent so well an object of a very different kind," Smith argues, "and upon our admiration of the art which surmounts so happily that disparity which Nature had established between them" (I.16.185). It is quite possible, then, to experience pleasure from imitation even though the original object is "indifferent, or even offensive" (I.7.179). Smith's discussion clearly carries loud echoes of Addison, but it is no less indebted to Hume's view of the imagination and the role he assigns the faculty in aesthetic experience, all of which was in plain view by the time Smith composed his own thoughts on the matter.[24] For Hume, the beauty of art – he focuses on literature

---

[22] Adam Smith, "Of the Nature of that Imitation which takes place in what are called The Imitative Arts/Of the Affinity between Music, Dancing, and Poetry," in *Essays on Philosophical Subjects, with Dugald Stewart's "Account of Adam Smith,"* ed. W. P. D. Wightman, J. C. Bryce, and I. S. Ross (Oxford: Oxford University Press, 1980), vol. 3 of *The Glasgow Edition of the Works and Correspondence of Adam Smith,* ed. J. C. Bryce et al., 7 vols. (Oxford: Oxford University Press, 1978–). All references are to part, paragraph, and page number. On dating the work, see the editor's introduction (171–5).

[23] Smith exempts instrumental music and dance from this general rule because their effects arise less from imitation than their power of "expression" or "representation," respectively. They produce feelings directly rather than through sympathy with another person.

[24] For Smith's debt to Hume's view of imagination, see D. D. Raphael, "The Impartial Spectator," in *Essays on Adam Smith,* ed. Andrew S. Skinner and Thomas Wilson (Oxford: Clarendon Press, 1975), 83–99.

and especially the poetic forms of lyric, drama, pastoral, and epic – is never a matter of the artist copying or presenting objects, but of re-presenting them in a way that satisfies certain criteria and determines in turn whether an artistic production effects the imagination and pleases its audience. These criteria are threefold: artists are obliged to transform ordinary experience into something extraordinary, create ideas that are agreeable to an audience, and bring about their effects deliberately.

First, Hume takes Addison's lead and argues that well-chosen words can produce more lively ideas in a reader than those arising from the representation of real being. Poets are like magicians who use their pens to represent the world with such "strong and remarkable" strokes that they "convey a lively image to the mind" (E 191–2); in so doing they transform ordinary experience into something extraordinary and marvelous. "All poetry," in Hume's view, "being a species of painting, brings us nearer to the objects than any other species of narration, throws a stronger light upon them, and delineates more distinctly those minute circumstances, which ... serve mightily to enliven the imagery, and gratify the fancy" (EHU 3.11). More than Hutcheson, however, Hume emphasizes that the transformative power of poetic language at once embellishes the world and makes what is otherwise ugly, repellent, or mundane appear beautiful, appealing, or in some way fascinating. "Sentiments, which are merely natural," by contrast, Hume writes, "affect not the mind with any pleasure, and seem not worthy of our attention. The pleasantries of a waterman, the observations of a peasant, the ribaldry of a porter or hackney coachman, all of these are natural, and disagreeable. What an insipid comedy should we make of the chit-chat of the tea-table, copied faithfully and at full length? Nothing can please persons of taste, but nature drawn with her graces and ornaments, *la belle nature*" (E 191–2). To represent the world in its "merely natural" aspect would be to replicate the empirical content of experience in all its mundane detail; the poet, by contrast, creates an alternative world adorned and rendered beautiful by the power of language.

Second, in transforming and embellishing experience, the poet also creates ideas that are agreeable to an audience and satisfies the imagination's desire for the satisfaction and pleasure it derives from relating ideas and completing a whole. Hume notes at one point that the imagination's love of totality and the satisfaction it finds there is the reason poets employ synecdoche and "frequently draw their images and metaphors" so that a part stands for the whole, such as a gate to represent a city (T 3.2.3n73.5). When poets achieve their affects they do so by transforming merely natural objects and scenes into things of beauty, deliberately arousing a corresponding pleasure in the audience. Although poetic genius reflects the active side of the imagination, its passive role is manifest as an audience's capacity to be moved by images created by the poet and have certain ideas raised in their minds as a result. Poets rely on the receptive capacity of the audience and the mechanism of sympathy that explains the "rule in criticism" that "every combination of syllables or letters, which gives pain to the organs of speech in the recital, appears also, from a species of sympathy, harsh and disagreeable to the ear" (EPM 5.37). A fundamental difference, however, between reality and its poetic counterpart is that poetic ideas are *always* a source of *pleasure* rather than pain and the agreeableness arises from the effect of sympathy and a quality immediately agreeable to ourselves. Pain, after all, is a real sentiment born of impressions or arising when sentiments are rekindled through memory; however weak a real sorrow may be, "yet in none of its gradations will it ever give pleasure" (E 221). In a poetical reality, by contrast, the passion is transformed; poetry does not simply *reproduce* the original sentiment, but *refashions* it in such a way that it becomes a source of pleasure rather than pain.

Clearly – and this is the third criterion the poet must satisfy – authors do not produce agreeable sentiments by accident, but employ their skills and techniques to bring them about deliberately as a particular response in the audience. This deliberate use of poetic skill is a double-edged sword, however, because one cannot embellish the world in a fictional way without exaggeration and artifice. On the one hand, to be effective in transforming the world poets must possess a certain genius, taste, or spirit as well have a firm grasp of principles governing human nature; without these qualities poets would create ideas that are dull and unable to convince, move, or otherwise affect an intended audience. Hume refers to this capacity as a "kind of magical faculty of the soul, which, tho' it be always most perfect in the greatest geniuses, and is properly what we call genius, is however inexplicable by the utmost efforts of human understanding" (T 1.1.7.15). On the other hand, Hume is sympathetic to Locke's criticism of "figurative speeches," and he is suspicious that poetry contains some inherent and unavoidable corruption. Hume goes so far as to call poets "liars by profession, [who] always endeavour to give an air of truth to their fictions" (T 1.3.10.5); skillful writers possess a "native enthusiasm" (E 139), which can sweep away writer and audience alike into a "kind of madness" (T 1.3.10.10). The "beauties [of poetry] are founded on falsehood and fiction, on hyperboles, metaphor, and an abuse and perversion of terms from their natural meaning" (E 231), which puts them in the company of priests and allegorists, who corrupted real events and heroes and thus "successively improved the wonder and astonishment of the ignorant multitude" (NHR 151). Hume manages these dangers of aesthetic representation by pointing out that unlike madness, poetic enthusiasm is a temporary state, and while poetry works by creating a fanciful world, neither poets nor readers actually believe in the reality they create. "In the warmth of a poetical enthusiasm, a poet has a *counterfeit* belief, and even a kind of vision of his objects ... [where the] blaze of poetical figures and images ... have their effect upon the poet himself, as well as upon his readers" (T 1.3.10.6).

One thing Hume valued in literature, not to mention in his own work and character as well, was simplicity in thought, expression, and composition;[25] a theme, it is worth noting, destined to work itself out in debates over the picturesque. For the noblest works of art are "beholden for their chief beauty to the force and happy influence of nature" (E 139), Hume writes, and demands of poets that they imitate nature. There is no reason for the poet to do more than put touches on a canvas already completed. When poets acknowledge themselves as understudies to the master and guide of nature, a world of poetic possibilities opens up as they at once discover techniques that can hardly fail to arouse sentiments to satisfy the imagination. Objects are beautiful, in part, because they are structured in such a way that fits our capacity to be affected; we take pleasure from harmonious compositions (EPM 5.37) and figures that are balanced (EPM 6.28), like the parts of an animal moving together in a perfect whole or a pillar slender at its top and wider at its base. In short, poets should avoid any hint of Locke's "figurative speeches," flourishes that distort natural language and inhibit the easy movement of the imagination. The imagination is pleased by the novelty of innovative productions, but those "which are merely surprising," Hume writes, "without being natural, can never give any lasting entertainment to the mind. To draw chimeras is not, properly speaking, to copy or imitate" (E 192). "Fine writing," however, " ... consists of sentiments, which are natural, without being obvious" (E 191), so that "Uncommon expressions, strong flashes of wit, pointed similes, and epigrammatic turns ... are a disfigurement, rather than an embellishment of discourse." Such flourishes in literary works are equivalent to the multiplicity of ornaments on a Gothic building: as the eye is "distracted ... and loses the whole by its minute attention to the parts; ... [so] the mind, perusing a work overstocked with wit, is fatigued and disgusted with the constant endeavour to shine and surprise" (E 192–3). For this reason, Hume considers the pastoral form of poetry to be the most entertaining because it mimics nature as closely as poetry is able and presents scenes that are best fitted to arouse agreeable sentiments in an audience.

Hume's idea of simplicity and refinement is manifest most clearly in the literature of Antiquity, the age of Augustus and the Greeks at the height of Athenian culture (E 196), distinguished by their "correctness and delicacy" (H 6.543) and "an amiable simplicity, which ... is so fitted to express the genuine movements of nature and passions" (H 5.149). Homer, Hume writes, "copies true, natural manners, which, however rough or uncultivated, will always form an agreeable and interesting picture" (H 4.386). From "the simple purity of Athens,"

---

[25] Hume wrote to Hugh Blair of an experience in Paris: "what gave me chief pleasure was to find that most of the elogiums bestowed on me turned on my personal character; my naivety and simplicity of manners, the candour and mildness of my disposition &c." (L I, 437), quoted in Leopold Damrosch, *Fictions of Reality in the Age of Johnson and Hume* (Madison: University of Wisconsin Press, 1989), 19.

however, Hume discerns an increasing desire for novelty, a gradual move away from the simple depiction of nature to increasing artifice and adornment, which leads authors "wide of simplicity and nature" and encourages a "degeneracy of taste" (E 196). "The glaring figures of discourse, the pointed antithesis, the unnatural conceit, the jingle of words; such false ornaments were not employed by early writers" (H 5.149). This "general degeneracy of style and language" becomes pronounced in "that tinsel eloquence, which is observable in many of the Roman writers, from which Cicero himself is not wholly exempted, and which so much prevails in Ovid, Seneca, Lucan, Martial, and the Plinys" (H 5.150); comes of age in the rebirth of letters in Europe in the sixteenth and seventeenth century; and reaches fruition in the Restoration dramas in the reign of Charles II. "The productions, represented at that time on the state, were such monsters of extravagance and folly," Hume declares, "so utterly destitute of all reason or even common sense; that they would be the disgrace of English literature, had not the nation made atonement for its former admiration of them, by the total oblivion to which they are now condemned" (H 6.542). Even before that, under Elizabeth Tudor and the Stuarts, learning was "attired in the same unnatural garb, which it wore at the time of its decay among the Greeks and Romans," as is evident in Shakespeare, whose works involve irregularities, absurdities, and deformities (H 5.151); in Johnson, who did little more than translate "into bad English the beautiful passages of the Greeks" (H5.151); and in John Donne, whose satire's, in Hume's view, while they contain "some flashes of wit and ingenuity ... are totally suffocated and buried by the harshest and most uncouth expressions, that is anywhere to be met with" (H 5.152).

Hume gives praise only when writers come close to the Augustan/Greek model, and then it is for elements or particular works rather than for a corpus as a whole. Spencer, he writes, for example, "contains great beauties, a sweet and harmonious versification, easy elocution, a fine imagination. Yet does the perusal of his work become so tedious, that one never finishes it from the mere pleasure which it affords: It soon becomes a kind of task-reading; and it requires some effort and resolution to carry us on to the end of his long performance" (H 4.386). In comparison with Homer the "pencil of the English poet [in the *Fairie Queen*] was employed in drawing the affectations, and conceits, and fopperies of chivalry, which appear ridiculous as soon as they lose the recommendation of the mode" (H 4.386). Hume also finds much to praise in the "great poet" Milton (DNR 97) and bemoans his neglect. Yet "Even in his Paradise Lost, his capital performance," he remarks, "there are very long passages, amounting to near a third of the work, almost wholly destitute of harmony and elegance, nay, all vigour of imagination" (H 6.150–1). Similarly, Hume sees great genius in some of Dryden's compositions – *Ode to St. Cecilia*, and *Absolom and Achitophel* – but considers his plays to be "utterly disfigured by vice or folly or both. ... Even his fables are ill-chosen tales, conveyed in an incorrect, though spirited versification." Some pieces, Hume concludes, constitute the "refuse of our language" (H 6.543). Hume's criticisms might be harsh,

but they are not arbitrary and are quite inconsistent with his views on literature and the rules he takes to govern compositions of taste and beauty.

WILLIAM HOGARTH

Although William Hogarth (1697–1764) is famous as engraver, painter, and
social critic, his work in aesthetic theory remains relatively obscure among
philosophers, especially in comparison to that of Shaftesbury, Hutcheson,
or Hume, and to this day his major theoretical work, *The Analysis of Beauty*
(1753), is routinely omitted from anthologies or writings on the history of aesthetics.[26] This is due in no small part to the fact that, even in his own time,
Hogarth's reputation was based primarily on his artistic productions and membership of the St. Martin's Lane Academy, which he founded in 1735. When the
Analysis was published, Hogarth's contemporaries – especially those associated with the rival Royal Academy of Arts founded by Sir Joshua Reynolds –
heaped scorn on the work and its central idea in the "line of beauty and grace,"
dismissing the whole as a misguided venture into theory; they even doubted
Hogarth's authorship.[27] The *Analysis* did not sell well, never went into a second edition in Hogarth's lifetime, and was soon eclipsed by Burke's *Enquiry*,
which appeared four years later.

Despite a poor reception in mid-century and its relative neglect now, the
Analysis did not fall into obscurity but had a significant and durable impact in
both theoretical and practical ways. It was read and admired by some, and had a
notable influence on Alexander Gerard and especially Alison, who, writing later
in the century (Alison's *Essays on the Nature and Principles of Taste* was published in 1790) cites the work critically but favorably. It also provided a mode
of philosophical expression for the influential school of eighteenth-century
English "landscape gardening," which championed gentle sweeps of land,
curves of lawn, and serpentine bodies of water. Hogarth's thought is also of
interest for the way it engages other aesthetic works of the period and stands
as one of only two works in the tradition of eighteenth-century aesthetics – the
other being Reynolds's *Discourses* – that stand as the fruit born by a major
artist reflecting on the nature of his craft through the categories of aesthetic
theory. The work of Reynolds and Hogarth certainly falls into the tradition of
the art treatise intended to offer practical advice to would-be artists, but at once
engages in what we might call an "empirical" aesthetics that emphasizes the
role of experience. Like Reynolds, Hogarth also frames rules for guiding good
artistic practice, but while the *Discourses* is aimed exclusively at students of the
Royal Academy of Arts, the intended audience of Hogarth's *Analysis* is quite

---

[26] William Hogarth, *The Analysis of Beauty*, ed. Ronald Paulson (New Haven, CT: Yale
University Press, 1997 [1753]). All references in the text are to chapter and page number of
this edition.

[27] See Paulson, editor's preface, xi.

clearly the spectator, consumer, or "public," educated and capable of appreciating art and understanding aesthetic theory. Hogarth is ruthless in his attacks on the "connoisseur," the "expertise" they profess, and the "authority" they claim. Hogarth considered the public to be in a better position to understand him, free as they are of professional investment and uncorrupted by the prejudice and pedantry of the experts who, despite their pretensions, could boast little or no "practical knowledge" of art and lacked any meaningful insight into the works over which their claimed expertise roamed. All one requires to follow his inquiry, Hogarth maintains, is an open mind and a willingness to consider its claims in light of the lessons of nature and wisdom born of observation.

As Hogarth makes clear in the preface, this point also applies to "mere men of letters" (2), philosophers and their ilk, whose misguided attempts to understand beauty find their purest expression in Shaftesbury's rarefied space of disinterestedness and contemplation. Great artists have long produced work that has "excelled in grace and beauty," Hogarth points out, by imitating nature and reproducing the lines of antique statuary, and have done so without the aid of explicitly formulated aesthetic principles or inquiring into the causes from which the beauty of their art follows as an effect. The likes of Rubens, Raphael, and Correggio could no more articulate a secret behind their work than the "day-labourer, who constantly uses the leaver, could give of that machine as a mechanical power" (6). When philosophers have turned their attention to discovering the basis of beauty – even to the point of framing a rule to direct its expression – they have foundered in bewilderment, contradiction, or obscurantism. In "All the English writers," Hogarth says provocatively, " ... *Je ne sçai quoi*, is become a fashionable phrase for grace" (4).

This opening gambit to fault philosophers has to be read ironically, however, because Hogarth borrows liberally and unself-consciously from other writers – the idiom of improving nature through representation, for example, the metaphors of sight and eye, the category of variety, and especially the power of imagination – and the title page of the book announces its author's debt to Addison and Hutcheson in particular: its subtitle reads "Written with a view to fixing the fluctuating ideas of taste," below which stands Hogarth's representation of the secret he is to reveal in the form of a three-dimensional triangle containing the line of beauty, resting on a plinth upon which is boldly emblazoned the word *variety* (Fig. 1).

In approach, then, the *Analysis* does not dispute the basic premise that some ordering principle underlies the experience of beauty, which can be extracted from artistic practice and given formal expression. Hogarth disagrees only in the particulars, with the specific principles proposed by others and the fact that they have been generated abstractly, independent, that is, of what artists actually do.

Hogarth's philosophical debts are also clear from the stated aim of his "short essay." "I shall endeavour to shew," he writes,

what the principles are in nature, by which we are directed to call the forms of some bodies beautiful, others ugly; some graceful, and others the reverse; by considering

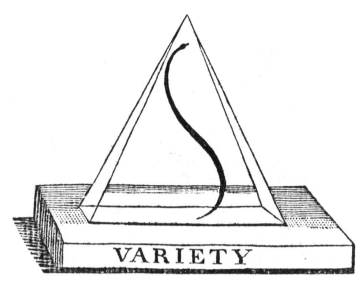

FIGURE 1. "Variety," detail from title page of *The Analysis of Beauty* by William Hogarth (London: J. Reeves, 1753). Image courtesy of The Lewis Walpole Library, Yale University.

more minutely than has hitherto been done, the nature of those lines, and their different combinations, which serve to raise in the mind the ideas of all the variety of forms imaginable. (17)

To achieve this end, Hogarth appeals to the imagination, the faculty affected by qualities of objects – artists "play" with and "entertain" it, he observes (50) – and the means through which readers are "to conceive, as accurate an idea as is possible, of the inside of ... surfaces" by considering every object "as if his eye were placed within it" (22). In an image reminiscent of Addison's discussion of the "concave and convex" previously discussed (*Spectator*, 3:556, no. 415), Hogarth asks the reader to picture a "thin shell" circumscribing a "vacant space" into which the "imagination will naturally enter." "[L]et every object under our consideration," he declares,

be imagined to have its inward contents scoop'd out so nicely, as to have nothing of it left but a thin shell, exactly corresponding both in its inner and outer surface, to the shape of the object itself; and let us likewise suppose this thin shell to be made up of very fine threads, closely connected together, and equally perceptible, whether the eye is supposed to observe them from without, or within; and we shall find the ideas of the two surfaces of this shell will naturally coincide. The very word, shell, makes us seem to see both surfaces alike. (21)

With this direction to conceive wholes as composed of lines that form shells around inner space, Hogarth proceeds to enumerate six "fundamental principles" that "please and entertain the eye" and are "generally allowed to give elegance and beauty, when duly blended together, to compositions of all kinds" (23): fitness (or utility) relates parts to whole; variety relieves the eye from the monotony of sameness; uniformity brings symmetry to elements in an object; simplicity facilitates perception; intricacy pleases the mind when solving difficult problems; and quantity (or the sublime) adds reverence and greatness. These principles can been seen in myriad objects – a bell or candlestick, for example, ornamentation on buildings and, most perfectly, the dome of St. Paul's Cathedral – and are "daily put in practice," Hogarth observes, even in something as mundane as "everyday dress" where "women of every rank, who are said to dress prettily, have known their force, without considering them as principles" (38). Thus an eye to utility fits dress to age and character, uniformity makes dress formal, variety recommends different color and form, simplicity restrains superfluous ornamentation, intricacy gives style and modesty, and quantity gives clothing a striking fullness (39–40).

These principles are all elements that confer aesthetic value on objects, but the most important is variety, because it explains the nature of beauty and grace. These involve, more specifically "*linear* variety," because, in Hogarth's thought experiment, lines are the mark that circumscribe the shell that encloses the empty space left from hollowing out the object in imagination. Experience suggests, Hogarth proposes, that things are bound within lines of different sorts – straight, circular, and waving – which combine in various ways and are most beautiful when united in the "precise serpentine line of grace." Readers are to imagine a horn dissected by a perpendicular line that has some beauty on account of the variation involved in its conical shape; beauty is increased when the horn is bent and circumscribed by a circular line, and reaches the "sublime in form" when the waving line is twisted to form a serpentine, "which, as it dips out of sight behind the horn in the middle, and returns again at the smaller end, not only gives play to the imagination, and delights the eye, on that account; but informs it likewise of the quantity and variety of its contents" (50) (Fig. 2). Hogarth sees this exemplified nowhere more dramatically than in the "twist" of the human body, both as a whole and in the individual parts of muscles and bones, which are displayed when, in imagination, the skin is removed.

Although, as noted at the outset, the *Analysis* stands very much in the tradition of aesthetics and is directed to the "public" rather than the connoisseur, Hogarth also casts an eye to the artist and artistic practice, and as the work proceeds he turns increasingly to matters of interest more to producers than consumers of art.[28] This is evident in the way he presents his aesthetic principles as recommendations or rules (similar to the rules of art of the sort established by Hume, Reynolds, and Kames) that artists should follow if they wish to produce beauty and grace in their work. Capturing just proportion of

---

[28] On this point, see Paulson, editor's introduction, xx.

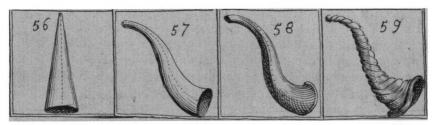

FIGURE 2. "The line of beauty and grace," detail from *The Analysis of Beauty* (London: J. Reeves, 1753), plate 2, second state. Image courtesy of The Lewis Walpole Library, Yale University.

figures is facilitated by general measurements of height and breadth of body, Hogarth points out for example, and the proper effects of light and shade are best achieved by following his categorization of different lines. Similarly, when considering which colors to use, the artist should choose those that give objects distinctness, opposition, and breadth, and further simplicity in the foreground, middle, and background of a canvas. Depictions of the human face, likewise, ought to follow the serpentine lines that express passions and mental states and capture differences in age, as the same most effectively depict the grace associated with a figure's attitude and movement.

Hogarth is keen to point out, however, that artists should not follow rules in a mindless or automatic fashion, and it is possible, as with Albrecht Dürer's near obsession with mathematical ratio, to become enslaved to them. Moreover, formal directives can hardly be of prime importance if, as Hogarth emphasizes early on, artists have long produced great work without formal knowledge of the lines of beauty and grace. Although Hogarth begins by criticizing philosophers for throwing up their hands in the face of beauty and resorting to the mystery of the "I know not what" as a substitute for real explanation, he does not abandon entirely the thought that artistic practice cannot be captured fully even by the lines of beauty and grace and the rules they suggest: artists still require a "good eye," he says, and must commit to sustained observation of the "works of art and nature" (59) and engage in a continual effort of imagination if they are to capture grace and beauty in their work. Real judges are those who know that "little more" – the *Il poco pui* of the Italians (56) – that separates even the best copy from the masterpiece. In addition to experience and observation, the artist also relies on intangible factors, varying, mixing, and compounding various elements "in imagination" (70) in pursuit of a model or perfect "ideal" out of which some new object is created; this ideal might not be reached in any actual work, but an approximation of it can successfully convey the qualities intended by the artist.

Before leaving Hogarth, two things are worthy of note. First, Hogarth's theory fits very well with highly ornate artistic styles and decorative flourish associated with Baroque and Rococo painters such as François Boucher

(1703–70), Michelangelo Merisi da Caravaggio (1571–1610), Jean-Honoré Fragonard (1732–1806), Thomas Gainsborough (1727–88), Peter Paul Rubens (1577–1640), and Jean-Antoine Watteau (1684–1721), but it is less satisfactory when applied to works outside this tradition. Hogarth clearly does not intend his theory simply as a justification for the taste of his own age, and insists that the lines of beauty and grace are found in nature and other artistic periods; many of his examples are drawn from the Renaissance and the Quattrocento. However, that other artistic traditions might not exhibit Hogarth's principle does not undermine his general theory, although it might well limit it to certain historical periods or styles. Second, it is not clear that Hogarth actually applies the principles developed in the *Analysis* in his own artistic productions, many of which are devoid of beauty and grace altogether and deliberately so. At the same time, Hogarth does not claim that beauty is the only function of art, and many of his now-iconic works such as *A Rake's Progress* (1732–3) and *Beer Street and Gin Lane* (1751) aim satirically at ends of a political and moral sort, a conviction that, according to Roger Fry, was to have unfortunate consequences. "For I think his [Hogarth's] influence on British art has been bad upon the whole," Fry writes. "It has tended to sanction a disparagement of painting as a pure art – has tended to make artists think that they must justify themselves by conveying valuable, or important, or moral ideas. ... It has obscured the truth that art has its own specific function, that it conveys experiences which are *sui generis*, not to be defined or valued by anything outside."[29] Whether or not Fry is correct in his assessment, he is surely right to recognize that the waving and serpentine lines are not appropriate to every style of art, Hogarth's included, especially where achieving beauty and grace is not the primary intention; however, this does not touch the claim the principle Hogarth offers to explain beauty and grace where those qualities are found.

EDMUND BURKE

Among eighteenth-century British writers (he was born in Dublin, but spent most of his life in London, and twenty years as Member of Parliament for Bristol) Edmund Burke (1729–97) enjoys the rare status of having made major contributions both to aesthetics and political theory. He is remembered today more as a leading Whig politician and eloquent voice of the counterrevolutionary response to the events of 1789, articulated powerfully in *Reflections on the Revolution in France* (1790), a founding text of conservative thought that has eclipsed the earlier *A Philosophical Enquiry into the Origin of Our Ideas of the Sublime and Beautiful* (1757) written while Burke was still in his twenties (it was finished by 1753) and a second edition two years

---

[29] Roger Fry, *Reflections on British Paintings* (New York: Macmillan, 1934), 42. I consider Fry's aesthetics in ch. 7.

later notwithstanding, on a subject matter to which he never returned.[30] The *Enquiry* should not be underestimated, however, for its systematic character, originality, and the influence it commanded on the tradition for decades to come. If Addison's essays in *The Spectator* set the direction for aesthetics to mid-century, Burke's *Enquiry* determines the course long thereafter, and well into the nineteenth century every subsequent writer, in some shape or form, as follower or critic, supporter or detractor, had to contend with the work and the views it expressed. Without it, the *Critique of the Power of Judgment*, as we know it at least, would be unthinkable, a fact reflected in the way Kant organizes the work (though he reverses Burke's ordering and treats beauty before sublimity) and in his acknowledgment of Burke as the "foremost author" of those who had undertaken an "empirical exposition of the sublime and of the beautiful" (CJ 5:277).

At first blush, the importance of the *Enquiry* is belied by the fact that much of Burke's philosophical language is, by the time of the work's composition in mid-century, conventional and familiar; its method, moreover, is distinctly empirical, the theory of mind on which it relies thoroughly Lockean, and the author is throughout in obvious dialogue (sometimes explicitly, though often not) with the likes of Addison, Hutcheson, Hume, and Hogarth.[31] Burke also appeals to principles of association, although he distances himself from Hutcheson's "accidental Ideas" and "fantastick Aversions" in favor of emphasizing the intrinsic nature of phenomena. Thus, as F. P. Lock points out, recalling an example from the *Enquiry* (IV.xiv.143) derived from Locke (*Essay* 2.23.10) and disseminated through Addison (*Spectator*, no. 110, July 6th, 1711), Burke rejects the idea that children are conditioned to be afraid of the dark due to the stories they hear of the creatures it conceals, but "derives the association from a *real and universal experience*. Darkness *is* a state of perpetual danger and insecurity, in which we feel vulnerable and therefore fearful." Burke backs this up, moreover, with a physiological theory that explains how darkness is "painful in itself, because of the way the eye reacts to it."[32]

At the same time, the *Enquiry* is strikingly innovative in a number of ways. It represents the first sustained treatment of the sublime since Longinus, and (as previously noted) effectively completes the movement intimated in Shaftesbury and initiated by Addison to free the sublime from its neo-classically inspired association with literary style, and isolate it as a category of aesthetic experience in its own right. Major contributors to the tradition that

---

[30] Edmund Burke, *A Philosophical Enquiry into the Sublime and Beautiful*, ed. James T. Boulton (London: Routledge and Kegan Paul, 1958 [1757]). Unless noted otherwise, all references in the text are to part, section, and page number of this edition.

[31] See F. P. Lock, *Edmund Burke: Volume I, 1730–1784* (Oxford: Clarendon Press, 1998), 91–4, who cites other influences on Burke's thinking, including Dubos and Étienne Bonnot de Condillac (1715–80). Lock also emphasizes the *Enquiry* as a response to moral relativism and secularism, which, he claims, makes it "at bottom a theological work" (98).

[32] Lock, *Edmund Burke*, 94, emphasis added.

preceded him had focused primarily on beauty, and (with the possible exception of Addison) given the sublime short shrift, regarded it as the lesser cousin of the beautiful or, in the very least, considered Longinus to have settled the matter to their satisfaction. Burke, by contrast, honors the sublime with the same attention as he does the beautiful, and thus treats them as equally important categories of aesthetic experience. This is reflected in the organization of the *Enquiry* in which each receive their own section (Part II and Part III, respectively), an innovation that finds its mirror image in Kant's later division of the "Critique of Aesthetic Judgment" into the "Analytic of the Beautiful" and the "Analytic of the Sublime." Not only does Burke give equal weight to the sublime and the beautiful, but he also goes further – and even to the extreme – of insisting on the "remarkable contrast" (III.xxvii.124) between the two categories and the impossibility of "reconciling them in the same subject" (III.xiii.114). This is a point he reiterates throughout and nowhere more forcefully (or more didactically) than in the formal comparison he makes at the end of Part III. "For sublime objects are vast in their dimensions, beautiful ones comparatively small," he writes,

beauty should be smooth, and polished; the great, rugged and negligent; beauty should shun the right line, yet deviate from it insensibly; the great in many cases loves the right line, and when it deviates it often makes a strong deviation; beauty should not be obscure; the great ought to be dark and gloomy; beauty should be light and delicate; the great ought to be solid, and even massive. They are indeed ideas of a very different nature, one being founded on pain, the other on pleasure; and however they may vary afterwards from the direct nature of their causes, yet these causes keep up an eternal distinction between them, a distinction never to be forgotten by any whose business it is to affect the passions. (III.xxvii.124)

Notwithstanding the later efforts of some to explode Burke's division – notably Dugald Stewart who wrote later that it is "to be ascribed chiefly to the weight of Mr. Burke's authority"[33] – this sharp line between the two experiences was never seriously challenged, and central for our story, made such a deep impression on Uvedale Price that he undertook to do for the picturesque what Burke had done for the sublime. The repercussions of these two innovations – raising the sublime to the same status as beauty, and delivering each to mutually exclusive realms of aesthetic experience – go much further than providing Burke with some organizing principle, however; they at once constitute a fundamental change in the way the experience of sublimity was understood. Burke stresses the emotional content of the sublime, and in so doing connects Addison's "pleasing Astonishment" and "delightful Stillness and Amazement in the Soul" with the Romantic subject developed later by Wordsworth. At

[33] Dugald Stewart, *Philosophical Essays* (1810), in *The Collected Works of Dugald Stewart*, ed. Sir William Hamilton, 11 vols. (Edinburgh: Thomas Constable and Co.; London: Hamilton, Adams and Co., 1854–60), 5:233n3.

the same time, Burke abandons the classically inspired connection of sublimity with elevation and the comforting feelings of admiration and wonder that attend it, replacing it with the decidedly more disturbing one of harm and ultimately death and the unsettling emotions of fear and terror it inspires.[34]

The Sublime and the Beautiful

Burke never says so explicitly, but he regards "sublime" and "beautiful" to denote ideas with which the mind (in the terminology of his Lockean model) comes to be furnished, and "passions" as the affective states ideas cause in the subject and constitutive of the aesthetic experience each term names. Burke thus conceives the *Enquiry* (as he expresses it in the preface to the first edition) as an attempt to rectify the "abuse" of the "sublime" and "beautiful" evident in their being "frequently confounded" and "indiscriminately applied to things greatly differing, and sometimes of natures directly opposite," and to do so "from a careful survey of the properties of things which we find by experience to influence those passions" (Preface, 1). Burke devotes Part I to examining the human passions in terms of final causes, that is, the ends to which each aims with respect to the pain or pleasure they invoke (novelty alone, he emphasizes, against Addison one assumes, is incapable of moving us). Burke emphasizes (contra Locke) that while neither pain nor pleasure can be defined, both share a "positive" and "independent" nature (I.ii.33) so that the removal of one does not necessarily herald the appearance of the other: a cessation of pain is not identical with pleasure, and an increase of pleasure is not the same as the absence of pain. Burke does allow that we experience "relative" pain and pleasure in the form of joy (sudden pleasure felt from escaping pain), indifference (the cessation of pleasure), disappointment (an abrupt end of pleasure), and grief (the total and irrevocable loss of pleasure), but his insight and guiding thought is that aesthetic experience can be understood – and its varieties distinguished – according to positive pleasures and pains and the different classes of human passions to which they give rise. These passions are connected either with "self-preservation" when they turn on pain and danger, or with "society" when they turn on pleasure. The latter divides further into society of the "sexes," which concerns propagation, and of "general society," the connections we enjoy with fellow human beings, animals, and inanimate nature. Objects or qualities that produce ideas of self-preservation are sublime, Burke reasons, and those that produce ideas of society are beautiful.

Burke then turns to describing the material causes of the different kinds of aesthetic experience, by enumerating the various properties of objects that give rise to the ideas of the passions that underlie and correspond to each. In Part II, he examines the sublime, "the strongest emotion which the mind

---

[34] On this point, see Lock, *Edmund Burke*, 103.

is capable of feeling," which he traces to "Whatever is fitted in any sort to
excite the ideas of pain, and danger, that is to say, whatever is any sort terrible"
(I.vii.39). The source of these ideas can be real or impending, in which case they
produce actual pain and involve what Shaftesbury and later Kant refer to as an
"interest" – in this case of self-preservation – that prevents the experience of
the sublime from developing. When the threat is removed or merely imaginary,
by contrast, so that we are not "actually in such circumstances" (I.xviii.51), the
passions then become a source of "delightful horror" (I.xviii.47) manifest in its
highest degree as "astonishment," and in lower forms as "admiration, reverence and respect" (II.i.57). For Burke, the source of the delight is pain in itself,
a view from which Kant obviously diverges when he urges that the experience
of sublimity does not reside in being overwhelmed or humiliated as such, but
in the subsequent pleasure taken in the feeling of respect that comes with realizing the superiority of reason to imagination or one's status as a person with
a moral vocation.

   For Burke, moreover, the sublime is not so easily or neatly reduced to one
or two causes – as it is later for Kant – in terms of magnitude (mathematical
sublime) and the power of nature (dynamical sublime). Burke includes both
of these as part of a long list of properties that produce the requisite feeling:
he cites magnitude in buildings of enormous dimension; vastness contained in
greatness or smallness of dimension in the ascending order of length, height,
and depth; infinity, where the eye cannot see the bounds of things; and succession in progress beyond actual limits, all of which can be accommodated
within Kant's two categories. For Burke, however, because the sublime lies
in the pleasurable experience of horror (when the threat is distance or imagined) and not in the subsequent feeling of having overcome it, any object that
stretches the imagination and excites the delightful horror that defines the
experience counts among the material causes of sublimity. As a result, Burke's
list is long and varied: the experience of sublimity can be excited by obscurity
(because both physical and metaphorical darkness suggests ignorance), power
(including the sheer physical strength of animals and, less tangibly, the institutional might of kings), privation (in vacuity, darkness, solitude, and silence),
uniformity (where the imagination advances unchecked), difficulty (involving
great force and labor), and magnificence (the profusion of what is splendid or
valuable). Burke also finds appropriate causes in colors, when they are great,
fast moving, or evoke the transition from light to darkness; in the gloominess
of light in building; in sounds that are sudden, intermittent, or express anger;
in the threatening cries of animals; in smells and tastes that involve an overwhelming stench or bitterness; and, finally, in the feeling of pain when it gives
rise to ideas of anguish and torment.

   In Part III, Burke offers a parallel treatment of beauty, which he begins
by rejecting the principles offered by other eighteenth-century writers; this
is illustrative in part, one assumes, of the charge in the preface of abuse and
indiscriminate application of aesthetic categories. The concept of proportion is

inadequate, Burke reasons, because it relates primarily to convenience, properly a function of the understanding, which judges relative quantity and leaves the imagination cold and indifferent. The appeal to custom and principles of association ignores the fact that beauty strikes immediately and without reflection; fitness or utility leaves unexplained how useful parts – the snout of a swine, pendulous bill of the pelican, quills of the hedgehog, or "springy limbs" of the monkey (III.vi.105) – lack beauty; perfection carries the idea of weakness, which is alien to beauty; and qualities of mind and virtues are of little help because far from inspiring beauty, they are properly the cause of terror (as in the case of justice, wisdom, and fortitude) and even the "softer affections" (such as compassion, kindness, and liberality) are connected with ideas of preventing danger, punishment, and trouble of various kinds.[35]

Burke's alternative is to trace beauty to anything that causes love, "that feeling of satisfaction that arises to the mind upon contemplating any thing beautiful" independent of use or any "creature of the understanding" (III.i.91). Unlike the sublime, which stretches, overwhelms, or otherwise upsets the soul, Burke takes beauty (much in the spirit of Addison, Hume, and Hogarth) as a feeling that soothes and calms, although the list is as long and varied as the material causes of sublimity. Beauty is found in objects that are small, such as little birds and small beasts; smooth like skin, streams, and the coats of animals; or that display gradual variation, as in the feathers of a bird. Similarly, Burke contends, the delicacy and fragility of certain trees and flowers renders them beautiful, as do colors that are clear, fair, light, and various. A physiognomy with the agreeable qualities of a clear eye and slow and languid motion that fits gradually with the face is likewise beautiful, as is grace found in posture and motion; the elegance of smooth and polished parts and regularity of shape; the feeling of slight resistance when one touches what is smooth and soft; sounds that are clear, even, smooth, and various; and, finally, taste and smells that are smooth and sweet.

Burke could quite easily have concluded his investigation here, but he proceeds in Part IV to examine the efficient causes or the laws by which the properties that give rise to the ideas of the sublime and beautiful affect bodies and excite the passions in question. One might expect Burke to draw on principles of association, but he rejects this account, reasoning that while "many things affect us after a certain manner ... by association," it would be "absurd ... to say that all things affect us by association only; since some things just have been originally and natural agreeable or disagreeable, from which others derive

---

35 Cf. Alison's later observation that, although Burke is no doubt correct to claim that no "natural" beauty resides in "unpleasing qualities" of snouts and quills, it does not follow that they cannot acquire that value form another source, viz., fitness. Having overcome any initial revulsion, then "in the light of the Fitness of their construction" they become "in some degree, objects of Beauty." See Archibald Alison, *Essays on the Nature and Principles of Taste* (Dublin: Byrne, Moore, Grueber, McAllister, Jones, and White, 1790), 381, and ch. 3 in this book.

their associated powers" (IV.ii.130–1). Burke opts instead for a physiological explanation in terms of nerves and muscles that contract to produce pain or relax to give gentle pleasure; this is intended to correspond in a direct (and rather simplistic) way to the disturbing passions of the sublime and the calm ones of beauty. In the case of the sublime, the nerves are stretched, but without the idea of danger present this produces the feeling of delight. Thus, for example, with sublimity, large visible objects make the eyes vibrate and darkness produces tension in them, as, in beauty, smoothness relaxes the fibers, and sweetness is found in liquids such as water and oil that consist of round parts.

This part of the *Enquiry* came in for rather harsh criticism. Richard Payne Knight pointed out one rather obvious oddity, remarking in *An Analytic Inquiry into the Principles of Taste*, and in apparent disbelief that anyone could seriously propose such a view, that

the slightest knowledge of optics would have informed him [Burke] that the sheet of paper, upon which he was writing, being seen thus close to the eye, reflected a greater, and more forcible mass of light; and, consequently, produced more irritation and tension, than the Peak of Teneriffe or Mount St. Elias would, if seen at the distance of a few miles: – yet, surely he would not say that the sheet of paper excited more grand and perfect ideas of the sublime.[36]

By the same lights, presumably, wearing fogged glasses would produce sufficient obscurity to make an otherwise unastonishing object sublime. This was not the only aspect of Burke's theory to come in for criticism and ridicule.[37] Reviewers took issue with the sharp distinction between pain and pleasure and the sublime and the beautiful. Some pointed out that beauty does not always calm and relax but often excites and stimulates, and others doubted his outright rejection of utility and proportion in favor of the small, smooth, and delicate. One of the extended and more trenchant critiques was that of Stewart who, in his *Philosophical Essays* (1810) and much influenced by Knight's *Analytic Inquiry*, objected that Burke had used *beauty* as a "generic word" and simply assumed that "in the objects of all our different external senses, there is some common quality to which the epithet Beautiful may be applied; and that this epithet, in all these different cases, conveys the same meaning." Burke is surely correct that smoothness is a source of pleasure – given the interconnectedness

---

[36] Richard Payne Knight, *An Analytic Inquiry into the Principles of Taste*, 4th ed. (London: T. Payne and J. White, 1808 [1805]), 1.5.5 (AI). All references here and in ch. 4, where I discuss Knight's views in some detail, are to part, chapter, and paragraph number.

[37] For a detailed discussion of Burke's contemporary critics and his response to them, see Lock, *Edmund Burke*, 109ff. More recent critics of note include Thomas Weiskel, *The Romantic Sublime: Studies in the Structure and Psychology of Transcendence* (Baltimore, MD: Johns Hopkins University Press, 1976), 88, and Hipple, *The Beautiful, the Sublime, & the Picturesque*, 91ff. More positive assessments are to be found in Monk, *The Sublime*, 96–8, and Vanessa L. Ryan, "The Physiological Sublime: Burke's Critique of Reason," *Journal of the History of Ideas* 62, 2 (2001): 265–79.

of the two senses, what is agreeable to touch is also agreeable to sight – but the further claim that smoothness defines beauty is "erroneous in itself and feebly supported": Burke simply converts one component of beauty into a universal maxim. This does not even hold empirically, Stewart observes, because there are objects disagreeable to touch, but beautiful to smell and sight, as well as natural objects that are beautiful when the reflecting rays of light make them rough and rugged. What Burke should have done, Stewart urges, was to move from the primary sense of beauty as objects of sight, to discover its other meanings that are based, on Stewart's own theory at least, with memory and association: a smooth lawn, for example, brings pleasure because it is connected with ideas of comfort, industry, art, and utility, or recalls delightful images from one's past. Had Burke taken this route, he would then have discovered the distinction between "intrinsic" or "absolute" beauty (objects pleasing in themselves) and its "relative" counterpart (objects pleasing when in combination – like a collection of colors or tastes – and thus "*in their proper place*" [228]); this would have complicated his account considerably, and perhaps saved him from the embarrassment of Part IV. "As for the physiological discussion itself," Stewart writes with the advantage of hindsight, "I am inclined to think that few, even of Mr. Burke's most partial admirers, will *now* be disposed to estimate its merits very highly."[38]

The treatment of the sublime – clearly the most influential and enduring part of the *Enquiry* – also came in for its fair share of censure, especially the claim that fear, terror, and astonishment should define the experience when the same feeling arises from increased esteem or love. The point is made explicitly by Reid who later charges Burke with having made "every thing grand or sublime that is terrible. Might he not be led to this," Reid wonders, "by the similarity between dread and admiration? Both are grave and solemn passions; both make a strong impression upon the mind; and both are very infectious." They differ, however, in that admiration presupposes "some uncommon excellence in its object, which dread does not." The sublime, Reid concludes against Burke's conflation, is really of some quality that excites admiration and has nothing to do with dread, which is a distinct experience ("Essay on Taste," IV.590.30–5, 591.1–5). In the first volume of *Modern Painters* (1843), Ruskin reiterates the objection, but then emphasizes dread – not fear – as definitive of the experience: anything "which elevates the mind is sublime," Ruskin observes, an effect achieved through the "contemplation of death ... [and] the deliberate measurement of the doom" involved.[39]

---

[38] See Stewart, *Works* 5:214ff., and for the details of Stewart's own view, see ch. 3. The italicized "now" suggests Stewart's appreciation of the high regard in which the *Enquiry* was once held. It is worth noting that, while Stewart's distinction between "intrinsic" and "relative" beauty clearly reflects Hutcheson, it had been given precisely this formulation already by Kames (see ch. 3).

[39] See ch. 6.

Further, despite the professed aim of the *Enquiry* to distinguish the beautiful from the sublime and raise both to equal status, the sheer number and variety of properties Burke enumerates to explain the origin of each tends to undermine the explanatory force at which his theory aims. This also tends to reduce otherwise quite different properties and objects to a single category – delightful horror and a feeling that soothes and calms – when they are in other respects quite different; the same is true of *passions*, a term under which Burke brings a bewildering variety of otherwise disparate phenomena. More recently commentators have raised issues concerning the obviously gendered character of the "masculine" sublime and the "feminine" beautiful, echoing in part earlier observations that Burke is preoccupied with female beauty and seems to take it as a standard of beauty; others have pointed to the tension in Burke's celebration of the radical and democratic nature of the sublime, on the one hand, and, on the other, his reaction against the very same in the shape of the French Revolution, which exemplifies the potential consequences of the suspension of reason and the ascendancy of the sublime passions.[40]

According to Knight, Burke came to acknowledge privately at least some of the oddities of his view and in retrospect found them highly amusing. "I shall merely observe, in justice to his memory," wrote Knight after Burke's death, "that, in his latter days, he [Burke] laughed very candidly and good-humouredly at many of the philosophical absurdities, which will here [in the *Analytic Inquiry*] be exposed" (AI 1.2.5.28). While Burke may well have softened in his later years, at the time he took the criticisms seriously, and published a second edition of the *Enquiry* – "something more full and satisfactory than the first" – in which he endeavored to "explain, illustrate, and enforce" the theory even if he saw no reason "for making any material change" to it (Preface, 2nd ed., 3), including the addition of a long section on power (II.v.64–70) that did not appear in the first edition. If Knight's report is correct, however, we can assume that Burke did not, on reflection, find these additions and corrections satisfactory.

The Standard of Taste

In addition to developing a comprehensive and original theory of the sublime and the beautiful, Burke also contributes to three central ongoing debates, namely, over a standard of taste, the paradox of tragedy, and the nature of

---

[40] See Stewart, *Works*, 5:220. Stewart also notes (220n2) a similar observation made by Price, and the gendered character of Burke's categories was not lost on other writers later in the century, including Knight and Mary Wollstonecraft (1759–97) (see Lock, *Edmund Burke*, 111). For a more recent consideration of the latter issue, see Linda M. G. Zerilli, *Signifying Woman: Culture and Chaos in Rousseau, Burke, and Mill* (Ithaca, NY: Cornell University Press, 1994), ch. 3, and on the tensions between Burke's aesthetics and politics, Tom Furniss, *Edmund Burke's Aesthetic Ideology: Language, Gender, and Political Economy in Revolution* (Cambridge: Cambridge University Press, 1993), esp. ch. 5.

poetry and poetic representation. The *Enquiry* proper contains *en passant* remarks that hint at Burke's view on the first of these – the question concerning a standard of taste (see I.xix.52–3) – but he only addresses the issue in a direct and systematic way in the "Introduction on Taste," a separate essay added to the second edition (1759) and generally regarded as a response to Hume's "Of the Standard of Taste," which had appeared too late for Burke to consider it in the first edition.[41] Burke makes unmistakable references to Hume's essay, and there are notable points of comparison between the two works. Burke was surely aware of Addison's essays for *The Spectator* as well as Hutcheson's remarks on the subject in the *Inquiry*, and for this reason the "Introduction" is more fruitfully read less as a direct response to Hume than as a contribution to the debate more generally.

Hume, as we have seen, argues that there is a standard – contained in qualities of objects, drawn from the test of time, and manifest in the true judge – even if it is routinely overlooked in the practice of making aesthetic judgments. Like him, Burke begins by emphasizing the apparent diversity of taste and evidence in favor of there being a standard. For "it is probable the standard both of reason and of Taste is the same in all human creatures" (IT 11), he writes, and the fact that there is no "obvious concurrence in any uniform or settled principles" is due to contingent factors such as the paucity of philosophers attempting to discover them or the negligence on the part of those who have. After all, Burke reasons, having discovered the principles underlying sublimity and beauty, it should *pari passu* be possible to find the "invariable and certain laws" (IT 12) that govern the imagination (IT 13). "Taste" is "no more than a faculty, or those faculties of the mind which are affected with, or which form a judgment of the works of imagination and the elegant arts" (IT 13), and its "Logic" should be no more mysterious than any other.

Burke's delineation of this logic, however, depends on distinguishing taste from knowledge, and takes a direction that anticipates the distinction Reid draws between perception and judgment and his discovery of a standard in "real excellence." As Gerard was to point out later in "Of the Standard of Taste," the fourth part added to the second edition of his *Essay on Taste*, Burke does not so much offer a solution to the question of a standard of taste as sidestep the issue altogether by denying that there are any "real differences to be adjusted."[42] As such, Burke steers away from the skeptical solutions of Hume and Hutcheson, who are inclined to accept variety and accommodate it within some universal principle that, all things being equal, should eventuate in correct judgment. Objects arouse the same pleasure and pain in all people, Burke reasons, and when taste "operates naturally" everybody is "agreed to call vinegar sour, honey sweet, and aloes bitter"; on this basis, we should conclude,

---

[41] "Introduction on Taste," in *Enquiry*, ed. Boulton, 11–27 (IT). All references are to the page numbers of this edition.
[42] See ch. 3.

"there is no diversity in … sentiments" (IT 14). There is, by contrast, diversity
in "preferences" – the equivalent of Hume's proverb *de gustibus* and Kant's
agreeable – and through custom and habit people come to prefer tobacco to
sugar or like the flavor of vinegar rather than milk. "[B]ut this makes no confusion in Tastes," Burke insists, because the same people are still aware that one
is "naturally" sweet and the other "naturally" bitter. If somebody were to deny
this and effectively claim that a preference changed the nature of the object –
that tobacco is actually sweet and sugar actually bitter – then one would be like
Hume's extravagant individual who puts Ogilby over Milton or takes molehills
as mountains; such a person is not "wrong in his notions," as Burke puts it
rather more bluntly, "but absolutely mad" (IT 14). On Burke's view, people
do not dispute about taste – although they might think they do – because that
is given in the nature of things; individuals do disagree, however, about the
degree of pleasure and pain that objects excite in them.

By analogy, Burke then insists, when it comes to making aesthetic judgments about beautiful objects, there is a single principle that shows everybody
to have the same taste, namely, resemblance: we all find the same object beautiful because it resembles the original. Taste is thus uniform, and there is a
standard governing beauty that exists in the nature of the objects. There is
variation, however, although what is often called "diversity of taste" is actually differences in the degree of pleasure different people take in the same
object and this is proportional to one's knowledge and thus appreciation of the
beauties in question. "The principle of this knowledge," Burke writes, "is very
much accidental, as it depends upon experience and observation, and not on
the strength or weakness of any natural faculty; and it is *from this difference
in knowledge* that what we commonly, though with no great exactness, call *a
difference in Taste proceeds*" (IT 18, emphasis added). If we lack natural sensibility we simply lack taste altogether (the capacity to be affected), Burke concludes, but without requisite knowledge we make false judgments and exhibit
bad taste instead of good.

The Paradox of Tragedy

Hume's "Of Tragedy" originally appeared alongside "Of the Standard of Taste"
in *Four Dissertations*, which means that Burke did not have it in mind when he
addressed the paradox of tragedy in the first edition of the *Enquiry*. This is supported by Burke's claim that extant solutions to the problem had ignored the
"mechanical structure of our bodies" or "natural frame and constitution of our
minds" in favor of the reasoning faculty, a charge of which Hume is clearly not
guilty. When he speaks of the paradox as a "cause of much reasoning," Burke
is no doubt referencing Aristotle, and certainly Fontenelle and Addison whose
theories (though not explicitly) he considers and rejects: that the pleasure arises
from the comfort we take in knowing the depiction to be fictitious, or that it
comes from being ourselves free from the evils represented. Burke develops

his own view of the subject in the context of discussing the social passion of sympathy, one of the three major "links" in the chain (the other being imitation and ambition) that binds individuals together through the pleasures of society; it is a "sort of substitution," he writes, "by which we are put into the place of another man, and affected in many respects as he is affected," and, depending on whether it turns upon pain or pleasure, is a source of sublimity and beauty. "It is by this principle," Burke continues, framing the paradox in his own terms,

chiefly that poetry, painting, and other affecting arts, transfuse their passions from one breast to another, and are often capable of grafting a delight on wretchedness, misery, and death itself. It is a common observation, that objects which in the reality would shock, are in tragical, and such like representations, the source of a very high species of pleasure. (I.xiii.44)

Burke addresses the issue by raising the more general question of how a spectator is affected by the feelings of others in "*real* distress." His answer, with a hint of the *Schadenfreude* that characterized Addison's discussion, is that people take a "degree of delight, and that no small one, in the real misfortunes and pains of others," revealed in the unnerving fact that typically we are not repulsed by such subjects, but "approach" and "dwell upon" them (I.xiv.45): consider the greater pleasure we take in the fall of kings, the ruin of great cities, or demise of heroes than we do in hearing of the success, continuation, and prosperity of the same. The reason for this, Burke maintains, lies in the passions that underlie sublimity and beauty: the delightful terror excited by the idea of distress and death (at the appropriate distance) is always pleasurable, as is the pity aroused by love and the social affections.

The same principle is at work in tragedy, Burke proposes, and explains why it is the source of such "high pleasure." The failure of philosophers who have addressed the issue, he argues, lies in their refusal to acknowledge real distress as a source of pleasure, which leads them to assign delight to literary representation alone. This mistake arises from confusing what we would not choose to do with what we would be eager to see had it already happened: nobody would wish the destruction of London, but were it to take place many would flock to the scene. Avoiding the sophism, Burke insists, shows that the only difference between the presentation of an original scene and a representation in the form of literary fiction is that the wretchedness, misery, and distress conveyed by the former are felt more keenly and with greater intensity than when depicted in the theater. The pleasure felt by the audience does not arise from comparing original to copy (as in Hutcheson's relative beauty), from relief of not being there oneself (as Addison suggests), or from aesthetic representation (as in Hume), but from the degree of similitude between real and "imitated distress," and the actual pain raised in the audience by the events (though fictional) unfolding on stage.

It follows, Burke reasons, that delight in the fictional events depicted in the theatrical depiction is proportional to the extent that fictional events excite similar terror and pity that arises from real events. This depends in turn on the extent to which the tragedy approximates real suffering, and that it does so "perfectly" is a mark of its success. The "nearer it approaches the reality," Burke writes, "and the further it removes us from all idea of fiction, the more perfect is its power" (I.xv.47). The fiction will always fall short of reality, however, and for this reason Burke thinks that an audience assembled in the theater to watch a feigned execution would leave the instance they heard of a real one taking place in the adjoining square. Whether or not this prediction is correct, the example does not, as Knight was to emphasize, prove Burke's point: the appearance of some foreign chief or dignitary in the same square would have like effect, as would the announcement of a "bottle conjuror, a flying witch, or any other miraculous phenomenon of the kind" (AI 3.1.4.322). Knight, one might note, takes Burke erroneously to be explaining the emptied theater as the effect of curiosity when his point is that the audience is driven by the prospect of circumstances in which terror and pity might be experienced with greater intensity and, correspondingly, increased pleasure.

Poetic Representation

In Part I of the *Enquiry*, while discussing the social passions and tragedy, Burke mentions *en passant* the connection between imitation and the arts of poetry and painting. When the object of these arts is such that we would never wish to see it in reality – a lowly cottage, for instance, a dunghill, or the "meanest and most ordinary utensils of the kitchen" (I.xvi.49) – then the pleasure arises not from the object, but from imitation or correspondence between the original and copy; the closer the resemblance, the greater the pleasure. By contrast, when the object is something from which we would derive pleasure in reality, then the "power of the poem or picture is more owing to the nature of the thing itself than to mere effect of imitation, or to a consideration of the skill of the imitator however excellent" (I.xvi.50). When Burke turns to discussing language and poetry in Part V, however, he seems to have forgotten these remarks – or at least thinks himself considering the issue from a different point of view – as he there argues unambiguously that the power of poetry to affect the passions and raise the ideas of sublimity and beauty lies not in imitation but in the representational power of its language.

Burke's emphasis on representation clearly brings to mind Hume's view of poetry, itself an extension and clarification of Hutcheson's principle of relative beauty in which the aesthetic value of art depends on the degree of resemblance between original and copy even if the former lacks beauty. Burke draws out the implication of this idea further by employing "representation" in two distinct senses. The first sense refers to picturing, of some original the poet copies in a description or, if there is no original, in the form of an image raised in the mind of the reader. Burke denies that poetry involves picturing in either sense. Many ideas conveyed by poetry do not fall within the experience of readers (e.g., war, death, and famine), if they exist at all are beyond possible experience (e.g., God, devils, angels, heaven and hell), or are simply fictions and known to be such. All can make a deep impression on readers, however. Poetic fictions should not picture reality, Burke insists, for that would undermine the "union of affecting words," which is the "most powerful of poetical instruments" at the writer's disposal (V.v.170). Poetry, then, is not, properly speaking, descriptive at all, and cannot be classed as an "art of imitation," because poets do not even intend their words to resemble anything (V.vi.172–3). Concomitantly, Burke emphasizes, the language of poetry does not achieve its effects by exciting images in the mind of the reader (a feature he finds in language more generally), and it is often impossible to find any specific idea involved in the poet language of which one could have an image: such is the case with Virgil's description of Vulcan's cavern in Etna, or Priam's words in the *Iliad* to convey the beauty of Helen (V.v.171–2).

Although poetry does not achieve its effects by picturing (through imitation or by raising ideas in the mind of the reader), it does so in a second sense of "representation," namely, by standing in for other things, although without referring outside (to recall Hume's phrase) the poetic reality in which fictional objects are contained. Words can give a "strong expression" insofar as objects depicted are "felt" by an audience, even if they do not give a "clear expression" of what that same object "is." In a striking observation that anticipates a distinction central to Romanticism, Burke points out that grasping the being of an object is a function of understanding and irrelevant to poetry, an art concerned wholly with the effect of words on the imagination. Poetic language strikes this faculty and moves the passions, and the "business" of the poet "is to affect rather by sympathy than imitation; to display rather the effect of things on the mind of the speaker, or of others, than to present a clear idea of the things themselves" (V.v.172). Burke discovers the causes of this phenomenon in the same principle of sympathy that underlies the paradox of tragedy: people have a natural proclivity to share and participate in the passions of others and the words of poetry are so many "tokens" that convey the subject and manner of the passions of others. The influence of things on our passions depends not on the nature of those things but on opinions that are often derived from the opinions of others that are conveyed through words.

Perhaps the most significant part of Burke's view of poetry, however, is the unique status he grants it in comparison to the plastic arts, which are confined to pictorial images and external sense. Poets are at liberty to combine words and, by adding "well-chosen circumstances," give "new life and force" to any simple object and create a fiction independent of reality. They do so, moreover, free of constraints imposed on the painter who must manipulate extant visual representations: on a physical canvas an angel is but a boy with wings or God an old man with a beard, but on the canvas of the mind the poet is liberated from the grossness of sense or clarity demanded by reason, and can rouse the passions of the reader with a single word or phrase: Milton's dark image of

"*Rocks, caves, lakes, dens, bogs, fens and shades*" is rendered sublime by adding
"*of Death*," a feeling intensified even further by the later "*universe of death*"
the author adds (V.vii.175).

SIR JOSHUA REYNOLDS

At first sight, it might seem an oddity to include Sir Joshua Reynolds (1723–
92) in a history of aesthetics. He is remembered not as a philosopher or Man
of Letters, although he did move in the highest literary circles and founded
the literary supper society, "The Club," which met at the Turk's Head Tavern
for some twenty years (active 1764–84) and counted Burke and Johnson (in
whose honor it was partly founded) among its small and highly select membership. Such activities notwithstanding, Reynolds is famous instead as the one
of the two great portrait painters of the eighteenth century, the other being
Gainsborough with whom he founded the Royal Academy of Arts (1768).
(Reynolds was knighted the following year and became official painter to
George III in 1784, but was forced to retire from painting five years later due
to failing eyesight.) At the academy's inception, Reynolds was appointed pres-
ident, a position he held until his death and under the auspices of which he
delivered the series of fifteen lectures (1769–90) later collected and published
together as *Discourses on Art* (1797), although the central philosophical ideas
it develops were essentially unchanged from views Reynolds had expressed in
three letters written for Johnson's "Idler" in 1759.[43]

The *Discourses* has long been criticized (prominently and vehemently by
William Blake, and less famously but more respectfully by Fry) both for the
content of the views it expresses and the apparent carelessness of their presentation: Reynolds has been cited routinely for his inconsistent terminology, unexplained paradox, and outright contradiction, although he might be
forgiven some of this considering the work was composed over the course of
two decades and was never intended as a complete theory or philosophical
system.[44] Fry considered the *Discourses* important enough to produce a new
edition of the work in 1905 complete with a general introduction and lengthy
comments preceding each discourse.[45] Reynolds's lectures are unabashedly

---

[43] Sir Joshua Reynolds, *Discourses on Art*, ed. Robert R. Wark (New Haven, CT: Yale University
Press, 1997 [1797]). All references are to *Discourse* followed by line and page numbers of
this edition. Reynolds's letters were first published in the *Universal Chronicle* on September
29, October 20, and November 10, 1759. All references are to the letters as they appear in
Samuel Johnson, *The Yale Edition of the Works of Samuel Johnson*, 18 vols. (New Haven, CT:
Yale University Press, 1958–2004), vol. 2, *The Idler and The Adventurer* (1963), ed. W. J. Bate,
John M. Bullitt, and L. F. Powell, nos. 76, 79, and 82, pp. 235–9, 246–9, and 254–8, respectively
(*Idler* followed by letter and page number).
[44] For a review of some of these problems, see Hipple, *The Beautiful, the Sublime, & the
Picturesque*, 134–6. Hipple is inclined to fault Reynolds for similar reasons.
[45] *Discourses Delivered to the Students of the Royal Academy by Sir Joshua Reynolds, with
Introduction and Notes by Roger Fry* (London: Seely, 1905).

didactic, written expressly for and directed explicitly to an audience of art students, but are at once informed by and articulate a particular approach to aesthetics. Weaknesses notwithstanding, the *Discourses* should be considered with Hogarth's *Analysis* as the fruits of a great artist's prolonged reflection on his own creative activity to yield a guide for the fledgling artist painting in the "great" or "Grand Style."

Not only does including Reynolds in a history of aesthetics require a word of explanation, so does considering him under the rubric of an imagination theorist. Reynolds has nothing to say about internal sense and appeals to association only briefly (in the course of discussing artistic education), and the theoretical thrust of his approach owes a great deal to the empiricist tradition we have been considering: this is evident both in the ubiquity of Lockean language that appears throughout – of memory "stored" and "stocked" with ideas to be "combined and varied," for example (II 32 and 66, 26–7 passim) – and in its focus on imagination. Like others before him, Reynolds identifies this faculty as the source of creativity on the side of the artist and the seat of aesthetic affect on the part of the audience, although with two notable additions. First, he effectively amends Hume's true judge to make imagination the *sine qua non* of good criticism – he quickly dismisses the "frigid mind" of those who judge pedantically according to rules of art "instead of giving up the reigns of their imagination into their author's hands" (*Idler* 76, 236) – and, second, in an image reminiscent of Hogarth's method of the scooped out shell, recommends that art students enter a "kind of competition" with great painters, by comparing them with their own efforts (II 96–8, 31). Reynolds insists that the artist aims at "captivating the imagination" of the spectator (III 27, 42), and says that the "great end of art is to strike the imagination" (IV 82, 59), "make an impression on the imagination," and produce a "pleasing effect on the mind" (XIII 384–9, 241); the "spectator is only to feel the result in his bosom" (IV 82–3, 59), as he points out elsewhere. At one point, Reynolds calls the imagination the "residence of truth" (XIII 36–45, 230), a notable turn of phrase that anticipates the later "truth of the imagination" so central to Romanticism.

What is most striking about Reynolds's conception of imagination, however, is the way it recalls Addison, not only his general emphasis on pleasure (also found throughout the *Discourses* [see, e.g., VII 324–32, 127 passim]), but also, more specifically, the feeling caused by "great" objects as the mind (to recall Addison's words) "naturally hates every thing that looks like a Restraint upon it" but loves to be "filled" by or "grasp" at objects "too big for its Capacity." The *Discourses* does contain a few references to Burke's *Enquiry* – Reynolds knew the work and admired it as he did its author (see VIII 561n, 162) – but with the exception of acknowledging a "certain degree of obscurity" as "one source of the sublime" (VII 70–71, 119), its influence on him appears minimal and he clearly rejects Burke's concept of astonishment born of pain, danger, and terror in favor of Addison's "Stillness and Amazement in the Soul" – "*repose*," as Reynolds characterizes it at one point – that comes when the imagination is expanded, uplifted, and free from "hurry and anxiety" (VIII 73–6, 147).

Reynolds often speaks of "beauty" it is true, but he effectively collapses this category into *great* and *sublime*, terms he uses synonymously (and no longer with any hint of the Longinian tradition) to refer to a style of painting and the effect it has on an audience.

Recognizing that Reynolds holds this view of the imagination is crucial because it leads directly to the central doctrines of his thought, expressed in both the *Discourses* and the letters to the *Idler*: that the mind feels pleasure when filled by "great and noble ideas" (*Idler* 79, 247) raised by the artist who employs techniques to draw the viewer's attention to the whole; the artist achieves this, in turn, through "imitations" that capture general features of the subject over and above extraneous details, which would not expand the imagination but result in "retarding" its "progress" (*Idler* 79, 247). The philosophical trope Reynolds employs to express and develop this doctrine is that of universal and particular, obviously of ancient pedigree, but likely inspired more immediately by the work of his close friend Johnson, especially his *Preface to Shakespeare* (1765) in which he juxtaposes "just representations of general nature" to the "accidents of transient fashions or temporary opinions."[46] Reynolds takes over Johnson's language verbatim, but fortifies it with a good dose of Platonic rationalism that recalls at moments Shaftesbury's disinterestedness and the enthusiastic rhapsodies of Theocles. Coupled with the language of Locke, the result is a strange and paradoxical affair with Reynolds deriving rules for artistic practice from experience that articulates a timeless pattern never manifest fully in the real world in which they originate. Reynolds finds this pattern in "Nature" – shorn, however, of the neo-Platonist metaphysics embraced by Shaftesbury – to which the enduring principles of art stand in the same relation as Ideas to their instantiations, reality to its apparent manifestations: they transcend and explain it even if the "great ideal perfection and beauty are not to be sought in the heavens, but upon the earth" (III 99–100, 44), discovered, that is, in and through experience of its worldly expression and subsequently reduced to "precept."

The force of the argumentative strategy underlying the *Discourses* derives from the strength of the analogy between beauty in nature and beauty in art. Reynolds effectively naturalizes Plato's metaphysics to suggest that as the philosophical mind moves from contemplating beautiful objects to beauty itself, so the empirical eye with the help of "observation" moves from sensing beautiful natural things to grasping the "general and invariable ideas of nature" (I 66–7, 16). Analogously, then, works of art can be studied to reach the

---

[46] See Samuel Johnson, *Preface to Shakespeare, 1756*, in *Works*, vol. 8 (1968), *Johnson on Shakespeare*, ed. Arthur Sherbo, 59–113, esp. 59–65 (the quotes are taken from 61 and 62). For the theme of universal and particular in the *Discourses*, see Hipple, *The Beautiful, the Sublime, & the Picturesque*, 136–7, and for a more recent discussion of some of the connections between Reynolds and Johnson, see Sarah Howe, "General and Invariable Ideas of Nature: Joshua Reynolds and His Critical Descendants," *English* 54 (2005): 1–13.

general and invariable ideas of artistic composition and as the former might be framed as principles that explain and constitute natural beauty, so the latter can be expressed as rules of art that explain and constitute artistic beauty. In a move familiar from Addison and Hume (although inspired by Johnson's Platonist language rather than the demands of literary style), Reynolds also insists that nature herself is "imperfect" and "deformed," so that the general and invariable ideas are really an ideal re-presentation of her in garments she would display were her timeless "central form" or "Ideal Beauty" made manifest. Given the argument by analogy that motivates his thinking, one would then expect Reynolds to make the same point about art, namely, that the central form of composition is an ideal re-presentation of artistic practice that overcomes imperfections and deformities of extant works of art. Reynolds, however, skips a number of steps and substitutes principles of natural beauty for rules of composition so that what artists come to enshrine in their work, he argues, are not the general and invariable ideas of composition but the general and invariable ideas of nature.

The artist, then, looks to nature as the "model" and final arbiter of taste; nature is a book open to all – she "denies her instructions to none, who desire to become her pupils" (III.145–6.45) – but the lesson (to extend the metaphor) must be inferred from her works and, to invoke the image from Locke, the empty cabinet of the artistic mind furnished with her general ideas through the activity of abstraction and recombination. The pupil can take instruction directly, by immediate contemplation of natural phenomena, or indirectly through studying the great Masters who have done so already; their best efforts are "faint and feeble" in comparison to the "splendour" of the original, Reynolds observes, but they have come close to realizing ideal beauty in their work (II 175–7, 30). In this regard, Reynolds recommends works of "established reputation" (II 232–3, 32), Claude Lorrain, Nicolas Poussin, Eustache Le Sueur, and Charles LeBrun from among the French, and from the Schools of Italy, Raphael, Titian, and especially the "divine" Michelangelo – the "Homer of Painting" (*Idler* 79, 248) – whose work speaks the "language of the Gods" (XV 431–2, 278) and in whose wake art has been in gradual decline (XV 495–6, 280). Reynolds is keen to emphasize that artists should not simply "copy" these masters, however, which generates but a "servile kind of imitators" who, as the history of art shows, are largely forgotten (see VI 381ff., 104–5).

Whether artists look to nature directly or indirectly, Reynolds urges that they "imitate" (rather than copy) her in order to capture general features and, in so doing, to perfect and correct what is deformed and defective. Reynolds evokes language by this time long familiar: artists "conceive and represent their subjects in a *poetical manner*" (IV 95–5, 59, emphasis added), a mode that renders the "grand style of Painting" as distinct from other styles as poetry is from history; where "Poetical ornaments destroy the air of truth and plainness which ought to characterize History," Reynolds intones, "... the very being of poetry consists in *departing from this plain narration*, and adopting every ornament that will warm the imagination" (*Idler* 79, 247, emphasis added). Imitating poetically, the artist "corrects nature by herself, her imperfect state by her more perfect" (III 116, 44), a process Reynolds compares to the method of the naturalist who extracts the "invariable" and "general form" of a species from a sample of particular specimens, the element in particular, one might note *en passant*, that drove Blake to cover his copy of the *Discourses* with words such as "fool," "knave," and "folly."[47] "Thus among the blades of grass or leaves of the same tree," Reynolds writes:

> though no two can be found exactly alike, yet the general form is invariable: a natural-ist, before he choose one as a sample, would examine many, since he took the first that occurred it might have, by accident or otherwise, such a form as that it would scarce be known to belong to that species; he selects as the painter does, the most beautiful, that is, the most general form of nature. (*Idler* 82, 255)

In the same way, although the perfect form of the human body is never exem-plified in any actual human being, it is possible to extract "all the characters which are beautiful in that species" and by combining them depict its "perfect beauty" (III 194–5, 47).[48]

In the realm of aesthetic practice this reconstruction of nature is translated into artistic representations that capture the central form and excite the imag-ination to the feeling of sublimity. The "whole beauty and grandeur of art," as Reynolds writes, "consists … in being able to get above all singular forms, local customs, particularities, and details of every kind" (III 102–5, 44); great art does not so much pass the test of time as it depicts what is changeless and ignores the transient altogether. For "works, whether of poets, painters, moral-ists, or historians, which are built upon general nature live for ever," Reynolds writes, "while those which depend for their existence on particular customs and habits, a partial view of nature, or the fluctuation of fashion, can only be coeval with that which first raised them from obscurity" (IV 506–11, 73). This is precisely what Fry later saw in Reynolds's work, namely, the transformation of individuals into actors playing roles on the stage of life, whose grand gestures and theatrical poses capture and reflect the timeless virtues of English society

---

[47] See William Blake, "Annotations to the Works of Sir Joshua Reynolds," in *The Complete Poetry and Prose of William Blake*, Newly Revised Edition, ed. David V. Erdman (Garden City, NY: Anchor/Doubleday, 1982), 635–62. Blake writes memorably by Discourse III: "Generalizing in Every thing the Man would soon be a Fool but a Cunning Fool" and that "Distinct General Form Cannot Exist Distinctness is Particular Not General" (649).

[48] Cf. Collingwood, *The Principles of Art*, 114, who rather spoils Reynolds's expansive descrip-tions by reducing it to its prosaic essence: "He [Reynolds] is quite right; if you want to pro-duce a typical case of a certain emotion, the way to do it is to put before your audience a representation of the typical features belonging to the kind of thing that produces it: make your kings very royal, your soldiers very soldierly, your women very feminine, your cottages very cottagesque, your oak-trees very oakish, and so on."

in the eighteenth century: "its special note of easy simplicity of manner, its unaffected and unconscious dignity, its discretion."[49]

Although, in Fry's assessment, he practiced what he preached, Reynolds is the first to acknowledge how difficult it is to specify exactly the "precise invariable rules" (III 89–90, 44) that encapsulate the changeless. His use of "precise" clearly registers a hostility to Hogarth (recall his "precise serpentine line of grace") and the proposition that one can reduce great art to simple formulae: in one of the *Idler* letters, Reynolds depicts a "gentleman connoisseur" (obviously Hogarth) recently returned from Italy who, armed only with the "remembrance of a few names" and a "few rules of the academy," has the audacity to criticize the great Masters hung in Hampton Court for lacking the "flowing line, which constitutes the line of grace and beauty" and ignoring the requisite "pyramidal principle" (*Idler* 76, 237–8) "To conclude," Reynolds writes after having his fun, "I would not be thought to infer from any thing that has been said, that Rules are absolutely unnecessary, but to censure scrupulosity, a servile attention to minute exactness, which is sometimes inconsistent with higher excellency, and is lost in the blaze of expanded genius" (*Idler* 76, 238).

Reynolds might scoff at him, but in the final analysis it is really only the content of Hogarth's principle and the kind of art it sanctions with which he disagrees; in the *Discourses* he discovers and presents quite literally a veritable book of rules that direct almost every aspect of artistic education and practice, and recommends that the "grand style of history painting" be placed at the highest pinnacle of art. First and foremost, artists should choose themes that address subjects of universal human appeal, instances of heroic action or suffering found in Greek and Roman fable, historical moments of great import, or iconic episodes from scripture. Subjects drawn from the vulgar details of ordinary life, by contrast, confine the artist and audience to a time and place, and although the works of David Teniers, the Younger, Adriaen Brouwer, Watteau, and even Hogarth are excellent "in their kind," Reynolds admits, "as their genius has been employed on low and confined subjects, the praise which we give must be as limited as its object" (III 320–1, 51). The same restriction applies to Reynolds's own *oeuvre*, portrait painting, inherently more humble because it focuses by necessity on a single individual. "An History-painter paints man in general," Reynolds remarks, "a Portrait-Painter, a particular man, and consequently a defective model" (IV 414–16, 70). The best portraits, however, are infused with elements of the grand style – iconically Reynolds's own *Mrs. Siddons as the Tragic Muse* (Fig. 3) – which the painter effects by "taking the general air, [rather] than in observing the exact similitude of every feature" (IV 68–70, 59), and giving the sitter bodily

---

[49] See Fry, *Reflections on British Paintings*, 54–5. Fry, it might be noted, faults Reynolds for his lack of technical skill: he manages to achieve but a charming flat pattern while "at every point Rembrandt is creating form in all its plenitude and relief" (56).

FIGURE 3. Sir Joshua Reynolds, *Sarah Siddons as the Tragic Muse*, 1783–4, oil on canvas, 94¼ × 58⅛ in. San Marino, CA: Henry E. Huntington Art Gallery. © Courtesy of the Huntington Art Collections.

posture and facial expressions that would suit anyone and in which the viewer instantly recognizes universal sentiments and passions (IV 126ff, 60–1).

Second, and in accord with the idea of perfecting nature, the artist should depart from "matter of fact" when required to impart the requisite dignity and nobility to their subjects. St. Paul, Reynolds reports, was as *"mean"* in *"bodily presence"* as Alexander the Great was of "low stature"; those are clearly deformities that should not be copied, but corrected in the process of artistic representation to depict the virtue and heroism that is the essence of each, respectively. The artist "cannot make his hero talk like a great man," Reynolds remarks, but "he must make him look like one" (IV 123–4, 60). There is no question here of "falsifying any fact," but simply a matter of "taking an allowed poetical license" (IV 108–9, 60), "improving" nature through paint on canvas as – in an idea that plays out in the aesthetics of the picturesque – the gardener "improves" a view by rearranging features of the landscape: in both cases the aim is to make nature look more like a reconstructed version of herself.

Third, even with the appropriate subject matter firmly impressed on the mind, artists should aim at "absolute unity" of composition (VIII 84, 147) – Rubens is Reynolds's model in this regard – and take care not to burden picture and viewer alike with unnecessary details that distract from the central image. The "sublime impresses the mind at once with *one great idea*; it is a single blow," and in their compositions artists should raise "that effect so indispensably necessary to grandeur, that of one complete whole" (IV 274–80, 65, emphasis added) in order to guarantee that the viewer's attention is "entirely occupied by the subject itself" (IV 383–4, 69). "The sublime in Painting, as in Poetry," as Reynolds expresses the same requirement later, "so overpowers, and takes such a possession of the whole mind, that no room is left for attention to minute criticism" (XV 362–4, 276).

As Fry was to point out later in the introduction to his edition of the *Discourses*, the clear weakness in Reynolds's conception of unity here lies in its narrowness, or more precisely, in the fact that it obscures other ways of achieving the same effect. For there are actually *"two* contending principles in art – one of which makes for richness of content, the other for unity of expression," and it might even be the case that "some kind of balance" between them is required for truly great works of art (xiv). Rubens's *Altarpiece of St. Augustine* (now in the National Gallery, Prague) (Fig. 4), as Fry goes on to show, conforms to Reynolds's principles and the "parts cohere like the atoms in a molecule, so that we feel that the detachment of one part would break up the whole conformation" (xv). In the *Adoration of the Mystical Lamb* by Jan Van Eycks (c. 1390–1441), the lower center panel of the Ghent Alter originally painted for St. Bavo Cathedral (Fig. 5), by contrast, one confronts a mass of detail, crowds of people, distractions for the eye that fragment the whole and, as Reynolds teaches, undoes or lessens its effect. There is no unity in Reynolds's sense, Fry observes, yet "if we examine the picture in detail we shall find the most marvelous sense of relationship in the parts" (xvi), albeit given in quite a different

FIGURE 4. Peter Paul Rubens, *Altarpiece of St. Augustine*, 1636–9, oil on canvas, 103⁹/₁₆ × 68⁷/₈ in. Prague: National Gallery. © National Gallery, Prague.

FIGURE 5. Jan van Eyck, *The Ghent Altar. Polyptych with the Adoration of the Mystical Lamb*. 1432, tempura and oil on panel, 11 × 15 feet (open). Detail lower half, center: the adoration of the mystic lamb by angels. Cathedral of St. Bavo, Ghent, Belgium. Image: Erich Lessing Art Resource, New York.

way: "as we in imagination walk over the enameled meadows, and address in turn each of these profound and stately, but intensely human, spirits, we experience an intense imaginative satisfaction at finding them thus brought together, and at finding in so delectable place such fit inhabitants" (xviii). The "hold upon the mind," as Fry puts in aptly, is simply different in the two cases.

Reynolds's narrow or partial conception of unity notwithstanding, from it a variety of rules follow, all intended to avoid anything that threatens to break the unity or fragment the whole. The artist should guard against placing too many figures in the painting and avoid excessive ornamentation (VIII 107–8, 148), curtail variety (VIII 73–6, 147), and resist resorting to "tricks," "trifles," and "petty effects" like the Dutch who represent candlelight as it appears during the day (red) rather than it does at night (white) (IV 378–81, 69). The same principle directs the artist's choice and use of color, which must reflect a proper grandeur by being uniform and simple, and applied with appropriate breadth, as in the chiaroscuro of the Bolognese School (Carevaggio), or the distinct and forcible use of blue, red, and yellow by the schools of Rome (Michelangelo) and Florence (Raphael). An excessive blending and softening of colors of the sort found in Hendrik Jansen and Anthony Van Dyck undoes the sublime by undermining the definite outlines of objects, as does the use of color in Venetian painting, for instance, that aims to "dazzle" rather than "affect" the viewer (IV 205–6, 63).

It is worth noting that Reynolds's remarks on color echo Shaftesbury's diminution of the senses, which he associates with interest, and anticipate

Kant's later claim that colors merely "charm" and "gratify" the senses, while only form is appropriately called beautiful. Reynolds recognizes the tension between two competing elements in aesthetic taste, that it claims a "kind of sensuality" but also a "love of sublime" (VIII 284–8, 153), the former being in the "external form of things" and the latter being "addressed to the mind," that is, the "imagination and the passions" and the invariable principles that govern it (VII, 458–62, 131). The two must be kept apart, Reynolds warns, for ultimately painting is not "merely a gratification of the sight" (IV 349–50, 68), but a contemplation of those general ideas of nature that constitute its eternal form and explain its beauty.

The Standard of Taste and Genius

As this last observation suggests, it is a few short steps from ideal beauty and rules of art to nominating a candidate for a standard of taste, and answering the question "whether," as Reynolds characterizes the issue, "taste be so far beyond our reach, as to be unattainable by care; or be so very vague and capricious, that no care ought to be employed about it" (VII 50–3, 118). For if "we can shew that there are rules for the conduct of the artist which are fixed and invariable, it follows of course, that the art of the connoisseur, or in other words, taste, has likewise invariable principles" (VII 210–12, 123). Reynolds understands "taste" conventionally as the capacity or power for "distinguishing right from wrong" when applied to works of art (VII 48–9, 118) or, more broadly, the "act of mind by which we like or dislike, whatever be the subject" (VII 151–2, 121). Reynolds insists that taste has been misunderstood by "general opinion" and treated erroneously as a "mere phantom of the imagination," because people have assumed it to be so mysterious "as to elude all criticism," a view expressed in the "common saying, *that tastes are not to be disputed*" (VII 38–43, 121).

Reacting against such obfuscation, Reynolds insists that taste, like the imagination on which it depends, should be recognized as involving a species of truth that the mind seeks no less in the realm of aesthetic experience than it does in science and mathematics. It is "the very same taste which relishes a demonstration in geometry," he remarks, "that is pleased with the resemblance of a picture to an original, and touched with the harmony of music" (VII 167–9, 122). In all these cases we find "unalterable and fixed foundations in nature" that stand in contrast to "*apparent* truth, or opinion, or prejudice" – "truth upon sufferance, or truth by courtesy" (VII 181–5, 122) – which yields a taste that is "secondary" (VII 197, 122). Reynolds's view tends more toward the conclusions of Hutcheson and Hume than it does to Shaftesbury and Reid; he is willing to admit that there is a standard of taste or beauty given in the invariable ideas or form of nature, but also acknowledges the diversity of taste or liking explicable by peculiarities of time and place. Thus "habit and custom cannot be said to be the cause of beauty, it is certainly the cause of liking it"

(*Idler* 82, 256), and it is only to be expected that different cultures attach differ-ent meanings to "beauty." We might speak of variations in beauty, but in such cases we "apply the word" not to mean a "more beautiful form, but something on account of its rarity, usefulness, colour, or any other property," that is, what we "like" (*Idler* 83, 258). Thus, temporary prejudices, fancies, fashions, familiar-ity, and accidental associations all give rise to different *opinions* (what we like), but that does not change the standard of taste, which is given in the beauty of nature.

The other issue on which Reynolds makes a contribution is that of genius, and his view is closely connected with his conclusions regarding a standard, the nature of taste, and the role of imitation and rules in artistic practice. The difference between genius and taste, he holds, "lies only in this, that genius has superadded to it a habit or power of execution: or we may say, that taste, when this power is added, changes its name, and is called genius" (VII 120–3, 120). Reynolds characterizes his position as "contrary to the general opinion" (VI 102, 96) that genius is a matter of enthusiasm or divine inspiration, a con-ception he attributes to ignorance and being easily dazzled by an effect that does little more than obscure its cause. "The untaught mind finds a vast gulph between its own powers and those works of complicated art," Reynolds writes, "which it is utterly unable to fathom; and it supposes that such a void can be passed only by supernatural powers" (VI 47–50, 94). Any artist looking to this "phantom" genius and finding himself "waiting on its inspiration" is "in reality at a loss how to begin" (II 378–9, 37). This is not to say that genius is transpar-ent or that it can be exhausted or captured by rules, and, in fact, "whatever part of an art can be explained or criticized by rules," he remarks, " ... is no longer the work of Genius, which implies excellence out of the reach of rules" (*Idler* 76, 236). Genius is properly understood as the "child of imitation" (VI 101, 96), a function of reason and the hard work involved in becoming an accom-plished artist, which for Reynolds means looking to the rule of nature and representing her Ideal Beauty. The erroneous conception of genius is thus dis-pelled by "invention" – the representation of an ideal mental picture aroused by the depiction of certain subject matter – and "mechanical performance," the "language of Painters" (IV 233–4, 64), which comes from habituation to the contemplation of excellence, transcending particulars that scatter the viewer's attention and draw the mind away from Ideal Beauty (IX, 30ff., 192).

3

Association Theorists

In this final chapter of Part I, we consider the third eighteenth-century school of aesthetics in the shape of "associationism," identified primarily with Henry Home (Lord Kames), Alexander Gerard, Archibald Alison, and Dugald Stewart. Like internal sense and imagination theorists, they too owe much to the empiricism of Locke, and to Hume of the *Treatise*, although they generally balk at the skeptical conclusions he drew there. These writers were all active in the second half of the century and therefore reap the benefits of being able to draw on the extensive body of work already completed; even Kames, who often writes as if in an intellectual vacuum, cannot help but, inadvertently or otherwise, draw on what his contemporaries and predecessors had achieved. More than the other contributors discussed so far, then, associationists knit together an eclectic array of elements to fabricate the most complex and systematic theories the tradition has produced, certainly in the eighteenth century and possibly in its long three-hundred-year history as well.

One element looming especially large for these thinkers is the imagination, which figures in their views as a compound and derivative faculty, and the seat of various principles that underlie association, the main explanans upon which Kames and others hit to account for the by-now-familiar desiderata of eighteenth-century aesthetics. There is also a notable emphasis on the same observation made by Reid (*Essays* I.575.5–8) that "beauty" and "sublimity" are predicated of objects with little or nothing in common, a feature of language that has sent many an unsuspecting philosopher scurrying into the alleys and byways of human nature or objective reality in search of some property or feature common to all phenomena of which the terms are predicated. Writing at century's end, Stewart, in particular, develops this point, finding in it a lens through which to cast a critical glance back to the likes of Hogarth and Burke with their "line of beauty" and "smooth and soft." The same insight also allows an entrée to contemporary debates over the picturesque, and opens the long tunnel of the nineteenth century, however vague still its distant shapes, toward the light (or darkness, depending on one's predilection) of post-Wittgensteinian analysis that would make decisive inroads into the landscape of philosophical aesthetics. These issues shall be met with in due course, but for the present it is to the work of Kames that we turn.

Henry Home, Lord Kames (1696–1782) spent his professional life ascending the ranks of the Scottish legal system becoming, by turn, solicitor, advocate, and Lawlord in the Court of Session (whence his title) culminating in his appointment (in 1763) to the High Court of Justice, the highest criminal court in Scotland. Much of Kames's writing, not surprisingly, is devoted to law and jurisprudence, and reflections in this and related areas led to what is generally considered his major work, *Sketches of the History of Man* (1774) organized around the theme of improvement. Kames was also engaged in other matters, including agricultural policy (his wife inherited a considerable estate), and, more to the point in the present context, nurtured throughout an interest in philosophy and the arts. His thoughts on these matters, and his main contribution to aesthetics, is contained in his *Elements of Criticism*, published in 1763.[1] Even among dedicated students of the canon, the *Elements* remains a lesser-known work, a marked contrast to its fame in the eighteenth century where it was both influential and widely read: the work was in a sixth edition by 1785 – the last authorized by Kames – and appeared subsequently in more than thirty others in Britain and the United States. The *Elements*'s fall into relative obscurity belies much in the work of potential interest to contemporary readers; Hipple describes it as "one of the most elaborate and systematic treatises on aesthetics of any age or nation," and ranks it with Alison's later *Essays on the Nature and Principles of Taste* (1790) as "the major effort of philosophical criticism in eighteenth-century Britain."[2]

As a work of criticism, the *Elements* is impressive, for the efficient and methodological way it proceeds from "facts and experiments" through general "principles" of human nature to eventuate in "rules" indispensable for artist, audience, and specialized critic alike; the *Elements* does for literature what Reynolds's *Discourses* did for painting. Philosophically, by contrast, the work is less striking, constructed as it is from materials purloined almost entirely and without acknowledgment from predecessors and contemporaries; even Hipple pauses in his narrative to note how Kames "writes as if he owed no debts and anticipated no objections." Even though he "must have been familiar with the books of Addison, Hutcheson, Hume, Hogarth, Burke, and Gerard," Hipple

---

[1] Henry Home, Lord Kames, *Elements of Criticism. The Sixth Edition. With the Author's Last Corrections and Additions*, 2 vols. (Indianapolis, IN: Liberty Fund, 2005 [1785; 1st ed. 1762). Unless indicated otherwise, all references in the text are to volume and page of this edition of the *Elements*.

[2] Hipple, *The Beautiful, The Sublime, & The Picturesque*, 99.

observes, "the aesthetic doctrines of these writers are nowhere canvassed in the *Elements*."[3] Of debts there are many, including, to mention only the most obvious, a thoroughly Lockean picture of mind, an experimental method familiar from Hume, and an appeal to "sense" in the manner of Hutcheson to denote the intuitive acquisition of knowledge of external objects and inner life. At the same time, credit is surely due Kames for anticipating central concepts of Reid and the "Common Sense" school, including their obsessive harping at the skepticism of George Berkeley and Hume, whose doctrines Kames saw as a threat to morality and religion, a point he drives home in his *Essays on the Principles of Morality and Natural Religion* (1751).[4] To Kames should also go the accolade of placing the principles of association central stage in aesthetic theory and in observing the "metaphorical" use of "beauty" in what, albeit anachronistically, might be considered the first tentative stirrings of "analysis": the *Elements* was published long before Alison's *Essays*, and although it appeared some three years after Gerard's *Essay on Taste* (1759), it was the culmination of work begun at least a decade earlier; for this reason, Kames must be reckoned the founding father of associationist aesthetics.

Pleasure and Criticism

Kames begins the *Elements* by identifying aesthetic pleasure as "mixed," traceable on the one side through the senses to external objects, and close to intellect on the other side in being similarly freed from "organic impressions" that restrict sense perceptions proper to the empirical world (1:11–12). Corresponding to this "middle place" between body and mind, Kames also locates aesthetic pleasure on a moral calculus, assigning it a transitional status between mere "gratification of sensual appetite" below and the "refined and sublime" pleasures of morality and religion above. There is a tendency in human nature to seek the latter, Kames declares, to move from what is low to high, inferior to superior, and in doing so realize the potential of our created natures; to pursue and enjoy the arts of poetry, painting, sculpture, music, gardening, and architecture, then, is part and parcel of our moral life. As a result, the *Elements* can be read as a manual of sorts, describing and prescribing the path ordained by God, a preparatory and revelatory guide to an aesthetic and moral vocation, and, as a philosophical investigation of the principles governing the process, a source of intellectual satisfaction as well. The *Elements* aims to "exhibit" with respect to the fine arts "their fundamental principles, drawn from human nature, the true source of criticism" (1.18), Kames intones, but this disarmingly simple description belies a didactic subtext and a set of far-reaching intentions.

---

[3] Ibid., 113.

[4] Henry Home, Lord Kames, *Essays on the Principles of Morality and Natural Religion. Corrected and Improved, in a Third Edition. Several Essays Added Concerning the Proof of a Deity* (Indianapolis, IN: Liberty Fund, 2005 [1779; 1st ed. 1751) (EPM).

In accordance with the plan to proceed from particular to general, Kames sets off in pursuit of these principles by establishing two basic points, one concerning the nature of mind, the other its affective states. First, he observes, our "train of our thoughts" are regulated and connected by various relations, chief among them being cause and effect, contiguity of time and place, high and low, prior and posterior, resemblance and contrast (1.21–2). When the mind is left to its own devices, the "natural order" of ideas continues according to the "strictest connection," although it can be redirected by an act of will, altered by some mental state or varied according to an individual's degree of natural acuity. Yet "we cannot dissolve the train altogether," Kames insists, "by carrying on our thoughts in a loose manner without any connection" (1.22). On the contrary, strict limits are imposed by an internal "principle of order" that is "implanted in the breast of every man," and while exceptions can always be found, the general bent of mind is to follow the order of nature and descend from high to low, superior to inferior, and whole to part; to follow the movement of objects downward, and to proceed according to the temporal arrangement of events along chains of cause and effect.

Kames then applies these principles, second, to the mental state we call "emotion," that "internal motion or agitation of the mind" that constitutes the "feelings" of pleasure and pain raised when external objects, agreeable or disagreeable in themselves, are seen or heard (or recalled as such). Some emotions are effectively disinterested – we simply feel pleasure at the sight of a beautiful garden or magnificent building – while others are accompanied by desire. When this feeling arises in response to a specific object (to reward a virtuous action or possess the goods of a fortune) the emotion is "converted" into a "passion" (1:37); when the object is general (e.g., a desire for fame or honor), it undergoes the same to become an "appetite." A passion in turn is then "instinctive," Kames explains, when it impels us to act blindly, "deliberative" when it involves reason, "social" if it advances another's happiness without gratification, "selfish" when the opposite, and "dissocial" when the desire has no other aim than the destruction of its object (1:38–41).

With this terminological apparatus in place, Kames moves to consider how emotions and passions are related to a variety of phenomena (sound, joy and sorrow, perceptions, opinion, and belief) including the "narrow inspection of such of them as serve to unfold the principles of the fine arts" (1:141). Kames enumerates these aesthetic emotions (as we might call them) under nine headings; some (the risible, ridicule, and wit) pertain specifically to criticism in the restricted sense of literary appreciation, or (as in his treatment of novelty and resemblance) repeat views developed earlier in the century, and others (congruity and propriety, dignity and grace) move the discussion more squarely into the realm of morals. The significant chapters for the tradition of philosophical aesthetics, then, are those concerning "beauty" and "sublimity and grandeur," and it is Kames's treatment of these phenomena that deserve our attention.

Beauty

Kames begins by affirming the long-standing assumption that in its "proper" or "native signification" the term *beauty* refers to sight, the objects perceived by other senses being "agreeable" but not "beautiful"; when it is applied to thoughts, events, discoveries, theorems, or the fine arts, it has a "metaphorical" or "figurative" sense. This extension comes about, Kames urges, because beauty is a "complex" idea, its component elements of color, figure, length, breadth, and thickness being productive alone or combined to give all objects that possess it a "common character … of sweetness and gaiety." "Hence it is," Kames concludes, "that beauty, a quality so remarkable in visible objects, lends its name to express every thing that is eminently agreeable: thus, by a *figure of speech*, we say a beautiful sound, a beautiful thought or expression, a beautiful theorem, a beautiful event, a beautiful discovery in art of science" (1:142, emphasis added). In an obvious echo of Hutcheson, Kames also distinguishes "intrinsic" from "relative" beauty, the former arising in response "to a single object of sense viewed independently," and the latter "founded on the relation of objects" and accompanied by an act of "understanding and reflection" of their purpose or utility (1:142–3). The two species are thus different, although not incompatible, and Kames follows Hume (and uses the same example) in seeing them combined in the same object, in which case they elicit "delight": a horse running pleases both by its symmetry (intrinsic) and unity of parts to the end of swift motion (utility).

Both species of beauty, moreover, are susceptible to degrees, being proportional in the case of relative beauty to the end furthered – the better arranged the limbs of the horse, the more beautiful the animal – and derived in the case of intrinsic beauty from the character of the compound elements: a beautiful tree – to use Kames's example – derives its value from its color (verdant and cheerful) and figure (where regularity, simplicity, uniformity, and order all contribute). Beauty, finally, is perceived as belonging to the object. Kames takes this to be self-evident in the case of intrinsic beauty, where sweetness and gaiety are inherent, but no less true of relative beauty as well where by a "natural propensity" – and in an explanation much exploited later by Reid – the beauty of some effect is transferred to the cause – the object – and taken as one of its qualities. Thus, an irregular house or an "old Gothic tower" – neither intrinsically beautiful by Kames's lights – becomes beautiful when understood as a convenient dwelling or proper defense against an enemy, respectively (1:143).

Grandeur and Sublimity

Burke's *Enquiry* (1757) had been in circulation for five years before the first edition of the *Elements* appeared, and although it came in for a fair share of criticism, most thought its author correct in distinguishing "sublimity" from "beauty," and justified in seeking some principle to explain the difference.

Later in the century, Reid and Stewart worked to reunite the parts into a single body – an effort renewed by their analytic successors in the twentieth century – but Burke's *coup de grâce* was to prove decisive and, especially with the weighty endorsement of Kant's third *Critique*, short of rejecting the idea of "aesthetic experience" altogether, no student of aesthetics has seriously doubted that beauty and sublimity are distinct modes of experience and require different philosophical explanations. Kames, however, appears largely oblivious to Burke's achievement, and the result is a curiously confused and confusing approach to what he terms "grandeur" and its close relation to the "sublime." On the one side, he emphasizes the features these share with beauty, which leads him to subsume them both as species under the genus "agreeable" (1:152): like beauty, "grandeur" and "sublimity" are sources of pleasure, he emphasizes; they acquire their proper signification of size (grand) and elevation (sublime) from the sense of sight, and their figurative ones through extension to objects that raise the same emotion, and require, moreover, regularity, proportion, order, and color that make something beautiful: a large pile of stones or the ruins of a massive house are simply "agreeable," but St. Peter's of Rome, the pyramids of Egypt, and the towering Alps are grand due to the dominant qualities of proportion, regularity, and color, respectively.

On the other side, Kames also acknowledges the clear and more fundamental differences between beauty and grandeur/sublimity. The latter are satisfied with a "lesser degree" of the qualities they putatively share with beauty, and even come to subvert them, for the "spectator is conscious of an enthusiasm, which cannot bear confinement, nor the strictness of regularity and order: he loves to range at large; and is so enchanted with magnificent objects, as to overlook slight beauties or deformities" (1:154). This division between beauty and sublimity reflects the profound difference between the two sets of emotions involved: beauty possesses the "common character" of sweetness and gaiety, while the grand/sublime is "serious," "occupies the whole attention," and "swells the heart into a vivid emotion" (1:52). Unlike beauty, moreover, "grand" and "sublime" have a "double signification," referring both to the requisite quality in the object that produces the emotion so-called and to the emotion itself. Kames draws this conclusion from his Lockean assumption that these emotions reveal primary qualities where the effects felt resemble the objects. So grand objects possess great magnitude (the sky, the ocean, or an elephant), to which the spectator responds by endeavoring "to enlarge his bulk," marking the emotion of grandeur with the same quality as its object. Similarly, sublime objects possess great elevation (the high place for a deity, a magistrate's throne, or a tree on a precipice seen from a plain below), which make the "spectator stretch upward, and stand on tip-toe" (1:151), rendering the attendant emotion sublime as well.

That Kames follows this line of reasoning is worthy of note because it obliges him to distinguish grandeur from sublimity. In itself, this puts him in the company of very few writers (Shaftesbury dimly, Reid clearly, and Hume tangentially), but he is in veritable exile when it comes to the grounds for doing so.[5] We have had occasion to remark already that, as the century progressed, the moderns gradually shed the ancient skin of Longinus that had tied "sublime" to elevated style, leaving "grand" for the effects of size and elevation; as the Longinian tradition and its emphasis on style waned, "sublime" emerged with its now familiar sense of what had earlier fallen under "grand." Kames moves still in the shadow of Longinus and speaks easily of "sublime poetry," yet it is not style and size or elevation that distinguishes grandeur from sublimity, but the differences of "internal feeling" and "outward expressions" that each involve, namely, the "double signification" of quality and emotion. This way of marking the difference might be singular, but it is also unstable, and Kames has barely made the distinction before he draws attention to its weaknesses. He is obliged to acknowledge straightaway that some objects have both emotions "mixed" together in a "complicated impression" (1:150), although he has sufficient poise to dodge the obvious question: do the Alps, say, containing both qualities, impress due to their grandeur (magnitude) or sublimity (elevation), and what is the experience of them when "mixed"? Is it a distinguishable element of each or some new and as yet unnamed emotion distinct from both? When the division is applied to the terms as they are applied to phenomena possessing moral and intellectual value (Kames names generosity, courage, magnanimity, and genius), it breaks down entirely: one is immediately in the company of elevated qualities predicated of great men, and Kames admits that in "such figurative terms, we lose the distinction between great and elevated in their proper sense; for the resemblance is not so entire, as to preserve these terms distinct in their figurative application" (1:159). One wonders, then, whether the distinction is worth drawing in the first place, and the fact that no subsequent writer follows Kames in this direction suggests that the answer is probably in the negative.

The Standard of Taste and Paradox of Tragedy

Kames's contribution to debate over the standard of taste occupies the final chapter of the *Elements*, and in form and content deviates little from Hume's earlier essay, repeating both its formulation of and solution to the problem (Burke's response to Hume had already appeared in the second edition of the *Enquiry* [1759], but Kames makes no reference to it). Kames begins with the same proverb as Hume – "That there is no disputing about taste" – pointing out that whether one means taste of the palate ("taste in its proper meaning") or of other external senses, why somebody might prefer a rude Gothic tower

---

[5] For a recent treatment of Kames's division compared to the other Scottish associationists, see Rachel Zuckert, "The Associative Sublime: Gerard, Kames, Alison, and Stewart," in Costelloe, *The Sublime*, ch. 5.

to a fine Grecian building, or take the smell of a rotten carcass over the "most odiferous flower" requires some explanation; failing to do so has the unfortunate result of sanctioning such poor taste as well. One might extend the observation further, Kames notes, to deny a standard altogether, and conclude with the "following general proposition":

> That with respect to the perceptions of sense, by which some objects appear agreeable some disagreeable, there is not such a thing as a *good* or a *bad*, a *right* or a *wrong*; that every man's taste is to himself an ultimate standard without appeal, and consequently that there is no ground of censure against any one, if such a one there be, who prefers Blackmore before Homer, selfishness before benevolence, or cowardice before magnanimity. (2:719)

Kames acknowledges that some genuine diversity always arises from the effects of habit, custom, and peculiarities of mind, but insists that "self-partiality" is always checked by accepting the "common nature" that holds within a species and functions as a timeless "model or standard for each individual that belongs to the kind" (2:721). Deviations from it (a child born without a mouth or disliking its mother's milk) are quickly condemned as abominations of nature, Kames observes, judged as such not by divergence from me, but "from what I judge to be the common standard" (2:723).

As in Hume's antinomy of taste, then, Kames frames the issue as a confrontation between individual liking and judgments of taste. Kames's solution proceeds by an equally familiar route: the standard is not given empirically in the actual judgments people make, he urges, but in some ideal or perfect one that judgments presuppose and at which they aim. Kames's point of analogy is morality where conduct is judged not in terms of what people actually do – they often do the wrong thing – but what they ought to do as an instance of the more perfect state of which they are capable. The same is true *mutatis mutandis* of the arts, Kames then suggests, where the standard is founded not on what is taken to be beautiful (a liking for the agreeable), but in what is general and lasting (a judgment of taste proper). Progress toward perfection in aesthetic judgment is slower and less important than in the case of morals, and there are also fewer people qualified to judge, namely, those with "good natural taste" and the "delicacy" that attends it, improved by education, reflection, experience, practice, and the tempering effect of moderation. This figure is much like a critic or "true judge" of Hume, and although Kames does flirt with the idea that the standard is set by minority rule, he concludes that the failure of these or anybody else to grasp properly the standard does not impugn the conclusion that one does in fact exist.

In contrast to the rather worn lines Kames's rehearses over the standard of taste, his discussion of tragedy is of considerable interest. He raises the issue in the *Elements* under the auspices of "Narration and Description," although he had already addressed it more generally in "Our Attachment to Objects of Distress," the first of the *Essays on the Principles of Morality and Natural*

Religion (1751). Hume, to recall, published his essay on the subject in 1757, though the evidence suggests that he had certainly completed it by 1755, and possibly earlier.[6] It is quite possible, then, that Kames had neither read the essay nor knew of its contents before he published the *Essays*, but it was hardly tenable to think that he had not done so by 1762 when the first edition of the *Elements* appeared. In the final analysis, the issue of timing is of little importance philosophically, but it would explain the shift in emphasis from the earlier to the later treatment: in the *Essays* Kames proposes a final cause argument to explain why we are not averse to pain, but in the *Elements* – after the publication of Hume's essay, that is – he provides a mechanism that makes it is possible. Kames's solution is Hume's conversion thesis with the addition of "ideal presence," which, whether it was Kames's intention or not, works to deepen and enrich what Hume had already proposed.

Kames begins the earlier essay by evoking (as does Hume) Dubos's attempt to "account for the strong attachment we have to objects of distress, imaginary as well as real" (EPM 11) in terms of avoiding languor; the pleasure of tragedy would then be due, as Kames characterizes it, to the "very horror of inaction, which makes men every day precipitate themselves into play, and deliver themselves over to cards and dice" (EPM 12). Kames is critical of Dubos's solution on the grounds that he mistakenly attributes all action to self-love as the reason that we seek pleasure and avoid pain, when in fact there are many painful emotions, grief being the primary example, that we "love to dwell upon." Not only do such objects "raise no aversion in us, though they give us pain," Kames observes, but also "they draw us to them, and inspire us with a desire to afford relief" (EPM 14–15). Individuals seem, perversely, to have an "appetite after pain" and inclination to render themselves "miserable" (EPM 16). Kames explains this curious phenomenon by emphasizing that painful passions in general might be accompanied by aversion, but when suffering involves concern for others, "we are willing to submit to it on all occasions with cheerfulness and heart-liking, just as much as if it were a real pleasure" (EPM 20). Tragedy, Kames then infers, pleases by the same principle: the audience enters into the sentiments of the characters depicted – inspired by their courage and bravery or moved by their distress – and because the history is "feigned" and the depictions fictional, the impression made is all the deeper, for the author selects subject matter in such a way that keeps spectators in "continual suspense and agitation, beyond what commonly happens in real

[6] Hume reveals in a letter to Andrew Millar (Letter 110, May 1755) that the essay was one of "four short Dissertations," which he had kept by him "some Years ... in order to polish them as much as possible." See *The Letters of David Hume*, 1:223. Mossner suggests that the four dissertations "had probably been composed 1749–51, after Hume's return from Turin and before he plunged into active compositions of the *History* in the spring of 1752." See *The Life of David Hume*, 321. I am indebted to Ted Gracyk for bringing these references to my attention. Dubos, it might be noted, was widely read for which reason his appearance in both Hume and Kames is hardly noteworthy.

life" (EPM 17). It is also fortunate, Kames ventures rather hopefully, that such entertainments have a humanizing effect on the temper and teach us to feel more deeply the natural impulse to do good that is already framed, albeit delicately, in our created nature.

This solution has a somewhat hollow ring, Kames's thesis being simply that we are attached to objects of distress and take pleasure in the emotions raised by them because that is how our Creator in his wisdom made us. When Kames turns to the issue later in the *Elements*, by contrast, his focus shifts to explaining *how* this effect comes about, namely, because an "object, however ugly to the sight, is far from being so when represented by colours or by words" (2:641). Kames proposes, obscurely, that a slight agitation of the mind through terror makes the mind more susceptible to impressions of beauty (2:643), and also suggests, as did Hume commenting on Rowe's *Ambitious Stepmother*, that even the liveliest description cannot overcome certain "scenes of horror"; poets, he urges, should simply avoid them (he faults Shakespeare's Iago and Milton's description of Sin for this reason). Caveats aside, Kames argues that in painting (representation through sight and a case of relative beauty), the pleasure arises from imitation, where "overbalancing the disagreeableness of the subject, makes the picture upon the whole agreeable" (2:641). In the case of literary description (representation by words and a case of intrinsic beauty), language conveys its own beauties directly to the audience: the "pleasure of language is so great," Kames writes, "as in a lively description to overbalance the disagreeableness of the image raised by it." This truth does not give reason to seek out the ugly and horrific, however, because descriptions of inherently agreeable subject matter always elicit an "incomparably greater" pleasure (2:642).

So far, there is nothing distinguishing Kames's solution to the paradox of tragedy from the one developed already by Hume: it is resolved through the effect of a lively representation on the mind that transforms the character of the painful object and "converts" the original painful passion into a new and pleasurable one. Kames's own contribution, however, is to deepen what Hume proposed by uncovering the condition that makes conversion possible, namely, the human capacity to bring past events into present time as an "ideal presence."[7] Kames observes that certain scenes or objects make such a deep impression – he writes of having witnessed a beautiful woman in distress over the loss of her only child – that it can be recalled to mind later in its entirety and with an intensity that annihilates past and future, and "perceived in our view ... as existing at present" (1:67). The object is clearly not real but neither is it merely remembered; it its ideal, as clear and distinct as a *"waking dream"* that dissipates, along with belief in its object, as soon as the spectator reflects

---

[7] Kames introduces this concept under the title "Emotions caused by Fiction." For a recent treatment of this part of Kames's thought and its philosophical significance, see Eva Dadlez, "Ideal Presence: How Kames Solved the Problem of Fiction and Emotion," *Journal of Scottish Philosophy* 9, 1 (2011): 115–33.

on the nature of the experience (1:68). In this concept, Kames finds the reason why a fictional character might influence the mind at least as powerfully as the "truth and reality" of one with "real existence" (1:66). "Ideal presence supplies the want of real presence," Kames writes, "and in idea we perceive persons acting and suffering, precisely as in an original survey; if our sympathy be engaged by the latter, it must also in some degree be engaged by the former, especially if the distinctness of ideal presence approach to that of real presence" (1:69). When language raises images of this sort, the passions are roused and occupy the mind as completely as if the object were before one. The object might be fictional, but the passions are real and genuinely felt. There is, then, a "conversion" of the sort described by Hume where pleasure of the lively description overbalances the pain produced by the object, but Kames shows that this phenomenon is possible only because characters or events in literature are ideally present and can make an impression as deep as those made by flesh and blood.

ALEXANDER GERARD

Alexander Gerard (1728–95) was educated at Aberdeen, where he subsequently became Professor of Natural Philosophy at Marischal College in 1750 and then Professor of Divinity (1760–71) before taking up the same position at King's College. The central aesthetic categories of his major work on aesthetics, the *Essay on Taste* (1759),[8] are familiar from writers considered already, and as his explicit references show, he was well acquainted with the work of Locke, Hume, Shaftesbury, Hutcheson, and Hogarth, as well as writers in the French tradition. The importance he attached to the latter is evident in the essays by Voltaire, D'Alembert, and Montesquieu that appear as addenda to the first edition of the *Essay* and account for fully a third of the book's length; they were subsequently omitted for the later third edition (1780) to which was added a fourth part entitled "Of the Standard of Taste." Given his sources, it is no surprise that Gerard's approach hangs very much within the general framework of empiricism and its variant applications: he endorses a Lockean picture of mind in which individuals are aware of internal representations of objects and their qualities in the form of ideas; like Addison, he emphasizes the pleasures of imagination; and insists with Reid (who cites Gerard's *Essay* favorably ["Of Taste," II.580.9–11]) that aesthetic experience is the result of "real" qualities in objects that affect certain "mental principles" in uniform

---

[8] Alexander Gerard, *An Essay on Taste with Three Dissertations on the same subject by Mr. De Voltaire, Mr. D'Alembert, F.R.S. Mr. Montesquieu* (London: A. Millar; Edinburgh: A. Kincaid and J. Bell, 1759) (ET). All references are to this edition except to "Of the Standard of Taste," which are to Part IV of the third edition: *An Essay on Taste. To Which Is Now Added Part Fourth, Of the Standard of Taste; with Observations Concerning the Imitative Nature of Poetry* (Edinburgh: J. Bell and W. Creech; London: T. Cadell, 1780) (ST).

and predictable ways (ET 77). Like Kames, Gerard also adopts Hutcheson's notion of "internal" or "reflex senses," which he combines with Hume's principles of association to compose an eclectic and innovative theory that might well make the *Essay*, as Hipple judged it, the "most elaborative investigation of the faculty of taste during the eighteenth century," even to the point that it treats its "subjects with such elaborateness as to discourage subsequent inquires of comparable detail."[9]

Judgment and Imagination

Much of Gerard's analysis is motivated by the distinction between imagination and judgment that gives the *Essay* its three-part division: Part 1 investigates the various principles of imagination; Part 2 examines how these combine and "co-operate" with judgment to form, refine, and perfect taste; and Part 3 considers various matters under the "province of taste," including its objects, pleasures, effect on character, and relation to genius, a subject to which Gerard later devoted an entire volume (considered under the heading of "Genius" later in this chapter). The role of judgment in these discussions is entirely conventional, the faculty appearing primarily to guide and ensure "good taste," and it is largely banished to the status of silent bystander in the subsequent discussion of the psychological processes underlying aesthetic experience. Judgment "distinguishes things different, separates truth from falsehood, and compares together objects and their qualities" (ET 90), or it "supplies materials, from which fancy may produce ideas and form combinations, that will strongly affect the mental taste" (ET 91). If through sense one "*feels* what pleases or displeases," as Gerard puts it succinctly, judgment "*knows* what ought to gratify and disgust" (ET 96).

More noteworthy is the treatment of imagination, which Gerard identifies as the faculty of taste, although he complicates the view of his predecessors by distinguishing two sets of principles. The first are "general laws of *sensation*," composed of seven "senses of taste" – novelty, sublimity, beauty, imitation, harmony, oddity/ridicule, and virtue – which, as the headings suggest, denote and explain the various ways in which qualities of objects affect the mind to elicit a "set of perceptions" through which pleasure or displeasure is felt. Gerard obviously and explicitly (ET 1–2n) follows the spirit (if not the letter) of Hutcheson in this regard, conceiving these senses as internal analogues of their external counterparts, which acquaint the spectator with "inherent qualities of things external" (ET 160). These internal perceptions of taste are also (as in Hutcheson) "uncompounded" (simple), "subsequent" (inconceivable prior to experience), and "immediately, necessarily, and regularly exhibited" in the circumstances that produce them. An object perceived through a sense

[9] Hipple, *The Beautiful, The Sublime, & The Picturesque*, 67.

of taste, Gerard explains, excites an "emotion" or "disposition" or "frame" of mind "suitable and analogous" to the qualities of the object and in virtue of which it receives its particular character relative to the sense in question (novelty, beauty, sublimity, and so on).

Subsequently, Gerard observes, the mind becomes aware or conscious of the state produced by an object perceived through a sense of taste, a metaperception or apperception that constitutes a second source of pleasure premised itself on the frame of mind in question. Thus "difficulty," Gerard writes,

produces a consciousness of a grateful exertion of energy: facility of an even and regular flow of spirits: excellence, perfection, or sublimity, begets an enlargement of mind and conscious pride; deficience or imperfection, a depression of soul, and painful humility. This adapting of the mind to its present object is the *immediate* cause of many of the pleasures and pains of taste; and, by its *consequences*, it augments or diminishes many others. (ET 165)

This activity of self-consciousness conforms to "general rules" that constitute a second set of principles, the "operations of imagination," to which those governing the senses of taste can be "justly reduced" (ET 160). These rules enable the imagination to carry out its primary function of "associating chiefly ideas which *resemble*, or are *contrary*, or those that are conjoined, either merely by *custom*, or by the connection of their objects in *vicinity, coexistence*, or *causation*" (ET 167–8). The result is varied, potentially long, and certainly complex "trains" of associated ideas of which the mind is often unaware. Yet the "union is so strong," Gerard observes,

and the transition from one to the other is so easy, that the mind takes in a long train of related ideas with no more labour than is requisite for viewing a single perception; and runs over the whole series with such quickness, as to be scarce sensible that it is shifting its objects. On this account, when a number of distinct ideas are firmly and intimately connected, it even combines them into a whole, and considers them as all together composing one perception … it is fancy which thus bestows unity on number, and unites things into one image, which in themselves, and in their appearance to the senses, are distinct and separate. (ET 168–9)

According to this complicated picture, then, the sensed qualities of objects affect the imagination to form ideas – a first source of pleasure – which produce a frame of mind consciousness of which forms another set of perceptions – a second source of pleasure – itself varied and diversified as the mind associates ideas in different ways to create new ones. These are sorted subsequently by judgment, under the guide of which (as described previously) taste is refined, improved, and perfected. As Gerard's discussion especially in Part I of the *Essay* shows, the bulk of aesthetic experience is explicable not from the first source of pleasure given immediately through the "impulses from external objects," but from the second, namely, self-consciousness and the trains of ideas that are subsequently forged by the associating imagination.

Before considering how Gerard draws on these principles to account for different kinds of aesthetic experience, it is worth pausing to emphasize some consequences of his approach. First, as Kames had hinted at certain junctures, most pleasure (or pain) arises immediately from the consciousness of the operations of the mind, and only mediately from external objects and their qualities. As a result, objects are not, strictly speaking, the cause of any such feeling, even though we ascribe that power to them; pleasure and pain, Gerard says explicitly, are "*ascribed* to those things, which give occasion to them" (ET 3, emphasis added). This implies, second, that the ideas of beauty, sublimity, and the like, as well as the pleasures they excite, can, and more often than not do, arise independent of and even despite any "real" qualities that objects might possess; Gerard also claims (like Hutcheson and Kames) that the presence of qualities "in themselves agreeable" tends to heighten the satisfaction. This tendency is due sometimes to disorder or weakness, but most often because the imagination and its principles are the primary source of the ideas in question. Chinese or Gothic architecture lacks "real beauty," for example, but gives pleasure by virtue of novelty in comparison to buildings, which, their "genuine elegance" notwithstanding, are judged inferior from our being long-exposed to and overfamiliar with them (ET 7–8).

Third, while Gerard speaks as if he were a realist of some stripe, his approach requires only that one have ideas (representations of objects) upon which the imagination works. In the final analysis, whether and in what sense qualities are "real" is moot and the concept could be dispensed with without touching the theory as a whole. Fourth, and clearly related to this latter point, in tracing pleasure to the workings of the mind rather than objects per se, Gerard is able to account for the effect of aesthetic ideas without resorting to a physiological explanation of the sort proposed, notably and unsuccessfully, by Burke; Gerard has a psychological alternative that enables him to discriminate the different kinds and degrees of pleasure obtained through the combinatory power of imagination: in one object beauty might combine with harmony, for instance, while in another it might combine with proportion, and the predominant quality in each case explains the particular effect and pleasure in question. This subtlety gives Gerard an advantage over internal sense and imagination theories both of which treat "pleasure" and "pain" as univocal categories or in the very least fail to explain exactly how different objects excite a range of feelings. As a result, Gerard's approach is richer and more nuanced than its rivals in reflecting the complexity and diversity of aesthetic experience.

The Senses of Taste and Operations of the Imagination

Gerard does not apply his prescribed laws of sensation and operations of imagination systematically, but draws on them pragmatically and on a case-by-case basis; what this approach sacrifices in systematicity is more than compensated in its flexibility and strength.[10] The first sense of taste, novelty, Gerard explains, produces pleasure because the mind attains a "lively and elevated temper" when it overcomes some "moderate difficulty," and "if its efforts prove successful, consciousness of success inspires new joy" (ET 3). This explains both the feeling of satisfaction that attends study and investigation, and the delight taken in objects previously unseen, such as new landscape or painting, or discoveries in science and philosophy where effort is required to move beyond previous experience. On some occasions, the feeling is simply the result of a mind at a "loss how to employ itself" becoming occupied (ET 7) and finding pleasure in being relieved from boredom; this pleasure is "augmented" when it involves release from the "uneasiness" brought on by unvaried study, business, or recreation, and even more so when the relief is unexpected and supplemented with surprise. In a similar way, the historian can make familiar facts more interesting by glossing them with the "appearance of novelty," and even a monster, notable otherwise only for its rarity, might acquire "charms." Pleasure of novelty is increased, finally, Gerard suggests, when the mind reflects on its success in having overcome an object "attended with very considerable difficulty" (ET 9). We then take added delight in having surmounted obstacles and improved ourselves through the acquisition of knowledge.

Gerard's second category is grandeur or sublimity, synonyms, one might note, rather than terms that denote different emotions, the sense in which Kames had used them. The discussion clearly recalls Addison and anticipates Burke (the *Essay* was written before the *Enquiry*, but published after it), and Gerard refers the reader to John Baillie's *An Essay on the Sublime* (published posthumously in 1747) for explanations of the principles he proposes (ET 13n). The "higher and nobler pleasure" of the sublime, Gerard explains, arises from objects such as the Alps, the Nile, the Heavens, and boundless space, where "*quantity* or amplitude" is combined with "*simplicity* in conjunction," or similarity of parts. Strictly speaking, both qualities are required, quantity to ensure the mind "expands itself to the extent of that object" (ET 14), and simplicity to focus the mind on contemplating a "single part [that] suggests the whole, and enables the fancy to extend and enlarge to infinity, that it may fill the capacity of the mind" (ET 16). Some phenomena lack amplitude, however – a vast army, eternity, and the discoveries of science, for instance – but are still sublime in virtue of their many simple parts, which "partake of the nature of *quantity*" and enlarge the mind sufficiently; in other cases, in which quantity or simplicity are lacking altogether, the same affect arises due to associations with "passions or affections of the soul" that make the object sublime: heroism, formidable dangers, and the power of nations all expand the mind as if they possessed quantity

---

[10] In what follows, I focus on the first five senses; the final three – harmony, ridicule, and virtue – function according to the same principles, but are less important for Gerard's aesthetic theory proper. His fourth category, imitation, is taken explicitly from Hutcheson's secondary or relative beauty, to which Gerard adds nothing of substance.

and simplicity. Gerard emphasizes this as a particular case of the more general effect of association, that "whatever excites in the mind a sensation or emotion *similar to* what is excited by vast objects is on this account denominated sublime" (ET 18, emphasis added). An object lacking the requisite qualities can thus produce the same pleasure as if it possessed them: although not vast, a storm arouses terror because it occupies the whole mind, and "superior excellence" displayed in strength, power, and genius is sublime both because it is uncommon and makes the mind aware of having overcome difficulties that would be insurmountable for others. As Gerard points out with reference to Hume's *Treatise* (T 2.3.8), through association an object can acquire sublimity that produces an easy transition of the mind from one to the other: words and phrases become lofty and majestic because we connect them to persons or objects that are elevated or distant in space and time.

Gerard's discussion of beauty follows a similar pattern. There is "no term used in a looser sense than beauty," he observes, "which is applied to almost every thing that pleasures us," and is "at least in part, resolvable into association" (ET 45). The pleasures involved, moreover, are similar enough to be collected as one genus, even though each arises from qualities sufficiently varied to constitute three distinct "species of beauty." The first species is "figure" and the qualities those of uniformity, simplicity, variety, and proportion. Each gives pleasure on its own to some degree, but when united – as they are in the human face (ET 47) – the pleasure is "exquisite." Gerard's guiding thought is that objects with these qualities "enter easily into the mind," with "facility," "easiness of conception," or "perspicuity of thought" from which the mind takes pleasure; the mind feels pain, by contrast, when forced to expend correspondingly greater labor on subjects that are difficult, obscure, or involve excessive variety, all of which produce strain, perplexity, and confusion (ET 31–2). The second species of beauty is "utility" or the "*fitness* of things" (ET 38), which arises from qualities of convenience and regularity. These are displayed most perfectly in nature, but also in the beauty of "instruments and works," structures suited to their proposed ends, as well as through the agreeableness of artistic composition where elements are appropriately subordinated to the design that gives unity to the whole. Finally, the third species of beauty is that of "colours," where the pleasure arises either from the quality of splendor that can "afford a lively and vigorous sensation" (ET 42), or, primarily, from association where they bear a natural resemblance or customary connection with agreeable ideas of various sorts – green fields suggest fertility, for example, and the color of clothing the character of the wearer.

"Of the Standard of Taste"

Gerard did not consider the standard of taste significant enough to address in either the first (1759) or second (1764) edition of the *Essay*, but after the subsequent efforts of Hume and Burke he changed his mind, and the third edition (1780) appeared with a new fourth part entirely devoted to the topic. In Part 2 of the first edition, Gerard does address the related question of whether the component parts of taste can be improved, which, with some caveats he answers in the affirmative. The reflex senses vary among people, he empha- sizes, and unlike the external senses, which are "ultimate" and lack flexibil- ity (ST 100), they are "*derived* and *compounded*" and liable to alteration and gradual perfection through exertion, habit, and the maturity of age. The same is true of delicacy, refinement, and correctness, all amenable to improvement through increased association of ideas, acquisition of knowledge, and exposure to objects of taste, respectively. As Gerard points out in Part 4 of the third edi- tion, however, this earlier discussion concerns only the "*perfection* of taste," an issue quite distinct from whether and in what sense there is a "*standard* of taste." The "tastes of men seldom coincide perfectly," Gerard reflects later, and this naturally raises a question: "when they disagree, by what rule can we determine, to which the preference is due?" This question, moreover, is con- siderably more difficult to answer than the earlier one concerning improve- ment, because although "general principles may be rendered unexceptionable ... in applying them to particular cases, there is room for an endless variety of sentiments" (ST 198).

Gerard develops his solution to the dilemma in obvious dialogue with Hume's "Of the Standard of Taste," adopting both its title and argumentative strategy: Gerard's tactic is to acknowledge the diversity of particular tastes and then find some general standard from which individual judgments might diverge, but do not thereby undermine. "On every subject, in every point of view, the taste of one man obviously differs from that of another" (ST 199), he observes at the outset, as "every age" is marked by "something peculiar, which distinguishes its taste, in dress, manners, and in the arts, from that of other ages" (ST 200). This diversity is "great and unavoidable" (ST 204), aris- ing as it does from variations among individuals with respect to the various powers enumerated earlier in the *Essay* – physical organs, internal senses, sagacity, quickness, skill of comparison, mental energy, and strength of asso- ciating principles – along with their exercise, development, and expression. To acknowledge diversity of taste, however, is not to deny a standard, a point Gerard makes by appealing to the same species of common sense articulated by Hume. On the one hand, he notes, we rely on the authority of a standard whenever we call into question the sentiments of others because "to find fault with any taste, necessarily implies that acknowledgment of right and wrong, and of a standard by means of which they may be distinguished" (ST 208; see 247). On the other hand, because taste is founded on imagination and subject to the inevitable variation and whimsy of that faculty, we also assume that the "pleasures of taste have no ... permanent foundation" (ST 210–11).

Gerard moves quickly, however, to distance himself from what he takes to be (part of) Hume's solution, namely, the latter's appeal to the "nature of sentiment" (ST 212). Gerard seems to have in mind Hume's remark that "All sentiment is right; because sentiment has a reference to nothing beyond itself, and is always real, wherever a man is conscious of it" (E 230), which he interprets as a commitment to the view that the standard would have to lie in the "congruence" between mind and perceived object without the intervention of judgment. This is not actually Hume's position – the passage cited is a report on rather an endorsement of one "species of philosophy" – although Gerard is correct to emphasize its drawbacks: it offers no help in deciding which sentiment is right or wrong, ignores the fact that qualities in objects should have the same effect on everybody, and overlooks the role of judgment in apprehending that there is "something beyond ourselves," an "external standard" in terms of which taste is either right or wrong (ST 214). Gerard exploits the view – ironically, given that he falsely attributes it to Hume – to stress the very conceptual difference Hume draws (to employ again the language of Kant) between a liking for the agreeable and a judgment of taste proper. For there is a difference, Gerard observes, between taste as a "species of *sensation*" and taste as a "species of *discernment*": the former is a matter of "mere feeling and perception" through which we receive pleasures (from beauties) and pains (from imperfections), while the latter involves reflection and discernment of the "several qualities fit to excite pleasure or disgust." There is clearly no standard when it comes to feeling and perception, but there may be a standard – and indeed there is one – "in respect of its [the mind's] *reflex acts*" (ST 215).

Gerard thus agrees with and adopts Hume's strategy of resolving diverse sentiments into a general principle and uses it to fix a standard, which, if denied, (recalling Hume's examples of Ogilby and Milton, mountains and molehills, a pond and the ocean) would make a man "monstrous" and beyond reason (ST 223). Gerard again takes issue with Hume, however – and this time he reads him correctly – for holding that the standard can then be "inferred *immediately*" from "general approbation" over time by seeing – in a clear echo of Hume's language (see E 233) – what has pleased "universally, in all countries and in all ages" (ST 225). This suggestion is dubious on empirical grounds alone, Gerard urges: there is no evidence for such consent; it generalizes from the specific case of European art; refers in practice only to the approbation of "very few" (ST 240); and tends to disqualify new work too young to have been fully disseminated or to have passed the test of general approbation. Gerard identifies this mistake with Hume's attempt to discover a "rule, by which the various sentiments of men may be *reconciled*" (E 229, emphasis added), and takes his own solution to be quite different and far superior. "A standard of taste is not something by which all tastes may be reconciled and brought to coincide," he writes in response, "it is only something by which it may be determined, which is the best among tastes various, contending, and incapable of coinciding perfectly" (ST 216). This does not mean that individuals actually revise judgments in light of discovering errors, although they might (a point Gerard takes explicitly from Kames), given that they often retain old sentiments (liking of sense) even when they agree with others in their judgments (taste proper): there is no contradiction in locating a standard for judgment with respect to discernment even though people reject it in practice due to sensation. The same point extends to criticism, Gerard insists, where reflection does not involve dispute about sentiments, but does "generally enable us to approve, as well as to feel them" and "prepare us for receiving more refined pleasures" (ST 270). Gerard clearly considers this a novel solution, although it is much the same position taken by Hume.

Gerard does part company with Hume, however, in his willingness to find the standard unequivocally in the nature of things rather than in the fit between mind and world, a conclusion that follows easily from his view of real qualities and the principles constituting the general rules of sensation and operations of imagination. Gerard's proposal for a standard is clearly adumbrated in the first edition of the *Essay* in which, in the concluding paragraph of Part 1, he writes the following:

There are qualities in things, determinate and stable, independent of humour or caprice, that are fit to operate on mental principles, common to all men, and, by operating on them, are naturally productive of the sentiments of taste in all its forms. If, in any particular instance, they prove ineffectual, it is to be ascribed to some weakness or disorder in the person, who remains unmoved, when these qualities are exhibited to his view. Men are, with *few* exceptions, affected by the qualities, we have investigated: but these qualities themselves are, without *any* exception, the constituents of excellence or faultiness in the several kinds. (ET 77–8)

Or, as he expresses the same idea in the third edition, the standard is "*internal*; it must be derived from some general qualities of taste itself, or from general principles of human nature" (ST 220), a proposal that Gerard takes to separate his own solution from that of Burke. The latter, to recall, argued that everybody has the same taste but that individuals differ in judgments based on the extent of their knowledge; or, as Gerard characterizes it, Burke "brings the question to a quick decision, by maintaining, that the differences of taste are only apparent, and that all men in effect, perceive nearly in the same manner" (ST 221) from which it follows that the "*principles* of taste are entirely uniform, but men possess very different *degrees* of these principles" (ST 222). As Gerard points out, there is nothing strictly wrong with Burke's solution, except (as noted in Chapter 2) it rather misses the point by simply denying the problem: Burke asserts that the "sentiments of all men concerning the individual objects of taste presented to them, are the same," and if this were true "there would be no need to enquire concerning a standard of taste, for there would no real differences to be adjusted" (ST 222). Gerard is willing to admit that Burke does not really mean what he says given that his illustrations actually show that men have different judgments, but "yet judge on the *same general principles*" (ST 222).

Gerard does not specify which "illustrations" he has in mind, and, one suspects, he reads a good deal into Burke's text either out of respect or to gain additional support for his own view. Whatever the case may be, Gerard's own solution comes finally in an appeal to "general principles," not empirical rules of the sort he finds wanting in Hume, but *a priori* ones derived from the proposition that with "taste, as in the material world, the phænomena are various and mutable; but the laws of nature, from which they proceed, are universal, uniform, and fixt" (ST 263). These principles are none other than the qualities of objects that, as enumerated in Part 1 of the *Essay*, affect the senses of taste and produce ideas that are combined in various ways by imagination. Gerard does not deny a role for "general approbation," but insists that it is not the standard so much as the "materials of which the standard is composed, ... the block from which it must be hewed out, ... the principal of those agreements from which it must be extracted" (ST 248). What actually pleases and displeases is but the ground for deducing general principles and rules from the qualities that are "more fixt and definite than the sensation which they excite" (ST 253) and are "capable of being measured with considerable accuracy" (ST 254). By paying attention to the general qualities of objects that gratify taste, we can "decide with certainty" what any given pleasure consists of: if it has uniformity, variety, and proportion then we know it to be beautiful; if amplitude and simplicity, then it is sublime. There will be marginal cases, the simplicity of Grecian architecture or variety in the Gothic, for instance, or the relative weight of magnitude and simplicity in two sublime objects. Gerard considers these reconcilable by looking at other qualities the object possesses and, in general, thinks his solution a potentially exhaustive way to describe the aesthetic value of objects and rank them according to the pleasure they produce. It also means, finally, that bad taste can be ruled out, although Gerard's ultimate expression of it in terms of what is "commonly agreeable" raises the very difficulties of "general approbation" he identifies as a weakness in Hume: "whenever it can be ascertained, which is the degree that commonly belongs to mankind, this decides which is in the present case right sentiment, and which the wrong" (ST 262).

Genius

Gerard devotes one short section of the *Essay* (Part 3, section 2, 173–80) to genius, but came to consider the issue important enough to warrant a treatise all its own, the *Essay on Genius*.[11] It appeared in 1774, although Gerard reports in the advertisement that the "first part [was] composed, and some progress made in the second part, so long ago as the year 1758" (EG, Advertisement, iii). The work is part of a sizable eighteenth-century literature on the subject, including, notably, William Sharpe's *Dissertation on Genius* (1755), Edward Young's *Conjectures on Original Composition* (1759), and William Duff's *An Essay on Original Genius* (1767).[12] At the same time, it stands out as the most

---

[11] Alexander Gerard, *An Essay on Genius* (London: W. Strahan; Edinburgh: W. Creech, 1774) (EG).

[12] William Sharpe, *A Dissertation upon Genius: or, an attempt to shew, that the several instances of distinction, and degrees of superiority in the human genius are not fundamentally, the result*

systematic and influential inquiry of its kind and, assuming that Gerard is accurate in reporting 1758 as the date of inception and composition, the most original as well.[13] The *Essay* also formed the basis for James Beattie's *The Minstrel; or, The Progress of Genius* (1771/2) and "Remarks on Genius" (1783), was read closely by Kant who clearly benefited from it in working out his own views on the subject,[14] and is an obvious herald of the Romantics' view of the poetic genius to come, albeit with a firmer foundation in the Scottish "science of man" than anything to be found in Keats or Shelley: Gerard aims to explain the origin of genius in imagination rather than abandoning it to the mysteries of unreason.[15]

Given that Gerard was developing his thoughts on genius in the 1750s, it is hardly surprising that his treatment of it should be closely allied to his view of imagination and judgment elaborated in the *Essay on Taste*, and although the later work adds a great deal of flesh, the philosophical bones remain those assembled in the earlier one. The concluding paragraphs of the third edition of this latter work hint squarely at the relation between taste and genius to be pursued later: fixing rules that express "ultimate principles of our pleasure," Gerard proposes, might seem to hinder creativity, but actually have the opposite effect and overturn the "tyranny of precedent," the idea that one is tethered slavishly to the achievements of predecessors (ST 272). Such rules indicate what has not yet been achieved and thus impels "imagination to strike into an unbeaten road, which blind deference to what has been universally approved, would have deterred … [an individual] from essaying" (ST 272–3). This, as Gerard explains at some length, is the mark of true genius.

Gerard denies that, properly speaking, genius is a capacity, which would render it so universal that anybody with sufficient judgment, memory, and

---

of nature, but the effect of acquisition (London: C. Bathurst, 1755); Edward Young, *Conjectures on Original Composition. In a Letter to the Author of Sir Charles Grandison* (London: A. Millar, and R. and J. Dodsley, 1759); and William Duff, *An Essay on Original Genius; and its Various Modes of exertion in Philosophy and the Fine Arts, particularly in Poetry* (London: Edward and Charles Dilly, 1767).

[13] See editor's introduction to Alexander Gerard, *An Essay on Genius*, ed. Bernhard Fabian (Munich: Wilhelm Fink, 1966 [1774]). Fabian makes a convincing case for taking Gerard at his word, marshaling a good deal of evidence available from the proceedings of the Aberdeen Philosophical Society before which Gerard seems to have presented and developed his views, independently of and prior to, that is, Duff and other contemporary treatments.

[14] James Beattie, *The Minstrel; or, The Progress of Genius* (1771; 1774), and "Remarks on Genius," in *Dissertations: Moral and Critical* (London: W. Strahan and T. Cadell; Edinburgh: W. Creech, 1783), 146–64. Kant refers to Gerard explicitly in one of the posthumously published *Reflections*: "Genius is not, as Gerard will have it, a special power of the soul (otherwise it would have a determinate object), but a principium of the animation of all other powers through whatever ideas of objects one wants." *Reflection* 949, KGS 15:420–1; Immanuel Kant, *Notes and Fragments*, ed. Paul Guyer, trans. Curtis Bowman, Paul Guyer, and Frederick Rauscher (Cambridge: Cambridge University Press, 2005), 516.

[15] See Fabian, *Essay*, Introduction, xvii–xxviii.

industry could lay claim to its possession. Certainly sense and memory give a glimpse of genius because they constitute specific stimuli that set imagination "at first in that road, by pursuing which it arrives at important inventions" (EG 98): Newton had to *see* the falling apple that led to the laws of gravitation, Pythagoras *heard* the smith's hammer from which he discovered a theory of music, and poets must *remember* some event or object in order to find a proper image for illustrating the conception they have in mind (EG 98). Genius cannot be explained by these powers, however, because that would be to confine individuals to real and present things (senses) and limit them to the review, copy, or mirroring of objects presented to sense (memory). Gerard also admits degrees of genius relative to the novelty, difficulty, and dignity of the works involved. The ancient poets, he holds for example, are greater geniuses because they were forced to invent and perfect work without the benefit of an extant tradition, while later writers enjoyed the benefit of using them as models for imitation. For this reason, Homer must be ranked over Virgil, and Chaucer and Shakespeare over Milton. Genius, although an innate and singular feature of imagination, might also be assisted and improved by diligence and acquired abilities, strengthened by culture and its efforts facilitated by knowledge. The effects of such are limited to the "capacity of expression," however – knowing mechanical skills of painting, the power of sounds, and the effects of words – and eventuate in a lower form of genius, the "genius of the improver."

Genius proper, then, Gerard concludes, is explicable in no other way than as a power of imagination, and a "fine imagination alone can produce it" (ET 175). This is due primarily to the fertility of the faculty that flows from the "leading quality of ... *invention*," a singular, bright, and "magical force" that enables its possessor to "strike out on a new track" (EG 11). It can do this because freed from matter of fact to which sense and memory are tied, and as a result "exhibits" ideas as "original" or as "independent existences produced by itself" (EG 29). The faculty

can lead us from a perception that is present, to the view of many more, and carry us through extensive, distant, and untrodden fields of thought; it can run with the greatest ease and celerity, through the whole compass of nature, and even beyond its upmost limits. It can transpose, vary, and compound our perceptions into an endless variety of forms, so as to produce numberless combinations that are wholly new. (EG 30)

As a magnet pulls together the "ferruginous particles" from a "quantity of matter," to use Gerard's metaphor, so genius draws elements from a heap of raw materials and orders them to "design a regular and well proportioned whole" (ET 173–4). As this image implies, Gerard also insists that genius must express its power through appropriate materials in an objective manifestation without which it would be "imperfect" and "for ever lie latent, undiscovered, and useless" (ET 175). Genius must be embodied, and, as Bernard Bosanquet (1848–1923) emphasizes in a similar vein later, the nature of that medium – be it clay, iron, wood, or words – affords possibilities and imposes limits on the work that results.[16]

Gerard traces this inventive capacity to association and the singular manner in which the person of genius accomplishes it, in a manner qualitatively distinct from the common and more usual motions of the imagination. There are three features of particular importance. First, the mind of genius has an increased vigor of association. This imbues connections among ideas with a "peculiar rigor" (EG 41) and bestows upon them a higher level of permanence and uniformity. Where imagination is enervated and sluggish, by contrast, memory and "diligent observation" must compensate, although they are poor substitutes that produce only followers, commentators, and servile imitators. Genius is marked, second, by regularity of association. Imagination must be fertile, yet some ordering principle is also required not only to "introduce proper ideas, but to connect the design of the whole with every idea that is introduced" (EG 46); without this ability to form a whole or unity, genius will "lose itself in a wilderness of its own creation" (EG 49). "As the bee extracts from such flowers as can supply them, the juices which are proper to be converted into honey," Gerard explains with the help of an unlikely metaphor, " ... so true genius discovers at once the ideas which are conducive to its purpose, without at all thinking of such as are unnecessary or would obstruct it" (EG 47–8). Third, and finally, genius requires alacrity of association, a particular *activity* of imagination" by which the faculty "darts with the quickness of lightning, through all possible views of the ideas which are presented" (EG 57). Gerard conceives this feature as a species of "internal stimulus" (EG 59) without which the mind remains idle and dormant, but when present maintains it in a constant state of spontaneous excitement. This has given rise, as Gerard notes, to the connection routinely made between genius and that "elevation and warmth of imagination, which we term enthusiasm" (EG 67). Genius has a "fire" like a "divine impulse," in which the imagination is roused and spurred on with new "force and spirit" that reaches, in some artists, a state of entrancement (EG 68–9).

As this latter feature suggests, the very fertility of imagination that underlies and constitutes genius also tempts it to roam, so although it thrives on liberty it should never be let loose unsupervised if the beauties of literature and painting are to flourish unblemished by anachronism and overornamentation (EG 76–7), and sublime works are to be protected from "madness and frenzy" (EG 74). Gerard awards the role of keeper to judgment, which in the man of genius will be accurate, sound, and piercing (EG 71 passim). It is never, strictly speaking, an inventive faculty, although it does revive ideas collected by fancy, perceive connections, infer conclusions, and "often supplies imagination with new materials" and inspires it into a "new track" (EG 91). Its role is more appropriately described as managerial, occupying a position from which it can

---

[16] See Bernard Bosanquet, *Three Lectures on Aesthetic* (London: Macmillan, 1915).

survey, examine, and scrutinize (EG 77); assist, moderate, and guide (EG 89); review, correct, and finish (EG 90); and, in general, stand as a constant "check on mere fancy" (ET 177). Judgment thus regulates the motions of the imagination as (in Gerard's various metaphors) the skillful rider directs a spirited horse, the farmer of a rich soil removes weeds from his crop, and the refiner of metal purifies gold from the "dross with which it is mingled" (EG 88).

Metaphors aside, when it comes to the details of the job description, Gerard is the first to admit that the role of judgment in the arts is less obvious than in "matters of science" where it has the unambiguous task of surveying "collections of ideas" produced by imagination and "infer[ing] truth" or detecting falsehood (EG 72). Discoveries in the sciences arise, as Gerard seems to understand it at least, from applying a set of rules framed and established prior to the subject of study. The fine arts, by contrast, have been "cultivated, and brought to perfection, *before* the rules of art were investigated or formed into a system: there is not a single instance of any art that has begun to be practiced in consequence of rules being prescribed for it" (EG 72, emphasis added). Thus Homer, Sophocles, and the Greek orators created original works of art that Aristotle later "points out" and codifies in his *Poetics* (EG 73). Gerard is quick to emphasize that those first inventors were surely possessed of fine judgment as well, because without it work of Shakespeare, Rubens, Tasso, Bacon, and Dryden would exhibit bad taste, irregular design, and want of correctness, none of which are faults generally associated with writers of this caliber.

ARCHIBALD ALISON

Archibald Alison (1757–1839) is unusual among leading figures of the eighteenth century in neither holding a university position nor spending his life as a man of letters. Alison was educated at the University of Edinburgh and Balliol College, Oxford, and took orders in the Church of England before occupying curacies in Durham and Shropshire in the North and West Midlands of England, respectively. In 1800 he returned to Edinburgh to take up the position of senior incumbent at St. Paul's Chapel where he remained for thirty-four years until his retirement, which he spent at Colinton, near Edinburgh. In his lifetime, Alison's reputation rested on his sermons, and his main philosophical work – *Essays on the Nature and Principles of Taste* (1790) – was little known until it went to a second edition in 1811.[17] Alison effectively abandoned the project, however, surprising perhaps given the outline he sketches in the introduction urging that a complete investigation of the nature and principles of taste would require no fewer than three major parts: an analysis of the effect of emotions on the mind, an inquiry into the qualities that produce these emotions,

[17] Archibald Alison, *Essays on the Nature and Principles of Taste* (Dublin: Byrne, Moore, Grueber, McAllister, Jones, and White, 1790). All references are to the pagination of this edition.

and an investigation of the faculty of taste by which the emotions are received; the latter would also include an answer to the question "Whether there is a STANDARD by which the Perfection and Imperfection of this Faculty may be determined?" (xii). As it stands, the *Essays* represents explicit fulfillment of only Part I of the projected whole, the investigation into the "nature of that effect produced upon the imagination, by objects of beauty and sublimity" (2) (Essay I, "Of the Nature of the Emotions of Sublimity and Beauty") and their origin in the qualities of matter or the "material world" (Essay II, "Of the Sublimity and Beauty of the Material World"). As Hipple observes, however, much of the material for the proposed second part is actually contained in the work as it stands, and the projected content of the remainder (involving primarily the pleasing effect of painful subjects and the standard of taste) can be easily inferred from it.[18]

Coming, as it does, toward the close of the eighteenth century, few if any elements of the *Essays* strike the reader as wholly original; that Alison assumes and incorporates a good deal of the tradition is reflected in the definition of "taste" with which the work begins: "that Faculty of the human Mind, by which we perceive and enjoy what is BEAUTIFUL or SUBLIME in the works of Nature or Art" (vi). Alison explicitly situates his efforts relative to the work of his predecessors, identifying them with a school of thought that "appears very early to have distinguished the PLATONIC School" of Shaftesbury, Hutcheson, and, most prominently, Reid. This is an odd characterization at first blush given the points of contrast separating these philosophers from one another, including many features that would disqualify Hutcheson and Reid from the epithet of "Platonism." The comparison is understandable, however, when one realizes the feature Alison takes them to have in common, namely, the thesis that "MATTER is not beautiful in itself, without reference to MIND; and that its Beauty arises from the Expressions which an intelligent Mind connects with, and perceives in it" (381). This is the extent of Alison's "Platonism," and he never deigns to enter the obscure regions of Shaftesbury's Theocles, nor does he accept the inference that all beauty and sublimity can be reduced to "mind," there being many qualities – relation, novelty, harmony, fitness, and utility – that produce the requisite emotions but are not properly mental. Alison's more "humble" proposal, and the philosophical message the *Essays* sends, is that the "BEAUTY AND SUBLIMITY OF THE QUALITIES OF MATTER, ARISE FROM THEIR BEING THE SIGN OR EXPRESSIONS OF SUCH QUALITIES AS ARE FITTED BY THE CONSTITUTION OF OUR NATURE, TO PRODUCE EMOTION" (383).

---

[18] See Hipple, *The Beautiful, the Sublime, & the Picturesque*, 159–60: "We may regard the existing *Essays*," Hipple concludes, "as constituting the basis and outline of the entire system" (160).

Emotions of Taste

This "Platonic" doctrine is the basis for the conceptual apparatus upon which the body of the Alison's work is hung, and its elaboration occupies the first and shorter of the two essays that compose it. Much of what Alison has to say is reminiscent of Gerard (whose name is conspicuously absent), although the emphasis on emotion and its associationist etiology points decisively toward developments in late Romanticism. It yields, more specifically, a fundamental distinction between perceived qualities of beauty and sublimity in objects, and the effect they have in the form of an "Emotion of Pleasure," or what Alison calls an "Emotion of Taste" to reflect the particular kind of (aesthetic) pleasure involved. Depending on the qualities in question, this will be either an "Emotion of Beauty" or an "Emotion of Sublimity," titles that methodize what everyday discourse already reflects, namely, that people routinely distinguish the "agreeable" – pleasure that attends gratification of sense – from "delight" – pleasure taken in the emotions of taste. "We are *pleased*, we say," as Alison writes,

with the gratification of any appetite or affection, – with food when hungry, and with rest when tired, – with the gratification of Curiosity, of Benevolence, or of Refinement. But we say, we are *delighted* with the prospect of a beautiful landscape, with the sight of a fine statue, with hearing a pathetic piece of music, with the perusal of a celebrated poem. Hence we can distinguish being pleased from delight. In these cases the term Delight is used to denote that pleasure which arises from Sublimity and Beauty, and to distinguish it from those simpler pleasures which arise from objects that are only agreeable. (106–7)

Like others of the associationist school, Alison does not deny that objects "possess" such qualities, but states explicitly that things are beautiful and sublime "in themselves" (see 134, 192) and "naturally expressive" of the relevant qualities (282), a point Stewart singles out later as one of Alison's great insights: that association aims not to explain the origin of pleasure, only how ideas of different sorts come to be connected.[19] Alison does insist that these qualities are not "objects of immediate observation" and also acknowledges – in a way reminiscent of Reid's notion of "occult" qualities – that "in all cases, while we feel the Emotions they express, we are ignorant of the causes by which they are produced" (viii). Like Gerard and Kames, then, Alison endorses the conclusion that objects and their qualities are a mediate source of the effects with which they are connected, the latter being traced immediately to some "operation of the mind," namely, the process through which ideas or thoughts

---

[19] Alison is equally clear that the beauty and sublimity of objects "is to be ascribed not to the Material, but to the Associated Qualities; and of the consequence, that the Qualities of Matter are not to be considered as sublime or beautiful in themselves, but as either sublime or beautiful from their being the Signs or Expressions of qualities capable of producing Emotion" (380).

are connected in a regular fashion to form a "train" that is "awakened [by the object] in ... imagination" and of which we become conscious in the course of experience (2). "Thus, when we feel either the beauty or sublimity of natural scenery," Alison writes illustrating the point with some flourish,

the gay luster of a morning in spring, or the mild radiance of a summer evening, the savage majesty of a wintry storm, or the wild magnificence of a tempestuous ocean, we are conscious of a variety of images in our minds, very different from those which the objects themselves can present to the eye. Trains of pleasing or of solemn thought arise spontaneously within our minds, our hearts swell with emotions, of which the objects before us seem to afford no adequate cause. (3)

The same principle explains the aesthetic pleasure taken in art. A painting, musical composition, or a poem produce only "feeble emotions" when attending to the qualities the work presents to the senses, but when the imagination is set in motion by objects – "freed," "excited," "exercised," or "kindled by their power" – the mind is filled with images in a "play of fancy" as if the spectator were lost in a romantic dream (3).

As Alison points out, however, if beauty and sublimity consist simply in this exercise of imagination, then all trains of ideas would produce emotions of taste when experience shows there to be many "ordinary" trains of ideas connected in regular and lawlike ways that fail to excite pleasure, leave one indifferent, or even produce pain; most trains do not arouse emotion at all. In response, Alison isolates two criteria that chains must meet if they are to qualify as emotions of taste and arouse specifically aesthetic pleasure. First, ideas must be "capable of exciting some affection or emotion" (45), "simple" ones – cheerfulness, tenderness, melancholy, solemnity, elevation, or terror – on the basis of which the "complex" emotions of beauty and sublimity arise (50). This transition comes about, second, in accord with the "nature" or "law" of succession that connects ideas so that the emotion is raised not only by a single idea, but also "pervades the whole, and gives them [the train of ideas] some certain and definite character." There is "not only a connection between the individual thoughts of the train, but also a general relation among the whole, and a conformity to that peculiar emotion which first excited them" (47); the "predominant relation" or "bond of connection" then stamps the chain in its entirety with a "character of emotion" (46). When, for example, the imagination is exercised to the point that ideas "fill the mind" (16), an otherwise ordinary object "becomes sublime": a common field associated with a glorious battle, the already majestic view of the Alps connected with Hannibal, or the Rubicon with Caesar. The addition of horror to an already sublime Middleton Dale in the Lake District increases the effect, as does the associations of solemn images with the sublimity of a deep wood covering the side of a mountain. Even the month of May, an object of only "vernal joy," can be rendered sublime even though not so "naturally" (19–20).

Granted that conditions are right and the "state of our imagination" is disinterested – "free and unembarrassed," "open to impressions," "vacant and … unemployed," as Alison variously describes it – factors can still intervene to interrupt the chain. Worry, grief, and the concerns of business have such an effect, Alison observes, as do restraints imposed by too intense a focus on the details of some object: when the critic reads poetry, the mathematician studies Newton, or the philosopher seeks the causes of beauty, the conditions of liberty that encourage the free flow of thought are compromised and the emotions of beauty and sublimity cease to flourish or fail to emerge at all. Age also effects the sensibility – the "fancy of youth has so much delight to wander" (8), Alison writes – as does variation in "original character" and "constitution of mind" that renders individuals more or less disposed to free their focus from what is useful, agreeable, fitting, or convenient (11). The most pervasive and fundamental cause of variation, however, is acquired associations and those "habits and employments of mind" that limit consideration to "single objects, [which] tend to diminish the sensibility of mankind, to the emotions of sublimity and beauty" (13).

The Material World

Having anatomized the emotions of taste and identified the chains of ideas that compose them, Alison turns in the second and by far longer of the two essays to discovering the "source" of the sublime and beautiful in the "material world." There are only two candidates possible, Alison surmises, either they arise directly (as the internal sense theorists hold) from material qualities "fitted" to raise emotions in a subject when perceived through external sense, or they are excited indirectly when these qualities are associated with other qualities that lead to emotions of taste being felt by the mind: such are utility, convenience, design, wisdom, skill, traits of character, and anything that produces the emotions and to which we apply the epithet "beautiful" or "sublime." In adopting the latter alternative, Alison is guided by the insight that "Matter" along with the qualities known through sensations – the smell of a rose, sound of thunder, sight of the color scarlet, taste of a pineapple (113) – lack any emotional content, in which case beauty and sublimity must arise indirectly as a function of the operations of mind that associates or connects sensed or material qualities with those productive of emotion and come to stand for or express the latter by "leading the imagination to the qualities they signify" (119). In art, for example, certain forms are signs of dexterity, taste, convenience, and utility; in nature, particular sounds and colors signify peace, danger, plenty, or desolation. "In such cases," Alison insists, "the constant connection we discover between the sign and the thing signified, between the material quality and the quality productive of the Emotion, renders at last the one expressive to us of the other, and very often disposes us to attribute to the sign, that effect which is produced only by the quality signified" (113–14). On Alison's view, then, a rose is not beautiful because it is red, for the color is a sign of some other quality and that, not the color, produces the emotion of taste.

Even though there is great scope here for objects to be rendered beautiful or sublime, this does not mean that the connections between associations and sensed qualities are arbitrary; on the contrary, they are determined by various causes that subsist in the "nature of things," and as Alison's subsequent treatments shows, he trusts experience to yield general rules that explain the associative connections in question. External objects that are useful, he observes for example, are distinguished by a particular form and color, and such qualities are then naturally and necessarily connected to utility and taken as signs of it: a ship, plow, printing press, or musical instrument come to express the different uses and pleasures they bring. In a similar way, certain qualities of people – such as power, strength, gentleness, and love – find "material signs" in bodily gesture, facial expression, and tone of voice through which they are typically manifest (115). These and other sources are all subject, moreover, to the singular experiences of any given individual, for there is no man who has not "from accident, from the events of his life, or from the nature of his studies, connected agreeable or interesting Recollections, with particular Colours, or Sounds, or Forms, and to whom such sounds or colours, &c. are not pleasing from such an Association" (118). For Alison, then, one and the same object can be rendered "beautiful" or "sublime" depending on the association or on whether an association exists at all: a rumbling cart mistaken for thunder is no longer sublime when one discovers the real cause of the sound.

Alison then proceeds to apply his insight to the various qualities of matter. First, sounds are sublime from the association of the heard quality with ideas of danger (howling storm, murmuring earthquake, rumble of artillery, or explosion of thunder); great power (noise of a torrent, explosion of gunpowder, or dashing of the waves); and majesty and solemnity (a trumpet, organ, and tolling of a bell). They are beautiful, by virtue of the same principle, when associated with qualities that express some particular character – the tranquility occasioned by the ringing of a bell, the peace of the murmuring of a rivulet, or the repose of a whispering wind are all beautiful, although if one lacks the temper of mind or experience in question, the sounds in themselves will produce indifference. The same applies, second, to objects of sight, colors being beautiful because they express "many pleasing and affecting Qualities" with which they are associated. Objects permanently colored establish regular connections, as white being the color of day expresses gaiety, and black being that of darkness produces gloom and melancholy; some colors depict dispositions or states of mind so that yellow is cheerful as red is strong, and others have accidental associations, such as purple, which, the chosen color of kings, expresses dignity and all that is regal. The beauty and sublimity of motion, however – the third material quality Alison enumerates – arises due to its being expressive of the "exertion of power" (373) and overcoming some obstacle: when power is great it produces awe and admiration, and when gentle, moderate, or slight the result is tenderness, interest, or affection. Power also varies in degree (rapid motion produces great power and sublimity, slow motion the idea of gentle power and beauty), and according to its direction (a straight line is sublime while curves, expressing ease, freedom, and playfulness, are beautiful).

Like the tradition as a whole, Alison clearly takes the sense of sight as primary, and his reflections on the fourth and final of his material qualities – form, the "essence" of the emotions of taste – yields the most elaborate discussion. Philosophers have been correct in focusing on this as a source of beauty, Alison acknowledges, but they have considered it to be "original and independent," a conclusion drawn from its being considered a primary quality and thus one that "cannot be destroyed without destroying the individual subject to which it belongs" (202). As a result, many systems resolve beauty of form into qualities in objects such as proportion, uniformity amidst variety, or utility, and – as in the case of Hutcheson and others – a "sense" has even been postulated to receive the putative quality in question (203). There may be an element of truth in each of these theories, Alison observes, and he praises Hogarth in particular for recognizing that the "Winding Line was of all others the most beautiful"; even Hogarth falls into the general trap of subsuming all diversity under a single principle, however, effectively ignoring the more reasonable conclusion that the line (or whatever feature one chooses) is "not of itself beautiful, but by association only and where that association is destroyed then so is the beauty of the object" (220).

Following this observation, Alison subsequently distinguishes three species of beauty and sublimity. The first, what he calls "natural," can be traced to the nature of inanimate bodies. Natural sublimity – the only source of the sublime as far as Alison is concerned – arises from certain ideas connected to the forms (danger, power, strength, splendor, magnificence, awe, and solemnity) or from the actual extent or "magnitude" of objects where the same ideas are expressed in size, height, depth, length, and breadth. Natural beauty, by contrast, arises from associations with angular and curved lines that enclose a form and can be "simple" (when composed by one of these) or "complex" (when they consist of both): thus natural objects with angular lines have strength, hardness, and durability; characterize maturity and age; or are rough, sharp, and hard to the touch, in which case they signify something forced, constrained, and uncomfortable. Objects with winding or curvilinear lines, by contrast, tend to the weak, fragile, and delicate, and characterize infancy and youth; or they feel soft, smooth, and fine, which are signs of growth, freedom, and ease.

The second species is "relative" beauty, which arises from objects that are subjects of art. Beauty here depends on excellence or wisdom of design, fitness or propriety of its construction, and the utility of its end, or from their various combinations. In each case, forms are associated with these qualities, which then become naturally and necessarily expressive of them and produce the emotions that belong to the qualities they signify: uniformity or similarity of parts considered separately, adaption of means to ends, and proportion or relation of parts to the designed end, respectively. Finally, Alison argues that in addition to the natural and relative – the "two great and permanent sources of the Beauty of Forms" (364) – there are other causes that produce the emotion in an "accidental" or "casual" way. These are confined to individual experience and consist, as one might expect, in the particular associations acquired due to peculiarities of education, habit, situation, and profession. The same principles apply, except that objects stand as "signs" of recollections and, unlike the associations stemming from the nature of objects, bestow only a temporary beauty upon the forms to which they refer. When these associations are more general, however, Alison acknowledges that they can sometimes replace the more permanent principles of beauty, and from this arise temporary fads and fashions of taste met with so often in art, architecture, furniture, dress, and ornamentation.

The Standard of Taste and Progress in the Arts

Alison does not enjoin explicitly the debate over a "standard of taste," it being, as noted already, a topic he reserved for part of the system never completed, but his expressed thoughts on the matter clearly follow in the spirit of Hume, Hogarth, Reynolds, and Kames in thinking that the principles of his system might be employed as "general rules, that may not be without their use to those Arts that are employed in the production of Beauty" (367). After all, the features that explain the origin of aesthetic emotions are "founded upon the uniform constitution of Man and of Nature," and it is a short step from here to set up a standard for "real and positive beauty" (369), which will be manifest in objects of art to the degree that these express the more or less permanent features of human nature. Art based on accidental expression is thus "as variable as the caprice or fancy of mankind" and "perishes often with the year which gave birth to it" (368); they take the shape of fads for different styles that are picked up and put down in succession, as with the Chinese, Gothic, and Antique (366). More durable is work that expresses the design and skill of the artist, but these remain relatively impermanent because "dependent upon the period of Art, in which it is displayed, and ceases to be beautiful, when the Art has made a father progress either in improvement or decline" (310).

The most advanced and beautiful art, by contrast, focuses on expressions of form in ornamentation, with the addition of those features that distinguish relative beauty, namely, excellence of design, fitness of construction, and utility of its end. The aim of any great artist, Alison thus proposes, is to dignify ornamental forms by utility and raise merely useful forms to the level of being beautiful; with some conceptual help from Hutcheson's "uniformity amid variety," Alison proposes that where utility is equal, beauty will be found in the most pleasing expression of form, and where expression of form varies, the object in which expression of utility is "most fully preserved" will be beautiful. They are not mutually exclusive, however, but must "be united" in some degree because "elegant or embellished design" gives an object unity and variety without which it could not be esteemed beautiful. For this reason, "Wherever both these objects can be attained, the greatest possible Beauty that Form can receive, will be produced." This seldom comes about, however, because the artist is condemned to the "Sublime distress" of seeking but never attaining "ideal Beauty," even though rules can be framed "for the direction of the Artist" (370). In the final analysis, Alison concludes, with reference to a "fine observation" of Hogarth (*Analysis* Chapter XI, "Of Proportion," 61–2), the artist must look "to the great school of Nature, and to observe the stupendous wisdom with which these expressions [of ornament and utility] are united in almost every Form" (371).

As the appeal to uniformity and variety makes clear, Alison also sees a temporal aspect to the way the more or less permanent principles of human nature find expression in the arts, a discernible "progress of Taste" as he puts it (285). At the early stage, artists are concerned primarily with exhibiting their skill and ingenuity in order to differentiate their efforts from nature and please an audience through the novelty of their productions; the uniformity achieved in these efforts is thus the governing principle. When an art matures, practitioners worry less about displaying their skill and an audience cares little for novelty; the stress is now on expressing and responding to the passion or the character of the subject matter, and variety replaces uniformity as the dominant principle. Thus there is no more important "rule of Criticism," Alison insists, than that works of art should be deemed faulty where the "Expression of the Art is more striking than the Expression of the Subject" or where the "Beauty of Design prevails over the Beauty of Character or Expression" (315). Correspondingly, it is a "first and fundamental principle" that

the Expression of design should be subject to the Expression of character; and that in every Form, the proportion of Uniformity and Variety, which the Artist should study, ought to be that which is accommodated to the nature of this Character, and not to the Expression of his own dexterity and Skill. (310)

Even when expression triumphs over and subsumes design, there will always be some artists intent on parading their skill; the powerful effect of novelty on the imagination will work its magic, and the public always tends to conform its tastes to perceived experts. The result of these factors is a third stage of "melancholy progress" (314), when, after a "certain period of perfection," the art in question inevitably suffers "decline and degeneracy" and falls into a "state of barbarity" where, absurd as it might be to sacrifice the superior and more permanent form of beauty for one inferior and fleeting, the arts become but a means again for artists to express their skill and an occasion for an audience to delight in novelty (313). There might be some remedy or at least "check" to this cycle of rise and fall: emulating periods of great art (the Golden Age of Greece, for example), looking to criticism and philosophy to foster a greater delicacy of taste, or increasing through the diffusion of knowledge the number of people qualified to judge. Alison considers such remedies and assessment of their potential efficacy to lie beyond the scope of his essay, however, and an issue independent of whether there is a standard that does and should underlie the production and reception of works of art.

DUGALD STEWART

While one would search in vain for a particular theory or thinker in which the Age of Taste culminates and ends, Dugald Stewart (1753–1828) stands as a convenient terminus and conclusion to the first hundred years of the tradition's history. This point is marked by his "Essays relative to Matters of Taste," the second part of *Philosophical Essays* (1810), which, although published a decade into the new century, belong thematically to the century of his birth. Stewart, fittingly, spent much of his career as Chair of Moral Philosophy at Edinburgh, a position he inherited from his mentor Adam Ferguson in 1785 and from which he attracted a generation of students some of whom would become leading figures of the nineteenth century, including James Mill (1773–1836), Sir Walter Scott (1771–1832), and Henry John Temple, third Viscount (Lord) Palmerston (1784–1865), future Prime Minister of Britain. In the *Essays*, Stewart does not introduce anything substantively original to the aesthetic tradition, but he refines and polishes, in an elegant, precise prose, certain ideas left coarse and rough by his predecessors, and the centerpiece of this effort – his notion that "beauty" and "sublimity" acquire their meaning "transitively" – provides him a valuable perspective from which to view critically central elements of the tradition, especially, as we had occasion to observe in Chapter 2, the influential theory of Burke. The same idea gives him some authority to comment on contemporary debates over the picturesque and, although in a way Stewart could hardly have imagined, anticipates the analytic turn aesthetics took in the mid-twentieth century.

Stewart's principal philosophical work is the *Elements of the Philosophy of the Human Mind*, published in three volumes in 1792, 1814, and 1827, respectively, and conceived as an attempt to "ascertain the simple and general laws on which complicated phenomena of the universe depend," and on that basis to "reason concerning the effect resulting from any given combination of them" (2:7).[20] Stewart conceives himself intellectually to stand in a direct line to Reid, whose classes he attended for a semester at Glasgow, where he also lodged and became firm friends with Alison. He saw Reid as having wrestled important philosophical truths out of the skeptical impasse of the empiricist tradition, notably to establish the principle that "As all our knowledge of the

---

[20] *The Collected Works of Dugald Stewart*, ed. Sir William Hamilton, 11 vols. (Edinburgh, 1854–60). All references are to volume and page of this edition.

material world rests ultimately on facts ascertained by observation, so all our knowledge of the human mind rests ultimately on facts for which we have the evidence of our consciousness" (2:8). Stewart's thought thus proceeds along lines established by the Common Sense school, but mixed with an array of philosophical wares culled eclectically from the history of philosophy generally and eighteen-century aesthetics in particular.

The third of the four essays that compose "Essays relative to Matters of Taste" – "Of the Faculty of Taste" – is intended to fill what Stewart sees as a lacuna in extant writings, by examining the "growth of Taste from its first seeds in the constitution of our nature" and exploring points of analogy between it and intellectual processes of the understanding (5:337). In the event, however, Stewart only summarizes what other writers had already proposed. He affirms that taste has an ineradicably subjective basis in sensibility, that it depends on "personal experience," includes the perceptual power to "distinguish" or "discriminate" qualities in objects (Sancho's kinsmen at the hogshead of wine from Hume's "Of the Standard of Taste" being Stewart's example [5:343]), and presupposes the same "instantaneousness" or "promptitude" as external sense in announcing its decisions. Such powers are acquired, moreover, through observation and comparison, and though one can talk of genius as an original or inventive taste, it still requires (as Stewart acknowledges Reynolds to have shown) models and precepts (5:356).

In the same essay, Stewart also ventures an opinion on the standard of taste, observing that disagreement can be settled only by an appeal to "philosophical principles of criticism" concerning what pleases and displeases, to be derived inductively from examining the constitution of human nature, or by reference to the somewhat narrower "rules" of the informed critics framed by the accumulation of what audiences find agreeable. Stewart sees disputes about taste as analogous to a disagreement among viewers over the distance of two oak trees. As the latter dispute is resolved by appeal to optics (seeing the details of foliage is good evidence that the tree is nearer than the other one), so in taste one can look to principles and powers discovered by philosophers. The final essay of the four – "On the Culture of Certain Habits of Taste" – focuses, as its title suggests, on how the power of taste is to be "gradually and slowly formed" by moving from an initial taste for the beautiful to a more comprehensive one for "external nature"; again, Stewart provides a summary and amalgamation of elements by this point long and well-established.

"Beauty," "Sublimity," and the Transitivity of Sense

Of considerably more interest than matters broached in the third and fourth essays is Stewart's treatment of the beautiful and sublime, which occupies the first two. Taste, he supposes, is "intellectual" in the sense urged by Reid, and involves the "Action of Mind" invoked early by Addison in his secondary pleasures of imagination (5:190n2; *The Spectator*, 3:559–60, no. 416). Stewart's own treatment of imagination is relatively brief and extends only to establishing that the causes of predicating "beauty" of images or representations are to be distinguished from the equivalent when the same epithets are applied to objects of sense. Stewart takes "imagination" as a compound faculty responsible for conception, abstraction, and judgment, and directs his examination of it exclusively to the language of the poet, whom he sees, very much in the manner of Hume, as manifesting the power to transform and perfect reality by selecting certain objects and qualities, and augmenting and changing them at will. One innovation worth noting is that Stewart reverses the observation made by his predecessors in debates over the paradox of tragedy. He observes not that the transformative power of imagination is inadequate in the face of some objects or scenes of horror, but observes how "some things which we see without offence, and even with pleasure, in real life, would excite disgust, if introduced into a work of imagination" (5:271). On this view, the power of imagination is potentially so great as to produce fictions too horrible even for the poetical reality that the faculty creates.

Stewart's main focus, however, is not the origin of beauty and sublimity in the imagination but on how these affects relate to sense. He begins by reiterating the point made by Reid that "beauty" and "sublimity" are predicated of many objects with different qualities – physical, intellectual, and moral – and, while these have nothing in common, philosophers have mistakenly assumed them to be signs of the same thing, each possessing some common feature that brings them as so many species under a single genus. On the side of "beauty," Stewart singles out for punishment Hogarth's "line of beauty and grace" (5:208), and Denis Diderot's claim that beauty consists in the "perception of agreeable relations" (5:192); on that of the sublime, Knight, Longinus, and Kames come in for censure, although the latter receives credit for treating the figurative meanings of beauty in literature (*Elements* 1:158–9) even if he falls into vague language of related emotions "similar" to the original (5:279). As we might expect from the discussion in Chapter 2, pride of place in the parade of shame goes to Burke, for his "smooth and soft" in the case of beauty and the "*terrible, operating openly or more latently*" in that of the sublime (5:277).

Stewart makes allowance for the innocent tendency of most writers to discover truths by generalizing their own taste, good or bad, to "maxims of universal application" (5:208), but this does not change the underlying cause of the problem, namely, that attempts to resolve all cases of aesthetic value into a single principle rest on a linguistic error, a trick played by language and easily overlooked by the unsuspecting philosopher. "Beauty" and "sublimity," Stewart observes, have not only a primary or "literal" sense but have a "metaphorical" or, more specifically, "transitive" one as well, and only having overlooked this fact might one be enticed to seek some feature that all objects so called possess. Stewart acknowledges intimations of the insight in Kames, as previously noted, and in D'Alembert who had already observed that words have meanings "*par extension*." The primary source for Stewart's distinction, however, is a passage in Knight's *Analytical Inquiry*, itself advertised as elaborating a general point made by Reid. "It is true," Knight observes,

that all epithets, employed to distinguish qualities perceivable only by intellect, were originally applied to objects of sense: for as such objects are the primary subjects of thought and observation, the primary words in all languages belong to them; and are therefore applied *transitively*, though not always *figuratively*, to objects of intellect or imagination. That expression only is properly figurative which *employs the image or idea of one thing to illustrate another*. (AI Intro. 7, second emphasis added)

Stewart illuminates and expands Knight's observation by imagining a series of objects – A, B, C, D, E – where each shares a property with its immediate neighbor in the row, but without there being a single quality that unites more than three of them. It is thus conceivable that the affinity between members of the single pair A and B leads the name of the first ("A") to be transferred to the second (B), and so on down the row as a result, again, of other affinities that hold between B and C, C and D, and D and E. In this way, Stewart observes, a "common application will arise between A and E, although the two objects may, in their nature and properties, be so widely distant from each other, that no stretch of imagination can conceive how the thoughts were led from the former to the latter" (5:196). "Beauty" and "sublimity," then, have specific and univocal primary meanings, but a whole range of transitive ones, and if one fails to make this distinction the tendency will be to regard all of them together as naming a single common property.

In the case of beauty, the original meaning of the term lies in its reference to objects of sight, for something that is beautiful is quite literally "pleasing to the eye," as "harmonious" is what is pleasing to the ear, and "sweetness" to the taste of the palate. The eye is pleased originally by colors, and then proceeds transitively to irregular and regular forms, and finally to motion, which is a modification of form, and can combine with the other two in myriad ways. "Beauty" is then applied transitively, the sheer number and variety of its meanings deriving from the "comparative multiplicity of those perceptions of which the eye is the common organ" (5:203). For "sublime," the eye is pleased by ascent and motion upward, from which arises its primary meaning of great altitude, reflected in conceptions of transcendent beings, "flights of fancy," and the sublime science of astronomy. Height and depth, by contrast, Stewart argues against Burke specifically, do not produce such a response alone, although it is allied; the imagination instead represents to us by an ideal change of place the feelings of those below, so that we compare apparent depth with apparent height, or become through sympathy somebody seen high up on a precipice (5:284–6).

"Beauty," "Sublimity," and Principles of Association

The second part of Stewart's account is to show how this process of transitivity proceeds through the principles of association. Stewart is clear that association cannot account for the origin of pleasures, its role being to "impart to one thing the agreeable or the disagreeable effect of another"; it must presuppose some provenance, however, for if "there was nothing originally and intrinsically pleasing or beautiful, the associating principle would have no materials on which it could operate" (5:242). One must proceed, like Alison, then, on the supposition that many qualities become beautiful when associated with objects that are already, namely, when through transitivity, the "literal sense" is transferred to other qualities. Stewart's paradigm is the scent of a rose, not itself beautiful because independent of sight, that receives that epithet when combined in "conception" with the "appearance" of form and color. The same process explains how qualities experienced through touch – a sense so often employed in concert with sight – are transferred imperceptibly to the realm of beauty, a subtlety lost on Burke, Stewart contends, who would not have otherwise reduced all beauty to the tactile qualities of smooth and soft. Beyond the senses, transitivity also explains how intellectual and moral qualities become beautiful, that is, when seen or imagined they are identified with forms and colors that embody them: thus the association of physical characteristics with expression comprises "Female Beauty," for instance, or the beauty of "Governing Intelligence" in the "Material Universe in general" (5:247). Finally, when "beauty" is used in connection with order, fitness, utility, symmetry, variety, and simplicity it is from the fact that they please the understanding, but as this arises from qualities "conveyed through the medium of the *eye*, they are *universally confounded with pleasing qualities* which form the direct objects of its physical perceptions" (5:249, second emphasis added). This cause becomes even more obscure, though no less effective, when the original source of beauty in appearance becomes remote and thus completely unnoticed.

Stewart applies the same reasoning to "sublime," which acquires its various transitive meanings due to the "great multitude of collateral associations" that come from the common basis of altitude (5:290). Stewart cites, first, a number of "natural associations," which fall under the "religious sublime" and develop as a result of our thoughts being carried upward toward the objects of worship; the heavens and heavenly bodies are conceived as the dwelling place of deities, and even our fates and fortunes are taken to depend on causes operating from above. Closely related, second, is the connection between sublimity and power, for the deity is not only conceived as being above, but also is regarded as omnipotent, the "Almighty." Likewise, the sublimity of natural phenomena – rocks, ridges of mountains, vast forests, rivers, and the ocean – arises from the idea of "Creative Power," and by extension, other divine attributes of eternity, immensity, omnipresence, and omniscience. Terror, Stewart thus urges against Burke, is not the essence of sublimity, but a further transference of the term from religious to related phenomena (5:297), as in the sublimity of the ocean due to its unfathomable depth, and the idea of dread that attaches to storms, wind, and waves, all threats to human life. The same process extends, finally, to various phenomena experienced on the surface of the earth that excite the analogous, albeit weaker, sentiments of admiration and wonder. Mountain torrents are sublime, Stewart urges, due to the association of elevated position and power, as vaulted ceilings inspire the same because they suggest overcoming obstacles and thus resisting the great force of gravity.

Although the origins of modern aesthetics and some of its central concepts lie indisputably with the eighteenth-century writers we have considered in the first part of this study, from a distance of two hundred years the modern reader might still wonder at the strangeness of the landscape viewed: the language of sense, imagination, and association; the foreign tenor of its explananda and the quaint naïveté of theories raised to address them; and the notion of "taste," which strikes many now as an anachronism best forgotten and left, along with its conceptual baggage, to the age it defined. Be this as it may, departing the Age of Taste, one detects a slight but decisive shift of momentum, a change of direction that only becomes visible more than a century hence, but discernible in Stewart's reflections on Burke, Hogarth, and the assumption of their contemporaries that aesthetics is really a search for some common feature or quality in the nature of things and/or the structure of human beings, which, once discovered, might unlock the door to understanding aesthetic experience. The "linguistic turn" lies far ahead, and there remains the long course of the nineteenth century to traverse – the land of Romanticism and its valorization of imagination – and the way through it is as desultory as the one winding from Shaftesbury to Stewart. The future is surely adumbrated, however, in the idea that "beauty" and "sublimity" are really epithets, tokens of language applied to various phenomena through the transitivity of sense or some such mechanism, and that the obscurity of this fact is a trick of the very medium through which philosophy proceeds. Stewart's insight in this regard gave him a splendid vantage point from which to look back on the preceding century; it also allowed him onto the margins of a debate that dominated the philosophical, literary, and popular imagination of his contemporaries: the nature, value, and theoretic significance of the "picturesque." Obscure as this might appear to the modern reader peering into the dim past of the discipline, it was this issue more than any other that contained the seeds, which would take root and, in the towering figure of William Wordsworth, grow into the concerns that would define the Age of Romanticism. It is to the first aspect of that age then, the picturesque, that we must now turn.

PART II

THE AGE OF ROMANTICISM

4

The Picturesque

Picturesque – literally, "like a picture" – entered English from Italian (*pit-teresco*) through French (*pittoresque*) and the term was common coin by the middle of the eighteenth century, well before it became part of the tradition of philosophical aesthetics.[1] Stewart suggests that its oldest and most general meaning was "that *graphical* power by which Poetry and Eloquence produce effects on the mind analogous to those of a picture," and cites for support its use by Joseph Warton (1722–1800) (*Essay on the Genius and Writings of Pope*, vol. 1 [1756]), and Johnson who writes of "a picturesque description of love" in his *Dictionary of the English Language*, although he does not deem it singular enough to warrant an entry for the term in its own right. The term was adopted in England, Stewart observes, with the more familiar meaning of "what is done in the style, and with the sprit of a painter," and was then attached as an "innovation" of meaning to the genre of landscape painting, which came increasingly into vogue as the century progressed (see PE, 230–ff.). Thus by the time *picturesque* became an aesthetic term of art, poetry had already found its "picturesque school" in James Thompson (1700–48) and Thomas Gray (1716–71) – *The Seasons* in particular was a literary and aesthetic landmark – and in fine arts the Baroque landscape artists of France and Italy, Niccolo Poussin (1594–1665), Gaspar Dughet (1613–75), Salvator Rosa (1615–73), and Claude Lorrain (c. 1600–82), provided well-established models for describing scenes witnessed by those on the Grand Tour; the works of Claude in particular were lauded as something akin to the Platonic Form of the picturesque style.[2]

[1] On the origin of the term *picturesque*, see Hipple, *The Beautiful, The Sublime, & The Picturesque*, 185–91.
[2] For a general account of the picturesque in the history of eighteenth-century literature, painting, and travel, see Christopher Hussey, *The Picturesque: Studies in a Point of View* (Hamden, CT: Archon Books, 1967 [1927]), ch. 4, and Malcolm Andrews, *The Search for the Picturesque: Landscape Aesthetics and Tourism in Britain, 1760–1800* (Stanford, CA: Stanford University Press, 1989), esp. chs. 1 and 2. Cf. Alison (*Essays*, 306), who cites a "very competent Judge," in the figure of a certain "Dr. Warton" (probably the literary historian, critic, and Poet Laureate Thomas

　　It is also possible to discern a hint of themes that compose the picturesque in the philosophical tradition already considered in Part 1: in Shaftesbury's juxtaposition of nature to the artifice of gardening, and in Hutcheson's equation of beautiful gardens with irregularity and lack of proportion, and his references to Chinese architecture and English (as opposed to French) landscaping (*Inquiry* I.IV.I and I.III.VIII); the same point was reiterated later by Burke (*Enquiry* III.iv.101), by which time ridicule of the formal garden was widespread. The same might be said of Reynolds's ubiquitous theme in the *Discourses* of perfecting and correcting nature, and, most explicitly perhaps, in Addison's *Spectator* articles in which he speaks of the "rough careless Strokes of Nature" (3:549, no. 414), proposes that "We find the Works of Nature still more pleasant, the more they resemble those of art" (3:549, no. 414), and suggests that poetry idealizes and improves on nature.[3] Even in Kames, a man obsessed with order and regularity, there is the "tree growing on the brink of a precipice, [that] looks charming when viewed from the plain below" (*Elements* 1:150). By the time Alison composed his *Essays* in the late 1780s the picturesque was all the rage, and he both incorporated the category seamlessly into his associationist aesthetics, and, in his "nature embellished and made sacred," pointed prophetically toward the Wordsworthian sublime to come.

　　The texts of the major picturesque writers are *pari passu* replete with the language of the Age of Taste and peppered with references to those responsible for it. The associationist theories of Gerard and Alison play a major role, and Burke's *Enquiry* casts a long, deep shadow over the latter part of the century and, whether as a source of authority or an object of criticism, forms the touchstone for those engaged in debates over the proper meaning of the picturesque and its role in the business of "improving" landscapes. Culturally and socially, the rise of the picturesque goes hand in hand with the growth of travel to the remoter and wilder parts of Britain – especially the "domestic Alps" of the Lake District and mountains of Scotland and Wales – "discovered" as the century progressed by increasing numbers of tourists with the leisure and resources to make use of the ever-expanding system of improved roads.

　　Although the term was widespread and its philosophical meaning adumbrated early on, it was not until the latter decades of the eighteenth century that the picturesque became an aesthetic category in its own right, fully formed and proud enough to stand beside and rival the beautiful and the sublime. This was principally the achievement of four main figures: the educator and country clergyman William Gilpin (1724–1804), Headmaster at Cheam School in Surrey and later Vicar of Boldre in the New Forest of Hampshire;

Warton [1728–90]) who observes that Thomson's *Seasons* "contributed in no small degree, both to influence and to direct the Taste of Men in this Art [of Landscape Gardening]."

[3] Addison and his followers, however, see art as an embellishment of nature, a point prominent later in Romanticism, but clearly rejected by writers of the picturesque who think of art as rearranging nature in the spirit of "improvement."

Sir Uvedale Price (1747–1829), Whig parliamentarian (services in the pursuit of which earned him the knighthood), classical scholar, and gentleman farmer of Foxley, Herefordshire; Richard Payne Knight (1715–1824), classicist, philosopher, poet, collector of paintings (including, apparently, the finest collection of Claudes in Europe) and antiquities (subsequently bequeathed to the British Museum), and noted all-round connoisseur with an estate in Downton in the northwestern corner of the same county as Price; and, finally, Humphry Repton (1752–1818), the last and, in the estimate of some, the greatest of the English "landscape gardeners" (a term he coined) that transformed the landed estates of eighteenth- and early nineteenth-century Britain.

Although these men draw on the tradition of British aesthetics – especially in the case of Price and Knight in whose hands the picturesque receives its most sophisticated philosophical treatment – none of them were professional philosophers, and what marks the writings of them all (albeit in different ways and to varying degrees) is the predominance of a practical element in their consideration of the picturesque and its relation to the beautiful and sublime. This is the case not only in the activity of painting that gives the picturesque its name (Gilpin and Repton were talented artists in their own right), but also through the physical pursuits that mark the lives of each: Gilpin's work is based on travels through various parts of the British Isles; the principles that Price and Knight explore philosophically are born in significant ways of work done on their country estates (including, in Knight's case, building a quasi-Gothic castle – still in existence – based in part on Horace Walpole's influential house at Strawberry Hill in London); and Repton's view of the picturesque is formed primarily through the pragmatic concerns of a gardener whose decisions are made in light of topographical contingencies, considerations of convenience, and the desires of paying clients. Although the picturesque finds its theoretical roots in Scottish and English philosophers, the formation of its character cannot be separated from the history of English gardening in the context of which it adopts its final form and becomes, as we shall see, a bridge to the writings of the Romantics as the century turns.

More specifically, the picturesque takes shape within and in reaction to the tradition that has its origins in the designs of Charles Bridgeman (1690–1738), and is made fashionable by William Kent (c. 1685–1748) and, most famously, his protégé Lancelot "Capability" Brown (1716–83), the latter so called for his habit of telling clients that their landscapes were "capable of improvement."[4] (Kent and

---

[4] For an informative introduction to Kent, Brown, and the school they founded, see Thomas Hinde, *Capability Brown: The Story of a Master Gardener* (New York: W. W. Norton, 1986), and Roger Turner, *Capability Brown and the Eighteenth-Century English Landscape* (New York: Rizzoli International, 1985). For the somewhat more obscure role of their predecessor in the story, see Peter Willis, *Charles Bridgeman and the English Landscape Garden* (Newcastle-upon-Tyne, UK: Elysium Press, [1977] 2002). The English landscape style is associated in the United States with Frederick Law Olmsted (1822–1903) and Calvert Vaux (1824–95), whose works include Central Park and Prospect Park in New York City. For a recent

Brown worked successively as head gardeners to Sir Richard Temple, Viscount Cobham [1675–1749] at Stowe, Buckinghamshire, in the 1730s and 1740s, respectively.) This tradition both reflects and forms the context of debates over the view of nature that the designs of the landscaper should present: whether and to what degree they should reflect nature or improve upon it through artifice, represented most spectacularly in Brown's damning of a stream at Blenheim Palace in Oxfordshire to create an artificial lake. The picturesque writers all place emphasis on rearranging and perfecting nature – making it "ideal," to borrow the language of Reynolds's *Discourses* – but disagree on the extent to which improvements should smooth out the rougher edges or preserve them all to make the landscape, paradoxically, look more like its "natural" self.

The call for "*Naturall wildnesse*" that lies at the heart of the picturesque ideal was made at least as early as Francis Bacon (1561–1626), who, in "Of Gardens" (1625), suggests that "heath" should take up some six acres of a thirty-acre garden,[5] and appears later in the call of Sir William Temple (1628–99) for "some parts wild" reflected in his enthusiastic descriptions of Moor Park in Bedfordshire: "very wild, shady, and adorned with rough rock-work and fountains."[6] The same sentiment is expressed in the eighteenth century by Alexander Pope in his fourth Epistle (1731), addressed to Richard Boyle, Earl of Burlington (1695–1753), student of architecture and admirer of Andrea Palladio (1508–80) after whose Villa Capra "La Rotonda" near Vicenza, he modeled his country house at Chiswick in the "Palladian" style that was to become all the rage; Kent aided Burlington with his plans and also designed the gardens. The Epistle reads as an homage to the burgeoning landscape gardening tradition, with woods, glades, and shades that follow nature's "intending Lines" before which "proud Versailles" in all her "glory falls." "To build, to plant, whatever you intend / ," writes Pope in praise of Burlington's taste and anticipating the later debates among picturesque writers, "To rear the Column, or the Arch to bend, / To swell the Terras, or sink the Grot; / In all, let Nature never be forgot."[7]

---

discussion of Olmsted and the picturesque, see Gary Shapiro, "The Pragmatic Picturesque: The Philosophy of Central Park," in *Gardening: Philosophy for Everyone: Cultivating Wisdom*, ed. Dan O'Brien (Oxford: Wiley-Blackwell, 2010), 148–60.

[5] Francis Bacon, "Of Gardens," in *Bacon's Essays*, ed. W. Aldis Wright (London: Macmillan, 1881 [1625]), 186–94, pp. 192 and 189.

[6] Sir William Temple, "Upon the Gardens of Epicurus; or, Of Gardening" (1685), in *The Works of Sir William Temple, to which is prefixed, the life and character of the author, considerably enlarged*, new edition, 4 vols. (London: F. C. and J. Rivington, 1814 [1754]), 3:202–45, pp. 223 and 236. Temple also reports how the Chinese scorn regular plantings of trees and employ their imagination in "contriving figures, where the beauty shall be great, and strike the eye, but without any order or disposition of parts that shall be commonly or easily observed" (237).

[7] See Alexander Pope, "Epistle IV. To Richard Boyle, Earl of Burlington" (1731), in *The Twickenham Edition of the Poems of Alexander Pope*, 6 vols. (London: Methuen, 1951), vol. 3, ii, *Epistles to Several Persons (Moral Essays)*, 130–51. The quotations are from pp. 139, lines 57ff., and 137, lines 47–50. Pope's first Epistle, it might be noted, is addressed to Sir Richard

As Pope's lines suggest, early intimations of wild nature notwithstanding, it was Kent, Brown, and their school that made *le jardin anglais* a reality, and introduced a style that stood in marked contrast to and departure from the formal, geometrical designs previously imported from France, Holland, and Italy. It found philosophical expression most easily in Hogarth's line of beauty, manifest in a taste for sweeps of smooth lawn, clumps of trees, shrubberies, belts of gravel path, and serpentine lakes that still grace or (depending on one's view) scar many a great estate of the British Isles. The aesthetics of the picturesque was not a denunciation of this new style per se, but a rejection of certain features of it, specifically those deemed artificial and born of an exclusive and erroneous commitment to principles of beauty (smoothness and gradual variation) over those of the picturesque (roughness and ruggedness). Nature "improved" by Brown and his school was not wild, not natural, *enough*. This point of contention unites and divides writers on the picturesque and forms the context for debates between the would-be defender of Brown (Repton) and his thoroughgoing critics (Price and Knight). These debates – often acerbic and personally charged – were carried on in print, and included a host of accusations, both major and minor, including charges of misrepresentation, plagiarism, unauthorized use of unpublished work and, perhaps worst of all, want of taste on both sides.

WILLIAM GILPIN

Gilpin was the first to explore the idea of the picturesque in any theoretical way and for that reason is rightly regarded as the philosophical father and founder of the aesthetic it defines; it is to him, and Dubos, that Stewart attributes the innovative use of the term with respect to landscape painting.[8] He employs the term in an early work, *A Dialogue upon the Gardens of the Right Honourable The Lord Viscount Cobham, at Stowe in Buckinghamshire* (1748), published anonymously, and develops it in the later and more widely read *An Essay on Prints; Containing Remarks upon the Principles of Picturesque Beauty, the Different Kinds of Prints, and the Characters of the Most Noted Masters* (1768) (also anonymous in its first two editions but bearing the author's name in the subsequent three). Gilpin's most sustained and developed treatment of the concept, however, is in *Three Essays: On Picturesque Beauty; On Picturesque Travel; and On Sketching Landscape to which is added a poem, On Landscape Painting*, composed in the 1770s but not published until 1792. This is the most

---

Temple, Lord Viscount Cobham, owner of Stowe; in the poem Pope has much to say about Cobham's character, but nothing of the gardens, although he does praise Stowe – "a work to wonder at" – and its owner in the Epistle to Burlington (139, lines 65–76).

[8] Stewart notes that Gilpin applies it chiefly to natural objects while Dubos refers mainly to art, although both "agree in one common idea, that of *a landscape so composed as to produce a happy effect in a picture*" (PE, 438).

philosophical of Gilpin's works and formulates the "picturesque principles" he drew on and applied subsequently in *Remarks on Forest Scenery, and Other Woodland Views, Relative Chiefly to Picturesque Beauty Illustrated by the Scenes of New Forest in Hampshire* (1791), and six volumes of travel writing published in his lifetime or shortly after his death. The title of each of these begins with "Observations on ..." followed by the part of the British Isles with which Gilpin is concerned, and in which he describes in words and sketches in aquatints, his impressions as he traveled the country during his summer holidays.[9] Gilpin had considerable knowledge of art (he was a great collector of prints and an artist himself), and an admirer of both Hogarth and Reynolds, whose names appear in the course of his writing. His work also reveals at least some familiarity with the tradition of eighteenth-century aesthetics (he cites Burke explicitly), and he draws freely on ideas familiar from the tradition, notably that of pleasure in the "sources of amusement" that inspire "picturesque travel," and the categories of variety and novelty in the form of enlarging the mind's stock of ideas to engage the imagination (TE 47ff.). At the same time, Gilpin generally distances himself from purely philosophical speculation and what he sees as its tendency to unproductive debate and unnecessary abstraction: at one point in *Three Essays*, he runs over various principles that had been framed unsuccessfully to explain the causes of beauty (cultivation, utility, common sense, a sense of beauty, proportion, and rules lost to ancients), the failure of which he takes as evidence for the futility of "inquiries into *first principles* ...[that] go on, without end, and without satisfaction" (TE 31–3). Gilpin's writings lack the rigor and systematic character of a Hutcheson or a Burke – or of Price and Knight, who take up and develop his views – but they mark the rise of a new aesthetic category and a nonacademic, even self-consciously amateur, way of articulating it.

Officially, at least, Gilpin treats the picturesque as a "species" of beauty, "which, tho among the most interesting, hath never yet ... been made the set object of investigation" (TE iii). Gilpin does not claim that "picturesque beauty" – the term he often employs – is superior to other kinds, but, in a way reminiscent of Hutcheson's category of absolute beauty, he holds that objects

---

[9] William Gilpin, *Observations on the River Wye and Several Parts of Wales* (1782), ... *on the Mountains and Lakes of Cumberland and Westmoreland* (1786), ... *on Several Parts of Great Britain, particularly the Highlands of Scotland* (1789), ... *on the Western Parts of England ... [and] ... the Isle of Wight* (1798), ... *on the Coasts of Hampshire, Sussex, and Kent* (1804), ... *on the Counties of Cambridge, Norfolk, Suffolk, and Essex ... [and] ... Several Parts of North Wales* (1809). The latter two volumes were published posthumously. In what follows I focus on Gilpin's theoretical treatment of the picturesque in *Three Essays: On Picturesque Beauty; On Picturesque Travel; and On Sketching Landscape to which is added a poem, On Landscape Painting*, 2nd ed. (London: R. Blamire, 1794 [1792]) (TE), and for purposes of illustration I refer chiefly to the first of his travel works, *Observations on the River Wye and Several Parts of South Wales Relative Chiefly to Picturesque Beauty made in the summer of the year 1770*, 5th ed. (London: A. Strahan, 1800 [1782]) (ORW).

might well be "more beautiful in themselves" outside of artistic representation (TE 15). At the same time, Gilpin clearly thinks that good art requires picturesque elements and holds that the artist (in a claim much criticized later by Price) can express "*the graces of his art more forcibly*" (TE 16) if he depicts a cart horse instead of an Arabian stallion even when the latter displays qualities more often associated with beauty. This claim follows from Gilpin's view that the qualities defining picturesque objects – "roughness" of surface and "ruggedness" of outline – are "more adapted to the pencil" (TE 22) than are those of symmetry, proportion, and smoothness, which (following Burke) Gilpin takes to be constitutive of beauty. As such, the picturesque would seem not to be a "species" of beauty but a separate and contrasting category, something Gilpin apparently confirms when he distinguishes scenes that are "*beautiful, amusing*, or otherwise pleasing" from those that are picturesque (TE ii), and opposes the latter to an "object simply beautiful" (TE 25).

A similar blurring of boundaries is apparent when Gilpin considers the sublime. On the one hand, he insists that "*Sublimity alone* cannot make an object *picturesque*" (TE 43) because the latter requires elements that the sublime necessarily excludes. He underscores this in a reply to Reynolds, who had been given an anonymous earlier draft of the *Three Essays* in 1776 and also received the later version from Gilpin in 1791 prior to publication.[10] Gilpin there acknowledges Reynolds's assessment that the picturesque is incompatible with the Grand Style, but urges its potential applicability to works of "inferior" schools (TE 35). On the other hand, Gilpin blends the "grand" and the "picturesque," especially in objects with roughness and ruggedness – iconically the "blasted oak, ragged, scathed and leafless," a favorite motif of Rosa – that occupies the foreground of a well-balanced composition.[11] There is also more than a hint of the sublime in Gilpin's observation that one source of the pleasure we take in the picturesque is the "comprehensive view" of entire scenes, which, at its height, "strikes us beyond the power of thought ... and every mental operation is suspended." This is a "pause of intellect" or "*deliquium* of the soul" (TE 49), Gilpin muses, in which "an enthusiastic sensation of pleasure overspreads it, previous to any examination by the rules of art ... We rather *feel*, than *survey* it" (TE 50).

This ambiguity of expression in Gilpin's attempt to distinguish the picturesque from the beautiful and sublime effectively pushes it into an uncomfortable middle ground between the other two: it must partake of beauty if it is to please and amuse, but can do so only if it invokes the qualities that in one way or another "ruffle" the smooth surface (TE 12) and usher in the elements

[10] For an account of this correspondence and the circumstances that occasioned it, see William D. Templeman, "Sir Joshua Reynolds on the Picturesque," *Modern Language Notes* 47, 7 (1932): 446–8.

[11] See William Gilpin, *Remarks on Forest Scenery, and Other Woodland Views, Relative Chiefly to Picturesque Beauty Illustrated by the Scenes of New Forest in Hampshire. In Three Books* (London: R. Blamire, 1791), 2 vols., 1:14, and ORW, 31, 35 passim.

that bring it closer to the sublime. A picturesque garden is one where smooth lawns, flowering shrubs, and elegant walks are supplanted by broken ground, rugged oaks, and wheel tracks scattered with brushwood (TE 8), and a picturesque portrait will convey the dignity of the sitter only when neat grooming and smooth complexion give way to disheveled hair and the furrows, wrinkles, shaggy beard, and other "rough touches of age" (TE 10). Similarly, achieving picturesque effect means replacing the horse – beautiful with its symmetrical proportions and glossy coat – with the worn-out cart horse, shaggy goat, scruffy ass, rough-maned lion, or bristly boar. As these and other examples make clear, Gilpin's picturesque is a development of the thought dominant from Hutcheson onward that representation brings its own kind of pleasure and does so through creating a species of beauty – in this case, "picturesque beauty" – that can exist nowhere but in the artifice of fictional wholes that lack corresponding originals. Objects and scenes in the "natural state" (TE 2) cannot be picturesque because the species of beauty they involve exists only in a world conjured through paint on canvas or words on a page, constructions composed of elements that the lens of the "picturesque eye" has isolated, rearranged, and combined. This is the message Gilpin conveys when he writes that the picturesque is "expressive of that peculiar kind of beauty, which is agreeable in a picture" (EP xii), and applies to "such objects, as are proper subjects for painting" (TE 36), or are "capable of being *illustrated by painting*" (TE 2). Similarly, as he proposes in the second of the *Three Essays*, the purpose of picturesque travel is to experience pleasure or amusement that one can receive only from objects with the specific kind of beauty in question.

Despite thus identifying the picturesque with artifice, Gilpin does on occasion suggest that natural scenes partake of the same or he at least uses picturesque language to describe them. "As we leave the gates of Glocester, the view is pleasing," Gilpin writes, for example, of his tour of the Wye. "A long stretch of meadow filled with cattle, spreads into a foreground. Beyond, is a screen of wood, terminated by distant mountains; among which Malvern-hills make a respectable appearance. The road to Ross leads through a country, woody, rough, hilly, and picturesque" (ORW 14). Similarly, on the water below Goodrich Castle, "A reach of the river, forming a noble bay, is spread before the eye," Gilpin observes. "The bank, on the right, is steep, and covered with wood; beyond which a bold promontory shoots out, crowned with a castle, rising among trees" (ORW 30). The same is true when Gilpin writes of the weather or other found features of the landscape: rain adds "gloomy grandeur" (ORW 63), fog softens the lines between parts of a landscape (ORW 28), and smoke from charcoal ovens blends the towers of Neath abbey with the sky above (ORW 117–18). Yet as one sees straightaway, these scenes are less natural than naturally occurring, punctuated as they are with unnatural elements constructed or placed by the hand of man – cattle grazing, castles on hills, industrial machinery. Gilpin's language, moreover, reveals how scenes of nature are only picturesque because they are composed of "picturesque materials"

(ORW 27) that combine in a way to coincide with or at least approximate a picturesque ideal; even the naturally occurring elements of ground, wood, and rock on the Wye are "ornaments" (ORW 20). In Gilpin's descriptions, nature becomes a picture and the spectator an artist who self-consciously views the scene through the specific lens provided by the picturesque eye, which transforms the original and freezes it as an image of itself. It is fitting, then, that this transformation of the real into the picturesque through the metaphor of sight should find physical expression in the visual apparatus of the Claude Glass (named after Claude Lorrain), without which no self-respecting tourist would leave home: a pocketbook-sized mirror on black foil that at once reflected and modified the landscape to which it was held: "fixed" in this manner, the scene could be sketched and, thus captured, taken away by the tourist much in the manner of a hunter leaving the field with a big-game trophy.[12]

This visual transformation of nature is also reflected in the language of theater and artistic technique that pervades Gilpin's descriptions. "The most perfect river-views," he writes of the Wye, " … are composed of four grand parts: the *area*, which is the river itself; the *two side-screens*, which are the opposite banks, and lead the perspective; and the front-screen, which points out the winding of the river" (ORW, 18). The views, Gilpin adds, are varied through the "*contrast of the screens*" in terms of elevation or the "folding of the side-screens over each other" in which case more or less of the front is obscured to the point where the folding side winds around to form an amphitheater, the very epitome of compositional unity and balance (ORW 19). Gilpin expresses the same idea in the language of the art sketch: the picturesque scene must exhibit balance among the depicted space of foreground, middle, and background, which are contrasted with each other through the features they contain – mountains back, forests mid, some relic, ruin or Gothic tower fore – yet unified through judicious selection of colors and application of the appropriate wash. The composition embodies variety, simplicity, the outlines and general shapes of figures in action, and an atmosphere that pervades the whole, emanating often from that rugged object in the foreground to which the eye is drawn.

As Gilpin often points out, however, more often than not materials fail to combine naturally for picturesque effect; the road to Ross and view of Goodrich Castle are rare examples of the "*correctly picturesque*," and most of the time nature just looks like itself. Nature is "seldom so correct in composition, as to produce a harmonious whole" (ORW 31), he observes, and "will rarely make a good picture" (ORW 31), the "elegant little touches of nature's pencil" (TE 23) being no match for the same instrument in the hand of an artist. Thus "in scenes like these," as Gilpin writes of the Welsh Borders, she "seems only to have chalked out her designs. The ground is laid in, but left unfinished" (ORW 147). Overwhelmingly, some element is missing or misplaced – an awkward line

---

[12] For this comparison and the history and use of the Claude Glass more generally, see Andrews, *The Search for the Picturesque*, 67–73.

disturbs, an ill-placed tree obtrudes, a disproportioned foreground or back-ground corrupts, a characteristic object is absent, or the whole is seen from too high a vantage point or broken into too many parts (the fields, fences, and walls that Gilpin abhors [ORW 6, 46]). Nature's "vistas are models to paint from" (ORW 119) and "ready prepared for the pencil" (ORW 116), so that Gilpin's assessment of Newport where a "few slight alterations would make it picturesque" (ORW 131), might be applied to nature in general. Because nature falls short, the production of picturesque effect requires some artifice, a self-conscious transformation of her order in a process in which elements must be extracted, collected, remembered, and rearranged on sketch pad and canvas, in description and poem, to look more like the ideal projected by the picturesque eye. At times, the transformation is (albeit metaphorically) vio-lent: the "mallet, instead of the chisel" is needed to make a beautiful Greek temple into a picturesque representation (TE 7), Gilpin observes, and the ruins of Tintern Abbey, not picturesque enough in their extant form, require a "mallet judiciously used" to refine the "vulgarity" of its gable ends (ORW 49). On some occasions, violence is real though, as in the satisfactorily picturesque condition of "Ragland-castle," where the traveler is delighted by an edifice already transformed by the wrath of Cromwell "who laid his iron hands upon it; and shattered it into ruin" (ORW 91).

Here, expressed in an appropriately dramatic way, is the paradox of Gilpin's picturesque. On the one hand, it is a species of beauty in which one delights; it amuses because within it the imagination has free reign and can "plant hills; can form rivers, and lakes in vallies; can build castles and abbeys; and if it find no other amusement, can dilate itself in vast ideas of space" (TE 56). The imagi-nation is an "active power [that] embodies half-formed images, which it rapidly combines; and often composes landscapes, perhaps more beautiful, if the imag-ination be well-stored, than any that can be found in Nature herself" (ORW 64). The picturesque eye finds little or nothing to disgust or bore it, and there are "few parts of nature, which do not yield [it] some amusement" (TE 54); even scenes apparently barren of beauty (like uninterrupted heathland) will yield variety in the form of light and shade, color, and wildlife. On the other hand, this delight can only be had when nature is pictured and transformed into something it is not. Picturesque beauty is an artifice that cares little for beauty as such, and so "universal are the objects of picturesque travel" (TE 46) that the picturesque eye delights equally in the tuftings of a tree and eddying stream as it does in the mechanical engines or iron forge on the banks of the Wye (ORW 36, 40).

There are limits to the reach of this transformative power, however, and as Hume observed that the magic of poetry dissipates in the face of graphic vio-lence (he cites, to recall, the self-mutilation in Rowe's *Ambitious Stepmother*), so Gilpin on the banks of the Wye confronts a scene that even the language of the picturesque cannot transform. At Tintern Abbey, Gilpin is shocked by the state of the impoverished individuals scratching a living for themselves among the ruins, and in his description the language of the picturesque drops away. The "poverty and wretchedness was remarkable," Gilpin writes.

They occupy little huts, raised among the ruins of the monastery, and seem to have no employment but begging; as if a place one devoted to indolence could never again become the seat of industry. ... One poor woman we followed, who had engaged to shew us the monks' library. She could scarcely crawl; shuffling along her palsied limbs and meager contracted body by the help of two sticks. She led us through an old gate into a place overspread with nettles and briars; and pointing to that remnant of the shattered cloister, told us that was the place. It was her own mansion. ... I never saw so loathsome a human dwelling. ... The floor was earth; yielding through moisture to the tread. Not the merest utensil or furniture of any kind appeared, but a wretched bedstead, spread with a few rags, and drawn into the middle of the cell to prevent its receiving the damp which trickled down the walls. ... – When we stood in the midst of this cell of misery, and felt the chilling damps which struck us in every direction, we were rather surprised that the wretched inhabitant was still alive, than that she had only lost the use of her limbs. (ORW 52–4)

Some eighty years later John Ruskin would describe similar feelings aroused by a scene at the Somme and, in the "The Mountain Gloom," describe in remarkably similar terms the horror of life for inhabitants of the Swiss Alps. For Ruskin, the experience was revelatory and life changing; for Gilpin, it was but an unpleasant scene and momentary interruption of his picturesque walk.

That the picturesque might require willful ignorance of real pain and suffering was a detail as yet unrealized in the 1770s and would remain hidden as the long as enthusiasm for its aesthetic endured. The more general paradox of the picturesque, however, that its pleasure comes only from nature reconstructed, was clearer to more insightful minds, as expressed later (c. 1814–17) in characteristically caustic terms by Hazlitt. Art, he observes, in an essay from *The Round Table*, can "draw aside the veil from nature," but is carried to an extreme in the "rage for the *picturesque*. You cannot go a step with a person of this class," Hazlitt quips, "but he stops you to point out some choice bit of landscape, or fancied improvement, and teazes you almost to death with the frequency and insignificance of his discoveries!"[13] The picturesque sensibility is really an example of art running into "pedantry and affectation" and a false genius for seeing beauty where others do not, in the "rough terrier dog" of Gilpin and his love of "wrinkles, deformity, and old age." Similar sport was had by Jane Austen around the same time – according to her brother she was an early reader and longtime admirer of Gilpin – who delights in deriding the mania for the picturesque aesthetic, most notably in *Northanger Abbey*, itself

[13] William Hazlitt, "On Imitation," Essay XXVIII of *The Round Table: A Collection of Essays on Literature, Men, and Manners*, 2 vols. (London, 1821–2), in *The Selected Writings of William Hazlitt*, ed. Duncan Wu, 9 vols. (London: Pickering and Chatto, 1998), 6:76/14–15 and 78/18. References here and elsewhere are to Wu's edition followed by page numbers of Hazlitt's original publications as supplied by Wu.

an extended parody of the Gothic novel, in which the picturesque and sublime make their strange union. Austen's heroine, Catherine Moreland, is lost in the romantic world of orphans, castles, secret passages, and happy endings, an image of the world that, as in the aesthetics of the picturesque and the Claude Glass, distorts and supplants the original in which she lives. Catherine listens to Henry and Eleanor Tinley (the former destined to be her husband) looking out on a local beauty spot near Bath. "They were viewing the country with eyes of persons accustomed to drawing," Austen writes,

and decided on its capability of being formed into pictures. ... The little which she [Catherine] could understand however seemed to contradict the very few notions she had entertained on the matter before. It seemed as if a good view were no longer to be taken from the top of an high hill, and that a clear blue sky was no longer proof of a fine day.

As the scene develops, Henry attempts to correct Catherine's ignorance "... and a lecture on the picturesque immediately followed. ... He talked of fore-grounds, distances, and second-distances – side-screens and perspectives – lights and shades; – and Catherine was so hopeful a scholar, that when they gained the top of Beechen Cliff, she voluntarily rejected the whole city of Bath, as unworthy to make part of a landscape."[14]

UVEDALE PRICE

Although, in the course of the novel, Catherine Moreland's summary dismissal of Bath might well say more about her own character than Gilpin's theoretical treatment of the picturesque, Austen's irony highlights nicely the absurdity of a view that allows nature beautiful only when transformed by the words of a writer or sketch pad of an artist. For Uvedale Price, this is precisely the problem that comes of combining "picturesque" and "beauty" in one unholy alliance, and a good deal of his main work in aesthetics, *An Essay on the Picturesque*,[15]

---

[14] Jane Austen, *Northanger Abbey*, ed. Barbara M. Benedict and Deirdre Le Faye (Cambridge: Cambridge University Press, 2006 [1817]), vol. 1, ch. 14, 111–12 and 113. See also *Pride and Prejudice*, ed. Pat Rogers (Cambridge: Cambridge University Press, 2006 [1813]), vol. 1, ch. 10, 58, where having been snubbed by Eleanor Bingley, Elizabeth Bennet responds to Mr. Darcy's invitation to rejoin the party walking in the grounds of Netherfield: "No, no; stay where you are. – You are charmingly group'd, and appear to uncommon advantage. The picturesque would be spoilt by admitting a fourth. Goodbye." See also Elizabeth's raptures at being invited by her aunt and uncle to accompany them on the "northern tour" of the Lake District (vol. 2, ch. 5, 174–5), and the criticism of Repton in *Mansfield Park*, especially for "leveling" and removing old avenues of trees to create an uninterrupted prospect; this was not, it should be noted, an *idée fixe* of Repton, although he did sometimes recommend the "axe rather than the spade" in his designs. See *Mansfield Park*, ed. John Wiltshire (Cambridge: Cambridge University Press, 2005 [1814]), vol. 1, ch. 6, 62–7.

[15] Sir Uvedale Price, *An Essay on the Picturesque, As Compared with the Sublime and the Beautiful, and On the Use of Studying Pictures, for the Purpose of Improving Real Landscape*

is directed toward dissolving the union once and for all. The *Essay* appeared in 1794, two years after the *Three Essays*, although Price claims that a "great deal" of it had been written before he found opportunity to read Gilpin's work (E 345). For this reason, one assumes, most, though not all (see E 38–9), of his references to Gilpin appear in footnotes (which in the later 1810 edition are collected in an appendix). Whether or not Price knew the *Three Essays*, the philosophical thrust of the *Essay* certainly reads as an elaboration, critique, and correction of Gilpin aimed chiefly at clarifying the ambiguities, which, as we have seen, pervade that latter's approach. At the same time, the *Essay* should not be read simply as a dialogue with Gilpin, but as a larger and more ambitious project to do for the picturesque what, in Price's view, Burke had done for the sublime: to raise it from being a species of beauty to an aesthetic category in its own right. After the *Essay*, one should speak not of pictur- esque beauty, but of the picturesque or "picturesqueness," the term (however unwieldy) Price feels compelled to coin from the "necessity of having some word to oppose to beauty and sublimity" (E 42n).

Price finds initial support for the claim that the picturesque has its own inde- pendent status by pointing to everyday experience, which seems to recognize a source of pleasure distinct from that underlying either beauty or sublimity. The only problem Price sees is that it has "never yet been accurately distin- guished from the sublime, and the beautiful" (E 38), but he is confident that when given the attention it deserves the picturesque will be revealed to have a "character not less separate and distinct than either the sublime or the beau- tiful, nor less independent of the art of painting" (E 40). In pursuit of this end Price is much indebted to Burke's system, the "general truth and accuracy" of which he accepts and takes as a "foundation" of his own (E 92–3). This includes adopting Burke's psychology of pain, pleasure, and the passions; his definitions of beauty and sublimity; and, most controversially, the physiological theory of contracted and relaxed fibers that account for them. Price acknowledges the criticism leveled against Burke's *Enquiry* (especially Part 4), but readily springs to its defense and insists that he need only find within Burke's schema some place for the picturesque between the calming effect of beauty and the violent power of the sublime. He discovers this in the state of excitement he calls "curiosity," with its efficient cause in the "full tone" of the bodily fibers. "In pursuing the same train of ideas [as Burke]," Price writes,

I may add, that the effect of the picturesque is curiosity; an effect, which, though less splendid and powerful, has a more general influence. Those who have felt the excite- ment produced by the intricacies of wild romantic mountainous scenes, can tell how

(London: J. Robson, 1794). This went to a second edition (1796), which appeared as Volume 1 of a three-volume edition of Price's works collected as *Essays on the Picturesque, As Compared with the Sublime and the Beautiful, and On the Use of Studying Pictures, for the Purpose of Improving Real Landscape*, 3 vols. (London: J. Mawman, 1810). All references to the *Essay* are to vol. 1 of the 1810 edition (hereafter E).

curiosity, while it prompts us to scale every rocky promontory, to explore every new recess, by its active agency keeps the fibres to their full tone; and thus picturesqueness when mixed with either of the other characters, corrects the languor of beauty, or the tension of sublimity. (E 88–9)

While he adopts and amends Burke in this manner, Price is at pains to emphasize (in response to criticism) that he does not consider the *Enquiry* to be definitive. Although he emphasizes that Burke "has done *a great deal towards* settling the vague and contradictory ideas" of beauty and sublimity, Price insists that they are not "clearly settled" (E 93), and only by engaging Gilpin on the picturesque can greater clarity be realized. Following Burke left Price open to objections similar to those raised against the *Enquiry*, a parallel exploited by Stewart who saw in Price the result of applying Burke's concept of "beauty" and, finding many features that would not fit under it, inventing a new category as a solution.

Before turning to the details of Price's view and points of divergence from Gilpin, it should be emphasized that there is something more than mere philosophical clarity at stake in the debates. For Price, the *Essay* is part and parcel of a plea to fellow landowners that they reject the destructive fashions of "modern improvers" in the style of Brown and his school, and the consequences that follow from disregarding the picturesque in favor of "dressing" wild spots through "clumps, belts, the made water, and the eternal smoothness and sameness of a finished place" (E 14). The antidote, Price urges, is to acquire the proper knowledge and develop the sound judgment that, Brown and his followers notwithstanding, actually composes the "whole science of improvement with *regard to its effect on the eye*" (emphasis added). For the "great object of our present inquiry," he writes of his *Essay*,

seems to be, what is that mode of study which will best enable a man of a liberal and intelligent mind, to judge of the forms, colours, effects, and combinations of visible objects; to judge of them either as single compositions, which may be considered by themselves without reference to what surrounds them; or else parts of scenery, the arrangement of which must be more or less regulated and restrained by what joins them, and the connection of which with the general scenery must constantly be attended to. (E 12)

This knowledge and judgment comes only with the study of natural scenery and the history of gardening and, crucial for overcoming the excesses of smoothness and gradual variation by the admixture of roughness, paying due attention to painters who have studied nature most closely and shown it at its best, *la belle Nature*. Although artists might have discovered "principles of painting" in the rules of composition for separating and combining objects, grouping and separating parts, depicting the effects of light and shade, and achieving a harmony of tints, these are "in reality," Price insists, nothing but "the general principles on which the effect of *all visible objects must depend, and to which it must be referred*" (E 14, emphasis added); in other words, both painting and improvement of landscape are governed by the same principles. This is not to deny that there are differences between the two practices (a point Price partly concedes to Repton), but while any common laborer who knows how to make an asparagus bed has the "essential qualifications" of an improver in the mold of Brown (E 103), only those who look with the "painters eye" (E 31) and understand what lies behind a Claude landscape can improve with taste and artistry.

This does not mean that the nature, origin, and effects of the picturesque are obvious or easy to grasp, a fact reflected in Gilpin who, Price charges, mistakenly conceives it only in terms of "proper subjects for" or "capable of being illustrated in" painting, a focus that yields a definition "at once too vague, and too confined" (E 39). The definition is "too vague," Price contends, because it effectively extends the term "to every object, and every kind of scenery, which has been, or might be represented with good effect in painting" (E 37). It is "very true," as he points out, "that picturesque objects do please from some quality capable of being illustrated in painting; but so does every object," he adds, "that is represented in painting if it please at all otherwise it would not have been painted" (E 39). We do recognize a difference among beauty, sublimity, and the picturesque, but representation is too imprecise a criterion to bring out the quality or qualities that would express formally what is implicit in experience; moreover, artists have also represented the beautiful and the sublime in their work, so being "proper subjects" for painting hardly distinguishes one aesthetic category from another. At the same time, the definition is "too confined" because it limits the term to the work of artist or poet, and restricts it to being a species of beauty only; this has the effect of obscuring the universal and consistent features that distinguish the picturesque as a category in its own right and leads to the idea of "picturesque *beauty*," a conceptual error that, Price urges, obliges Gilpin to embrace a number of contradictions and inconsistencies.

First, and despite protestations to the contrary, Gilpin claims that artists always prefer picturesque elements over others that are simply beautiful; thus regular, finished architecture will always give way to the ruin. As Price notes, however, the evidence speaks against him. With "regard to entire buildings in contradistinction to ruins, the back grounds [*sic*] and landscapes of all the great masters are full of them," Price writes, including those of Claude and Gaspar, whose work is replete with elegant symmetrical buildings of regular design. Second, while insisting that roughness is the mark of the picturesque, Gilpin also admits that certain smooth objects fall under the same description: "the lake spread upon the canvas; the *marmoreum aequor*, pure, limpid, smooth, as the polished mirror," the horse with sides that "shine with brushing, and high-feeding" (TE 22), and the soft, smooth touch of a bird's plumage (TE 23). Surely, Price emphasizes, these cannot be called "picturesque" when they lack the very quality that defines that class of object. Even Gilpin's attempt to avoid the inconsistency by appealing to ostensibly rough and broken elements – undulations and reflections on the water, the swell of muscles under the skin, and the change and variety of colors in feathers – involves the very features that make an object beautiful rather than picturesque. Third, as noted previously, Gilpin expresses what to Price is the strange view that the "graces" of artists and their art are best displayed in painting the picturesque cart horse rather than the obviously more beautiful Arabian thoroughbred. Art and artists insisting on this principle would be judged "preposterous," Price retorts, and artists achieve picturesque effects not by "downgrading" a beautiful horse to a beast of burden, but by depicting the former through "sudden and spirited action": physical exertion, a disordered mane, freedom of movement, and elegance and grandeur of form (E 360).

In general, Price thinks Gilpin has laid himself open to these charges "by his exclusive fondness for the picturesque, and by having carried to excess his position, that roughness is that particular quality which makes objects chiefly please in painting" (E 358–9). Had he curbed his enthusiasm, Gilpin might have recognized the picturesque as a distinct category and arrived at a position both more precise, by distinguishing it from the beautiful and sublime, and more open, by admitting under it objects other than those represented by the artist: "it surely would have been more simple and satisfactory," Price observes in summarizing his criticism of Gilpin's position, "to have named things according to their obvious and prevailing qualities; and to have allowed that painters sometimes preferred beautiful, sometimes picturesque, sometimes grand and sublime objects, and sometimes objects where the two or three characters, were equally, or in different degrees mixed" (E 357). Price is willing to admit theoretically what he finds practically in art and nature, that objects or scenes with elements that make them beautiful or sublime might combine – "mix" or "blend" – with others that are picturesque, but he insists that one should speak clearly and definitively in a way that reflects the overwhelming presence of one over the other: one cannot, that is, with sense and without contradiction, speak of "picturesque beauty" or "picturesque sublimity." For the picturesque "appears to hold a station between beauty and sublimity and more happily blended with them both, than they are with each other. It is, however, perfectly distinct from either" (E 68). Or, as Price expresses the same thought with a different metaphor, the picturesque "fills up a vacancy between the sublime and the beautiful, and accounts for the pleasure we receive from many objects, on principles distinct from them both" (E 114).

Having thus placed the picturesque between the sublime and beautiful, Price attempts to specify, first, the features that define it, and show, second, how these distinguish it from its two aesthetic kin. The distinctive character of the picturesque he discovers in the relationship between the sources of pleasure in picturesque objects and the qualities (or what he also calls efficient causes) in those objects that explain them. There is, one has to admit, a lack of care on Price's part in making clear whether and how the "sources of pleasure" differ from "qualities"; one might expect him to refer the former to the affective state of the subject and the latter to objects that give rise to it, but as he presents it at least, both appear to belong to the object. This notwithstanding, he traces pleasure (like Gilpin) to variety and intricacy, which are "distinct" from each other but at once "connected and blended" (E 21–2) in a way to produce the distinct pleasure of the picturesque: variety consists in the "forms, the tints, and the lights and shadows of objects," while intricacy is "that disposition of objects, which, by a partial and uncertain concealment, excites and nourishes curiosity" (E 22). This picturesque pleasure can be traced in turn to three qualities. The first, roughness, Price adopts from Gilpin, but the other two, sudden variation and irregularity, are clearly derived as the "most diametrically opposite" to gradual variation and regularity identified with beauty by Burke (E 49). Price's favorite example is the pleasure produced by winding lanes, hollow trees, and overgrown ground, features that contrast with and exclude the "monotony and baldness" displayed by places "improved" by Kent, Brown, and their followers (E 22–3).

With these characteristics in place, it is but a short step for Price to specify what distinguishes the picturesque from the beautiful. Where one finds smoothness, gradual variation, and regularity, the pleasure will be of something beautiful; where roughness, sudden variation, and irregularity constitute intricacy and variety, the pleasure will be of something picturesque. Thus a calm lake, smooth beech tree, a "pampered steed," greyhound, and Greek temple, are all *beautiful*, Price urges, whereas broken water, "rugged old oak or knotty wych elm" (E 57), carthorse, rough waterdog, and Gothic spire are picturesque. The picturesque also increases with agitation and movement – the bristling whiskers of the boar or the erect quills of the porcupine – as it does with age and decay that stands opposed to youth and freshness that often attends the beautiful. This latter point brings a temporal dimension to Price's picturesque. Gilpin, we might recall, describes the transformation of a beautiful Greek temple – regular, symmetrical, and smooth – into the rough, rugged ruin that is its picturesque counterpart in a process through which a real object is converted into a linguistic or pictorial representation; the artist takes his metaphorical mallet to the building in question. For Price, however, who uses the same example, there is a "process by which time, the great author of such changes, converts a beautiful object into a picturesque one" (E 51), a "transition" that takes place not through an artistic medium, but by the play of efficient causes that deform the uniform surface with moss and incrustation, turn the stones into tumbled heaps, and cover the whole with vines, creepers, and other wild plants. Parallel to how such a "beautiful *artificial* object becomes picturesque," Price identifies the same process in "*natural* objects" (E 78) where the smooth, fresh gloss that gives beauty to young plants and animals decays into the dry, craggy appearance of picturesque old age. Time also works its effects on human characters we find depicted in story and poem: when happy they are beautiful, but when warring passions have reduced them to a "state of ruin" they are picturesque (E 64).

Although Price's delineation of the picturesque makes for easy points of contrast with the beautiful – after all, the presence or absence of the respective pleasures and relevant qualities automatically rules them in or out – it is less decisive when it comes to the sublime. Price accepts that picturesque phenomena "must always have a tincture of the sublime" because "caused by those dreaded powers of destruction" (E 58–9) to which sublimity attests (such are the "limbs of huge trees shattered by lightening or tempestuous winds"), or the picturesque and sublime might be "finely united" as in lines from Book 1, verse 65 of Ludovico Ariosto's epic poem *Orlando Furioso* (1516):

> Quale stordito, et stupido aratore
> Poi ch'e passato il fulmine, si leva
> Di la, dove l'altissimo fragore
> Presso agli uccisis buoi steso l'aveva;
> Che mira sense fronde, et senza onore,
> Il Pin che da lontan veder soleva,
> Tal si levo'l Pagano.

> As the bewildered and astonished clown
> Who held the plough (the thunder storm o'erpast)
> There, where the deafening bolt had beat him down,
> Nigh his death-stricken cattle, wakes aghast,
> And sees the distant pine without its crown,
> Which he saw clad in leafy honours last;
> So rose the paynim knight with troubled face,
> The maid spectatress of the cruel case.[16]

Unlike Gilpin, however, who glosses over any similarities, Price insists that the picturesque is as distinct from the sublime as it is from the beautiful because

---

[16] Price omits the concluding lines of the stanza: " ... a piè rimaso/Angelica presente al duro caso." The translation is by William Stewart Rose (London: J. Murray, 1823–31). A somewhat freer rendering is that of John Hoole, *Orlando Furioso: Translated from the Italian of Lodovico Ariosto; with notes by John Hoole*, 2nd ed., 5 vols. (London: George Nicol 1785 [1783]), 1:27–8, lines 448–61:

> The knight unknown, beholding on the mead
> His foe lie crush'd beneath the slaughter'd steed,
> And deeming here no further glory due,
> Resolv'd no more the contest to renew;
> But turning swift, again pursu'd his way,
> And left the fierce Cirassian where he lay.
> As when, the thunder o'er, the ether clears,
> Slow rising from the strike the hind appears,
> Where stretch'd he lay all senseless on the plain,
> Where fast beside him lay his oxen slain;
> And sees the pine, that once had rais'd in air
> Its stately branches, now of honours bare:
> So rose the Pagan from the fatal place,
> His mistress present at the dire disgrace.

although there are "some qualities common to them both, yet they differ in many essential points, and proceed from very different causes" (E 83). The sublime arises from greatness of dimension, while dimension is irrelevant to the picturesque whose objects can be large or small; sublimity also involves awe and terror in contrast to the playfulness of the picturesque, and where the latter is bounded and marked by variety, the sublime tends to uniformity and moves out to infinity.

RICHARD PAYNE KNIGHT

While Price was going to such lengths to articulate the distinct character of the picturesque, Richard Payne Knight was doing his level best to move in the opposite direction by showing that the picturesque is, as Gilpin vaguely grasped, actually a species of beauty. Knight's first foray into aesthetics (he had already published an essay on the Greek alphabet and a rather controversial work, *The Worship of Priapus*, on sexual symbolism) was *The Landscape, a Didactic Poem in Three Books. Addressed to Uvedale Price, Esq.*, a long poem running to some fifteen hundred lines accompanied by footnotes expounding or otherwise elaborating Knight's views.[17] The ideas expressed in the poem were, to some degree at least, a result of Knight's discussions with his neighbor Price (hence the dedication of the title) concerning principles governing picturesque land improvement in which both were engaged on their respective estates. The personal nature of their relationship, however – not to mention the physical propinquity of their seats – did not prevent Knight from adding a long footnote to the second edition of the work criticizing Price for his "imaginary" and "supposed distinction between the picturesque and the beautiful" (which inspired Price in turn to compose a lengthy rebuttal in the form of a dialogue),[18] which was elaborated in many passages of *An Analytic Inquiry into the Principles of Taste* published a decade later.

Against Price, Knight insists that the picturesque "is merely that kind of beauty which belongs exclusively to the sense of vision; or to the imagination, guided by that sense" (L 19). This deceptively simple definition presupposes a good deal of theoretical work that Knight had already undertaken when he composed *The Landscape*, and although it is fair to describe the work as applied aesthetics concerned principally with urging the adoption of a particular taste in gardening, it sits on a sophisticated and well-constructed

[17] Richard Payne Knight, *The Landscape, a Didactic Poem in Three Books. Addressed to Uvedale Price, Esq.*, 2nd ed. (London: G. Nicol, 1795 [1794]), 18–19 (L). Page numbers refer to Knight's footnoted text, and other numbers to the lines of the poem.

[18] Uredale Price, *A Dialogue on the Distinct Characters of the Picturesque and the Beautiful, in Answer to the Objections of Mr. Knight. Prefaced by an Introductory Essay on Beauty; with remarks on the Ideas of Sir Joshua Reynolds & Mr. Burke upon That Subject* (London: J. Robson, 1801), in *Essays on the Picturesque*, 3:181–400.

philosophical foundation. Knight refers to this explicitly in the poem (as in "For nought but light and colour can the eye / But through the medium of the mind, descry" [L 264–5]), elaborated in a footnote (L 20–4), which amounts to a remarkably concise summary of the detailed exposition presented in the *Analytic Inquiry*. The jab at Price is also noteworthy because it hints at Knight's view that there are two ways in which the picturesque can be experienced and articulated. He accepts roughness and ruggedness as desiderata, but argues that such qualities can be grasped either through the sense of sight alone or through sight with the addition of association. The first of these – what we can call for convenience the *sense-picturesque* – is based on sense alone and yields a correspondingly narrow form of pleasure; the second – the *association-picturesque* – engages in addition both imagination and intellect, and given the seemingly inexhaustible ways in which ideas can be combined, provides pleasure of a richer and deeper sort.

Like Price, Knight is inspired in no small part by Burke, but unlike his neighbor who defends and adopts the content of the *Enquiry* without emulating its form, Knight largely rejects the specifics of Burke's doctrine but is inspired by its systematic structure. Knight, as noted in Chapter 2, is critical of Burke's naïve optics and devotes a good deal of space in Part 3 of the *Analytic Inquiry* ("Of the Passions") to showing up the limitations of what he refers to at one point as the "brilliant, but absurd and superficial theories of the *Inquiry into the Sublime and Beautiful*" (AI 2.2.74). Much of Knight's criticism is aimed at confusions and obscurities following from Burke's attempt to discover qualities of sublimity in objects and trace them subsequently to physiological states. Terror, Knight argues in particular, necessarily excludes the feeling of exultation that sublimity involves and is really the power in which the latter originates.[19] At the same time as he criticizes Burke, he supports the general attempt to discover a physical theory of impressions, and the first part of the *Analytic Inquiry*, "Of Sensation," is aimed at developing an alternative account to the one proposed in the *Enquiry*. Where Burke speaks of tension, Knight emphasizes "action" and "motion," and the "irritable" nature of the "organic parts" of animals and plants (AI 1.1.4). On this picture, all such parts, sense organs included, are in a constant state of irritation as part and parcel of their normal functioning, although it varies, being "either increased or decreased by external impressions, accordingly as they are stimulant or narcotic; or its modes may be changed according to the different qualities of the substances applied" (AI 1.1.4). The ultimate explanation for how these changes take place Knight considers beyond the limits of the human faculties, but he speaks with confidence about the sensations, both pleasant and unpleasant, that result

[19] See especially AI 3.1.59–84. It is worth recalling in this context Reid's criticism of Burke for equating terror with sublimity as a result of being misled by the "similarity between dread and terror" (they are both grave and solemn) when, in fact, the two emotions are quite different ("On Taste," III.590.30ff.).

from the increase or decrease of irritation. "If the irritation be weak, the result is insipidity or flatness," he concludes, "if it be too strong, it is pain or uneasiness" (AI 1.1.4).

Knight applies this general principle to all the senses and their respective organs, but the one of primary importance for his view of the picturesque is sight. The pains and pleasures of vision depend upon the "exciting cause" responsible for moderating the degree and mode of irritation: the degree is given by light "reflected, from the objects seen, upon the retina of the eye" (AI 1.5.1) and the mode by color, the "different colors ... being only collections of rays variously modified, separated, and combined, according to the different textures of the surfaces of bodies, from which they are reflected, or the substances of those through which they are refracted" (AI 1.5.7). Knight thus distinguishes between sensation (the physical modification of the sense organ through impressions), and perception, which depends upon but cannot be reduced to it; after all, the sense of sight gives only a two-dimensional plane, and only through "habit and experience" are distance and depth perceived (AI 1.5.2). With this distinction in mind, Knight observes (as had Reid earlier and would Stewart later) that "beauty" is a "general term of approbation, of the most vague and extensive meaning, applied indiscriminately to almost every thing that is pleasing, either to the sense, the imagination, or the understanding." It is predicated of diverse phenomena, Knight emphasizes, "to a problem, a syllogism, or a period, as familiarly, and ... as correctly as to a rose, a landscape, or a woman" (AI Intro 6). Diverse its applications might be, but this does not change the fact that all beauty results from the "sensuous pleasure" afforded by a "moderate and varied irritation of the organic nerves," and if the transitions of color are "too violent and sudden" or the contrast of light and shade "too vigorous and abrupt" then the irritation will be too strong and the effect painful or unpleasant; concomitantly, if the same effects are "too monotonous and feeble," the irritation will be "flat and insipid, and the sensation too languid to be pleasing" (AI 1.5.9). In short "visible beauty," or beauty to sense, consists in "harmonious, but yet brilliant and contrasted combinations of light, shade, and colour; blended, but not confused; and broken, but not cut, into masses: and it is not peculiarly in straight or curve, taper or spiral, long or short, little or great objects, that we are to seek from these; but in such as display to the eye intricacy of parts and variety of tint and surface" (AI 1.5.16).

On the basis of this theory Knight concludes that the picturesque is a particular kind of beauty that gives sensual pleasure by virtue of the play of light and color on the organ of sight. It is, as Gilpin insisted, beauty "capable of being *illustrated by painting*" or "*after the manner of painters*" (AI 2.2.17), but what an artist does in effect is to imitate the visible qualities of objects that contain the roughness and ruggedness that irritate the eye and bring pleasure. Thus the figures and objects that (in Knight's ironic words) "Mr. Price has so elegantly described as picturesque" (AI 1.5.17) actually qualify as beautiful: shaggy animals, irregular trees, broken foliage, ruined buildings, agitated streams, and massy rocks. Knight then marshals support for his claim by appealing to the history of landscape painting. Early painting, he argues, fancifully but persuasively, was slavishly imitative, distinguishing individual blades of grass, leaves on a tree, or hairs of the head. Artists soon realized, however, that this method did not make for a "true" representation at all, because it failed to reflect what the eye *actually* sees when it takes in objects at a distance; not, that is, individual elements, but the "masses," which in visual experience compose the sweep of lawn, an entire tree, or a whole human figure. Thus the "mode of imitation was changed," Knight speculates, "as this *massing* gave breadth to the light and shadows, mellowed them into each other, and enabled the artist to break and blend them together" (AI 2.2.21). The conclusion to this process – beginning with Giorgione (c. 1477/8–1510), perfected by Titian (c. 1488/90–1576), and exemplified by Claude – is that particular style of representing objects and compositions of objects that we call picturesque, characterized by hazy lines, blended colors, a "playful and airy kind of lightness, and a sort of loose and sketchy indistinctness not observable in the reality" (AI 2.2.20).

Knight's identification of beauty with the qualities of contrast, break, and intricacy, goes to the heart of his disagreement with Burke and his "leading disciple" (as Knight describes Price), both of whom made the mistake of equating beauty with smoothness and identifying that quality as the primary source of pleasure. Smoothness, Knight emphasizes, is not a part of visual experience at all but "properly a quality perceivable only by touch" (AI 1.5.10), and only "applied metaphorically" to the sense of sight and then "very improperly" (AI 1.5.11). Even in the realm of the tactile, moreover, beyond warmth and coolness, the pleasures of smoothness are few and far between. The "elegant author," namely, Burke, Knight writes in his characteristically acerbic way, "... has expatiated upon the gratifications of feeling smooth and undulating surfaces in general: but, I believe, these gratifications have been confided to himself; and probably to his own imagination acting through the medium of his favorite system" (AI 1.3.1).[20] This improper application of terms has the unfortunate effect of glossing what would be obvious to anyone who has grasped what brings pleasure to the eye: a surface might be smooth to the touch, Knight emphasizes, but that does not make it smooth to sight, which depends at the level of sensation on the "sharp, harsh, and angular reflections of light upon the eye" (AI 1.5.11). Smoothness is a phenomenological deception, for what the eye perceives as "smooth" – Gilpin's *marmoreum aequor*, for example, the surface of polished metal, or the sleek coat of an animal – actually consists of impressions that are "harsh and edgy" (L 20). The same is true of Brownian landscapes with their level lawns, winding canals, and shaven banks,

---

[20] Knight considers this erroneous equation of smoothness with beauty to be an example of the common error to mistake a specific "sexual sympathy" – the erotic quality of smooth skin – for a general principle: the quality occupies a fixed and narrow space of human experience, but once isolated it forms part of complex chains of association and becomes a powerful influence on other areas of human life, philosophical aesthetics included (AI 1.3.2).

all of which might be called smooth, but actually consist of harsh, discordant shapes, broken by lines and diversified by light and shade all of which irritate the eye. The only objects that Knight is willing to admit might come close to being visibly smooth are the monotonously green billiard table and bowling green, but he doubts that many would actually "find much beauty in either of these objects" (AI 1.5.14). Beauty and the picturesque, then, are really inseparable because at the level of sight the qualities of both are one and the same. The picturesque is simply the name we give to that particular kind of beauty "after the manner of painters," an artistic style that represents the world on canvas or describes it in words by way of the rough and rugged qualities corresponding to the reflections of light that irritate the eye. Notwithstanding Price raising it to rival the beautiful and the sublime, this is precisely what it had meant from the beginning, and Knight is really showing how and why it acquired that meaning in the first place.

Because this view of the picturesque is based on the function of the eye, we can think of it, as previously suggested, as the sense-picturesque (or the "merely picturesque" as Knight calls it [AI 2.2.27]) and the pleasure it provides is available to anybody with well-functioning organs of sight that are properly irritated by the objects represented by the artist. Knight, however, considers this to be a narrow definition of "picturesque" and, despite a disparaging reference to Alison (AI 2.3.49n), he suggests that the wider and more usual meaning of the term involves the addition of principles of association through which the mind (in the form of imagination) combines ideas. Knight regards association as something that begins at an early age and becomes so "spontaneous and rapid" in adult life as to be mechanical and largely beyond any direct influence or control: "those ideas, which we have once associated, associating themselves again in our memories of their own accord; and presenting themselves together to our notice, whether we will or not" (AI 2.2.1). These trains of thought might begin with some painful thought that produces a pleasant chain of association or, on the contrary, begin with a pleasant memory that generates an unpleasant series of associations. In addition, the extent and intensity of associations vary among people according to "natural constitutions of their minds and bodies" (AI 2.2.2), "vivacity of spirits" (AI 2.2.6), and power of memory, and will vary with the effects of intoxication and physical states.

Unlike the case of sense-picturesque, which brings pleasure through the faculty of sense alone, the association-picturesque involves the gratification of intellect: its power to contrast, expand, imitate, discriminate, and above all compare one idea of an object with another.[21] The pleasure of the picturesque arises

---

[21] Cf. Stewarts's observation that many objects called picturesque by Price and Gilpin are so in a *"poetical sense"* (236), that is, not in terms of what is "actually represented; but what sets the imagination at work, in forming pictures of its own; or, in other words, those parts of a picture where more is meant and suggested than meets the eye" (PE 236). Thus cattle grazing recall earlier impressions of similarly bucolic scenes, and a ruined castle conjures romantic ideas of ages past.

from "comparing nature and art," Knight proposes, through which "both the eye and the intellect acquire a higher relish for the productions of each; and the ideas excited by both, are invigorated, as well as refined, by being thus associated and contrasted" (AI 2.2.25). Those in the habit of viewing pictures will take pleasure in seeing objects in nature that have inspired the artistic representations of them, as well as the skill, taste, and genius of the artist who has imitated, combined, and embellished them in such striking ways. Correspondingly, viewing the objects on canvas will bring to mind the originals, which leads in turn back to their representations "through an improved medium – that of the feeling and discernment of a great artist" (AI 2.2.24). The picturesque proper is still a matter of beauty "after the manner of a painter," but something altogether richer, nuanced, and more complex than what can be obtained by sense alone.

Further, because the pleasure taken in the picturesque is primarily intellectual and based on association, "objects and circumstances called *picturesque* ... afford no pleasure, but to persons conversant with the art of painting, and sufficiently skilled in it to distinguish, and be really delighted with its real excellence" (AI 2.2.15). It can be felt fully only if one has acquired an appropriate stock of ideas and the alacrity of association to combine them, and the picturesque effectively becomes a realm of experience available to the connoisseur or true judge who has access to works of art and the leisure to appreciate them. "Such persons being in the habit of viewing, and receiving pleasure from fine pictures," Knight thus writes, "will naturally feel pleasure in viewing those objects in nature, which have called forth those powers of imitation and embellishment; and those combinations and circumstances of objects, which have guided those powers in their happiest exertions" (AI 2.2.24). There is, moreover, a "scale of enjoyment" due to the direct relationship between the ideas stored up in the mind and available for association and the degree of pleasure that the habit of association brings; the more extensive one's exposure to art, the richer the possible associations and greater the corresponding pleasure. For as "all the pleasures of intellect arise from the association of ideas," Knight observes, "the more the materials of association are multiplied, the more will the sphere of these pleasures be enlarged. To a mind richly stored, almost every object of nature or art, that presents itself to the senses, either excites fresh trains and combinations of ideas, or vivifies and strengthens those which existed before: so that recollection enhances enjoyment, and enjoyment brightens recollection" (AI 2.2.12).

It is worth noting that Knight's description of the picturesque effectively (though perhaps unknowingly) reiterates Hume's point about art being a double-edged sword. On the one hand, it has the power (in Hume's language) to "convert" what is otherwise ugly and painful into something beautiful and pleasurable. For Knight, this transformation occurs because the painter separates out and displays only those qualities that are pleasing to the eye in terms of the appropriate degree and mode of light and color; qualities displeasing to the eye (albeit pleasing to other senses or faculties) are simply dispelled.

It is for this reason that otherwise unpleasant objects – decayed trees, rotten thatch, crumbling plaster, tatty clothes, and market tables of meat and fish – are rendered beautiful because light and colors combine in a "harmonious" and "brilliant" way (AI 1.5.18). On the other hand, this conversion is only possible because artists represent the real and manipulate their images for effect. Knight's painters trade in "imitative deceptions," and take their stand with Hume's poets who are "liars by profession." As ventriloquists deceive the ear by throwing their voice, so do painters deceive the eye by giving a "semblance" of things, of depth and distance on a flat surface, for example, that only ever resembles what is real (AI 1.5.17).

HUMPHRY REPTON

The art of deception that Knight sees as part and parcel of the particular kind of beauty called picturesque finds its most complete expression in the figure of Humphry Repton, who dedicated a good deal of his adult life to the theory and practice of landscape gardening. He began his career in 1788, at the relatively late age of thirty-six after trying his hand unsuccessfully at a variety of occupations including textile merchant and transport entrepreneur.[22] He soon established a reputation and over the next thirty years carried out more than four hundred commissions for leading figures of British landed society, and more than succeeded in his ambition of becoming the "successor" to Kent and Brown. Unlike Gilpin, Price, and Knight (even granting that the latter two practiced their principles on estates of their own), Repton's attention to the picturesque and other aesthetic matters is inspired less by a deep interest in their philosophical underpinnings, than by the concerns of a "professor," namely, a professional engaged in the practical business of improvement.[23] It is true that he

---

[22] For a biography of Repton's life and career, see Stephen Daniels, *Humphry Repton: Landscape Gardening and the Geography of Georgian England* (New Haven, CT: Yale University Press, 1999).

[23] The writings most pertinent in the present context are Humphry Repton, *A Letter to Uvedale Price, Esq.* (London, 1794), later published as a footnote to the appendix of *Sketches and Hints* (LUP); *Sketches and Hints on Landscape Gardening. Collected from Designs and Observations Now in the Possession of the Different Noblemen and Gentlemen, for Whose Use They Were Originally Made. The Whole Tending to Establish Fixed Principles in the Art of Laying Out Ground* (London, 1795) (SH); and *Observations on the Theory and Practice of Landscape Gardening. Including Some Remarks on the Grecian and Gothic Architecture, Collected from Various Manuscripts, in the Possession of the Different Noblemen and Gentlemen, for Whose Use They Were Originally Written. The Whole Tending to Establish Fixed Principles in the Respective Art of Laying Out Ground* (London, 1803) (O). All references are to pagination of the 1840 edition of Repton's *Works: The Landscape Gardening and Landscape Architecture of the Late Humphry Repton, Esq. Being His Entire Works on These Subjects. A New Edition: with an Historical and Scientific Introduction, a Systematic Analysis, a Biographical Notice, Notes, and a Copious Alphabetical Index. By J.C. Loudon, F.L.S.* (London: Longman & Co.; Edinburgh: A. & C. Black, 1840).

draws easily on the language of the tradition (he cites Gerard's *Essay on Taste* as well as Burke, with whom he corresponded), and clearly regards his art to be governed by principles of human nature no less than the "other polite arts" pursued by painter, sculpture, or poet: "true taste in *landscape gardening*," as he writes in his first major work, *Sketches and Hints on Landscape Gardening*, in a far echo of Locke and a nearer one of Knight, is "not an accidental effect, operating on the outward senses, but an appeal to the understanding, which is able to compare, to separate, and to combine, the various sources of pleasure derived from external objects, and to trace them to some pre-existing causes in the structure of the human mind" (SH 38). This notwithstanding, Repton's contribution to the picturesque is driven overwhelmingly by the practical busi-ness of landscape design and effecting successful improvements on the estates of his clients. For this reason his "theoretical" observations read as inferences drawn from professional experience, couched as general rules to guide the gar-dener's art. Much of Repton's published writings are summaries or verbatim reproductions of material contained in the "Red Books" (so called from the Moroccan leather in which they were bound) that he would compile for com-missions, each being an amalgam of site-specific plans and sketches for the proposed improvement and interspersed with more general observations on the theory and practice of landscape gardening.

Repton coins the term *landscape gardening* to underscore the "affinity" between painting and gardening, and to distinguish his art from the nar-row associations with horticulture, thus expanding the meaning of "English Gardening" to emphasize that displaying "native beauties ... with advantage" requires viewing scenery as if arranged in a picture or (to use Gilpin's phrase) through the lens of the picturesque eye. On the one hand, the meeting of gar-dener and painter speaks to the practical side of landscaping, emphasizing that its progress requires elements only the artist can provide. "I have adopted the term *Landscape Gardening*," Repton reports, "as most proper, because the art can only be advanced and perfected by the united powers of the *land-scape painter* and the *practical gardener*" (SH 29). Most obviously, the painting or sketch works as a blueprint and imaginative projection of the proposed changes, and enables the landscape gardener to grasp the effects of otherwise isolated elements – a hill raised, a lake created, trees planted – as they compose a whole. Repton's writing is correspondingly replete with the language of fore-ground, middle, and background; of screens and contrasts; and the "balance of composition" that indicate the artistic representation of space (SH 89).

On the other hand, uniting gardening and painting reveals that the effects of "improving" scenery are achieved not by presenting or reproducing nature as it is found, but representing it as ideally conceived. The "perfection of land-scape gardening," as Repton expresses the thought, "depends on a conceal-ment of those operations of *art* by which *nature* is embellished" (SH 52). It is the "business of taste, in all the polite arts, to avail itself of stratagems, by which the imagination may be deceived," Repton writes, and the landscape gardener is one with poet and painter in seeking to "seduce the mind to believe their fictions" (SH 76). It is the *sine qua non* of the improver's art to gloss the real with the apparent, to fool eye and mind with invention: a hill built to raise the ground, banks of a brook opened to form a river, a damn built to create a lake, or fences removed to produce "imaginary extent" (SH 76). The mind is not offended by these pleasing deceptions, Repton emphasizes, any more than it is repelled by characters in a tragedy known to be fictional; the characters of literature and artifice of the improved landscape must "look natural" to give pleasure, and in both cases it is "enough, if so much as we are shewn of the character appears to be a just resemblance of nature" (SH 77). This deception is evident in the four elements that Repton enumerates as goals of landscape gardening and distinguish it from its older counterpart: to hide natural defects and display the natural beauties of every situation, give the appearance of extent and freedom by disguising or hiding boundaries, conceal the means of art by which scenery is improved, and to remove objects of mere convenience or comfort if they cannot be blended with the environment or made ornamental (SH 84).

Although the notion of landscape gardening exploits the affinity between gardener and painter, Repton at once underscores the differences between the painterly and picturesque eye, the divergence of a "scene in nature" from a "picture on canvas." Painters can vary their creations at will – place a blasted oak or romantic church where the gardener is faced with a recalcitrant lawn or gravel path – but they are also limited by the principles of art: a two-dimensional canvas; prescribed materials and techniques; the "fixed state" to which they are frozen in time and place and that determines the effects of season, weather, light, and shade. The gardener, by comparison, is free: "in motion" (SH 96) and at liberty to take different views of the same landscape, including those that confound and contort the painter's art, such as the instant foreshortening of looking down a steep hill, Repton muses, one of the most pleasurable features of natural scenery. There is also, at bottom, a difference in perspective between the imagined landscape of the painterly eye and the view of an actual scene – the way light reflects on water, for example, or the appearance of white objects in the landscape – which the gardener must regard with a view to their real and permanent effects (SH 75–6). In short, a landscape might be the proper subject for a painter, but it is the prospect with which the gardener is occupied and in which the viewer of nature delights. Thus, at Matlock Bath, Repton points out in a direct response to an example raised by Price, visitors are only satisfied when they have seen the town from a bird's-eye view that "no painting can represent." In the final analysis, painting and gardening are not sister arts (as Price and Knight had urged) but "congenial natures" brought together in a marriage (LUP 19).

These differences between gardening and painting provide the context in which to appreciate Repton's view of the picturesque, which he articulates in response to the criticism leveled at him (and his Brownian principles) first by

Knight in *The Landscape* and then by Price. Both Knight and Price knew of
Repton, and met him personally in 1789 when he was engaged by the owner of
Ferney Hall, an estate just over the border into Shropshire and close to Knight,
who took a personal interest in the prospect of improvements so close to home.
Initially, both saw in Repton a potential ally, and Price was so impressed that
he helped him secure commissions early in his career. Early enthusiasm turned
to dismay, however, when the plans for Ferney and other estates appeared and
as Repton's resumé and stature grew. Knight communicated his displeasure
by letter before he published *The Landscape*, and Price accused him publicly
of being only a "defender of Mr. Brown" (LHR 30), one of those "Brownists"
who have been "universally and professedly, smoothers, shavers, clearers, lev-
elers, and dealers in distinct serpentine lines and edges" (LHR 71–2).[24] Repton
was none too pleased. He had obtained an advance copy of Price's *Essay on the
Picturesque* and read it while traveling in Derbyshire. His swift response was
published and distributed as *A Letter to Uvedale Price, Esq.*, which inspired
Price in turn to compose *A Letter to Humphry Repton, Esq.* that grew to such
length (some eight times longer than Repton's original rebuttal) that it came to
form a "supplement" to the *Essay*. The tone of debate among the three interlocutors (Price and Knight had their own quarrel as well) is sometimes personal and points of disagreement often petty, exemplified best by Knight's use
of Repton's unpublished Red Book for Tatton Park (he had come across it on
display in a London bookshop to promote *Sketches and Hints*) to charge him
unfairly with urging the owners of the estate to place their family arms on local
turnpike milestones. Repton was more than justified in complaining of being
misrepresented, but this did not stop him from accusing Price in turn of steal-
ing ideas from his Red Book for Wembley.[25]

   If one moves beyond the personal and petty, however, it is easy to discern
the real differences between Price and Knight (philosophers and gentlemen
farmers) on one side, and Repton (practically minded professional) on the
other. Throughout the debates, Repton emphasizes the broad agreement
among all three of them with respect to their general principles,[26] but he at

---

[24] Sir Uvedale Price, *A Letter to H. Repton, Esq., on the Application of the Practice As Well as
   the Principles of Landscape-Painting to Landscape-Gardening. Intended As a Supplement to
   the "Essay on the Picturesque," to Which Is Prefixed Mr. Repton's Letter to Mr. Price* (London:
   J. Robson, 1795). Repton's *A Letter to Uvedale Price, Esq.* (London: G. Nicol, 1794) had
   appeared the year before and was later reprinted as a footnote to the appendix of *Sketches
   and Hints*. All references are to both letters as they appear in Price, *Essays on the Picturesque*,
   vol. 3 (LHR and LUP).

[25] For a historical recounting of the relations and squabbles among Knight, Price, and Repton,
   see Daniels, *Humphry Repton*, ch. 3, and for a detailed assessment of the theoretical differences informing them, the latter chapters in Hipple, *The Beautiful, the Sublime, & the
   Picturesque*.

[26] See LUP 3 and Humphry Repton, *An Inquiry into the Changes of Taste in Landscape
   Gardening. To Which is Added Some Observations of Its Theory and Practice, Including a
   Defence of that Art* (1806), in *Works*, 353ff. (ICT).

once insists in a principled and sustained way that landscape gardening is governed by its own set of considerations, which often dictate departing from or simply rejecting what the picturesque eye might otherwise recommend. At the same time, he is not beyond accusing Price and Knight of a false taste born of living among picturesque scenes unavailable except to the privileged few, itself indicative of the precarious position that Repton occupied with respect to the politics of landownership and use that surrounded the picturesque: Repton saw a clear connection between improvement, pleasure, beauty, and private property and had no qualms in extending his own cottage garden in Essex to enclose what was common land, but was quick to criticize the *nouveaux riche* for doing the same when they contravened the aesthetic principles of landscape gardening.[27] Hypocrisy under a different name this might be, but for Repton such worries disappear, if they ever surfaced at all, in emphasizing the importance of aesthetic considerations above all others.

Thus, paramount for Repton is the fact that in the practical business of improvement, critics have failed in "duly considering the *degree* of affinity betwixt painting and gardening" (SH 95, emphasis added). Consider the lines Repton quotes from Knight's *The Landscape*:

> The quarry long neglected, and o'ergrown
> With thorns, that hang o'er mouldering beds of stone,
> May oft the place of natural rocks supply,
> And frame the verdant picture to the eye;
> Or, closing round the solitary seat,
> Charm with the simple scene of calm retreat. (II 260–5)
> …
> Bless'd is the man in whose sequester'd glade,
> Some ancient abbey's walls diffuse their shade;
> With mouldering windows pierced, and turrets crown'd,
> And pinnacles with clinging ivy bound.
> Bless'd too is he, who, 'midst his tufted trees,
> Some ruin'd castle's lofty towers sees;
> Imbosom'd high upon the mountain's brow,
> Or nodding o'er the stream that glides below.
> Nor yet unenvy'd, to whose humbler lot
> Falls the retired and antiquated cot; –
> Its roof with weeds and mosses cover'd o'er,
> And honeysuckles climbing round the door;
> While mantling vines along its walls are spread,
> And clustering ivy decks the chimney's head. (II 280–93)

---

[27] For an excellent discussion of this issue, see David Worrall, "Agrarians against the Picturesque: Ultra-radicalism and the revolutionary politics of land," in *The Politics of the Picturesque*, ed. Stephen Copley and Peter Garside (Cambridge: Cambridge University Press, 1994), 240–60.

Images of a more picturesque cast it is hard to imagine, and that they are charming in a poem or picture Repton freely acknowledges, but that does not qualify them as proper subject matter for the gardener, let alone models from which to work. A quarry long neglected might be a suitable home for swallows and martens, the mouldering abbey a haven for ravens and jackdaws, a ruined castle ideal for bats and owls, and even the antiquated cot "may perhaps yield a residence for squalid misery and want"; they remain, however, "situations ill-adapted to the residence of man" (SH 100). (Even Gilpin, we might recall, hardly found the living conditions furnished by the ruins of Tintern Abbey charming, and escaped quickly to more pleasant vistas further down the Wye.) The same is true of urging the growth of wild vines and weeds around a residence. These are picturesque in a painting and even in keeping with the wild woods beyond a house, but they are hardly desirable as a view from one's drawing-room window, and the gardener who knows his duty will replace them with "trim mown grass and swept gravel-walk," however much abhorred these are by the painter (SH 101). People do not live in the fantastic scenes depicted on canvas as they do in the real world created by the gardener; "a dwelling-place is an object of comfort and convenience, for the purposes of habitation," Repton points out, "and not merely the frame to a landscape, or the foreground of a rural picture" (SH 99). For this reason "utility must often take the lead of beauty, and convenience be preferred to picturesque effect, in the neighbourhood of man's habitation" (SH 99). Repton simply refuses to admit Price's distinction between picturesqueness and beauty into landscape gardening at all because the latter involves a set of considerations remote from the concerns of painting and requires arranging objects in ways that fall beyond the representative powers of the painter. That phenomena fall beyond the limits of painting, however, does not affect their beauty in a landscape, for "*in whatever relates to man, propriety and convenience are not less objects of good taste, than picturesque effect*," Repton writes, "and a beautiful garden scene is not more defective because it would not look well on a canvas, than a didactic poem because it neither furnishes a subject for the painter or the musician" (LUP 6).

This emphasis on the practical dimensions of landscape gardening goes to the heart of Repton's view of the picturesque and explains his reaction to what he regards as unjust attacks by Price and Knight, who cast him into the company of Brown and his school. Repton is careful to distinguish himself from those who claim to continue Brown's principles – "Brown *copied Nature*," he writes at one point, "his illiterate followers *copied him*" (ICT 327) – and credits Price and Knight for exempting him from the "tasteless herd of Mr. Brown's followers" (LUP 4). At the same time, he is not shy in praising the "immortal Brown" (HS 30) and the "innumerable beauties in that self-taught master" (LUP 8) – especially his use of water features exemplified at Blenheim (SH 77) – and is more than willing to defend his clumping of trees and use of belts to enclose a park (LUP 10ff. and ICT 334ff.). That some nurserymen or laborers have badly copied his designs does not impugn Brown's own practice or remove any considerations of propriety and convenience that governed it.

Repton's defense of Brown does not have the hollow ring of dogmatism so much as solid sounds of a pragmatist who has "learned by practice" (LUP 17) and must forego the luxury of relying exclusively on a single principle, aesthetic or otherwise, in an art than demands knowledge of surveying, mechanics, hydraulics, agriculture, botany, and architecture. There is also a range of sources that give pleasure in landscape gardening (he lists sixteen in all), four of which – congruity, utility, order, and symmetry – are "generally *adverse* to picturesque beauty" (SH 112, emphasis added).[28] Gardening, moreover, "must include the two opposite characters of native wildness, and artificial comfort," Repton writes, but each will be "adapted to the genius and character of the place" (SH 102), which dictates possibilities and choice: the shape and species of the available species of trees; the extant scenery and shape of the ground (whether concave, convex, plane, or inclined plane); the play of shadow and light on a building; and whether consequently the horizontal lines of the Gothic should prevail over the perpendicular of the Grecian, or whether the two should be combined. Repton is willing to condemn the uniformity and sameness characteristic of avenues of trees (beloved by Brown) because they destroy variety and novelty and often obscure more interesting features of the landscape, but he also recognizes that avenues contain elements that gratify the mind's love of order, unity, antiquity, greatness of parts, and continuity, and that simply cutting down the trees in the name of the rugged and rough, although an easy solution, does not always improve the prospect. The same flexibility is apparent in Repton's approach to the use of symmetry and straight lines – despised in principle by Gilpin, Price, and Knight – which might have a place if useful, as in small flower gardens in front of a greenhouse or in an orangery where irregularity would be an affectation. Symmetrical designs should neither contradict the natural shape of the land nor extend beyond the human artifices near a house – a walk or fence, for example – but landscaping near regularly shaped buildings should involve lines that reflect the immediate vicinity, otherwise, Repton observes, the house would appear "twisted and awry" (SH 87).

Repton does not reject the picturesque out of hand, but justifies his criticism of it practically, modifying its principles and the aesthetic it circumscribes in light of demands made upon the landscaper gardener. It is understandable, then, that he should feel attacked unfairly by the "unprovoked sally of Mr. Knight's wit" (LUP 21), and see in Price's censure an assault on the "very existence" of his profession. Repton inspired criticism, perhaps, less because he was prepared to defend Brown, but because in doing so he offered a frank assessment and statement of the limits imposed by adopting and slavishly

---

[28] The other sources Repton lists are picturesque effect, intricacy, simplicity, variety, novelty, contrast, continuity, association, grandeur, appropriation, animation, and seasons and times of day (SH 112–13).

adhering to a single aesthetic view, whether the "*genius* of the bare and bold" or "capable of being illustrated by painting." As an aesthetic category, the picturesque has not disappeared entirely, but it is a pale ghost of its former self, condemned to roam with only the memories of its past glory for company. If Gilpin heralds the rise of the picturesque, and Price and Knight announce its mature form, then Repton surely portends its fall, to be realized, as we shall see, in its self-overcoming first as the Romantic sublime and then in its truth as a moral category. The fate of the picturesque and its connection to a time and a place in which it had already grown old, is captured perfectly and with an appropriately gloomy pathos, in the images conjured by William Wordsworth of Price who, in his final years, personified the aesthetic he championed, and became at the end a sort of anachronism of his own doomed experiment: "striding up the steep sides of his wood-crowned hills, with his hacker, *i.e.* his sylvan Hanger [a short cutlass-like sword used by woodsmen], slung from his shoulder, like Robin Hood's bow." On his final visit, only a year or so before Price's death (in 1829), Wordsworth described the eighty-one-year-old Price "as active in ranging about his woods as a setter dog"; not a greyhound, one might note, but a rough and therefore picturesque animal.[29]

[29] See Wordsworth to Samuel Rogers, January 21, 1825, and Wordsworth to unknown recipient, January 25, 1828, in *The Letters of William and Dorothy Wordsworth: The Later Years Part I 1821–1828*, 2nd ed., arr. and ed. Ernest de Selincourt; rev., arr., and ed. Alan G. Hill (Oxford: Clarendon Press, 1978), 175 and 290–1, respectively.

5

Wordsworth and the Early Romantics

Despite the efforts of Price and Knight to raise the picturesque to the stature of the beautiful and sublime, its fate as an aesthetic category was predicted, albeit unwittingly, by Gilpin, the ambiguities of his work like so many tea leaves from which the future state of things might be read. The intensity of debate surrounding it in the closing decades of the eighteenth century notwithstanding, the picturesque proved inherently unstable. It was to receive its startling swan song and dénouement in Ruskin (in whose hands it is transformed into a moral category), find its way tangentially (as the superiority of art to nature) into the writings of Oscar Wilde ("The Decay of Lying" and "The Critic as Artist") and James McNeill Whistler ("Ten O'Clock" Lecture), and to appear *en passant* in George Santayana (as the effect of interruption of symmetry by an interesting object); it was also deemed worthy of mention by Fry (in the artistic rearrangement of objects for emotional effect). Despite these persistent echoes, however, the picturesque was to lose its precarious and short-lived independence by being absorbed into the concept of sublimity developed by Wordsworth and the "early" Romantics, a term employed here to distinguish them from the "late" Romanticism of Hazlitt and Ruskin. There are facets of the picturesque and elements of the debates considered in the last chapter that hint at this, its protosublime character, and go some way to explaining its instability and eventual demise; the picturesque finds its culmination and full expression only when it capitulates to its more powerful aesthetic kin.

There are two general points worth emphasizing in this regard. First, the picturesque finds its characteristic mode of expression in the language of sight: the eye views scenes arranged (by imagination or in reality) for effect according to compositional rules abstracted from painting. At the same time, the picturesque also involves a viewer who sees and in whom pleasure arises, and it is on this side of the duality that the philosophical spirit of Romanticism settles: it emphasizes not the object viewed, but the subject viewing, the being who actively experiences and is moved by a profound state of mind (the sublime). This inward turn, as we might appropriately call it, is not invented by the Romantics; it was present throughout the eighteenth century's ontology of aesthetic qualities, and clearly adumbrated in the philosophical treatment of the picturesque, notably by Knight in the *Analytic Inquiry* who charges Price with committing the "great fundamental error" of "seeking for distinctions in external objects, which only exist in the modes and habits of viewing and considering them" (AI 2.2.74). This being said, with Romanticism comes a distinct emphasis if not on the subject per se, then on the subject's emotional state, and a conspicuous shift to a newly idealized view of nature as the occasion for the affective response of the subject: nature is no longer constrained by the myopic lens of the picturesque eye, but appears, as if through a visionary haze, in her wild state, in which – to recall Addison's early and memorable description of the sublime – restraints fall away and the unbounded imagination is free to grasp at objects "too big for its Capacity" and "flung into a pleasing Astonishment at such unbounded Views, ... feel a delightful Stillness and Amazement in the Soul at the Apprehension of them" (3:540, no. 412). For this conceptual shift, credit should go to the picturesque, for, as Alison had recognized a decade before the turn of the new century, to landscape painting and the aesthetic it occasioned goes credit for "awakening our taste to natural Beauty, and in determining it," free, moreover, of the influence of foreign models and the assumed inferiority of the domestic British landscape (*Essays* 302–3). With this in mind, we might say that the picturesque was a victim of its own success.

Second, in addition to its characteristic language, the picturesque centers around the qualities of the rough and the rugged, and the objects at the heart of its iconic images – the blasted oak, craggy peak, and Gothic ruin – transfer seamlessly into the fabric of Romanticism. Gilpin and Price had both emphasized, albeit in different ways and to different ends, how the picturesque occupies an awkward place between the beautiful and the sublime, and Gilpin was inspired to admit not only that the picturesque involves a sensation of pleasure felt by the subject, but also that it is "enthusiastic" and consists of a "*deliqium* of the soul" (TE 49–50). The idea of picturesque pleasure, in other words, already included elements of the sublime from which it could never free or disassociate itself. When faced with the shift of emphasis from object to subject, and from nature constrained by rules of art to nature wild and untamed, the picturesque is confronted with the truth of its own inner nature, and sees in Romanticism the realization of a fate already written, albeit in small and indistinct letters, by Gilpin and the debates he inspired.

WILLIAM WORDSWORTH

The year 1798 has long been considered a watershed in the history of English poetry, marking as it did the publication of *Lyrical Ballads*, the innovative collaboration between the young William Wordsworth (1770–1850) and Samuel Taylor Coleridge (1772–1834), the two having met in Bristol in 1795 when both were still in their twenties. For the history of aesthetics, however,

1800 is a more significant date, it being the year when Wordsworth added "a few words of introduction" that formed the Preface and appendix to the second edition (revised and enlarged for the third edition in 1802), in which he attempted a theoretical defense of his and (to some extent and ambiguously) Coleridge's artistic intentions; the result has become at least as famous as the poems it explicates.[1] It is generally acknowledged that although the Preface is an original essay in aesthetics insofar as it contains Wordsworth's reflections on poetry and his own creative process, the philosophical ideas it contains are drawn entirely from the eighteenth-century tradition, the main elements of which had become not only familiar but also commonplace by 1800; this is true even if, as the editors of the standard edition of Wordsworth's prose writings remark, it is "only rarely possible to point to specific sources."[2] This assessment of "specific sources" with respect to the Preface might well be a fair one, but there is good reason to emphasize the specific and ubiquitous presence of the picturesque as a deep and pervasive influence on Wordsworth's aesthetic thought. The preceding assessment notwithstanding, the Preface becomes a clearer and perhaps more interesting document when understood as presupposing and expressing views born of Wordsworth's engagement with picturesque literature. His relationship to the tradition is complex, not least because he shares its sentiments and often draws on its language while excoriating the narrow parameters of its principles and exposing its limitations for expressing the powerful emotions inspired by the natural world. Wordsworth develops what we might call a *natural picturesque* that rejects the emphasis on compositional rules and the rearrangement (metaphorical or actual) of the natural world in conformity with them, urging instead that aesthetic value be sought in nature outside of a picture and unimproved, the proper expression of which is the sublime.

Wordsworth and the Picturesque

Wordsworth witnessed the height of picturesque mania, including the popular discovery of his beloved Lake District and its environs, which by the turn of the century had become a favorite and well-established destination for middle-class tourists who made the journey north seeking the pleasures of nature armed with their Claude Glass and a variety of guidebooks replete with the language and principles of picturesque beauty.[3] Wordsworth was steeped in writings on the subject, both popular and philosophical: he was a longtime admirer

---

[1] Almost as well-known is the preface to the *Poems* of 1815 in which Wordsworth distinguishes *fancy* from *imagination*. For reasons that will become clear, I discuss this part of Wordsworth's contribution in connection to Coleridge in the next section of the current chapter.

[2] See the editors' general introduction in *The Prose Works of William Wordsworth*, ed. W. J. B. Owen and Jane Washington Smyser, 3 vols. (Oxford: Clarendon Press, 1974), 1:111–14.

[3] For the rise of the Lakes as a tourist destination, see Hussey, *The Picturesque*, 97ff.

of Gilpin's work,[4] and read Knight's *The Landscape* in 1800 and the *Analytic Inquiry* with Coleridge sometime around 1806; their copy with extensive marginalia survives.[5] In his review of Wordsworth's *The Exursion* (1814), moreover, Hazlitt, with his customary insight, recognized the picturesque elements of Wordsworth's aesthetic: "Here are no dotted lines, no hedge-row beauties, no box-tree borders, no gravel walks, no square mechanic enclosures. All is left loose and irregular in the rude chaos of aboriginal nature."[6] Wordsworth also carried on a long acquaintance with Price, both at a distance through the latter's work (Dorothy Wordsworth reports that her brother had read the *Essay* by 1806)[7] and personally through their mutual friend Sir George Beaumont at whose estate at Coleorton in Leicestershire they were both frequent visitors (Price had given Beaumont advice on landscaping his grounds). Wordsworth declares that he never felt close enough to call Price a "friend," but he was a guest at Foxley for visits of up to a few days on at least three occasions in 1811, 1824, and 1827 (and from which his picturesque descriptions of Price quoted at the end of the last chapter originate). There is also evidence that the two men exchanged letters on a range of subjects (aesthetics and the picturesque included) between 1806 and 1827, though sadly none of this correspondence seems to have survived.[8]

The fact that Wordsworth knew the picturesque literature is hardly evidence that he embraced its contents, any more than his long acquaintance with

---

[4] Evidence suggests that Wordsworth first read Gilpin in 1787 (*Observations on the Mountains, and Lakes of Cumberland, and Westmoreland*) and continued to do so for the next thirteen years, through 1810 (*Observations on the River Wye*). See Duncan Wu, *Wordsworth's Reading 1770–1799* (Cambridge: Cambridge University Press, 1993), 66–7, and *Wordsworth's Reading 1800–1815* (Cambridge: Cambridge University Press, 1993), 93.

[5] The copy of the *Analytic Inquiry* belonged to Coleridge, although the marginalia – largely critical and often dismissive to the point of contempt – are in Wordsworth's hand. For a detailed discussion and reproduction of the written comments, see Edna Astor Shearer, "Wordsworth and Coleridge Marginalia in a Copy of Richard Payne Knight's *Analytic Inquiry into the Principles of Taste*," *Huntington Library Quarterly* 1, 1 (1937): 63–99. Coleridge also mentions Knight disparagingly in his *Lectures on Shakespeare* of 1808, and in *Principles of Genial Criticism* (1814), which is an attack on Knight in the spirit of Kant (though both go unnamed). See Wu, *Wordsworth's Reading 1800–1815*, who lists both 1806 and 1808 as suggested dates of reading of the *Analytic Inquiry*, and for the suggested date of reading for *The Landscape*, see *Wordsworth's Reading 1770–1799*, 123.

[6] William Hazlitt, "Character of Mr. Wordsworth's New Poem, *The Excursion*," *The Examiner*, August 21 and 28 and October 2, 1814, in *The Selected Writings of William Hazlitt*, ed. Duncan Wu, 9 vols. (London: Pickering and Chatto, 1998), 2:325–40, p. 325. See ch. 6.

[7] See Dorothy Wordsworth to Lady Beaumont, January 19, 1806, *The Letters of William and Dorothy Wordsworth: The Middle Years Part I 1806–1811*, 2nd ed., arr. and ed. Ernest de Selincourt; rev. Mary Moorman (Oxford: Clarendon Press, 1969), 3. Wu, *Wordsworth's Reading 1800–1815*, suggests that Wordsworth read the *Essay* both by mid-January 1806 and again in 1809–10, as well as a manuscript of Price's *Essay on Decorations near the House* sometime after January 19, 1806.

[8] See John R. Nabholtz, "Wordsworth's *Guide to the Lakes* and the Picturesque Tradition," *Modern Philology* 61, 4 (1964): 288–97, p. 290n8.

Price is an indication that he accepted the man's principles or approved of the landscaping carried out in their name; there is much to suggest the very opposite.[9] In a letter to Beaumont dated August 28, 1811, Wordsworth describes the day and a half he had recently spent at Foxley and reports how Price was "very kind and took due pains" showing him the "beauties of the place." Although he admits being out of sorts (upset in part by the "strange speech, looks, and manners" of Price's daughter), Wordsworth raises deep and principled objections to what Price had accomplished, suggesting above all – and reminiscent of the same charge made by Repton – that he had fallen victim to an obsession for the picturesque, which had blinded him to the beauties of nature and led to "improvements" that actually enervated further the already somewhat impoverished scenery. There is an ironic justice in this charge given, we might recall, that Price had criticized Gilpin for having "carried to excess" an "exclusive fondness for the picturesque." "Wanting both rock and water," Wordsworth writes of Foxley,

> it necessarily wants variety, and in a district of this kind, the portion of a Gentleman's estate which he keeps exclusively to himself, and which he devotes wholly or in part to ornament, may very easily exceed the proper bounds. … A man by little and little becomes so delicate and fastidious with respect to forms in scenery, where he has a power to exercise a controul [*sic*] over them, that if they do not exactly please him in all moods, and every point of view, his power becomes his law; he banishes one, and then rids himself of another, impoverishing and *monotonizing* Landscapes, which, if not originally distinguished by the bounty of Nature, must be ill able to spare the inspiriting varieties which Art, and the occupations and wants of life in a country left more to itself never fail to produce. This relish of humanity Foxley wants, and is therefore to me, in spite of all its recommendations, a melancholy spot – I mean that part of it which the owner keeps to himself, and has taken so much pains with.[10]

Wordsworth had this reaction to Foxley in 1810, but the view of the picturesque it expresses is evident much earlier in a note to a passage from *Descriptive Sketches* (1793). In rather pointed terms, he there condemns picturesque principles as wholly inadequate for expressing the profound feelings aroused by the grandeur of the Alps; only the language of the sublime, Wordsworth urges, can honor the scene of storm and sunset appropriately:

> 'Tis storm; and hid in mist from hour to hour
> All day the floods of deeper murmur pour,
> And mournful sounds, as if a Spirit lost,

---

[9] There is also evidence that Wordsworth and Price saw eye to eye on some aesthetic matters: Dorothy reports (to Lady Beaumont, January 19, 1806) that her brother not only "read Mr. Price's Book on the Picturesque" but "thinks that Mr. Price has been of great service in correcting the false taste of the layers out of Parks and Pleasure-grounds," and Wordsworth (to Lady Beaumont, June 3, 1806) reports receiving a letter from Price who "seems much pleased with what I said upon the sublime." See *Letters, Middle Years Part 1*, 3 and 35, respectively.

[10] Wordsworth to George Beaumont, August 28, 1811, *Letters, Middle Years Part 1*, 505–6.

Pipe wild along the hollow-blustering coast,
'Till the Sun Walking on his western field
Shakes from behind the clouds his flashing shield.
Triumphant on the bosom of the storm,
Glances the fire-clad eagle's wheeling form;
Eastward, in long perspective glittering, shine
The wood-crown'd cliffs that o'er the lake recline;
Wide o'er the Alps a hundred streams unfold,
At once to pillars turn'd that flame with gold;
Behind his sail the peasant strives to shun
The west that burns like one dilated sun,
Where in a mighty crucible expire
The mountains, glowing hot, like coals of fire.[11]

In the note added to this last line, however, Wordsworth says that he "had once given to these sketches the title of Picturesque; but the Alps are insulted," he retorts, "in applying to them that term." The language of the picturesque and its "cold rules of painting" are too narrow to capture the warm, expansive feelings such scenery inspires, and whoever chooses them, Wordsworth insists, "would give his reader but a very imperfect idea of those emotions which they [the sublime features of the Alps] have the irresistible power of communicating to the most impassive imaginations. The fact is," he concludes, "that controul-ing influence, which distinguishes the Alps from all other scenery, is derived from images which *disdain the pencil*" (emphasis added). Where Price looked at Foxley with the narrow lens of the picturesque eye and its attendant rules of composition, Wordsworth consulted nature and his feelings; he thus rejected the temptation to "make a picture of the scene" by casting the Alps in subdued light and shadow – the very features that gave Foxley its want of "humanity" and pall of "melancholy" – but instead flooded the mountains with a "deluge of light, or rather fire" that express the unity and grandeur of the scene.[12] As Wordsworth makes clear later in letters written in the mid-1820s, he does not deny that objects like the Alps are capable of being depicted on canvas, but resists adamantly the idea that they can be identified with the picturesque as if to be "like a picture" exhausted their aesthetic value. "Many objects are fit for the pencil which are not picturesque," he writes in a letter to Jacob Fletcher, " – but I have been in the habit of applying the word to such objects only as are so"; a month or so later to the same he explains this comment by refer-ring to "Italian Artists, in whom beauty and grace are predominant." These artists depict the Madonna and Holy Family and arrangements of still life, Wordsworth points out, all of which are fitted to the pencil, but "we never think

[11] *Descriptive Sketches by William Wordsworth*, ed. Sally Bushell, James A. Butler, Michael C. Jaye, and David García (Ithaca, NY: Cornell University Press, 2001) (1793), 70–2, lines 332–47.

[12] *Poetical Works*, 1:62n1. The footnote appears in the first (1793) version, but omitted in edi-tions from 1815 onward, including the final one of 1849 where the lines to which the note is attached are completely rewritten to become: "A crucible of mighty compass, felt / By moun-tains, glowing till they seem to melt" (283–4).

of [them] ... as picturesque – but shall I say as something higher – something that realizes the idealisms of our nature, and assists us in the formations of new ones."[13] Fundamentally, at the Alps and later at Foxley, what Wordsworth finds abhorrent is the limitations inherent to the language and principles of the picturesque and its inadequacy for expressing exulted emotions inspired by nature. The picturesque, moreover, lacks the advantage of poetry, which can (as Burke had insisted in the final part of the *Inquiry*) employ the more indefinite and sublime aspects of literary language in a quasipictorial way that prose, even in Gilpin's masterly descriptions, cannot approach.[14]

It is worth noting in this context that the strength of the language in *Descriptive Sketches* and elsewhere can be seen as a reaction on Wordsworth's part to his own experience of having succumbed to the charms of the picturesque and developed something of that "delicate and fastidious attention" he detected in Price. In lines from *The Prelude*, Wordsworth admits how from arrogance and slavish adherence to rules of aesthetic convention, he, too, came to suffer, albeit it briefly, from the same "infection of the age":

> O soul of Nature, that dost overflow
> With passion and with life, what feeble men
> Walk on this earth, how feeble have I been
> When thou wert in my strength! Nor this through stroke
> Of human suffering, such as justifies
> Remissness and inaptitude of mind,
> But through presumption, even in pleasure pleased
> Unworthily, disliking here, and there
> Liking, by rules of mimic art transferred
> To things above all art. But more – for this,
> Although a strong infection of the age,
> Was never much my habit – giving way
> To a comparison of scene with scene,
> Bent overmuch on superficial things,
> Pampering myself with meager novelties
> Of colour and proportion, to the moods
> Of Nature, and the spirit of the place,
> Less sensible.[15]

---

[13] See Letters to Jacob Fletcher Esquire, January 17 and February 25, 1825, in *Letters: Later Years* 1:303 and 321–2, respectively. In the latter, Wordsworth also observes that if certain objects that ordinarily disgust (insides of stables, dung carts, dunghills, and "foul and loathsome situations") might produce more agreeable effect upon canvas than in reality, and if so can be said to have picturesque qualities (322).

[14] In the preface of 1815, it is Milton and the Hebrew Bible – both antivisual – that Wordsworth regards as sublime in the highest degree. The visually oriented Greeks, by contrast, lack sublimity. I owe this observation to Adam Potkay.

[15] William Wordsworth, *The Prelude* XI (1805), in *William Wordsworth: The Prelude 1799, 1805, 1850*, ed. Jonathan Wordsworth, M. H. Abrams, and Stephen Hill (New York: W. W. Norton, 1979), 422–4, lines 102–21.

The change of heart from "rules of mimic art" to "moods" and "spirit" expressed here is also evident in "Lines composed a few miles above Tintern Abbey," which Wordsworth wrote while touring the Wye in the summer of 1798. The poem is famously a meditation on the narrator's return to a spot visited five years earlier and dramatizes the difference between youth and maturity and, for our purposes at least, the change of taste that the intervening years have brought. The theme and setting is tantalizing given that Wordsworth could hardly have looked on the scene then (and one assumes in 1793) without recalling Gilpin's impressions of the Abbey recorded some twenty years before (Gilpin was there in the summer of 1770); it is surely plausible that he had *Observations on the River Wye* in mind or even in hand while composing the lines. Whether the case or not, the poem is certainly replete with picturesque tropes, although, significantly, they are associated not with the man of 1798 but with the youth of 1793, a self as unrecoverable as the aesthetic sensibility it held; the poem "curls its way toward the word *sublime* and a redefinition of it," as one commentator characterizes the progress of the poem, "but it seems to open with the picturesque."[16] "Once again I see," Wordsworth's narrator declares, describing a correctly picturesque scene in language worthy of Gilpin,

> These hedgerows, hardly hedgerows, little lines
> Of sportive wood run wild; these pastoral farms
> Green to the very door; and wreaths of smoke
> Sent up, in silence, from among the trees,
> With some uncertain notice, as might seem,
> Of vagrant dwellers in the houseless woods,
> Or of some hermit's cave, where by the fire
> The hermit sits alone.[17]

This arrangement of compositional elements dissipates, however, in face of the realization that

> ... – I cannot paint
> What then I was. The sounding cataract
> Haunted me like a passion: the tall rock,
> The mountain, and the deep gloomy wood,
> Their colours and their forms, were then to me
> An appetite: a feeling and a love,
> That had no need of a remoter charm,

---

[16] Carl Woodring, "The New Sublimity in 'Tintern Abbey,'" in *The Evidence of the Imagination: Studies in the Interaction Between Life and Art in English Romantic Literature*, ed. Donald H. Reiman, Michael C. Jaye, and Betty T. Bennett (New York: New York University Press, 1978), reprinted in *Critical Essays on William Wordsworth*, ed. George H. Gilpin (Boston: G. K. Hall, 1990), 11–23 and 12, respectively.

[17] "Lines composed a few miles above Tintern Abbey, on revisiting the banks of the Wye during a tour, July 1798," in *Lyrical Ballads and Other Poems, 1797–1800 by William Wordsworth*, ed. James A. Butler and Karen Green (Ithaca, NY: Cornell University Press, 1993), 116–20, lines 15–23.

> By thought supplied, or any interest
> Unborrowed from the eye. (76–84)

The realization at once marks a change of aesthetic sensibility, a rejection of the picturesque in light of deeper emotions it is unable to express. "For I have learned," the narrator muses,

> To look on nature, not as in the hour
> Of thoughtless youth, but hearing oftentimes
> The still sad music of humanity,
> Nor harsh nor grating, though of ample power
> To chasten and subdue. And I have felt
> A presence that disturbs me with the joy
> Of elevated thoughts; a sense sublime
> Of something more deeply interfused,
> Whose dwelling is the light of setting suns,
> And the round ocean and the living air,
> And the blue sky, and in the mind of man,
> A motion and a spirit, that impels
> All thinking things, all objects of all thought,
> And rolls through all things. (89–103)

The picturesque and its principles are shallow and phenomenal, and compose a language inadequate to the feelings that arise from somewhere deep and real and that soar upward in a "sense sublime" of the interanimation and interfusion of all things.[18]

The "Guide" and the Natural Picturesque

What Wordsworth articulates poetically in "Tintern Abbey" finds prosaic expression a decade later in *A Guide through the District of the Lakes in the North of England*, a work that reveals a liberal borrowing of picturesque tropes while casting doubts on the principles they involve.[19] Notably, the *Guide* was composed and revised over a span of some twenty years of Wordsworth's mature life – not, that is, in the "hours of thoughtless youth" – a period that extends long after the self-declared revolutions in taste recounted in *The Prelude* and "Tintern Abbey."[20] In the opening sentence Wordsworth

---

[18] See in this context Adam Potkay, "Wordsworth and the Ethics of Things," *Proceedings of the Modern Language Association* 123, 2 (2008): 390–404, and for discussion of Wordsworth's closely related conception of "joy," Adam Potkay, *The Story of Joy: From the Bible to Late Romanticism* (Cambridge: Cambridge University Press, 2007), ch. 5.

[19] *A Guide through the District of the Lakes in the North of England, with A Description of the Scenery, &c. for the Use of Tourists and Residents*, 5th ed., with *Considerable Additions* (Kendal and London, 1835), in *Prose Works*, 2:152–259 (GL followed by line numbers).

[20] The *Guide* began life as a text commissioned to accompany etchings by Reverend Joseph Wilkinson (with his wife a longtime acquaintance of the Wordsworth family) and was first

announces in unequivocal terms his disagreement with the picturesque tradition. He emphasizes that the work has a loftier goal than other guides with which it might share a name, and in doing so replaces the central metaphor of the picturesque – sight and the eye – with that of the Romantic – feeling and mind: "In preparing this Manual," Wordsworth writes, "it was the Author's principal wish to furnish a Guide or Companion for the *Minds* of Persons of taste, and feeling for Landscape, who might be inclined to explore the District of the Lakes with that degree of attention to which its beauty may fairly lay claim" (GL 4–8). Readers of the *Guide* are not to be content with "observations" that please the eye, rest only on the surface of things, and amount to a species of appearance constructed mechanically from rules of composition. They are to enjoy instead a superior subject matter that will bring a more profound pleasure, the origins of which lie in experience rather than phenomena viewed. The causes are explicable and the pleasure forthcoming, however, only when the mind of man is opened up to nature free of artifice, whether imposed by the improvers of industry or picturesque landscapers.

At the same time as Wordsworth signals his break with the picturesque tradition, the *Guide* echoes it in its language, with some passages having clear and identifiable precedents in the literature.[21] Wordsworth reiterates Gilpin's procedure of comparing the Lake District to Scotland, Switzerland, and America (GL 505ff.; 2440ff.), for example, and explicitly adopts his reasoning (also accepted by Price) against the use of white in landscape (GL 1970ff.).[22] Wordsworth also writes extensively of architecture and gardening in ways reminiscent of Price's *Essay* and Repton's *Sketches and Hints*. "The rule is simple; with respect to grounds – work, where you can, in the spirit of nature, with an invisible hand of art" (GL 1833–5), Wordsworth advises, and (much in the spirit of Repton's nod to utility) urges that modern internal conveniences of a residence can be adopted without compromising the external appearance, which should always "harmonise with the forms of nature" (GL 1840–1). On this basis he accepts that artificial ornament may without censure be employed around a house as long as it does not contradict nature (GL 1910–12), as exotic plants are acceptable providing the transition from shrubbery to plantation beyond (of native rather than imported trees) is not abrupt (GL 2080–9). The "house must harmonise with the surrounding landscape" (GL 1936–7),

---

published as *Select Views in Cumberland, Westmoreland, and Lancashire* (London, 1810). A second edition appeared in 1821, but Wordsworth had already published the text by itself in 1820 (he thought Wilkinson's etchings "intolerable"), and with additions and alterations the work went to further editions in 1822, 1823, and 1835. For the history of the work and the various changes it underwent between 1810 and 1835, see Owen and Smyser, *Prose Works*, 2:123–49.

[21] See Nabholtz, "Wordsworth's *Guide to the Lakes* and the Picturesque Tradition," 293–5.

[22] See William Gilpin, *Observations, relative chiefly to Picturesque Beauty, Made in the Year 1772, On Several Parts of England; particularly the Mountains, and Lakes of Cumberland, and Westmoreland*, 2 vols. (London: R. Blamire, 1786), 1:117–18, and Price, *Sketches and Hints*, 75–6.

Wordsworth emphasizes, a general and overriding principle that should determine both the size and color of the residence.

In addition to specific parallels of this sort, the *Guide* is striking generally for the picturesque images and phraseology employed throughout, and nowhere more than when Wordsworth extols the Lakes for exhibiting qualities he found so lamentably lacking at Foxley: "variety in influences of light and shadow" (GL 637), the "diversified" forms of its mountains (GL 659), the "general tint" of lichen on rocks (GL 680), and "variety in colouring" (GL 716). He likewise praises the area's numerous small and middle-sized lakes for the variety they bring (a principle of water established earlier by Price), and delights in the level areas of vales when "diversified by rocks, hills, and hillocks, scattered over them" (GL 949–50). The "contrasted sunshine and shadow" on walls and roofs of traditional dwellings give a similar effect (GL 1546–7) as does the rudeness and "graceful neglect of danger" found in the traditional stone bridges that span valley streams and rivers (GL 1601ff.). Wordsworth is also willing to view scenes with a distinctly picturesque eye and employ the terminology of artistic composition. At the "outlet of Gowbarrow Park," he writes, "we reach a third stream, which flows through a little recess called Glencoin, where lurks a single house, yet visible from the road. Let the Artist or leisurely Traveller turn aside to it, for the building and objects around them are romantic and picturesque" (GL 412–16). He also speaks of the "minute beauties" of lichen and moss that "adorn the foreground" (GL 730–1), and describes the "bay of Morcamb" in terms that make the seaside town into an amphitheater to rival that of Naples, so beloved of landscape painters: "sloping shores and back-ground of distant mountains are seen," Wordsworth writes, "composing pictures equally distinguished for amenity and grandeur" (GL 1062–4).

It is clear from such examples that Wordsworth did not reject the picturesque outright, but continued to employ and identify with elements of it. The version he fashions, however, is not that of Gilpin but closer to the one glimpsed in the romantic image of Price striding Robin Hood–like through a facsimile of Merry Olde England, or expressed in Repton's mourning for a land destroyed by the *nouveaux riche* with their bad taste and unpicturesque fences. Wordsworth does not embrace the Gilpinesque fascination for rearranging and improving nature that Austen found so amusing, but he is drawn to the sentiments it expresses and the mood it captures; when Wordsworth expresses his attachment to these strains of the tradition he tends to elide the picturesque with the feeling or "sensation," which, as we shall see in the next section, he identifies as the sublime: "For sublimity will never be wanting," he remarks at one point,

where the sense of innumerable multitude is lost in, and alternates with, that of intense unity; and to the ready perception of this effect, similarity and almost identity of individual form and monotony of colour contribute. But this feeling is confined to the native immeasurable forest; no artificial plantation can give it. (GL 2188–93)

Or, similarly, writing of the tarns – small, rain-filled lakes – Wordsworth observes how they lie mostly at the foot of steep precipices so that the water in them "appears black and sullen" with masses of rocks and stones scattered around their edges, "some defying conjecture as to the means by which they come thither. ... A not unpleasant sadness is induced by this perplexity, and these images of decay," he reports, "while the prospect of a body of pure water unattended with groves and other cheerful rural images by which fresh water is usually accompanied, and unable to give furtherance to the meager vegetation around it – excites a sense of some repulsive power strongly put forth, and thus depends the melancholy natural to such scenes" (GL 1036–43).

Wordsworth's picturesque is shorn of rules and compositional elements adopted from painting, but it follows the principle he frames with respect to planting and ornamentation: "let the images of nature be your guide" (GL 2240–51). In this version, the picturesque is a naturally occurring phenomenon – a *natural picturesque* – inscribed in the powerful, untamed force of nature within which human beings dwell organically, nestled, as it were, in her protective bosom; human beings and their works are themselves of nature, elements that combine with the beauty of lake, mountain, forest, and vale to create a seamless whole. The *Guide* articulates and celebrates this ideal while also telling a tale of its passing in the shift from a prelapsarian idyll of rural life to a landscape scarred and a community dissipated by the effects of deforestation, improvement, and industrialization (see GL 1466ff.). In this spirit, Wordsworth's juxtapositions are typically of nature and artifice overlaid with the moralizing language of modesty and affectation: the "mountain-cottage ... beautifully formed in itself, and ... richly adorned by the hand of nature" (GL 1583–5) is contrasted with gaudy buildings designed only with the aim of impressing others; ancient dwellings that "ornament" the landscape by sitting "snug" in its vales and valleys (1825–30) stand against modern houses placed ostentatiously on the summits of naked hills only for the sake of a view, and the life and liberty of woods "self-planted" through wind, water, birds, and animals are juxtaposed to the "insipid and lifeless" avenues placed for profit by the "artificial planter"; so lacking in natural variation are these plantations, Wordsworth laments, that even the beauties of sunshine and shadow cannot adorn them (see GL 1805–11, 2115ff. and 2181–3).[23]

In Wordsworth's mind, modernity and the picturesque share a common strain of violence – recall Gilpin's imaginary mallet at Tintern Abbey and the

---

[23] Cf. Alison's observations on the "progress of taste" (see ch. 3) with respect to gardening (*Essays on the Nature and Principles of Taste*, 289–90). In early garden design, regularity and uniformity predominated over irregular forms – even though the latter are both more convenient and agreeable – because, Alison ventures, they "immediately excited the belief of Design, and with this belief, all the admiration which follows the employment of Skill or even of Expence" (289). Alison observes that same desire to display the "spirit of industry" and "improvement" still prevailed toward century's end even though the uniform lines and regular divisions violated Nature's tendency to the opposite.

salutary effects of Cromwell's iron fists at Ragland Castle – for whether one improves in the name of progress or taste, the result is the same "disfigurement," damage inflicted by "persons who may have built, demolished, and planted, with full confidence, that every change and addition was or would become an improvement" (GL 1915–17). Consider the island at Windermere, "disturbed" by those who effect changes in the name of "taste": the church docked of its steeple and turned into a boathouse, the fort demolished, ancient Druid stones swept away, and the native hollies and ash once "scattered over" the main shore replaced with the lifeless plantations of ubiquitous larch. "The present instance has been singled out," Wordsworth remarks, "extravagant as it is, because, unquestionably, this beautiful country has, in numerous other places, suffered from the same spirit. ... What could be more unfortunate than the taste that suggested the paring of the shores, and surrounding with an embankment this spot of ground, the natural shape of which was so beautiful!" (1760–9). Wordsworth acknowledges (in an echo of Repton's comment on avenues of trees) that "transgressions" against nature please insofar as they satisfy certain features of human nature: we "delight" in "formality and harsh contrast" (GL 1790–1) and take pleasure "from distant ideas, and from the perception of order, regularity, and contrivance" (GL 1786–9). If people would only pay attention to what is there, they would discover a beauty more valuable and a pleasure more satisfying than any improver can provide. For Wordsworth, nature has not (to recall Gilpin's phrase) simply "chalked out her designs," but finished them to perfection; scenes are already naturally picturesque, exemplified in that "peaceful harmony of form and colour, which have been through a long lapse of ages most happily preferred" (GL 1783–5).

Given that picturesque means "like a picture" or "capable of being illustrated by a painting," it might seem that removing the element of compositional rearrangement in this manner would denude the concept of its meaning: if Wordsworth rejects the artifice of the picturesque, then surely he rejects the picturesque altogether. This is too quick, however, not only because (as we have seen) Wordsworth both sympathizes with elements of the tradition and finds value in its language, but also because the vision of nature he holds as the source of sublimity is not far removed from the rough and rugged that occupied the likes of Gilpin, Price, Knight, and (with qualification) Repton. The important point for Wordsworth, however, is that nature herself is the source of aesthetic value and not some version of her represented on canvas or constructed by the landscape gardener. Wordsworth's natural picturesque rejects rules of composition but at once frees the mind for the "sense sublime."

Wordsworth's Sublime

Although Wordsworth mentions sublimity in the *Guide* and expresses what he means by it poetically, the single most informative document for his systematic thinking on the subject is the eponymously titled *The Sublime and the Beautiful*, an unfinished manuscript probably composed in 1811–12 and the only work written in a mode (as Wordsworth describes it) "almost entirely aesthetic and philosophical" (SB 132).[24] This is an appropriate description, because the work is, in effect, a philosophical defense of the shift of emphasis announced at the beginning of the *Guide* from the external observation of objects through the picturesque eye to the internal constitution of the subject that moves the Romantic mind.[25] Despite its title, the work is primarily concerned with the sublime (Wordsworth obviously abandoned it before developing fully his thoughts on beauty), and his discussion draws on elements from different strands of eighteenth-century thought mixed in a way that by happenstance or design bring nature and human experience to the fore: Wordsworth's emphasis on the subject and his various references to "moral nature" and the "moral law" carry strong overtones of Kant; the prominence of fear, awe, and above all power is clearly indebted to Burke; and the description of the sublime as an "elevation of our being" (SB 284) and the importance Wordsworth accords principles of association brings to mind Gerard, Alison, and Kames.[26]

Such debts notwithstanding, Wordsworth's treatment of the sublime is informed fundamentally by an older and more familiar piece of philosophical lore: the distinction between qualities of an object and the mind of a subject affected by them. Wordsworth does not take issue with the distinction as such, but he observes critically that too great an emphasis has been placed on the objective side and too little attention paid to the role of the subject. The result, he insists, are "difficulties and errors" and, above all, the misguided assumption that beauty and sublimity are in objects themselves, a charge, one might note, that makes sense with reference to Burke and Price, but hardly to the likes of Hutcheson, Hume, and especially the complex associationist theories of Gerard and Alison. For "the attention of those who have been engaged in them [disquisitions on the sublime and beautiful]," Wordsworth maintains,

has been primarily & chiefly fixed upon external objects & their powers, qualities, & properties, & not upon the mind itself, and the laws by which it is acted upon. ...

---

[24] *The Sublime and the Beautiful*, published as Appendix III to the *Guide*, in *Prose Works* 3:349–60 (SB followed by line numbers). The unpublished manuscript bears no date, but Owen and Smyser place its composition sometime between September 1811 and November 1812. Wordsworth put it aside to take up the commission of the *Guide* and, though he mentions in correspondence the possibility of returning to it, he never did. For a full history, see the editor's introduction, esp. 128–32.

[25] Some have seen a tension between the subjective emphasis of *The Sublime and the Beautiful* and the (arguably) more objective view of nature presented in the *Guide*. See Theresa M. Kelley, *Wordsworth's Revisionary Aesthetics* (Cambridge: Cambridge University Press, 1988), ch. 2.

[26] Wu finds no evidence that Wordsworth read these latter thinkers, but suggests September 1798 as the latest date for his reading of the third *Critique* and is confident that Wordsworth had the work "in mind" when composing the *Guide*. See *Wordsworth's Reading 1770–1799*, 80–1.

To talk of an object as being sublime or beautiful in itself, without references to some subject by whom that sublimity or beauty is perceived, is absurd; nor is it the slightest importance to mankind whether there be any object with which their minds are conversant that Men would universally agree ... to denominate sublime or beautiful. It is enough that they there are, both in moral qualities & in the forms of the external universe, such qualities & powers as have affected Men, in different states of civilization & without communication with each other, with similar sensations either of the sublime or beautiful. (SB 258–73)[27]

Wordsworth acknowledges that beauty and sublimity are "not only different from, but opposite to, each other" (SB 26); the former speaks more to our "placid and gentle nature" that comes with maturity and old age (SB 16), he urges, as the latter concerns "those obtrusive qualities in an object sublime" more suited to youth (SB 17). Speaking accurately, however, objects themselves are not sublime or beautiful, but they "have the power of affecting us both with the sense of beauty & the sense of sublimity" (SB 23–4). For this reason the same object "may have the power of affecting us both with the sense of beauty & the sense of sublimity," albeit at different times (SB 22–4).

This move from the object to the subject in describing and explaining the sublime is a decisive one, although (as noted at the outset) clearly not original to Wordsworth and the Romantic tradition. The idea that objects are not themselves sublime, but a trigger or the occasion for a feeling so-called, was adumbrated as early as Addison's celebration of the pleasures of the imagination, was developed by Burke, and given decisive philosophical voice by Kant; it is well-known that Wordsworth was exposed to Kant's philosophy – his aesthetics included – through Coleridge. There is, however, also a more immediate and direct precedent and source in works of the picturesque tradition that Wordsworth read himself. As noted earlier, Gilpin had already spoken of picturesque effects in decidedly sublime terms – recall again his "*deliquium* of the soul" through which we "rather *feel*, than *survey*" the "enthusiastic sensation of pleasure" – but it is in Knight's criticism of Burke's "absurd and superficial theories" and their application in the hands of Price that we find an explicit and dramatic shift *from* the external and visible qualities of objects that makes something beautiful, sublime, or picturesque (the language of the eye and sight), *to* the inward pleasure that arises in the subject through association (the language of feeling and mind). Knight emphasizes that "those exalted or enthusiastic feelings, which are called sublime" are connected with "subjects of taste" by the human capacity for sympathy (AI 3.1.1), and the sublime is thus a passion that arises from the effects of literary representation. Thus objects need not be sublime – that is, possess "qualities" (whatever those might be)

---

[27] See also Letter to Jacob Fletcher Esquire, February 25, 1825, *Letters, Later Years*, 1:183–4, where Wordsworth reiterates that the main issue is not to ask whether objects are beautiful, sublime, or picturesque, but to discover the "law under which they are contemplated."

in order to produce the feeling of exaltation (see AI 2.2.70–3), which means, Knight emphasizes, criticizing Burke in particular, that pleasure should be traced not to the objects but to ideas those objects produce in the subject; something can thus be "*displeasing to sight*" and yet "*pleasing objects of sight*" (AI 2.2.74). "All these extra pleasures are from the minds of the spectators," Knight writes, drawing on the language of associationism,

> whose pre-existing trains of ideas are revived, refreshed, and reassociated by new, but correspondent impressions on the organs of sense; and the great fundamental error, which prevails throughout the otherwise able and elegant *Essays on the Picturesque*, [of Price] is seeking for distinctions in external objects, which only exist in the modes and habits of viewing and considering them. (AI 2.2.74)

Knight, in other words, emphasizes the side of the distinction that Wordsworth finds neglected: the affective state of the subject over qualities of the object and the importance of association in explaining aesthetic pleasure. Philosophically speaking, then, Knight takes a decisive step away from the Gilpin and toward the natural picturesque, effectively articulating what Wordsworth denominates the "law" of sublimity and beauty that is the focal point of his essay: to discover the "several grand constitutional laws under which it has been ordained that these objects (of Nature) should everlastingly affect the mind" (SB 50–5).

For his part, Wordsworth does not deny that an object called sublime contains or exhibits certain "attributes or qualities" (in *Descriptive Sketches*, recall, the Alps had "sublime *features*" [emphasis added]) but he understands these (albeit not explicitly) along the lines of Locke's distinction between primary and secondary qualities: the ocean or a mountain (Wordsworth's central examples) has the potential or "*power* of affecting the mind with a sensation of sublimity" (SB 109–10, emphasis added) given in the motion of flowing waves of the one and "abrupt and precipitous" lines of the other. An object also needs to be large (though in the *Guide* Wordsworth warns against simply identifying grandeur with magnitude [GL 839–40]) and be the "sole object before our eyes"; the mountains at Windermere give only a "grand impression, and nothing more" when seen at a distance (SB 63–5), but are sublime when they fill one's field of vision. None of these attributes or powers renders the object sublime, however, because, as we have seen already, that term applies properly to the affective state of the subject: the sublime is properly called a "complex impression" or "sensation," as Wordsworth variously describes it, a "feeling or image of intense unity, without a conscious contemplation of parts" (SB 141–4). Analytically, this intense unity consists of three "elementary parts" or distinguishable feelings experienced by the spectator: a "sense" of individual form or forms, of temporal duration, and, most importantly, of power (SB 68–73).[28]

---

[28] Later, in the preface to the *Poems* of 1815, Wordsworth adds a psychological dimension by identifying the imagination as the faculty that makes this sense of power possible. I consider this in the next section.

Wordsworth is willing to accept that "works of Man" (SB 88) are capable of producing the impression of sublimity, and in such cases it is sufficient that the object has a combination of form and duration; he offers no examples, but one can assume that he is talking of the plastic rather than literary arts because it is unclear how poetry or prose could meaningfully contain the latter elements. The sublime as a response to nature, by contrast – in Wordsworth's view clearly the fullest expression of the feeling – and requires the addition of power (not the violence of the improvers), which "awakens the sublime" according to two different principles: "union and communion" and "humiliation and submission" (SB 188–9). In the former we participate in the object through sympathy, and in the latter we meet resistance in something that inspires fear and dread; in both cases the result is that same "intense unity," which completely occupies or possesses the soul (see SB 159–60 and 192–3). The sense of power has this effect, Wordsworth writes,

either when it rouses us to a sympathetic energy & calls upon the mind to grasp something towards which it can make approaches but which it is incapable of attaining – yet so that it participates [*sic*] force which is acting upon it; or, 2dly, by producing humiliation or prostration of the mind before some external power, &, as far as it has any consciousness of itself, its grandeur subsists in the naked fact of being conscious of external Power at once awful & immeasurable. (SB 150–60)

Wordsworth clearly considers the second alternative – humiliation before an overwhelming and terrifying force – the more profound of the two, because it puts the mind in a state of "opposition and yet reconcilement" that modifies intense unity into the even stronger impression of infinity. Wordsworth likens this phenomenon to parallel lines in mathematics, which are simultaneously connected and separated in a tension that is "infinitely prolonged" because they "can never come nearer to each other" (SB 250–5). There is a delicate balance to be struck if the sensation of sublimity is to have its full effect: it presupposes that our "physical nature" has not been threatened with annihilation and that our "moral Nature has not in the least degree been violated" (SB 197–9). Without the requisite participation or resistance, the sensation of sublimity will not arise at all, and, once it has, the feeling of sympathy and union will dissipate if the attention of the spectator is divided, as an excess of fear will draw him away from consciousness of and submission to the immeasurable power.

In a strong echo of eighteenth-century writers considered in Part I – Addison, Hume, and Kames, for example – Wordsworth also emphasizes that although human beings have a "sense" for the sublime, the feeling will be absent "without a preparatory intercourse with that object or with others of the same kind" (SB 342–4). The impression is not spontaneous, but presupposes a certain "state or condition of the mind" with respect to habits of "accurate observation" and to "knowledge" that render the experience "more lively and comprehensive" (SB 6–7 and 112–14). The sublime is not weakened by familiarity or enervated by loss of novelty, but one's capacity to experience it grows with time and attention. First contact with objects considered a source of the sublime may prove disappointing and only later through reflection does one attain the state of mind and feel its full force. Such was Reynolds's experience on first seeing the work of Raphael in the Sistine Chapel, Wordsworth relates anecdotally; of a woman native to the barren Orkney Isles underwhelmed on seeing real trees after years of living with the more spectacular specimens of her imagination; and of another transported suddenly from the flat plains of Lincolnshire to the mountainous regions of Scotland. In a letter to Dorothy, Wordsworth confesses a similar reaction to the famous falls on the Rhine at Schaffhausen: he had raised his "ideas" of them "too high" and was disappointed.[29]

The most important factor Wordsworth cites for determining the frequency and intensity of a sublime impression, however, is the associations brought to mind by the image of an object or view (actually perceived or remembered) and, to borrow Alison's terminology, the chain of ideas that emanate from it. The disappointment of Reynolds in Rome or Wordsworth at the Rhine are essentially cases of being "excluded" from "communication with the sublime in the midst of objects eminently capable of exciting that feeling" (SB 326–7), where, that is, union dissolves or the tension between opposition and resistance is relaxed by excess fear. Images of barren landscape, moreover, might cause feelings of depression as the appearance of chaotic crags could bring to mind unfinished and unstable buildings; they might also conjure associations related to childhood or ideas of lesser works of art. Personal associations of fear and wonder can also destroy the sublime by mitigating the effect of power: the former gives way to "comprehensive awe," Wordsworth maintains, as the latter to "religious admiration" (SB 134–5), neither of which are sublime.

The Preface to *Lyrical Ballads*

We have seen so far how Wordsworth develops the "natural picturesque," a phrase designed to indicate how he at once rejects the picturesque and its principles as too narrow, but retains certain elements taken or at least absorbed from his reading and/or contact with Gilpin, Price, and Knight; it also reflects Wordsworth's shift of focus from the object to subjective experience as the source of aesthetic value found, specifically, in the feeling of intense unity that constitutes the sublime. With this picture in mind, we are now in a position to appreciate the Preface to *Lyrical Ballads* as Wordsworth's application of his aesthetic principles to poetry and the process of poetic composition.[30]

---

[29] "Magnificent as this fall certainly is I must confess I was disappointed in it. I had raised my ideas too high." *Letters, Early Years,* 35, (1790, Wordsworth to Dorothy), quoted in Owen and Smyser, *Prose Works,* 2:456n.

[30] *Lyrical Ballads, Advertisement, Preface, Appendix,* in *Prose Works,* 1:118–65 (PLB followed by line numbers). Unless noted (as PLB [1800]), all references are to the final version of 1850, which, with minor changes, preserves that of 1802. I shall assume that the preface reflects

Anticipating what he would write later in the "aesthetic and philosophical" mode of *The Sublime and the Beautiful*, Wordsworth advertises the Preface as an attempt to elucidate "certain inherent and indestructible qualities of the human mind, and likewise ... certain powers in the great and permanent objects that act upon it, which are equally inherent and indestructible" (PLB 178–80). The "law" of the sublime in poetry is to be sought in the language (the objective side) with the inherent power to elicit a feeling in the reader (the subjective side) according to principles that act "permanently" upon and affect the mind.[31]

On the objective side stands the poetic equivalent of the qualities and attributes of the ocean (motion of flowing waves) or mountains ("abrupt and precipitous" lines) that have the "power" to affect the mind with a "sensation of sublimity." With a poem before them, readers are in a very different position than Wordsworth's imagined spectator gazing at the actual mountains of Windermere; the former confronts instead a literary representation of some natural phenomenon, be it the Lakes of the *Guide*, the Alps of *Descriptive Sketches*, or scenes and characters that compose the themes of the poems in *Lyrical Ballads*. In poetry and prose (Wordsworth claims, controversially, that there is no essential difference between them, a point I take up later), the qualities or attributes are contained in the language, those features that comprise its "style," which no less than motions and lines have the potential to "gratify certain known habits of association" (PLB 53–4) and thus "excite" feelings in the reader. This is the "worthy purpose" of all good poetry, Wordsworth maintains, and makes *Lyrical Ballads* an "experiment" to see "how far, by fitting to metrical arrangement a selection of the real language of men in a state of vivid sensation, that sort of pleasure and that quantity of pleasure may be imparted, which a Poet may rationally endeavour to impart" (PLB 16–19).

This "vivid sensation" and "pleasure" arises in and through poetry according to the same "law" that governs the experience when occasioned by objects in nature, and for this reason one might consider it of the same species as the effect Wordsworth describes in *The Sublime and the Beautiful*. The effect cannot be the sublime of "humiliation and submission," which, as we have seen, requires a power emanating from the actual presence of some object "awful and immeasurable" that fills one's visual field. The effect of poetry, rather, lies in the direction of "union and communion," where "sympathetic energy" calls the mind to grasp at something unobtainable, but in which it participates

---

the views of Wordsworth, although Coleridge's role in forming the ideas it expresses, and the degree to which he did or did not share or endorse what Wordsworth wrote, is complex. I touch on the issue below, but see the remarks by Owen and Smyser, *Prose Works*, 1:112–14, and editor's general introduction to *Lyrical Ballads*, 2nd ed., ed. Michael Mason (London: Longman, 2007 [1992]), esp. 4–9.

[31] For an informative discussion of the notion of "permanence" in the preface, see W. J. B. Owen, *Wordsworth as Critic* (Toronto: University of Toronto Press, 1969), ch. 1, esp. 7–15.

nevertheless. In the poems of *Lyrical Ballads*, this criterion is satisfied by the *power* of the sentiments – the "great and simple affections of our nature," as Wordsworth calls them – which the reader confronts when expressed through the characters and themes of the poems. These are literary representations of passions, and thus weaker than any original, but with sufficient power to excite communion and the feeling of intense unity that Wordsworth identifies with the sublime. Wordsworth highlights some of the affections that occasion this feeling on the part of the reader: maternal passion ("The Idiot Boy" and "The Mad Mother"), the last struggles of a human being as death approaches ("The Complaint of a Forsaken Indian Woman"), the perplexity and obscurity of death to a small child ("We are Seven"), the strength of moral attachment when associated with the beauty of nature ("Simon Lee"), dejection and desolation ("The Female Vagrant"), the pull of avarice ("The Two Thieves"), and the quietude of tranquility ("Old Man Travelling/Animal Tranquility and Decay") (see PLB [1800] 140ff.).

It is worth noting that Wordsworth also speaks of power in the later *Essay* added to the Preface of the *Poems* of 1815.[32] Much of the work is a response to critical reviews that Wordsworth had received (and expected to receive), which he counters by arguing that much literature (including his own) that is great and destined to stand the test of time is routinely neglected by contemporary audiences.[33] This articulates the same tension evident in Shaftesbury onward, that art appeals to features of human nature – the "pathetic participates of an *animal* sensation," as Wordsworth expresses the thought (ESP 781) – which do not always yield the expected response, although the excellence of some passage is "proved by effects immediate and universal" (ESP 785–6). Wordsworth explains this phenomenon in two ways. First, he suggests, in an adage he attributes to Coleridge, that an original writer of genius cannot assume an extant taste for his work, but must create it in his audience; he is a "Hannibal among the Alps" who must "shape his own road" (ESP 693ff.). Second, drawing on observations made by Dennis,[34] Wordsworth maintains that the degree to which poetry brings about its effects are relative to the kind of emotions evoked: "simple and direct," "complex and revolutionary," and – pertinent to the present discussion – "sublime." The first presents no

---

[32] *Essay, Supplementary to the Preface*, in *Prose Works*, 2:63–84 (ESP followed by line numbers).

[33] See Owen, *Wordsworth as Critic*, 88–9, who says that this argument is "passable rhetoric but poor logic" – it has the structure of an invalid syllogism – and that much of the evidence Wordsworth marshals to support his thesis is inconclusive. More generally, however, Owen considers Wordsworth's overall position coherent, although it does raise interpretive issues for the reader (see esp. 195ff.).

[34] See John Dennis, *The Advancement and Reformation of Modern Poetry* (1701), in *The Critical Works of John Dennis*, ed. Edward Niles Hooker, 2 vols. (Baltimore, MD: Johns Hopkins University Press, 1939), 1:197–278, esp. 216ff.

real difficulty because the "heart yields [to them] with gentleness." The second is more recalcitrant because against them the mind "struggles with pride" and arbitrary associations, which the poet "melts down for his purpose" (ESP 786ff.) The real difficulty lies with the sublime emotions, because they are remote from the concerns of daily life and unfamiliar to the reader who confronts them in a poem. As Wordsworth predicted earlier of the "experimental" *Lyrical Ballads*, readers find poems that elicit sublime emotions difficult, challenging, and obscure; the audience will inevitably "struggle with feelings of strangeness and awkwardness" (PLB 68–9) in the face of poems that are in form and content removed from those to which they are accustomed.

The poet, then, is faced with the task – as eighteenth-century writers would have considered it – of educating taste or refining delicacy of passion, and like others before him Wordsworth is keenly aware that poets must employ techniques and draw on their knowledge of human nature to elicit deliberately a particular response in the reader. Poets have a *choice* concerning the style they employ, dictated in turn by the *kind* of emotion they intend to arouse. For Wordsworth, as we have seen, the sublime is feeling that originates in nature, and is characterized by freedom and a forceful communication that (with the proper attention and reflection, and barring any intervening obstructions) can be comprehended easily by the mind. On this basis, and in a way reminiscent of Hutcheson's view that representative or relative beauty increases when the object represented is absolutely beautiful, Wordsworth infers that poetry is more likely to achieve its end of bringing about the vivid sensation of sublimity if the *objective qualities and attributes of the poem (its style) are essentially the same as the feeling (the sublime) it is intended to elicit.* "The principal object ... proposed in these poems," Wordsworth writes accordingly,

was to choose incidents and situations from common life, and to relate or describe them, throughout, as far as was possible in a selection of language really used by men, and, at the same time, to throw over them a certain colouring of imagination, whereby ordinary things should be presented to the mind in an unusual aspect; and further, and above all, to make these incidents and situations interesting by tracing in them ... the primary laws of our nature: chiefly as far as regards the manner in which we associate ideas in a state of excitement. (PLB 81–90)

Consequently, poetry should employ "simple and unelaborated expressions" (PLB 107), which represent the original emotions of human beings and reflect nature to the degree that they are themselves natural. The poet should only "interweave any foreign splendour of his own with that which the passion naturally suggests" (PLB 298–9).

This conviction is reflected in what Wordsworth calls a "sublime notion of poetry" (PLB 471–2) with a style that puts it in sharp contrast to the work of his predecessors and contemporaries concerned only with "conferring honour on themselves and their art," and intent on gratifying "fickle tastes, and fickle appetites" (PLB 110–14). The techniques of these poets – Gray, Pope, and

Cowper come in for particular scrutiny[35] – amount to what Wordsworth calls "poetic diction," a rarefied, artificial language that relies on the personification of abstract ideas, and an extravagant "falsehood of description" (PLB 189–92, 212) that *distances* readers from the work and thus dissipates the intense unity that the poem arouses or even prevents that feeling from arising in the first place. Poetic diction does violence to language in the name of art, as modern improvers do violence to landscapes and the organic order of communal life in the name of beauty and progress. In normative terms reminiscent of the *Guide*, Wordsworth juxtaposes poetry that is natural, healthy, pure, and light – sublime – to one artificial, enervated, adulterated, and depraved: the former expresses primordial passions in the same natural "language of men" in which they are ordinarily expressed; the latter eviscerates these passions and clothes them in an "improved" language that satisfies a taste blunted by a false relish for "gross and violent stimulants" and reduces the mind to a "state of almost savage torpor" (PLB 154ff.).

Wordsworth, moreover, takes this thought a step further and (albeit obliquely) links the sublime style of his poems to their *subject matter*: the characters and forms of life he chooses for *Lyrical Ballads* exhibit the same (or at least similar) qualities as the language and sensation they inspire; fittingly, they are apiece with those that comprise the rural idyll portrayed later in the *Guide*. The inhabitants of the idealized pastoral life of the Lakes enjoy not only a country unscathed by improvers but also are at liberty to experience and express human feelings both spontaneously and in their original form. Under conditions of "humble and rustic life," Wordsworth writes, employing a metaphor that explicitly binds simple affections to the land on which those who feel them dwell, "essential passions of the heart find a better soil in which they can attain their maturity, are less under restraint, and speak a plainer and more emphatic language." Elementary feelings exist there "in a state of greater simplicity, and, consequently, may be more accurately contemplated, and more forcibly communicated"; manners are "more durable" and "more easily comprehended"; and, finally, "in that situation the passions of men are incorporated with the beautiful and permanent forms of nature" (see PLB 90–100). Here Wordsworth completes the circle and makes poetry natural through and through: it is of nature, expresses nature, and excites sentiments that are natural.

It does not follow that sublime poetry achieves it effects automatically, creative effort and exertion being required on the part of both poet and audience. This is obscured by the language of "taste," Wordsworth contends, because it emphasizes the "*passive* sense of the human body," including the domain of "intellectual *acts* and *operations*" (ESP 721–3) to which "taste" has been

---

[35] See appendix "by what is usually called Poetic Diction," in *Prose Works*, 1:160–5, lines 81ff. (App). Wordsworth added this to the 1802 edition of the preface.

metaphorically extended. For "without the exertion of a co-operating power in the mind of the Reader," he writes, "there can be no adequate sympathy with either of these emotions [the pathetic and the sublime]: without this auxiliary impulse, elevated or profound passion cannot exist" (ESP 744–6). Primary responsibility falls to the poet, whose task it is to "call forth and communicate *power*" (ESP 762–3) or "bestow power" (ESP 778–9), and draw on that same "accurate observation" and "knowledge" that renders the sublime experience of ocean or mountains "more lively and comprehensive" to the observer of nature. The feeling of sympathy and union dissipates when the poet fails and the spectator's attention is divided. Successful poets are those who effectively mediate the originals of nature through the "real language of nature" (PLB 482), and while poets differ from other men in degree rather than kind, they are possessed of "more than usual organic sensibility" (PLB 139) and a "greater promptness to think and feel without immediate external excitement, and a greater power in expressing such thoughts and feelings as are produced in him in that manner" (PLB 494–7). This finer sensibility and power of expression are reflected above all in poets' ability to connect and combine ideas and associations and thus draw in themselves those "fluxes and refluxes of the mind when agitated by the great and simple affections of our natures" (PLB [1800] 137–8). This is a creative process, which (as we will see in the next section) Wordsworth identifies with the faculty of imagination. Poets are then able to educe the same in others and thus excite in the reader the vivid sensation of sublimity and the pleasure it brings.

The role Wordsworth assigns to the poet cannot but bring to mind the issues raised by Hume (discussed in Chapter 2) concerning the dangers of representation and the potentially damaging character of fictions toward which the mendacious poetic mind is inclined. Wordsworth's aesthetics exhibit a certain naïveté, not only in his moralizing assumptions about the passional purity of humble and rustic life, but also in the philosophical premise that poetic language is sufficiently transparent to reflect affections accurately and without distortion. Wordsworth often shows that he is aware of this difficulty, but is unable or unwilling to come down firmly on one side or the other. He does not share Hume's suspicion that poets are "liars by profession," but he knows that poetry works in part through its magical ability to transform ordinary experience. Wordsworth acknowledges that a representation is always less vivacious than the original it copies and approximates the real so that even the "greatest Poet … must often in liveliness and truth, fall short of that which is uttered by men in real life, under the actual pressure of those passions, certain shadows of which the Poet thus produces, or feels to be produced, in himself" (PLB 341–6). He also recognizes that the aim of "bringing pleasure" obliges the poet to engage the "principle of selection" in order to "remov[e] what would otherwise be painful or disgusting in the passion" (PLB 387–9), and accepts that poetic language is "unusual" and "not heard in ordinary conversation" (App 50–5). (Many of the poems, one might note, were revised over time to remove some of the more rustic and affected-sounding turns of phrase). At the same time, Wordsworth insists that his own style, albeit unusual, is "still the language of men," and he feels entitled to speak of poetic "truth" because the poems he writes speak of and to the reality of human beings and their natural condition. The mark of poetic genius is to glimpse this truth and articulate it: the poet "considers man and nature as essentially adapted to each other," Wordsworth writes with the aid of a revealing metaphor, "and the mind of man as naturally the mirror of the fairest and most interesting qualities of nature" (PLB 425–7). In the final analysis, Wordsworth is of a piece with his eighteenth-century predecessors who also felt the tension between the original and the copy, the real and the represented, and unable to remove it, focused their efforts on articulating and moderating its effects.

SAMUEL TAYLOR COLERIDGE

As we have seen, Wordsworth draws in various ways on the aesthetic tradition of the eighteenth century, and this is one reason why *The Sublime and the Beautiful* is such a rich, provocative, and informative essay. Its "aesthetic and philosophical" mode makes it a singular occurrence in Wordsworth's literary output, however, and it would be inaccurate and unnecessary to put him in the same company of the philosophers on whom he draws. In this respect, Coleridge is a point of contrast: not only was he widely read in the history of philosophy, but his voluminous output also contains numerous discussions, lectures, analyses, and translations of figures from the Ancients onward.[36] Although it is fair to say that Coleridge made no original philosophical contribution, his writing reveals a remarkable ability to collate, synthesize, and clarify the eclectic sources on which he draws, and when considered together the result at least approximates a system of thought reminiscent of those in the German tradition from whom he took his greatest inspiration: Kant, in particular, was a source for much of Coleridge's thinking, followed closely by the Idealist philosophies of Johann Christoph Friedrich von Schiller (1759–1805) and Friedrich Wilhelm Joseph von Schelling (1775–1854). Coleridge's philosophical bent is also evident in his literary style; he writes in a deliberate, self-conscious, and sometimes pompously technical language in which the search for definitional clarity and "just distinction" finds pride of place. This affectation was not lost on Keats who, in a telling remark in one of his letters, notes how Coleridge would rather forego insight than be "content with half-knowledge." Coleridge stands somewhat apart from others in the Romantic tradition with his passion to bring order to and discover explanations for phenomena that Wordsworth, Keats, and Shelley are willing to celebrate as an ineffable part of the quasidivine

---

[36] *The Collected Works of Samuel Taylor Coleridge*, 16 vols. (Princeton, NJ: Princeton University Press, 1983) (*Works*).

mystery that underlies and facilitates the poetic art in which they are engaged. Despite deep differences between the two men, Hazlitt described Coleridge as the only person he had ever known "who answered to the idea of a man of genius" and the only person from whom he "ever learnt any thing"; this must speak in some way to the originality of Coleridge's mind.[37]

Whether or not Coleridge was a philosophical mind of the first order, there is certainly a general tendency among commentators to see him as bringing to fruition or completing aesthetic principles that Wordsworth left obscure or undeveloped, especially with respect to the distinction between imagination and fancy (of which more follows). This is to overstate the case, however. Despite his extensive writings on philosophical matters, Coleridge's theoretical contribution to the aesthetic tradition is relatively slight, even bearing in mind the complexities of deciphering where his views begin and those of Wordsworth leave off. The *Collected Works* (running to some sixteen volumes) contain a number of undeveloped fragments and notes on aesthetic matters, as well as *The Principles of Genial Criticism*, which consists of three essays occasioned by an exhibition of the American artist Washington Allston (whom Coleridge had first met in Rome in 1805) and first published in *Felix Farley's Bristol Journal* in August and September 1814. Apart from the fact that passages are directed at Knight and the *Analytic Inquiry*, the *Principles* is of little philosophical interest, consisting as it does almost entirely of an unacknowledged restatement of Kant's treatment of beauty and aesthetic judgment in the *Critique of the Power of Judgment*, which Coleridge had read sometime around 1810 and considered the greatest of Kant's works.[38] Not until *Biographia Literaria*, however, composed quickly and in some desperation between late May and early September 1815 (he was despairing of his creative and literary progress and struggling with opium addiction), does Coleridge collect and present his thoughts on aesthetics (and many other subjects besides) in any organized way, and even here his views are scattered through the so-called philosophical chapters (Chapters 5–13 of 24).[39]

The work began life as a preface modeled on and in response to the one that had graced *Lyrical Ballads*, and was intended to articulate Coleridge's own views of poetry and to clarify points of divergence between himself and

---

[37] The quote is from the final lecture of Hazlitt's *Lectures on English Poetry*. See ch. 6.

[38] *The Principles of Genial Criticism*, in *Works*, vol. 1, *Shorter Works and Fragments*, ed. H. J. Jackson and J. R. de J. Jackson, 1:356–86. See also "Hints Respecting Beauty," "Aesthetic Terms," "On Aesthetic Problems," "Definitions of Aesthetic Terms," and "On the Distinction between the Picturesque and the Sublime," in ibid., 277–80, 345–6, 347–8, 350–1, and 352–3, respectively.

[39] *Biographia Literaria or Biographical Sketches of My Literary Life and Opinions*, in *Works*, vol. 7 (two parts), ed. James Engell and W. Jackson Bate. (BL followed by part, chapter, and page number.) For an informative discussion of the work's origin, see editor's introduction, BL I, esp. xlv–lxxiii, and for an overview of Coleridge's philosophical views and possible sources and influences, ibid., esp. lxxiii–civ.

Wordsworth; it soon grew into something much larger, becoming finally the wide-ranging if unsystematic work that reflects, as the subtitle indicates his literary life and opinions. One immediate impetus for composing *Biographia Literaria* was Wordsworth's new Preface to the *Poems* of 1815, and it is noteworthy more generally that Coleridge's contributions to philosophical aesthetics are framed largely in terms of his reaction to Wordsworth. There is remarkable consistency in the themes the two men emphasize – *inter alia* the search for permanent principles of human nature, the importance of sympathy and imagination, pleasure and sublimity, the organic unity of a whole, and the privileged place of the poet – and although this is not to deny points of disagreement between them, it is to underscore that there is more that unites than separates them. There are two areas are of particular interest in the present context: first, Coleridge's claims for poetry and the poem, which he develops by way of contrast with the Preface to *Lyrical Ballads*, and second, his celebrated discussion of the nature and function of "imagination," which draws heavily on Kant and German Idealism, but is formulated in response to Wordsworth's attempt in the Preface of 1815 to distinguish that faculty from "fancy."

Poems and Poetry

As already noted, the role Coleridge took in the composition and publication of the Preface to *Lyrical Ballads* is a complex one, as is the part he played in the emergence of the ideas its expresses and the degree to which he shared or endorsed them. A telling example of this is the marginalia to Knight's *Analytic Inquiry* previously mentioned (see n. 4): the copy was certainly used and owned by Coleridge and contains extensive comments decidedly Coleridgean in tone, but which are written in Wordsworth's hand and sometimes in the first-person plural. Coleridge reports in *Biographia Literaria* that the collection was planned to fall into two parts. The first was to consist of poems by Coleridge in which "incidents and agents, were to be in part at least, supernatural; and the excellence aimed at was to consist in the interesting of the affections by the dramatic truth of such emotions, as would naturally accompany such situations, supposing them real"; the second part was to contain poems by Wordsworth in which "subjects were to be chosen from ordinary life; the characters and incidents were to be such, as will be found in every village and its vicinity, where there is a meditative and feeling mind to seek after them, or to notice them, when they present themselves" (BL II 14.6). The task of writing a preface for the work had originally fallen to Coleridge, but because, as it transpired, he contributed fewer poems than planned, it was Wordsworth who appropriately penned the published version. Given this history of its origin and development it is not surprising that the Preface should focus on poems of "ordinary life" rather than those of "supernatural" subjects, and reflect the views of Wordsworth rather than Coleridge. So obvious was it that Coleridge's *Christabel* did not fit the principles proposed that Wordsworth asked the printer to omit it from the final version of the volume, a turn of events that upset its author considerably.

As one might expect, then, Coleridge's attitude to the Preface is decidedly ambiguous (though he remains unfailing, one might note, in his praise for Wordsworth's genius and in condemning the scathing reviews and parodies of his work). On the one hand, Coleridge embraces the Preface as (at least in part) a collaborative effort. In letters written as early as 1802, he describes it as "half a child of my own brain" and the product of conversations between him and Wordsworth so numerous that it became almost impossible to say "which first started any particular Thought."[40] The fact that the Preface reflected primarily the poetic muse of Wordsworth, moreover, did not change the fact, as Coleridge reports later in *Biographia Literaria*, that he and Wordsworth were of a similar mind when it came to the "two cardinal points of poetry" – exciting the sympathy of the reader through adhering to the truth of nature, and producing novelty for the reader "by the modifying colours of imagination" (BL II.14.5) – or that he saw a fundamental continuity between the aims of their respective poetry. The ends are "analogous," Coleridge emphasizes, for they both seek to arouse a state of excitement, the supernatural poems by moving readers to a "willing suspension of belief ... which constitutes poetic faith," and those of ordinary life by awakening the mind to the same and directing attention "to the loveliness and wonders of the world before us" (BL II 14.6–7). On the other hand, Coleridge distances himself from the Preface and the aesthetic principles it contains. He attributes its composition to Wordsworth alone and, likewise, responsibility for adding it to the 1802 edition; he also declares not only his disagreement with what the "words undoubtedly seem to authorize," but also insists that "on the contrary [he] objected to them as erroneous in principle, and as contradictory (in appearance at least) both to other parts of the same preface, and to the author's own practice in the greater number of the poems themselves" (BL II.14.10). Coleridge clearly considered the differences between himself and Wordsworth significant enough to warrant a formal expression of his own views on poetry, both "in *kind*, and in *essence*" (BL II.14.11).

A major point of contention concerns Wordsworth's elision and effective denial of any meaningful distinction between poetry and prose. In the Preface, Wordsworth had declared that "there neither is, nor can be, any *essential* difference between the language of prose and metrical composition.... They both speak by and to the same organs," he continues, "the bodies in which both of them are clothed may be said to be of the same substance, their affections are kindred and almost identical, not necessarily differing even in degree; ... the same human blood circulates through the veins of them both" (PLB 266–78).

---

[40] *Collected Letters of Samuel Taylor Coleridge*, ed. Earl Leslie Griggs, 6 vols. (Oxford: Clarendon Press, 2000 [c. 1956–71]), 2:830. See also 811–12.

Coleridge responds by admitting that one might "choose to call every composition a poem," but that doing so evades the cardinal point, which is to reach the "definition ... of a *legitimate* poem." Coleridge does not deny that poetry and prose consist of the same elements, but emphasizes against Wordsworth that one is distinguished from the other by the way these elements combine and the object on which each focuses. A "legitimate" poem, as Coleridge explains it, has two components. First, its object is pleasure; not, however, pleasure that arises incidentally from seeking some other end (as in the search for a scientific fact or mathematical truth), but as its intended and thus "*immediate* object." Second, this pleasure comes about because a poem (and by extension any work of art) succeeds "by proposing to itself such delight from the whole, as is compatible with a distance gratification from each component part"; that is, a poem must be a composition "the parts of which mutually support and explain each other; all in their proportion harmonizing with, and supporting the purpose and known influences of metrical arrangement" (BL II.14.13). A poem is thus a "selection and artificial arrangement" that succeeds in "exciting" the attention of the reader in a way "more continuous and equal" than does the language of prose (BL II.44.15.). Coleridge likens this effect to a traveler who delights in the pleasurable activity of the journey rather than succumbing to the restless desire for consummation that comes only when the final destination is reached.

Imagination and Fancy

On the face of it, these criteria do little to distinguish a "legitimate" poem from an illegitimate one: surely prose also involves the mutual support of parts in a whole (though this might reduce its length) as well as the "selection and artificial arrangement" of elements, and there is no reason to deny that it too excites the reader's attention in a "continuous and equal" way. The significance of the difference Coleridge has in mind, however, is suggested in his remark that defining poetry is part and parcel of clarifying the nature of poetic genius, which demands in turn understanding the difference between "fancy" and "imagination," and it is here that Coleridge's idea of a legitimate poem makes more sense: the question "What is poetry?," he contends, "is so nearly the same question with, what is a poet? that the answer to the one is involved in the solution of the other" (BL II.14.15). Like his philosophy generally, Coleridge's treatment of the imagination is an attempt to assimilate and elucidate a range of material drawn from a variety of philosophical sources; his treatment of the imagination bears closest comparison to that of Schelling's *System of Transcendental Idealism* (1800) and Johannes Nikolaus Tetens's *Philosophical Inquiry into Human Nature and Its Development* (1775–6), although no single source can be cited definitively.[41] As previously noted, the immediate impetus

---

[41] On this point, see the editor's introduction, LB I.lxxxviii.

was Wordsworth's treatment of the same subject in the Preface to the *Poems* of 1815, and although one should not forget that Coleridge had been concerned with the question for many years before composing *Biographia Literaria*, Wordsworth forms an appropriate and informative way for considering his views.[42]

As we have seen already, for the most part writers in the eighteenth century tended to use the words *imagination* and *fancy* interchangeably. If there was a difference, it was largely implicit, reflected in the tendency from Shaftesbury and Addison onward to award the serious business of creativity to *imagination* while leaving *fancy* with the more playful pastime of forming amusing yet frivolous associations. This is expressed nowhere more forcefully than in Hume's identification of imagination with the "*creative* power of the human mind" (EHU 2.5) and its "unlimited power of mixing, compounding, separating, and dividing ... ideas, in all the varieties of fiction and vision" (EHU 5.10). As the century progressed, this implied division between the creative imagination and associative fancy crystallized and hardened into something like a principled distinction. As early as 1767, in his *Essay on Original Genius* Duff hints at such a difference, although ambiguously as he also suggests that both faculties require judgment and thus taste. Still, he credits imagination with the "plastic power of inventing new associations of ideas and of combining them with infinite variety," enabling it to "present a creation of its own, and to exhibit objects which never existed in nature," but says the "proper office of Fancy, is only to collect the materials of composition; but, as a heap of stones, thrown together without art or design," he continues, "can never make a regular and well proportioned building; so the effusions of Fancy, without the superintending and directing powers ... [of judgment], can never produce a masterly composition."[43] This philosophical trend, however, was actually a reversal of an older tradition with roots in classical and medieval thought that assigned roles to the faculties on the basis of etymology: *fancy* being associated with the Greek *phantasia* – from *phantazein*, "causing to appear" – was awarded the power of creativity, while *imagination* from the Latin *imaginatio* was given the more concrete task of copying percepts in the shape of images. It was this older division that found its way into William Taylor's *British Synonyms Discriminated*,[44] criticism of which formed the starting point for Wordsworth in the Preface of 1815: he accuses Taylor of being "enthralled by Etymology"

---

[42] William Wordsworth, "Preface to the Edition of 1815," in *Prose Works*, 3:26–39 (P followed by line numbers). In the later edition, the earlier preface of 1800/1802 was relegated to an appendix suggesting to readers that it was now a historical curio rather than an indispensable guide to the poems.

[43] Duff, *An Essay on Original Genius*, 7 and 70–1, respectively. See Stewart, *Elements of the Philosophy of the Human Mind* (1792), 284–5, 305–9, and 477. I am indebted to the editor's introduction for the references to Duff and Stewart. See also Owen, *Wordsworth as Critic*, 158–9.

[44] See William Taylor, "*Imagination, Fancy*," in *British Synonyms Discriminated* (London: W. Pople, 1813), 242.

(P 157), of equating fancy with fantasy and the production of "ideal representations of absent objects," and connecting imagination with the "power of
depicting" (P 143–6) that generates pictures or copies. The result of this error,
Wordsworth concludes, is "nothing more" than a reduction of both terms to a
"mode of memory" (P 162–3).

Wordsworth, then, is very much part of the philosophical rather than etymological tradition in raising imagination above fancy, but at once connects the faculty with his view of poetry and poetic creativity, emphasizing its passive role in
enabling readers to feel and be moved by vivid impressions, and its active role
as the creative source of poetic images that affect the reader. Wordsworth thus
speaks of the "poetical imagination," which has "no reference to images that are
merely a faithful copy, existing in the mind of absent external objects; but is a
word of higher import, denoting operations of the mind upon those objects, and
processes of creation or of composition, governed by certain fixed laws" (P 168–
74).[45] The poetic imagination works upon some image or idea through its "powers" of "conferring," "abstracting," "modifying," and "endowing," and thus gives
to objects properties they would not otherwise possess; the result, Wordsworth
urges, is something "like a new existence" (P 239–43). In the realm of poetry, these
new existences have "attributes and qualities" that mark a creative extension of
the literal meaning of words in such a way that stretches, fills, and exercises the
imagination, making it "conscious of an indestructible dominion" (P 385–6). This
is the psychological basis for that feeling of intense unity without a conscious
contemplation of parts, which, as we saw in our discussion of *The Sublime and
the Beautiful*, Wordsworth sees as the province of the sublime. The imagination
is the basis of this experience because it is the faculty that soars upward to the
indestructible and infinite, displaying the singular power of "consolidating numbers into unity, and dissolving and separating unity into number, – alterations
proceeding from, and governed by, a sublime consciousness of the soul in her
own mighty and almost divine powers" (P 279–82). Such is the effect, he urges
by way of example, of Virgil's description of goats "hanging" from a cliff ("Never
again shall I, reclining in some green dell, watch you my goats hang far above
from the bushy cliffs"), or, more dramatically and sublimely, Milton's use of
the complex phrase "hangs in the clouds" (*Paradise Lost* II. 636–43) to express
the magnificence and extent of a fleet of ships moving as one mighty person.

The fancy, by contrast, is defined by opposite characteristics and performs
quite a different function. Wordsworth accepts that it has the "power of evoking and combining" (P 346) or, in an explicit reference to a remark by Coleridge
in an essay contributed to Robert Southey's *Omniana*, that it has "aggrega-
tive and associative power."[46] Against Coleridge, he finds this definition "too

---

[45] Wordsworth also distinguishes the poetical imagination, the province of the sublime, from
the "human and dramatic" imagination, which is affected by the pathetic. Shakespeare is the
prime example of the latter. See PE 229–30.
[46] William Southey, *Omniana*, no. 174. Reproduced in BL I:193–4 (1907 edition).

general" on the grounds that "to aggregate and to associate, to evoke and to combine, belong as well to the Imagination as to the Fancy" (P 346–50). The main difference, Wordsworth insists in his customary language, is that the two faculties work according to different laws: "Fancy is given to quicken and to beguile the temporal part of our nature, Imagination to incite and to support the eternal" (P 388–90); where the principles governing the imagination confers on it the freedom to create new existences, the fancy is prevented from changing the constitution of the materials on which it works by the associative principles that govern it; its images are thus "bounded."

In *Biographia Literaria* Coleridge reports that he had not yet seen Taylor's work on synonyms, but endorses nonetheless Wordsworth's criticisms and in so doing he too rejects the tradition that defined *fancy* and *imagination* on the basis of etymology: there is no more "apposite" translation of *phantasia* than *imaginatio* (BL I.4.82), he insists, thus attributing creativity to the imagination and association to fancy. At the same time, Coleridge insists that there are differences between him and Wordsworth born primarily of the divergent ends for the sake of which they consider the distinction. For "it was Mr. Wordsworth's purpose," Coleridge writes,

> to consider the influences of fancy and imagination as they are manifest *in poetry*, and from the different effects to conclude their diversity in kind; while it is my object to investigate the *seminal principle*, and then from the kind to deduce the degree. My friend has drawn a masterly sketch of the branches with their *poetic* fruitage. I wish to add the trunk, and even the roots as far as they lift themselves above ground, and are visible to the naked eye of our common consciousness. (BL I.4.88, emphases added)

As our discussion of the 1815 Preface makes clear, this is neither a fair nor accurate description of either Wordsworth's views or his method of expressing them: he does not deduce a principle from the effects of poetry (the fruitage), as Coleridge would have it, but finds first a "seminal principle" (the trunk) to distinguish fancy and imagination on the basis of which he shows how sublime effects come about. Moreover, on the basic distinction between the two faculties there is no substantive disagreement between them: like Wordsworth, Coleridge holds that "fancy and imagination [are] two distinct and widely different faculties" (BL I.4.82), that imagination is both active and passive (BL I.7.124), and a "plastic" power that synthesizes, shapes, and unifies the materials upon which it works: imagination has what Coleridge calls "ensemplastic power," a term he coins from the Greek "to shape into one" (BL I.10.168) and takes to be analogous to the German *Einbildungskraft*, the faculty that forms the many into one, *in eins Bildung*.[47] Like Wordsworth, Coleridge also

---

[47] Etymologically, we might note, Coleridge is mistaken because the relevant preposition in *Einbildungskraft* is *ein* (in) rather than *Eins* (one). Schelling does use the phrase "*In-Eins-Bildung*," however, which may be the source of Coleridge's conjecture and/or confusion. See editors' note 2 in BL I.10.168.

connects the fancy with association; it is "no other than a mode of Memory emancipated from the order of time and space; and blended with, and modified by that empirical phenomenon of the will, which we express by the word CHOICE. But equally with the ordinary memory it must receive all its materials ready made from the law of association" (SB I.13.305).

What then does Coleridge have in mind when he insists that, unlike Wordsworth, his interest is in the seminal principle, the trunk rather than the branches and fruit of poetry? An answer to this question can be gleaned from the distinction he draws between the "primary" and "secondary" imagination:

> The primary IMAGINATION I hold to be the living Power and prime Agent of all human Perception, as a repetition in the finite mind of the eternal act of creation in the infinite I AM. The secondary I consider as an echo of the former, co-existing with the conscious will yet still as identical with the primary in the *kind* of its agency, and differing only in degree, and in the mode of its operation. It dissolves, diffuses, dissipates, in order to re-create; or where this process is rendered impossible, yet still at all events it struggles to idealize and to unify. It is essentially vital, even as all objects (as objects) are essentially fixed and dead. (SB I.13.304)

Although this is expressed in the somewhat esoteric language of the German Idealists, Coleridge's point is a familiar one in the history of modern philosophy. The primary imagination is Coleridge's version of Kant's productive imagination as the latter describes it in the *Critique of Pure Reason*, and, specifically, in the Deduction of the Categories. It is the seat of the involuntary mechanism whereby impressions of sense are brought together in a "necessary unity in the synthesis of what is manifold in appearance" (A124), the "faculty of representing in intuition an object that is not itself present" (B151). The imagination also provides content for the empirical self (Coleridge's "I AM"), moments of which are held together by what Kant calls the "transcendental unity of apperception," the mysterious yet necessary condition without which the self-identity of a being through time would be impossible (see A107/B153-4). Coleridge considers this power of the imagination to be creative insofar as it is spontaneous and active, but at once limited to generating copies without originality. The secondary imagination, by contrast (the equivalent of Wordsworth's "poetical imagination"), exhibits the same kind of creative power as the primary imagination, but is guided or employed by the will of the poet and through his power it imitates and recreates. It does so by rearranging materials provided by sense (diffusing, dissipating, idealizing, and unifying), and produces what Wordsworth calls a "new existence." The individual in whom this secondary imagination is manifest is the poet, an individual whose genius "sustains and modifies the images, thoughts, and emotions of the poet's own mind" and in doing so "brings the whole soul of man into activity" (BL II 14.15-16).

Similarities notwithstanding, one can see how Coleridge might consider this view of the imagination to be a "seminal principle" in a way not conceived by Wordsworth and one that explains why he might consider the doctrine of the preface to be "erroneous in principle." The primary imagination is a common feature of human nature and thus possessed by everybody; in the language of Kant's Critical Philosophy, it is the condition for the possibility of all knowledge and any self-consciousness. The secondary imagination, by contrast, though similar in kind, is a special application of the primary power, and possessed by only a few individuals – "poets" – who have the will to direct and employ it appropriately. This is the creative act proper and requires a particular mode of expression and peculiarity of language – poetic diction – that departs from the characters, incidents, and language of "ordinary life." Poetry is not, on this view, the domain of the unschooled rustic, but a rarefied place to which a privileged and talented minority have access. Thus, while he and Wordsworth might agree on the two cardinal points of poetry and take the aims of their respective work to be "analogous," one can understand how Coleridge might at once insist that his own views differ "in *kind*, and in *essence*."

PERCY BYSSHE SHELLEY AND JOHN KEATS

While Wordsworth and Coleridge represent the most significant contribution made by the Romantics to the tradition of philosophical aesthetics, the picture would be incomplete without considering two other founding figures, Percy Bysshe Shelley (1792–1822) and John Keats (1795–1821). Their presence is felt despite the fact that both died young, and tragically, Shelley in a sailing accident off the coast of Italy, and Keats of consumption in Rome, hastened in all probability by the therapeutic bleeding and near-starvation diet recommended by his physician. The contributions of each follow in paths well marked for them by Wordsworth and Coleridge – the nature of imagination and its manifestation in the art of poetry – but they emphasize more the rarefied, divine nature of poets and their connection to certain enduring principles that engage the poetic mind in a spontaneous and inexplicable way. As such, they effectively endorse Coleridge's idea of the secondary imagination, although they at once reject his poetic "will" and "just definition" in favor of Wordsworth's emphasis on feeling and sensation. In both, and especially in the Platonist language that pervades Shelley's thinking, one finds a return to, and an unapologetic celebration of, Shaftesburian enthusiasm, with the poet as an instrument through which, in a process equally opaque, the mysteries of the universe are expressed.

Shelley's contribution to the history of aesthetics is contained in the justly celebrated *A Defence of Poetry*, an essay composed shortly before his death in response to the half-facetious and at times highly amusing *The Four Ages of Poetry* (1820) written by his friend Thomas Love Peacock (who also wrote *Memoirs of Percy Bysshe Shelley* in honor of his departed friend).[48] The *Defence*

---

[48] *The Four Ages of Poetry*, in *The Works of Thomas Love Peacock*, ed. H. F. B Brett-Smith and C. E. Jones, 10 vols. (London: Constable and Co., 1934), 8:3–25 (FAP). (The *Memoirs*

was scheduled to appear twice in literary magazines that failed before the date of planned publication, and it was not until 1840, and through the efforts of Shelley's second wife, Mary Shelley, that it saw the light of day. Peacock had sketched a cyclical history of poetry (reminiscent in striking ways of the *curso i recurso* of Giambattista Vico's *New Science*)[49] in which the art progresses from iron through gold to silver only to reach that of brass, which represents a return to the barbarism of its beginnings. In the first age, "the bardic," poetry takes the form of unwritten panegyrics to individuals of wealth and power (the age of the great Norse myth); the second, or "Homeric," comes into being under established civil polity and celebrates the history of nations and kings (exemplified by Greek epic); and the third, "the Virgilian," develops as the "poetry of civilized life," producing either original works in the form of the comic, didactic, and satiric or ones that imitate and give "exquisite polish" to those of the age of gold (Menander and Aristophanes, Horace and Juvenal). Peacock contends that the "state of poetry" in this third age already constitutes a "step towards its extinction," revealed in the tendency to supplant "ornamental and figurative language" that speaks to the passions with the "simplest and most unvarnished phrase" that marks the growing ascendancy of reason (FAP 11). This reaches its culmination in the age of brass, "the Nonnic," "which, by rejecting the polish and learning of the age of silver," Peacock writes, "and taking a retrograde stride to the barbarism and crude traditions of the age of iron, professes to return to nature and revive the age of gold" (FAP 13). As one might expect, this last is aimed pretty squarely at the Romantics and while Shelley (as a friend one assumes) is spared, the Lake Poets – that "egregious confraternity of rhymesters" (FAP 18) and the "morbid dreamer" Wordsworth in particular – receive the full brunt of Peacock's wit: "Mr. Wordworth," he quips at one point, "picks up village legends from old women and sextons; and Mr. Coleridge, to the valuable information acquired from similar sources, superadds the dreams of crazy theologians and the mysticisms of German metaphysics" (FAP 19–20).

Part of Shelley's response (notably more serious in tone and considerably more sophisticated in content than the essay that inspires it) takes the form of a sketch for an alternative history of poetry, and in the course of doing so – and more interesting for present purposes – he proposes a view of imagination and poetry that draws on and extends the treatments of the same by Wordsworth and Coleridge. Shelley's view also recalls eighteenth-century thinkers who emphasized the role of the imagination, but unlike his Romantic forebears

---

is to be found in the same volume, 39–141.) Percey Bysshe Shelley, *A Defence of Poetry: or, Remarks Suggested by an Essay Entitled "Four Ages of Poetry,"* in *Shelley's Poetry and Prose*, ed. Donald H. Reiman and Neil Fraistat, 2nd ed. (New York: W. W. Norton, 2002), 510–35 (DP followed by paragraph and page number).

[49] See *The "New Science" of Giambattista Vico, unabridged translation of the third edition (1744) with the addition of "Practic of the New Science,"* trans. Thomas Goddard Bergin and Max Harold Fisch (Ithaca, NY: Cornell University Press, 1984).

he also recalls an earlier tradition represented by Sir Philip Sidney (1554–86) and Herbert Spenser (1542–99), and explicitly juxtaposes the faculty to reason rather than to fancy.[50] In Shelley's hands, this is intended not (as in the case of Hume) to suggest any mendacity on the part of imagination, but to emphasize and confirm its relation to truth and to celebrate without apology its creative power. Reason, for Shelley, is inert and functions through the principle of analysis, the effect of mind regarding the relation between things "simply as relations," whereas imagination is alive, the "imperial faculty" (DP 5.513) that creates according to the principle of synthesis, the effect of mind acting upon thoughts, which it colors "with its own light" to compose (as in Wordsworth's "new existence") other thoughts "each containing within itself the principle of its own integrity" (DP 1.510–11). Imagination alone confers value, and stands in relation to reason (to use Shelley's similes) as an agent to the instrument he employs, as spirit to the body it animates, or as substance to the shadow it casts.

Shelley emphasizes above all the mysterious and unknown workings of imagination, which, as he presents it in the "Hymn to Intellectual Beauty," feels the shadow cast by the Spirit of Beauty and grasps it in a moment of "extacy":

> The awful shadow of some unseen Power
> Floats tho' unseen among us; visiting
> This various world with as inconstant wing
> As summer winds that creep from flower to flower;
> Like moonbeams that behind some piny mountain shower
> It visits with inconstant glance
> Each human heart and countenance;
> Like hues and harmonies of evening,
> Like clouds in starlight widely spread,
> Like memory of music fled,
> Like aught that for its grace may be
> Dear, and yet dearer for its mystery.[51]

Imagination connects to this mystery as a "power that arises from within, like the colour of a flower which fades and changes as it is developed" (DP 39.531).

---

[50] Herbert Spenser, "Fowre Hymnes" (1796), in *The Works of Edmund Spenser*, A Varorium Edition, ed. Edwin Greenlaw, Charles Grosvenor Osgood, and Frederick Morgan Padelford, et al., 9 vols. (Baltimore, MD: Johns Hopkins University Press, 1932–49), *The Minor Poems*, ed. Charles Grosvenor Osgood and Henry Gibbons Lotspeich, 7:193–230. Sir Philip Sidney's *The Defence of Poesy; Otherwise Known as An Apologie for Poetry* was extant in 1580–1 in manuscript form and was published in two separate editions in London 1595 (printed by J. Roberts for Henry Olney, and by T. Creed for William Ponsonby). The definitive critical version is found in Katherine Duncan-Jones and Jan Van Dorsten, eds., *Miscellaneous Prose Works of Sir Philip Sidney* (Oxford: Clarendon Press, 1973).

[51] "Hymn to Intellectual Beauty," *Poems*, in *The Complete Works of Percey Bysshe Shelley*, ed. Roger Ingpen and Walter E. Peck, 10 vols. (New York: Gordain Press, 1965), 2:59–62, lines 1–12.

Its fruits come unbidden, adventitiously, unlike those with their basis in the transparent workings of reason whose mechanical operations can be exposed and commanded at will. In this sense poetry is properly understood as the "expression of the imagination" (DP 2.511), Shelley emphasizes, manifest both in the act of creation and as the cause of an affective state in the reader. The "functions of the poetical faculty are twofold," he writes, "by one it creates new material for knowledge, and power and pleasure; by the other it engenders in the mind a desire to reproduce and arrange them according to a certain rhythm and order which may be called the beautiful and the good" (DP 38.531). This latter function might not, strictly speaking, be original to Shelley, but he casts it in a new and striking light by comparing the sentient nature of human beings to the play of wind across the strings of a lyre (an image already familiar from Coleridge and others):[52]

Man is an instrument over which a series of external and internal impressions are driven, like the alternations of an ever-changing melody ... and produces not melody, alone, but harmony, by an internal adjustment of the sounds or motions thus excited to the impressions which excite them. It is as if the lyre could accommodate its chords to the motions of that which strikes them, in a determined proportion of sound; even as the musician can accommodate his voice to the sound of the lyre. (DP 2.511)

Like Wordsworth and Coleridge before him, Shelley thus highlights the unity of self and object, subject and external world, and sees the synthetic activity of imagination as the substance that unites them. "Poetry turns all things to loveliness; it exalts the beauty of that which is most beautiful, and it adds beauty to that which is most deformed; it marries exultation and horror, grief and pleasure, eternity and change, it subdues to union under its light yoke, all irreconcilable things" (DP 41.533). The faculty is also a plastic power, however, and unlike a musical instrument whose strings must be tuned to a predetermined pitch, contains the requisite sensitivity and pliability to conform itself to the object that affects it. Thus, emotions that arise as the effect of some perception are expressed in gesture, language, and the mimetic arts, but these latter are themselves images of the emotions they express and change in harmony with them. Art is thus both the effect and expression of passions, the "representation and the medium," as Shelley expresses it, "the pencil and the picture, the chord and the harmony" (DP 2.511).

Each form of representation, Shelley then emphasizes – be it language, music, dance, sculpture, painting, or architecture – has a particular rhythm or order that manifests the relation between perception and expression, which composes it. This order imparts pleasure to the audience and *any* art form that

---

[52] Coleridge writes: "and what if all of animated nature / Be but organic harps diversely framed, / That tremble into throught, as o'er them sweeps / Plastic and vast, one intellectual breeze, / At once the Soul of each, and God of All?" (lines 44–8). "The Eolian Harp" (1795) *Works*, 16, I:232–5. On the lyre as a characteristic metaphor of expression for the Romantics, see Abrams, *The Mirror and the Lamp*, 50–3.

produces this effect deserves the name of "poetry": not only the fine or creative arts as we have come to think of them, but the framers of laws and erectors of civil society as well. In its widest sense all representative art is poetic, and any human creation that reflects the principles of the imagination is art. For "what is called poetry in a restricted sense," Shelley writes, "has a common source with all other forms of order and of beauty, according to which the materials of human life are susceptible of being arranged, according to which Poetry is poetry in a universal sense" (DP 47.535). The narrower and more customary meaning of "poetry" is then but the highest expression of this "universal" sense, because it manifests the same principles only in a way that approximates more closely or instantiates most fully the beautiful, which is nothing other than the "relation between this highest pleasure and its cause" (DP 3.512). In Shelley's language, a poem is thus the "image of life expressed in its eternal truth" and captures what is universal about human nature. A poet, concomitantly, is an individual in whom this capacity or "faculty of approximation to the beautiful" exists most fully. At his most Platonic, and like Shaftsbury's Theocles contemplating the Supreme Principle of Beauty, Shelley unites the various elements of his view into a mystical union of poet, poetry, and the universal principles of human nature: poetry is "something divine" (DP 39.531) that acts in a "divine and unapprehended manner, beyond and above consciousness," with the poet "belonging ... to all time," a "nightingale, who," in an image appropriately sublime, "sits in darkness and sings to cheer its own solitude with sweet sounds; his auditors are as men entranced by the melody of an unseen musician, who feel that they are moved and softened, yet know not whence or why" (DP 12.516). A more esoteric and Romantic image of poetry and the poet it is hard to imagine.

Safely back to earth, there are two consequences of the position proposed in *A Defence* worth emphasizing. First, although he does not do so explicitly, Shelley clearly sides with Wordsworth against Coleridge in finding no essential difference between poetry and prose, or "measured and unmeasured language" (DP 8.514) as he terms it. His reasons for doing so are decidedly Platonic, but he effectively shares Wordsworth's view that the affections aroused by both are "kindred and almost identical," and thus rejects as ungrounded the search for a "legitimate" poem on which Coleridge placed such emphasis. He clearly acknowledges that the intrinsic harmony of language tends over time to produce poetic meter and versification – what Peacock celebrates as ornamentation appropriate for the expression of emotion, and Wordsworth dismissed as "poetic diction" – and concedes that successive generations of writers are obliged to innovate if they are not simply to reproduce their predecessors' achievements. At the same time, Shelley also insists that the imagination can be expressed poetically without such artifice so that ultimately the "distinction between poets and prose writers is a vulgar error" (DP 8.514).

The second point of note arises in connection to Shelley's fascination with Platonic metaphysics and his use of its language to express the conviction that

poetry reflects or manifests some ideal and eternal order emanating myste-
riously in the opaque workings of imagination. For Plato the Form or Idea
of Beauty is never experienced – though it can and should be sought by the
philosophical mind – but is manifest in the grosser phenomenal world of sense
perception; in other words, representations of beauty in the realm of appearance are necessarily corruptions of something higher and infinitely finer. Poetry,
however, on Shelley's view, and ironically given Plato's derision of the art and
recommendation that practitioners should be cast from the ideal city, *corrects* or
purifies the distortions of Beauty in its apparent forms; it is the means whereby
the mind might rise above the heavier stuff of appearance and glimpse the eternal order above. As the closest approximation of the beautiful, poetry has the
memorial power to preserve or, in Shelley's language, "reproduce":

> Poetry lifts the veil from the hidden beauty of the world, and makes familiar objects
> be as if they were not familiar; it reproduces all that it represents, and the imperson-
> ations clothed in its Elysian lights stand thenceforward in the minds of those who
> have once contemplated them, as memorials of that gentle and exalted context which
> extends itself over all thoughts and actions with which it coexists. (DP 13.517)

Poetry has the power to reflect the immutable order behind appearances: it
"makes immortal all that is best and most beautiful in the world; it attests the
vanishing apparitions which haunt the interlunations" (DP 40.532), and is effectively a "mirror," as Shelley describes it, "which makes beautiful that which is
distorted" (DP 9.515). Beauty experienced in this way "awakens and enlarges
the mind itself by rendering it the receptacle of a thousand unapprehended
combinations of thought" (DP 13.517), and the emotional impact is one with
Wordsworth's sublime, though cast in the shape of Rationalist metaphysics.

Keats's views on poetry and imagination are shorn of Platonic metaphysics,
but they put him very much in the company of Shelley, and carry strong echoes
and even borrowings of views expressed by Hazlitt whom he met early in 1818
and who remained a companion for, and influence on, Keats until his early and
untimely death. Keats was a regular attendee of Hazlitt's *Lectures on the English
Poets* delivered in 1818 and published later that year, and was also a self-avowed
enthusiast of Hazlitt's other work, especially the essays for *The Examiner* written between 1814 and 1817 and published as *The Round Table* in 1817.[53] Keats
did not compose anything remotely comparable to the well-worked sentences of
Wordsworth's *Guide* or *The Sublime and the Beautiful*, the dense philosophical
prose of Coleridge, or an equivalent of Shelley's polished *Defence*. His contribution to Romantic criticism is found exclusively in passages of varying length

---

[53] The connections between Keats and Hazlitt are explored by various commentators. See, e.g.,
R. M. Wardle, *Hazlitt* (Lincoln: University of Nebraska Press, 1971); David Bromwich, *Hazlitt:
The Mind of a Critic* (New Haven, CT: Yale University Press, 1999 [1983]), ch. 11; Andrew
Motion, *Keats* (London: Faber and Faber, 1999); and Duncan Wu, *William Hazlitt: The First
Modern Man* (Oxford: Oxford University Press, 2008), 197 and 210. I discuss Hazlitt's own
views in ch. 6.

contained in letters written to friends and family, and like the faculty of imagination and the art of poetry he celebrates, these remarks exhibit spontaneity of
expression, free of either ponderous technical language or difficult conceptual
schemes.[54] Perhaps it is a function of Keats's youth and want of opportunity for
pursuing much formal study, but the result is a purity of passion that often leaps
from the page. This is not to say that Keats despised knowledge; on the contrary,
he conceived his future as a road of "application, study and thought" that would
lead to a "continual drinking of Knowledge," which he expected would take him
into seclusion "for some years" (W 6.62.192–3). Keats also valued knowledge
as a weight to anchor him in the abyss of enthusiasm: the "difference of high
Sensations with and without knowledge," as he writes at one point, "appears
to me this – in the latter case we are falling continually ten thousand fathoms
deep and being blown up again without wings and with all <the> horror of a
bare-shouldered creature – in the former case, our shoulders are fledge, and we
go thro' the same air and space without fear" (W 7.64.5).

At the same time, Keats is one with Shelley in juxtaposing the creative imagination to the analytic faculty of reason. He credits it with reaching out to its
own kind of truth – "What the imagination seizes as Beauty must be truth"
(W 6.31.98), he writes – and identifies it with emotional affect and intense feeling tantamount, perhaps, as John Dewey later interpreted it, to the "wisdom by
which men live."[55] This is nowhere better expressed than in a passage written
after viewing Benjamin West's painting *Death on the Pale Horse*, which Keats
describes as a "wonderful picture," but containing "nothing to be intense upon;
no woman one feels mad to kiss, no face swelling into reality" (W 6.32.102–3).
Even "axioms in philosophy are not axioms until they are proved upon our
pulses," he remarks elsewhere. "We read fine things but never feel them to the
full until we have gone the same steps as the Author" (W 7.64.7). Keats goes further than the other Romantics, however, in emphasizing that imagination not
only opposes reason but also suspends or "obliterates" it, an effect required if
the mind is to be opened to insights that arise only from some secret and hidden
place of mystery closed to those – like Coleridge – who place limits, set demar-
cations, and frame "just distinctions." Keats captures this feature of imagination
that defines the "Man of Achievement" in the idea of "Negative Capability,"

that is, when a man is capable of being in uncertainties, mysteries, doubts, without any
irritable reaching after fact and reason – Coleridge, for instance, would let go by a fine
isolated verisimilitude caught from the Penetralium of mystery, from being incapable
of remaining content with half-knowledge. This pursued through Volumes would perhaps take us no further than this, that with a great poet the sense of Beauty overcomes
every other consideration, or rather obliterates all consideration. (W 6.32.103–4)

---

[54] *The Poetical and Other Writings of John Keats*, ed. H. Buxton Forman, rev. Maurice Buxton
Forman, 8 vols. (New York: Phaeton Press, 1970) (W). The letters comprise vols. 6–8. All references are to volume, letter, and page number.
[55] See John Dewey, *Art and Experience*, 40. See ch. 7 in this book.

Poetry, as one would expect, originates in and reflects this "Penetralium of mystery," and finds expression through the spontaneous and inspired act of poetic creativity; it should come, moreover, as naturally to the poet as "Leaves to a tree" and if not "it had better not come at all" (W 6.51.155). One cannot know whether one has this gift until one engages in the activity, just as one learns to swim, to use Keats's metaphor, by plunging into the water headlong and not by lingering on shore to develop first some theory of how to do it. For the "Genius of Poetry must work out its own salvation in a man," Keats writes,

it cannot be matured by law and precept, but by sensation & watchfulness in itself. That which is creative must create itself – In Endymion, I leaped headlong into the Sea, and thereby have become better acquainted with the Soundings, the quicksands, & the rocks, that if I had stayed upon the green shore, and piped a silly pipe, and took tea & comfortable advice. (W 7.90.122)

The same shock and spontaneity is reflected in the way Keats describes the effect poetry should have on an audience: it "should *surprise* by a fine excess and not by Singularity," he remarks, " – it should *strike* the Reader as a wording of his own highest thoughts, and appear almost as a Remembrance"; it should make the reader "*breathless* instead of content," as if the sun has come over him and then setting leaves him "in the Luxury of Twilight" (W 6.51.155, emphases added).

Keats clearly considers Wordsworth a model and as having come closest to manifesting the workings of the poetic mind in a way that articulates the "Penetralium of mystery"; for Wordsworth thinks "into the human heart" (W 7.64.11), which was the "main region of his song" (W 7.64.7). Keats develops a complex and provocative metaphor to express his thinking, in which (obviously recalling John 14.2) he compares human life to a "large Mansion of Many Apartments," only two of which he can describe: the "infant or Thoughtless Chamber" where one remains for a long time until, having discovered thinking, one enters the "Chamber of Maiden Thought" where one understands that the life of man is governed by misery, heartbreak, pain, sickness, and oppression. The chamber darkens and many doors open from it, all leading to dark passages, and to be here, Keats proposes, recalling the line from "Tintern Abbey," is to feel the "burden of the Mystery." "To this Point was Wordsworth come when he wrote 'Tintern Abbey,'" Keats observes, "and it seems to me that his Genius is explorative of those dark Passages. Now if we live, and go on thinking, we too shall explore them – he is a Genius and superior <to> us, in so far as he can, more than we, make discoveries, and shed light in them" (W 7.64.9–10).

At the same time as he celebrates Wordsworth's genius, Keats also expresses what he sees as its fundamental flaw in what (no doubt under the influence of Hazlitt) he calls the "wordsworthian or egotistical sublime," a "thing per se and [that] stands alone." Wordsworth, as we have seen in detail, understands the sublime as "intense unity" that completely occupies or possesses the soul whether it arises from "union and communion," through which we participate in the object, or from "humiliation and submission," where we meet resistance in something that inspires fear and dread. Keats, however, clearly thinks that Wordsworth does not go far enough, holding fast to the "I" when poetry involves and demands the *negation* of identity and *dissipation* of the self into someone or something other. For the "poetical Character itself" – of which Keats considers himself a "Member" – "is not itself,"

– it has not self – it is everything and nothing – It has not character – it enjoys light and shade; it lives in gusto, be it foul or fair, high or low, rich or poor, mean or elevated. ... A Poet is the most unpoetical of any thing in existence; because he has not Identity – he is continually in for – and filling some other Body – The Sun, the Moon, the Sea and Men and Women who are creatures of impulse and poetical and have about them an unchangeable attribute – the poet has none; no identity – he is certainly the most unpoetical of all God's Creatures. (W 7.93.129–30)

On this view, the act of poet creation is a sublime experience, because it involves expanding the imagination to the point where it explodes its own limits and is freed to become some other being; the imagination is released from a cage to "wander" and "cloudward soar," as Keats expresses the thought memorably in "Fancy":

> Ever let the Fancy roam,
> Pleasure never is at home:
> At a touch sweet Pleasure melteth,
> Like to bubbles when rain pelteth;
> Then let winged Fancy wander
> Through the thought still spread beyond her:
> Open wide the mind's cage-door,
> She'll dart forth, and cloudward soar.[56]

This is clearly how Keats saw himself: he too, he declares, had reached the Chamber of Maiden Thought and began to wander the dark passages of human life. Wordsworth, after all, had explored but a fraction of that space into which Keats was better prepared to enter, unhindered by the ego, in a rhapsodic experience that pushed Wordsworth's "intense unity" to its conceptual limits and returns us to Shaftesbury and the character of Theocles with his flights of fancy and philosophical deliriums. Like any *recorso*, however, the culmination of Romanticism in Keats's "winged Fancy" is not simply a recapitulation of some earlier movement of thought: Theocles, we should recall, is a philosopher pulled in two directions by the competing forces of imagination and reason – he returns from his reveries apologetic and embarrassed. When Romanticism finds its apotheosis in Keats's unselfing poet, however, the imagination reigns triumphant, and that is a victory to be embraced, celebrated, and explored.

---

[56] "Fancy," W 3:164, lines 1–8.

6

Victorian Criticism

Wordsworth died in 1850, and although the nineteenth century still had half its course to run, the writings of its greatest poet had already penetrated so deeply into the body of British aesthetics that, like Burke's *Enquiry* a century before, their influence would be felt long after their author had passed on. The principal writers who came to bear the legacy of Wordsworth and the early Romantics were not poets, nor were they, strictly speaking, philosophers; one of their number – John Stuart Mill – obviously qualifies for that epithet, but his contribution to the tradition bears little resemblance to the works on ethics, politics, and logic for which he is remembered and read. The body of writings in question is better thought of as "criticism," and the first proponent of the trade, William Hazlitt, holds sufficient credentials to be considered the father of the modern, professional variety with which we are familiar today.

To characterize these writers as "Victorian critics" – the epithet under which I propose to collect them – is not to deny that they developed striking and theoretically sophisticated views, nor is it to suggest – especially in the case of John Ruskin – that they did not hearken back to eighteenth-century themes and thinkers. Their work, however, is focused primarily on understanding and appreciating the form and content of creative work: poetry and literature in the case of Hazlitt and Mill; art and architecture in that of Ruskin; and for Walter Pater, in his idiosyncratic and rebellious assessment of the Renaissance, the entire range of the fine arts from medieval French prose to the Herculean scholarship of the nineteenth-century classicist, Joachim Winckelmann. As we shall see throughout this chapter, the faculty of imagination championed by Wordsworth, Coleridge, Keats, and Shelley remains center stage albeit now manifest as the creative and expressive power of the artist; in Ruskin one finds the full realization of the picturesque, in whose hands it undergoes a startling transformation from the "aesthetic" version familiar from Gilpin through Stewart and into its moral or "Turnerian" alternative. Pater, finally, in a dramatic subversion of everything Ruskin admired and valorized, produces perhaps the first self-consciously antiphilosophical text of the tradition, shaped rebelliously around a fully aestheticized and decadent subject. It is with Hazlitt that we begin.

WILLIAM HAZLITT

William Hazlitt (1778–1830) is remembered today as a great critic, essayist, and one of the finest stylists of the English language. The standard edition of his collected works runs to some twenty-one volumes and covers a career of almost continuous writing from his first book-length publication, *An Essay on the Principles of Human Action* (started in 1796 and published anonymously in 1805) to his last major work, the four-volume *Life of Napoleon* (1828–30); he was still writing through his final illness, and only the pain and weakness of his last days stilled his pen. The intervening years saw an enormous body of brilliant work on a wide range of subjects from the world of art, literature, philosophy, and politics, including most famously perhaps, *Characters of Shakespeare's Plays* (1817) and *The Spirit of the Age: or, Contemporary Portraits* (1825).[1] A recent biographer has not only credited Hazlitt with founding modern literary criticism, but also for being responsible in large part for what is now thought of as journalism, including the first article to cover a sporting event (the occasion being an illegal prize fight).[2] Hazlitt's father, William senior, was a Unitarian minister with an intellectual bent, who had studied at Glasgow under Adam Smith, and wrote and published volumes of sermons in his own right; he was also a staunch supporter of the English Dissenters and Reform Movement, counting Joseph Priestly and Richard Price among his friends.

The young William was thus raised in the heady atmosphere of ideas and radical politics, including a brief sojourn (1783–6) in the United States where his father had secured a position, and two seminal years at the recently founded New College at Hackney, a short-lived (1786–96) dissenting college in what was then a town north of London (dissenters were not allowed to enter the old universities of Oxford and Cambridge). Hazlitt was to remain true to this upbringing throughout his life, expressed appropriately in his unwavering support for the ideals of the French Revolution and their inheritor in the shape of Napoleon Bonaparte. Hazlitt was eleven when news of the events of 1789 reached Britain, and, by his own accounting, they left a deep and indelible mark. His political persuasion was a major cause of the later rift with Wordsworth and Coleridge, both of whom grew increasingly conservative and

---

[1] The standard edition remains *The Complete Works of William Hazlitt*, ed. P. P. Howe, 21 vols. (London: J. M. Dent, 1930–4). In what follows I use the more recent and, in certain respects, more reliable *The Selected Writings of William Hazlitt*, ed. Duncan Wu, 9 vols. (London: Pickering and Chatto, 1998). Unless otherwise indicated, all references are to volume number and pagination of the latter edition, followed by page numbers of Hazlitt's original publications as and when supplied by Wu.

[2] See Wu, *Hazlitt*, 212 and 304–6 passim.

came not only to reject the Revolution but also actively supported the English Crown and monarchical system that opposed and fought against it; this was a *volte-face* in Hazlitt's eyes that betrayed the principles of humanity and spirit of liberty that he detected in both men when he first visited them in Coleridge's cottage at Nether Stowey in the spring of 1798 – an episode described later by Hazlitt with great poignancy ("My First Acquaintance with Poets" [1823]) – and as he came to know them in the early years of the new century.[3]

Hazlitt is often described as a philosopher, and late in life still thought of himself as a "metaphysician," though he was never a system builder in the mold of Coleridge or other thinkers he read. It is more accurate to say that his criticism was philosophically informed or set upon a philosophical base cemented and made firm by a lifelong opposition to sensationalism and the associationist psychology of David Hartley and his followers. In his adolescent years, Hazlitt read deeply in the empiricist tradition of Hobbes, Locke, Hume, Priestly, Price, Condillac, and D'Holbach, and came to admire Berkeley, Rousseau, and Joseph Butler, in particular. His knowledge of Aristotle, Plato, and modern German philosophers, by contrast, seems to have been slight, sometimes inaccurate, and, for the most part, secondhand. Hazlitt's Greek was limited and his German nonexistent, which means that Coleridge was likely the principal source for his knowledge of Kant's Critical Philosophy, elements of which he clearly absorbed and made his own.[4] Hazlitt's interest in the British and French tradition is reflected in the course he offered in 1812 and published as *Lectures on the History of English Philosophy*, and formed an early impetus for what was to become the *Principles*, his only strictly philosophical work and matched nowhere in his corpus by any comparable exposition of his views on aesthetics, which emerge largely piecemeal through his essays and other critical writings. In various pieces, Hazlitt does consider discrete aesthetic issues and concepts, but these often betray more general theoretical concerns and, for the most part, add little or nothing to the eighteenth-century tradition from Shaftesbury and Addison onward. In "On Beauty," for example, one of a collection of essays published as *The Round Table* in 1817, Hazlitt sides with the view that beauty is "inherent to the object" and explicable by "a symmetry of parts and principle of proportion, gradation, harmony," but his allegiance is born more fundamentally of his opposition to the "association of ideas," which he considered "manifestly absurd," because without something "in itself pleasurable or painful" there would be no feelings that could be

---

[3] See "My First Acquaintance with Poets," in *Selected Writings* 9:95–109 (FAP). For a vivid reconstruction of the meeting, see Wu, *William Hazlitt*, 1–19.

[4] For an overview of Hazlitt's philosophical background, see Elisabeth Schneider, *The Aesthetics of William Hazlitt: A Study of the Philosophical Basis of His Criticism* (New York: Octagon Books, 1969 [1933]), ch. 1. Schneider also supplies a useful list of Hazlitt's known reading list (App. 3, 186–91). See also Bromwich, *Hazlitt*, ch. 1, and A. C. Grayling, *The Quarrel of the Age: The Life and Times of William Hazlitt* (London: Weidenfeld and Nicolson, 2000), ch. 8.

"transferred from one object to another" (2:71/2). Similarly, in "On Imitation" Hazlitt repeats the familiar point that "Objects in themselves disagreeable or indifferent, often please in imitation" (2:75/11), and the main concern of the piece is clearly to explore the "*ideal* in art" (2:77/16) along lines laid out by Reynolds, whose views come in for a good deal of criticism.[5] The same is true of "On the Picturesque and Ideal" (6:106–27/289–345), which, albeit elegantly, only reiterates elements isolated and discussed in the debates among Gilpin, Price, Knight, and Repton, and approaches neither in detail nor originality Wordsworth's theoretical treatment of similar issues in *The Sublime and the Beautiful* and the *Guide*.

If Hazlitt's inclusion in a history of aesthetics cannot be defended by his essayistic forays into these and related areas, it is more than justified by the contribution he makes to the Romantic themes broached by Wordsworth, Coleridge, Shelley, and (Hazlitt's protégé) Keats. Hazlitt was artistically inclined, and tried unsuccessfully to earn a living as a painter before he became established as a writer and critic (though he always struggled financially), taking the likenesses of Coleridge and Wordsworth (who hated the result and had the portrait destroyed); he was not, however, a poet, nor did he see the world through a poet's eyes. His views are conclusions of theoretical reflection from outside rather than abridgments of experience from within that come only to those who practice the art. Hazlitt learned this lesson early from his youthful encounter with the authors of *Lyrical Ballads* and fully acknowledged the lack he saw in himself: "Wordsworth," Hazlitt wrote years later, recalling his visit to Nether Stowey, "looking out of the low, latticed window, said, 'How beautifully the sun sets on that yellow bank!' I thought within myself, 'With what eyes these poets see nature!' and ever after, when I saw the sun-set stream upon the objects facing it, conceived I had made a discovery, or thanked Mr Wordsworth for having made one for me!" (9:105). Hazlitt's most important work and only systematic treatment of the art he saw thus personified bears the title "On Poetry in General," and formed the first of a public course of eight lectures on the English poets delivered at the Surrey Institution near Blackfriars Bridge (the building is now lost) from late January to early March 1818. The series was so successful that it was repeated immediately in March and April at the Crown and Anchor Tavern in the Strand (where Coleridge also lectured); the lectures were published later the same year.[6] "On Poetry in General" bears deep marks of the position developed in the *Principles*, in which Hazlitt defends a "metaphysical principle" concerning the imagination

---

[5] See "On Certain Inconsistencies in Sir Joshua Reynolds's Discourses," Essays XIII and XIV of *Table Talk; or Original Essays*, 2 vols. (London, 1821–2), *Selected Writings* 6:106–14/284–309 and 115–27/313–45, respectively. Hazlitt's younger brother, John, it might be noted, became a painter and studied under Reynolds.

[6] "Lecture 1. Introductory – On Poetry in General," *Lectures on the English Poets: Delivered at the Surrey Institution* (London, 1818), *Selected Writings* 2:165–320/1–331 (OPG).

and its relation to sensations and ideas.[7] A proper appreciation of "On Poetry in General," then, requires some consideration of what Hazlitt took himself to have established in the earlier work.

The Principles of Human Action

In the *Principles*, Hazlitt takes a stand against the widespread doctrine of moral egoism – the writings of Hobbes and Bernard Mandeville (1670–1733) being the most famous contemporary expressions – and defends the alternative view that human beings are actually "disinterested," no less concerned, that is, with the welfare of others than they are with their own. This thesis is not original to Hazlitt – he acknowledges that he had "adopted" it "in common with Butler" and reports that it was already known to Coleridge (9:108) – and his defense of it, albeit ingenious, takes the form of a transcendental argument strikingly similar to Kant. One's own welfare, he argues, is always directed at a future self with which one sympathizes through the "projective" power of the imagination, the same faculty and mechanism that enables one to share in the happiness and well-being of others. The "imagination," Hazlitt writes,

by means of which alone I can anticipate future objects, or be interested in them, must carry me out of myself into the feelings of others by one and the same process by which I am thrown forwards as it were into my future being, and interested in it. I could not love myself, if I were not capable of loving others. Self-love, used in this sense, is in its fundamental principle the same with disinterested benevolence.[8]

Because they rely on the same condition, Hazlitt concludes, interest in both one's own welfare and in that of other people are inseparable and mutually conditioning. Admittedly, Hazlitt does not always use "imagination" consistently – he associates it with the pleasure taken in novelty, for example, and with discriminating between kinds of similarity – and nowhere shows any interest in distinguishing it from "fancy," even gropingly, in the manner of Wordsworth, let alone with the decisiveness of Coleridge. In general, he steers a course similar to the one laid by Locke and the eighteenth-century imagination theorists, emphasizing the faculty's power to manipulate ideas, but firmly rejecting the

---

[7] Hazlitt took the *Principles* to mark a genuine advance in the history of philosophy and remained proud of it to the end. "There is no work of mine which I should class as even third rate," he wrote in the course of defending himself against a libelous attack by *Blackwoods Magazine* in 1818, "except my Principles of Human Action." For an account of the affair that occasioned the remark, see Grayling, *The Quarrel of the Age*, 238–42, and Wu, *William Hazlitt*, ch. 15.

[8] William Hazlitt, *An Essay on the Principles of Human Action: Being an Argument in Favour of the Natural Disinterestedness of the Human Mind. To Which Are Added, Some Remarks on the System of Hartley and Helvetius* (London, 1805), *Selected Writings* 1:3–82/1–263, 3/3 (PHA). For a concise presentation and useful overview of the argument (much of which is not relevant in the present context), see Grayling, *The Quarrel of the Age*, 362–5.

passive picture of mind on which it is based, namely, Locke's "empty cabinet," a "sort of inner room," as Hazlitt characterizes it, containing images locked safely away like "pictures in a gallery" (PHA 63/200–1).

The problem with this empiricist model, Hazlitt emphasizes – much in line with Leibniz's earlier criticism of Locke in the *Nouveaux essays sur l'entendement humain* (*New Essays on Human Understanding*) (completed 1704) – lies primarily in ignoring the obvious need for some active principle, without which it becomes impossible to explain how sensations, or impressions of sense, are connected to their corresponding ideas, and how these latter phenomena are subsequently combined in the way empiricist philosophers proposed. Hazlitt discovers this principle in the imagination, the seat of two distinct but related powers, which he explains by way of an example, a child who is burnt by fire and comes consequently to dread it. The first belongs to the "projectivist imagination" and consists in the synthesizing power (familiar from Locke and his followers) of "multiplying, varying, extending, combining, and comparing ... original passive impressions," but with the temporal dimension central to Hazlitt's claim about disinterestedness: without projection to extend the self ecstatically forward in time, the child "must be utterly blind to the future and indifferent to it, indifferent to any thing beyond the present moment" (PHA 20/59). The second power, by contrast, belongs to what Hazlitt calls the "reasoning imagination" (PHA 21/61) with the capacity to connect the result of synthesis with a consciousness or self. The dread of fire felt by the child, Hazlitt observes, "does not consist simply in the apprehension of the pain itself abstractedly considered, but together with this apprehension of pain he connects the idea ... of himself as about to feel it" (PHA 18/53). Hazlitt goes further and observes, in a move that parallels Kant's Deduction and Refutation of Idealism of the first *Critique*, that a consciousness unifying an aggregate into a manifold also requires consciousness of one and the same self, the very insight that led Kant to posit the mysterious "transcendental unity of apperception" (CPR A107–11). "To perceive the relation of one thing to another it is not only necessary that the idea of the things themselves should co-exist," Hazlitt writes, "but that they should be perceived to co-exist by the *same conscious understanding*, or that their different actions should be felt at the same instant by the *same being in the strictest sense*" (PHA 63/201, emphases added). Thus the "relation between fire and the pain of the child is impossible," Hazlitt insists, referring to his example, unless we posit a "power" that forms a "collective idea, comprehension, or *consciousness* of those sensations" and thus "unite different actions in the same consciousness" (PHA 63/200).

Given its strong Kantian flavor, not to mention treatments of imagination and sympathy developed by the likes of Hume in the *Treatise* and Smith in *The Theory of Moral Sentiments* (1759), it is doubtful that Hazlitt's "metaphysical principle" is quite the "discovery" he thought. In the context of English Romanticism, however, it stands as an original development of views expressed by Wordsworth and Coleridge, with which it bears comparison, and informs

Hazlitt's distinct treatment of poetry. His "reasoning imagination" forms much the same function as Coleridge's "primary imagination" – the synthetic faculty and condition for its possibility in a unified self – while the "projectivist imagination" corresponds to his "secondary imagination" and Wordsworth's "poetical imagination," the creative power to rearrange at will the materials provided by sense. This is no doubt what Hazlitt has in mind when he contrasts the faculty with understanding: the "province of the imagination is principally visionary, the unknown and undefined," he writes, while "the understanding restores things to their natural boundaries, and strips them of their fanciful pretensions" (OPG 2:172/18). He departs company from Coleridge, however, in rejecting the latter's idealistic proclivity to see imagination reaching beyond possible experience – the "eternal act of creation in the infinite I AM" (SB I.13.304) – remaining securely in the empiricist camp by limiting the imagination to the material of impressions; in this respect he is actually closer to Kant's Critical Philosophy than Coleridge from whom he learned it.[9]

Of greater interest in the present context, however, is the way Hazlitt differs from Wordsworth, at whose poetry and character he directs a good deal of critical and, on occasion, personal animosity. He takes Wordsworth to have missed or ignored the projective capacity of the imagination that enables one to sympathize both with one's future self and, crucially, with others.[10] The recognition of this element of imagination is central for Hazlitt because it leads him to a different way of approaching the duality of mind and world, which he sees as being bridged "not through assimilation of all *other* in the *self*," as Elisabeth Schneider expresses it concisely, "but through the projecting of *self* into all *other*"; rather than incorporating other people and objects in the ego, human consciousness always dissolves the perceived barrier between the "experiencing power and thing experienced."[11] Or to express the point another way, human beings identify with what is outside them, and in the process of doing so they effectively un-master, un-self, and discharge themselves in what they are not: this is precisely what Hazlitt articulates in the *Principles* – that individuals extend themselves through sympathy to include and presuppose the welfare of others in their own – and finds wanting in Wordsworth and his poetry.

"On Poetry in General"

Poetry, for Hazlitt, is part and parcel of this same process of dissolving the barrier between self and other: poets imitate nature and give themselves to a transcendent experience, which they communicate to the reader, but without aggrandizing the self or claiming to have knowledge of ultimate reality.

---

[9] On this point, see Schneider, *The Aesthetics of William Hazlitt*, 100–1.

[10] For a view of Wordsworth that takes issue with Hazlitt, see Adam Potkay, *Wordsworth's Ethics* (Baltimore, MD: Johns Hopkins University Press, 2012), ch. 8.

[11] Schneider, *The Aesthetics of William Hazlitt*, 39–41.

Poetry articulates the "natural impression of any object or event, by its vividness exciting an involuntary movement of imagination and passion, and producing, by sympathy, a certain modulation of the voice, or sounds, expressing it" (OPG 165/1). It is a "language" (OPG 2:167/6 passim), as Hazlitt often describes it, made possible by the imagination that represents in words the effect that impressions, synthesized and related to a self, have on an individual who imitates the world as poet, or, as a reader, experiences the world mediated through poetic language. For the "imagination is that faculty which represents objects," as Hazlitt describes it,

> not as they are in themselves, but as they are moulded by other thoughts and feelings, into an infinite variety of shapes and combinations of power. This language is not less true to nature, because it is false in point of fact; but so much the more true and natural, if it conveys the impression which the object under the influence of passions makes on the mind. (OPG 167/7)

Hazlitt recalls having experienced Wordsworth reading "Peter Bell" "in the open air" where, like Macbeth, the poet's "face was as a book where men might read strange matters" (9:105). There is something in Hazlitt of Coleridge's insistence that poets are those in whom the imagination works with greater alacrity and increased delicacy than in the mass of humankind: in poets one finds "heightenings of the imagination" (OPG 167/5), an "excess of imagination beyond the actual or ordinary impression of any object or feeling" (OPG 167:6), and impressions "impatient of all limit" (OPG 167/6–7).

As the language of imagination, moreover, poetry is the *most refined* expression of sensation. When poetry communicates, it does so with the "highest eloquence of passion, the most vivid form of expression that can be given to our conception of any thing, whether pleasurable or painful, mean or dignified, delightful or distressing. It is the perfect coincidence of the image of the words with the feeling we have, and of which we cannot get rid of in any other way" (OPG 170/14–15). The "light of poetry is not only a direct but also a reflected light," as Hazlitt writes employing a particularly vivid metaphor, "that while it shews us the object, throws a sparkling radiance on all around it: the flame of the passions, communicated to the imagination, reveals to us, as with a flash of lightening, the inmost recesses of thought, and penetrates our whole being. ... Poetry puts a spirit of life and motion into the universe" (OPG 167/5–6). Poetry, consequently, is not a trifling amusement to be identified with the verse composed, published, and read for purposes of light entertainment. It is rather the most profound expression of what transpires when human consciousness confronts the world. "Wherever there is a sense of beauty, or power, or harmony, as in the motion of a wave of the sea, in the growth of a flower," Hazlitt writes enthusiastically, "... *there* is poetry, in its birth" (OPG 165/2). It is, in an echo of Shakespeare's *Tempest*, "the stuff of which our life is made" (OPG 165/3), which means that "Fear is poetry, hope is poetry, love is poetry, hatred is poetry; contempt, jealousy, remorse, admiration, wonder, pity, despair, or madness, are all poetry" (OPG 165/2). Poetry is an "imitation of nature, but the imagination and the passions are part of man's nature" (OPG 166/5) and even an "emanation of the moral and intellectual part of our nature, as well as of the sensitive – of the desire to know, the will to act, and the power to feel" (OPG 169/12).

This expansive view of poetry immediately puts Hazlitt in the company of Coleridge when it comes to driving a wedge between poetry and prose, emphasizing the importance of the very "poetic diction" that Wordsworth disparages as doing violence to language in the name of art. Hazlitt equates prose and its ascendancy over the poetic with the "necessary advances of civilization," which are "unfavourable to the spirit of poetry": a world grown calculable, predictable, safe, where awe for the preternatural is lost (OPG 172/19). There is nothing inherently musical to language, Hazlitt observes, and prose is often harsh and contains jerks, breaks, and inequalities that poetry can smooth over: it "makes these odds all even" (OPG 174/24) by supplying the "inherent defect of harmony in the customary mechanism of language" (OPG 175/25). At the same time, poetic technique alone is not sufficient. "All is not poetry that passes for such," Hazlitt writes, "nor does verse make the whole difference between poetry and prose" (OPG 176/27), but, recalling Reynolds recommendations that artists look to the "grand" events of history and fable, has much to do with recognizing and isolating a proper subject matter: that "which lifts the spirit above the earth, which draws the soul out of itself with indescribable longings, is poetry in kind, and generally fit to become so in name" (OPG 176/27). "Common prose differs from poetry," he thus insists, "as treating for the most part either of such trite, familiar, and irksome matters of fact, as convey no extraordinary impulse to the imagination, or else such difficult and laborious process of the understanding, as do not admit of the wayward or violent movements either of the imagination or the passions" (OPG 176/27).

In light of these views, one can begin to make sense of Hazlitt's consistently ambivalent and sometimes hostile attitude toward Wordsworth, both in "On the Living Poets," the last of his *Lectures on the English Poets*, and the earlier three-part review of Wordsworth's *The Excursion* written for and published in *The Examiner* in August and October 1814. Hazlitt produced a revised version of the same – omitting the passages in praise of Wordsworth, and therefore more strident and directly critical in tone – for *The Round Table* that was published in 1817, only a few months before the lecture series began.[12] In both

---

[12] See *Lectures on the English Poets*, Lecture VIII, "On the Living Poets," *Selected Writings* 2:298–320/283–331, pp. 319–20/328–9 (OLP), and *The Round Table*, nos. XXXVII, "Observations on Mr. Wordsworth's Poem, 'The Excursion,'" and XXXVIII, "The Same Subject Continued," *Selected Writings* 2:112–25/96–162. I use and quote from the text of *The Examiner* review: "Character of Mr. Wordsworth's New Poem, *The Excursion*," *The Examiner*, August 21 and 28 and October 2, 1814, *Selected Writings* 2:325–40 (ER), with references to Wu's pagination. For a sympathetic account of Hazlitt's criticism that emphasizes his disappointment with the poem on political grounds, see Wu, *William Hazlitt*, 168–71.

essays, Hazlitt praises Wordsworth for working in the poetic "spirit" that the advances of civilization undermine, seeing his as a mind "coeval with the primary forms of things, [that] holds immediately from nature" (ER 326). "In power of intellect, in lofty conception, in depth of feeling, at once simple and sublime, which pervades every part of it," Hazlitt writes of *The Excursion*, "and which gives to every object an almost preternatural and preterhuman interest, this work has seldom been surpassed" (ER 325). In "Of the Living Poets," Hazlitt extends similar praise to Wordsworth's poetry in general, calling him the "most original poet now living" and saying that it is impossible to speak of many of the poems in *Lyrical Ballads* "in terms of too high praise"; they are of "inconceivable beauty, of perfect originality and pathos," he observes. "They open a finer and deeper vein of thought and feeling than any poet in modern times has done, or attempted" (OLP 309/309).

At the same time, Hazlitt is highly critical of Wordsworth, faulting his work in technical matters of style and versification, and his poetic ability: for lacking a "constructive faculty," being incapable of "form[ing] a whole," and being "totally deficient in all the machinery of poetry," all failings for which *The Excursion* furnishes "proof" (OLP 309/309–10). These problems are a result, Hazlitt charges moreover, of Wordsworth's general and fundamental failure to appreciate or understand the "metaphysical principle" articulated in the *Principles*: rather than projecting the self into the other, Wordsworth incorporates the other into self and, more specifically, *his* self; the duality of mind and world is not dissolved and transcended, but objects and people refracted through and resolved into Wordsworth's own ego. (In *The Excursion*, Hazlitt charges, every character is really a version of its author!) The poetry of Wordsworth is thus "internal," less about the objects that putatively compose its subject matter than the expression of an extended and sustained reflection on the "workings of his own mind" (ER 326). The "object is lost in the sentiment" (ER 326), as Hazlitt puts it, and in Wordsworth's sympathy with "simple forms of feelings" and the "general stream of humanity," an "intense intellectual egotism swallows up everything" (ER 327), terminating at a point where there is "nothing but himself and the universe" (ER 327). For Hazlitt, this egotism is all-consuming and defines Wordsworth's very being: "he does not even like to share his reputation with his subject," Hazlitt writes, in what is surely a moment of great psychological insight,

for he would have it all proceed from his own power and originality of mind. Such a one is slow to admire anything that is admirable; feels no interest what is most interesting to others, no grandeur in anything grand, no beauty in anything beautiful. He tolerates only what he himself creates. ... He sees nothing but himself and his universe. He hates all greatness and pretensions to it, whether well or ill-founded. His egotism is in some respects a madness; for he scorns even the admiration of himself, thinking it a presumption in any one to suppose that he has taste or sense enough to understand him. (OLP 316/323)

This "egotism" is manifest, further, in the kind of poetry Wordsworth writes, falling as it does under the rubric of "sentiment" (or the "moral"), involving "depth of feeling" and dependent on the "strength of the interest which it excites in given objects" arising "from the food of our moral sensibility" (ER 334). It stands in contrast to and excludes features exhibited in poetry of the "imagination" (or the "intellectual"), characterized by "richness of invention" and "conversant with the world of external nature" (ER 334). When these two species unite – as they do in Chaucer, Spenser, Shakespeare, and Milton – poetry reaches its greatest heights, but in the case of Wordsworth, Hazlitt charges, "his writings exhibit all the internal power, without the external form of poetry" (ER 335), and resolve into a matter of "mere sentiment" furnished "from his own mind" and "his own subject" (OLP 309/309). His sentiments are "subtle and profound," yet they are presented in a style of "extreme simplicity" (ER 335) that overpowers and undoes the creative faculty. The result is a leveling down, a display of "paradox" in the assertion that "all things are by nature equally fit subjects for poetry; or that if there is any preference to be given, those that are the meanest and most unpromising are the best, as they leave the greatest scope for the unbounded stores of thought and fancy in the writer's own mind" (OLP 315/320). Gone in Wordsworth are images of pomp and decoration (palaces, temples, knights, and adventure), or grand subject matter that "draws the soul out of itself," all of which is supplanted by "common every-day events and objects of nature" – "most simple and barren of effect" (ER 335) – which (to employ the language of Addison) restrain and confine the imagination and reduce, enervate, or destroy the pleasure it might otherwise bring.

What Hazlitt finds more startling is the inversion this egoistic magic effects; Wordsworth not only miscalibrates the proper focus of poetry, but also manages to magnify the littleness of his subject matter and, in a feat of poetic transformation of which Hume was so suspicious, lend to the petty, mean, and small a grandeur they do not really possess: through the distorting lens of Wordsworth's ego, a molehill becomes a mountain and a puddle agitated with the storms of passion. One might be able to appreciate Wordsworth's attachment to "groves and fields," Hazlitt observes, but not his celebration of "peddlars and ploughmen" as "heroes" (ER 335) or (and here Hazlitt includes the Coleridge of *Lyrical Ballads*) his courting "bosom friends" in a "mixed rabble of idle apprentices and Botany Bay convicts, female vagrants, gipsies, ... ideot [*sic*] boys and mad mothers" (OLP 315/321). "We take Mr. Wordsworth himself for a great poet, a fine moralist, and a deep philosopher," Hazlitt freely acknowledges, "but if he insists on introducing us to a friend of his, a parish clerk, or the barber of the village, who is as wise as himself, we must be excused if we draw back with the same little want of cordial faith" (ER 335–6). The reality of rural life, as Hazlitt describes at great length in the concluding paragraphs of *The Examiner* review, is one of squalor, poverty, stupidity, lack of refinement, petty-mindedness, selfishness, and insensibility, not as it appears in Wordsworth valorization, the seat and origin of joy and moral perfection.[13]

Hazlitt's criticism is at times harsh and unmistakably personal, a mixture of philosophical conviction and the contingencies of a life lived, replete with complex and competing passions forged in the heat of friendships won and lost.[14] It would be disingenuous to reduce Hazlitt's views to biographical details, but at the same time they cannot be separated entirely from circumstances in which they were formed; a more expansive reflection on Wordsworth and his work might reveal a partiality in Hazlitt's perspective. In the present context, it is worth recalling the Wordsworth of the Preface to *Lyrical Ballads* and *The Sublime and the Beautiful*. As we saw in Chapter 5, in these works Wordsworth understands poetry as the expression of feeling aroused as a response to nature that "awakens the sublime" according to the principle of "union and communion" and "humiliation and submission" (SB 188–9). Wordsworth's language is of "possession" to be sure, but this does not distinguish him markedly from previous writers on the subject, and there is much in Wordsworth's mode of expression that suggests, if not a dissolution of the distance between mind and world, then at least a response of the self to the other as a being that resists and transcends: "intense unity," "grasping towards" something that one is "incapable of attaining," the result of which is "humiliation and prostration

---

[13] Hazlitt was raised in the country and routinely expresses the pleasure and joy he takes in rural life. There is much truth in Hazlitt's description of the realities of country life, though *The Examiner* review also reflects the animosity that had grown between him and Wordsworth. Some commentators have even seen it as revenge for the "Keswick incident" when Hazlitt was run out of town by villagers angry at his overzealous pursuit of a local girl, which included "smoting her on the bottom" when she denied his advances. According to Grayling (*The Quarrel of the Age*, 98–9) and Wu (*William Hazlitt*, 98–9), Wordsworth later used the affair to discredit and embarrass Hazlitt after *The Examiner* review, and deliberately exaggerated and embellished what had been regarded at the time as an amusing trifle. Hazlitt's sexual exploits with prostitutes and country girls were well-known, and counted by Wordsworth and Coleridge as a mark against him, their own indulgence in the same and thus hypocrisy, as Wu points out, notwithstanding: Wordsworth kept secret the fact of the illegitimate child fathered and abandoned in France, and both he and Coleridge frequented the same West End establishments as Hazlitt. "The fact is," Wu observes, "that Hazlitt was remarkable less for his sexual appetite than for the honesty with which he wrote about it" (99).

[14] It is worth emphasizing that Hazlitt's remarks about Coleridge are similarly ambiguous. Hazlitt describes him (as noted already) as the only person he ever knew "who answered to the idea of a man of genius" and the only one from whom he "ever learnt any thing," but he is also critical of Coleridge's volubility, and finds little of merit in Coleridge's verse or *Biographia Literaria* (he published excoriating reviews of *Christabel* and "Kubla Khan"). See, for example, OLP 320/330 and OFP 100ff. Hazlitt ends OLP with great praise for the Coleridge *he once knew* ("His mind was clothed with wings; and raised on them he lifted philosophy to heaven"), but ends with words that could hardly be more bittersweet: "And shall I, who heard him then, listen to him now? Not I! …That spell is broke; that time is gone for ever; that voice is heard no more: but still the recollection comes rushing by with thoughts of long-past years, and rings in my ears with never-dying sound" (OLP 320/330).

before some internal power ... awful & immeasurable" (SB 150–60). There is
much here that speaks against "appropriation" and "egotism," and suggests
that Hazlitt's criticism should be tempered by a more nuanced appreciation of
Wordsworth, both as man and poet.

JOHN STUART MILL

John Stuart Mill (1806–73) is a name not generally associated with aesthetics.
He is celebrated as a stylist certainly, but one whose eloquence was put in service of major contributions to political theory, philosophy of social science, and,
ethics, most famously through interpreting and popularizing the doctrine of
Utilitarianism developed by Jeremy Bentham (1748–1832). Although not the
central focus of his writing, early in his career – mostly in the 1830s when in his
mid- to late twenties – Mill also wrote a number of short works on criticism and
aesthetic matters, the most important of which are the essays "What is Poetry?"
and "Two Kinds of Poetry," noteworthy both for the theoretical nature of views
they express and the characteristic precision with which their author treats his
subject matter. These appeared first in *The Monthly Repository* in January and
October 1833, and were published later, revised and combined, in *Dissertations
and Discussions* (1859) as "Thoughts on Poetry and its Varieties."[15]

Mill takes as his starting point a distinction Wordsworth draws in the
Preface to *Lyrical Ballads* between the "Man of Science," who slowly accu-
mulates facts about parts of nature through dint of hard work and in solitude,
and the "Poet" whose subject matter is everywhere, and who, in articulating
the passional relationship between man and nature, "binds together ... the vast
empire of human society." For Wordsworth, these two character types are connected by the common presence of pleasure, and because the crucial element
is "impassioned expression" through the "real language of nature," he denies
any essential difference between poetry and prose. Mill accepts and endorses
the general idea that poetry is singular, consisting as it does of "the thoughts
and words in which emotion spontaneously embodies itself" (TPV 356) that
intend to "bring thoughts or images before the mind for the purpose of acting
upon the emotions" (TPV 344); he thinks the unique character of poetry is
recognized intuitively by everybody as a "vague feeling," and it is the task of
the philosopher to discover and frame the "distinct principle" that underlies
it (TPV 344). It is a mistake, however, to proceed to this end by juxtaposing
poetry to prose, Mill insists, which only stirs fruitless debate over the merits of
the comparison – that among Wordsworth, Coleridge, and Hazlitt being a case
in point – and eventuates in the error of "confound[ing] poetry with metrical
composition." The real point of contrast, Mill emphasizes – drawing on and

---

[15] "Thoughts on Poetry and its Varieties," 2nd ed. (1867 [1859]), in *Collected Works of John Stuart
Mill*, ed. John M. Robson and Jack Stillinger, 33 vols. (Toronto: University of Toronto Press,
1963–), 1:343–77 (TPV). All references are to the pagination of this edition.

redirecting Wordsworth's original distinction – is with "matter of fact or science," an activity that addresses itself to beliefs and seeks to convince or persuade by "presenting a proposition to the understanding"; poetry, by contrast, appeals to feelings, and aims to move its audience through offering up "interesting objects of contemplation to the sensibilities" (TPV 344).

By itself, however, the claim that poetry produces images that act upon the emotions does not demarcate it meaningfully from the fictions of the novelist (or even the narratives of the historian). The more fundamental difference lies elsewhere: the interest one takes in a novel (or historical reconstruction) is "derived from incident," Mill observes, and the emotion felt is excited by "a series of states of mere outward circumstances"; interest in poetry, by contrast, derives from the "representation of feeling," and its emotional impact originates in the "exhibition of a state or states of human sensibility" (TPV 344–5). Poetic truth, moreover, diverges from the novelist's concern to fashion a "true picture of life" for the reader, because it lies instead in the poet's desire "to paint the human soul truthfully." Mill does not deny that poetry is descriptive, but, as Wordsworth of *The Sublime and the Beautiful* took such pains to emphasize, what the poet describes is not "in" any object so much as "in the state of mind" through which any phenomenon is contemplated. Its mode is not the "delineation" of objects "as they are," but the employment of "imagery" to represent objects as they "appear" (TPV 346). The poet "paints them not in their bare and natural lineaments," as Mill writes echoing the long tradition reaching back to Addison, "but arranged in the colours and seen through the medium of the imagination set in action by the feelings" (TPV 347).

Poetry, then, in Mill's rather extreme version of expressivism, is not really about objects at all. Poets go directly to the "deeper and more secret workings of the human heart," and the product of their artistic labors is "interesting only to those to whom it recalls what they have felt, or whose imagination it stirs up to conceive what they could feel, or what they might have been able to feel had their outward circumstances been different" (TPV 345–6). The poetic description of a lion, for example, works by suggesting likenesses and comparisons that might occur to a mind contemplating the object, and what makes the whole poetic is ultimately the emotional "state of awe, wonder, or terror, which the spectacle naturally excites, or is, on occasion, supposed to excite" (TPV 347). As a consequence, the issue of there being a proper subject matter for poetry, a point upon which Hazlitt insisted, is rendered moot. For Mill, *any* outward impression can be poetic, for what counts, and indeed, what defines poetry, is that the object in question be invested or colored with some emotion – joy, grief, pity, reverence, awe, hatred, or terror being the most usual and powerful.

What makes this possible, moreover, is the very egotism of the poet that Hazlitt found so disturbing in Wordsworth, and which Mill pushes to its logical conclusion. Poets are not only "ignorant of life," he maintains, but also turn their gaze upon themselves in a movement of pure inwardness:

What they [poets] know has come by observation of themselves; they have found within them one highly delicate and sensitive specimen of human nature, on which the laws of emotion are written in large characters, such as can be read off without much study. Other knowledge of mankind, such as comes to men of the world by outward experience, is not indispensable to them as poets. ... (TPV 346)

This solipsistic retreat to the "inner man" produces not the eloquent speech of the rhetorician *heard* by an audience and intended to influence belief or move listeners to passion or action. The poet's conversation is *with himself*; it is in the "nature of soliloquy" (TPV 349), and *overheard* by readers eavesdropping on a drama that unfolds in "utter unconsciousness of a listener" (TPV 348). "Poetry is feeling," Mill writes, in lines that capture his view concisely, "confessing itself to itself in moments of solitude, and embodying itself in symbols, which are the nearest possible representations of the feeling in the exact shape in which it exists in the poet's mind" (TPV 348).

Because poetry is nothing but the expression of emotion in moments of solitude, Mill is obliged to accept that anybody can be a poet; for whosoever "writes out truly any human feeling, writes poetry," and there are few people who have not, at some moment in their lives, if only in thought, satisfied this criterion (TPV 356).[16] Because poetry is also a rarefied and singular activity – a "higher" rather than a lower "pleasure," as Mill draws the distinction in *Utilitarianism*[17] – he is uncomfortable enough with this conclusion to insist that writing genuine poetry is not equivalent to being a poet. Those who achieve the former are "poets of culture" to whom poetry is "extraneous and superinduced" (TPV 356): they view their objects from the external perspective of everyday life rather than from within the parameters of the poetic world, forever a foreign land to which they travel as an occasional visitor. The title "poet," however, denotes a certain "variety of man" (TPV 356) with a particular "nature," namely, a "mental and physical constitution or temperament peculiarly fitted for poetry" (TPV 355). While the poet of culture "sees his object in prose, and describes it in poetry," this "poet by nature" sees his object "in poetry" (TPV 356), as part and parcel, to borrow Hume's phrase, of a poetic reality of the sort in which Wordsworth appeared in Hazlitt's vision of him at the window in Nether Stowey: "Whatever be the thing which they are contemplating ... the aspect under which it first and most naturally paints itself to them, is its poetic aspect" (TPV 356).

Mill equates the genuine poet, moreover, with a certain activity of imagination reminiscent both of Gerard's identification of genius with increased vigor,

---

[16] Cf. "On Genius," in *Collected Works* 1:329–39, where Mill treats genius in parallel terms: rather than being the purview of any particular faculty, the essence of genius is thought, and whoever thinks for himself being an original thinker is therefore a genius. The discovery of new facts or creation of new art – the sense of genius familiar from the eighteenth century onward – is but a specific manifestation of a capacity that is common to all.

[17] See *Utilitarianism* (1861), in *Collected Works*, esp. 10:210–14.

regularity, and alacrity of association, and Alison's account of the difference between "ordinary" chains of ideas and those constituting the peculiar emotion of taste he isolates in the "predominant relation" or "bond of connection" that stamps the latter in its entirety with a "certain and definite character." In Mill's version (he mentions neither Gerard nor Alison by name), poets "by nature" are those in whom feelings or emotions are the "links of association by which their ideas, both sensuous and spiritual, are connected together" (TPV 356), and the chains thus formed acquire "unity and consistency" from some particular "dominant feeling" that pervades the whole (TPV 357). In the poet of culture, by contrast, the same is achieved by a "dominant *thought*" (TPV 357, emphasis added), and "with however bright a halo of feeling the thought may be surrounded and glorified," Mill insists, "the thought itself is always the conspicuous object; while the poetry of a poet is *feeling itself*, employing thought only as the medium of its expression" (TPV 357, emphasis added).

Given Mill's point of departure with the Preface to *Lyrical Ballads*, and his highly expressivist view of poetry, one might expect Wordsworth to stand as the exemplar of the poet "by nature." As one learns from the later *Autobiography* (1873), Mill had read Wordsworth only a few years before, in 1828, and in the midst of a deep depression brought on by intense study and gloomy contemplation, finding in the *Poems* of 1815 writing with "feeling" that communicated the existence of "real, permanent happiness in tranquil contemplation" and with it a cure for his own "mental wants."[18] Mill admits himself drawn immediately by the rural objects and natural scenery that formed Wordsworth's subject matter, but it was less the "beautiful pictures" contained in the descriptions that appealed – less pleasing themselves, Mill maintains, than those of Sir Walter Scott or the actual view of even a second-rate landscape – than the emotions conveyed. "What made Wordsworth's poems a medicine for my state of mind," he writes, echoing the views expressed in his earlier essays, "was that they expressed, not mere outward beauty, but states of feeling, and of thought coloured by feeling, under the excitement of beauty. ... In them I seemed to draw from a source of inward joy, of sympathetic and imaginative pleasure, which could be shared in by all human beings; which had no connexion with struggle or imperfection, but which would be made richer by every improvement in the physical or social condition of mankind" (A 151).

Despite his place in Mill's personal development, however, when it comes to illustrating the distinction between the poet of culture and the poet by nature, Wordsworth is equated with the former, and it is Shelley who Mill celebrates "as perhaps the most striking example ever known of the poetic temperament" (TPV 358). Wordsworth, in Mill's estimation, and in an ironic reversal of Hazlitt, is not egoistical enough; his poetry valorizes thought rather

[18] *Autobiography* (1873), in *Collected Works* 1:1–290 and 153 (A). Mill limits his praise to the poems; he says he had "looked" into *The Excursion* a few years earlier and "found little" (A 151).

than emotion, for "first in his mind" is the need "to impress [on the reader] some proposition, more or less distinctly conceived" (TPV 358). Wordsworth's poetry as "never bounding, never ebullient," Mill contends; it lacks spontaneity, and is divorced from the man behind it, who "never seems possessed by any feeling" or ever gives himself up to the emotions he describes: exultation, grief, pity, love, admiration, or devotion (TPV 358–9). Shelley's verse, by contrast, relies on the "vividness" of its author's emotions and sensations (TPV 359), remains untouched by the mediation of thought, and therefore achieves the pure inwardness that Mill takes to be the mark of the poet: Shelley is a "great poet" because he writes "under the overruling influence of some one state of feeling, either actually experienced, or summoned up in the vividness of reality by a fervid imagination ... unity of feeling being to him the harmonizing principle ... and supplying the coherency and consistency which would else have been wanting" (TPV 360).

At first blush, Mill's identification of Shelley rather than Wordsworth with the genuinely poetic temperament might come as a surprise, especially given the special place the *Poems* of 1815 occupied in Mill's life. If one recalls the thrust of Shelley's *The Defence of Poetry*, however, the judgment is easier to understand: Shelley celebrates enthusiasm, and paints a picture of the poet as an instrument expressing the mysteries of the universe, all of which comes much closer than Wordsworth to Mill's vision of poetry as a soliloquy overheard by an audience. Shelley's motif of the nightingale that "sits in darkness and sings to cheer its own solitude with sweet sounds" is almost one with Mill's own image of "feeling confessing itself to itself in moments of solitude." Mill could have chosen no better metaphor to express poetically his philosophical reflections on poets and the art they pursue.

JOHN RUSKIN

If Hazlitt was the first modern man, John Ruskin (1819–1900) is surely the last great Romantic. A prolific writer of boundless energy and singular mind, Ruskin ranged across a wide variety of subjects and material: his collected works run to thirty-nine volumes and, in addition to his famous multivolume tomes on art and architecture – covering his celebrated championing of J. M. W. Turner, support for the Pre-Raphaelite Brotherhood, and defense of the style he termed "Northern Gothic" – include writings on geology, geography, botany, meteorology, education, economics, and political economy.[19] Ruskin

---

[19] *The Complete Works of John Ruskin (Library Edition)*, ed. E. T. Cook and Alexander Wedderburn, 39 vols. (London: George Allen, 1903–12). The works containing Ruskin's contribution to philosophical aesthetics and of primary interest in the present context are as follows: *The Poetry of Architecture; or The Architecture of the Nations of Europe Considered in its Association with Natural Scenery and National Character, by Kata Phusin* (1837–8), *Works* 1 (PA); *Modern Painters*, 5 vols. (1843–60), *Works* 3–7 (MP); *The Seven Lamps of Architecture* (1849), *Works* 8 (SLA); and *The Stones of Venice*, 3 vols. (1851–3), *Works* 9–11

was also a fine draftsman (he worked primarily in pen and ink and illustrated many of his volumes himself), was appointed the first Slade Professor of Fine Art at Oxford (1870–8), and holds the rare honor of having an Oxford college – Ruskin College (founded in 1899) – named after him. His services were also in constant demand to catalogue and evaluate collections of art, including the enormous bequest made by Turner of his works to the nation, for which he named Ruskin executor. In addition, Ruskin left behind a body of poetry from his youth (as an undergraduate at Oxford he won, on the third attempt, the Newdigate Prize), an enormous correspondence carried on with family and friends (including many luminaries of Victorian Britain), and three volumes of diaries with entries spanning the length of his long life. Ruskin's work also left a tangible legacy. His writing not only became founding texts for criticism in the visual arts, but also inspired the design work of William Morris and the Arts and Crafts movement, encouraged Gothic Revival, and had a direct influence on Frank Lloyd Wright and the Prairie School, and through him, on the development of Modernist architecture well into the twentieth century.[20]

Compared to other writers we have considered, Ruskin was not particularly well read in philosophy, and not only claimed (or feigned) slight interest in abstract modes of investigation, but also actively disdained them in favor of his own doggedly empirical methods, which yielded the enormous mass of detail that gave his work content. As an undergraduate he studied Aristotle, notably the *Poetics* (which he claimed to despise) and the *Ethics* (to which his thought is heavily indebted), and was a lifelong reader of Plato (whose metaphysics he Christianizes to his own ends). He was also an admirer of Addison, and mentions various other writers from the aesthetic tradition – notably Burke, Reynolds, Smith, Alison, and Stewart – though dismissively and without detailed discussion.[21] Professed animosity to philosophers and their notions notwithstanding, there is actually a good deal of theoretical sophistication behind Ruskin's writing, and whether his focus be chimneys, clouds, Venetian churches, or a Turner seascape, he deliberately presses his material into an eclectic mélange of ideas that frames his studies to form an aesthetics that, like those of Hogarth and Reynolds, purports to explain the origin of aesthetic value, identify great art, and recommend rules of good taste and sound judgment for producing and appreciating it.

(SV). All references are to individual works, volume (where relevant), and page number (e.g., MP I, 24), and do not therefore correspond to volume numbers assigned by Cook and Wedderburn.

[20] For a consideration of Ruskin's role in the development of Lloyd Wright's work, see John D. Rosenberg, *The Darkening Glass: A Portrait of Ruskin's Genius* (New York: Columbia University Press, 1986), 71ff.

[21] See MP II, 66–75, where Ruskin summarily rejects theories of beauty that focus on truth, usefulness, custom, and association of ideas. For an explication and overly generous defense of Ruskin's criticisms, see George P. Landow, *The Aesthetic and Critical Theories of John Ruskin* (Princeton, NJ: Princeton University Press, 1971), 91ff.

Whatever the true breadth and depth of Ruskin's reading, he certainly seems to draw a good deal on the tradition he officially rejects, both for his major categories of beauty, sublimity, and the picturesque, and for more specific and clearly identifiable lines of thought that crisscross his writing: like Shaftesbury, he valorizes intellect, disinterestedness, and "truth" (he even rejects the term *aesthetics* as relating too much to the senses [MP II, 35ff.]); speaks like Reid of "excellence" and power "signified" (MP 1, 96); adapts Locke's "ideas" for his own purposes and, in general, finds much nourishment in a range of empiricist philosophy without which his treatment of sympathy, imagination, and understanding (in *Modern Painters* I and II) would be impossible. There are also deep veins of associationist psychology marbling his work (PA 108, 127, passim), strong hints of Hume's true judge (MP II, 56ff.), whiffs of Gerard on genius (MP II, 239ff.), and a good deal of Coleridge (mentioned by name), whose presence is indicated not only through Ruskin's own attempt to distinguish fancy from imagination (MP II, 229ff.), but also (despite his official derision of German thought) in the generally rationalist atmosphere that surrounds and pervades everything.

Although these are all notable elements in Ruskin's approach, however, they are really parts of a whole fashioned from two fundamental and abiding influences on his life and thought: the poetry of Wordsworth and Evangelical Protestantism. Ruskin read and absorbed Wordsworth's poetry early – lines from *The Excursion* provide the epigraph for *Modern Painters*[22] – and imbibed it so deeply that only with a hint of exaggeration might one regard the aesthetic theory he develops through the late 1850s as a

---

[22] The lines are spoken by the Wanderer in Book IV, lines 978–94, although Ruskin seems to be quoting from memory or selectively because his epigraph does not correspond exactly to any single version Wordsworth wrote. This version follows the 1850 line numbers in the standard critical edition, *The Excursion, by William Wordsworth*, ed. Sally Bushell, James A. Butler, Michael C. Jaye, and David García (Ithaca, NY: Cornell University Press, 2001), 157. The brackets indicate the lines omitted by Ruskin.

> "Accuse me not
> Of arrogance, [unknown Wanderer as I am],
> If, having walked with Nature [threescore years],
> And offered, far as frailty would allow,
> My heart a daily sacrifice to Truth,
> I now affirm of Nature and of Truth,
> Whom I have served, that their Divinity
> Revolts, offended at the ways of men
> [Swayed by such motives, to such ends employed;]
> Philosophers, who, though the human soul
> Be of a thousand faculties composed,
> And twice ten thousand interests, do yet prize
> This soul, and the transcendent universe,
> No more than as a mirror that reflects
> To proud Self-love her own intelligence;
> [That one, poor, finite object, in the abyss
> Of infinite Being, twinkling restlessly!]"

monumental effort to do for painting and architecture what Wordsworth had done for poetry: to show that great art should imitate nature and inspire in the beholder the same reverence and awe crystallized in Wordsworth's concept of the sublime. Ruskin's Wordsworth, however, is refracted through the other influence on his outlook, namely, the dogmatic theology contracted in childhood, nursed in adult life, and retained (albeit in softer, humanist, and more mystical form) to the last. Throughout his work, this thick religious lens focuses all aesthetic and moral value on a single point and turns everything it touches, down to the pebbles beneath Ruskin's feet, into the tangible product of Creation and an expression of God: in Ruskin's hands Wordsworth's naturalism becomes theophany, the appearance of the Divine to human beings through the medium of nature.[23] This outlook is crystallized in Ruskin's "assumption" that man has a "use and function, ... to be the witness of the glory of God, and to advance that glory by his reasonable obedience and resultant happiness." Whatever enables human beings to fulfill that function is "useful," Ruskin asserts, in a more expansive sense of the term he mourns as lost in the myopia of the Benthamites and their obsession with "things that only help us to exist" (MP II, 28–9).

There is great emotional appeal in this worldview and the critique of modernity it generates, though its darker side is visible in the sometimes offensive moralizing, disturbing narrow-mindedness, and irritating arrogance that too often rises to the surface of Ruskin's writing, all couched in a prose style – as Ruskin later (in the 1880s) came to see it – as pompous and tendentious as it is tedious and prolix. At times, Ruskin's aesthetics appear less a sincere attempt to develop a serious aesthetics than it does a sustained effort to generalize and justify an individual taste and personal point of view. Despite such faults, there is much of interest for the student of aesthetics in Ruskin's work, especially as it represents the culmination and end of the romantic love affair with the picturesque, heard *sote voce* in Gilpin's innocent descriptions of the British countryside, and in full-throated ease through Wordsworth's natural sublime. Those inclined to view the past providentially might say that Ruskin, or somebody very much like him, was required to inherit, consummate, and find wanting the rhapsody of Wordsworth's naturalism that looked, as the years marched toward a new century, increasingly like a partial truth, an optimistic vision, and a flimsy defense against the rise of industrialism and the materialism, degradation, and poverty, that came with it. Ruskin was long seduced by Wordsworth's rural fantasy, but ultimately found it an unsatisfying refuge and unethical escape from the real world, and came instead to confront head-on, both intellectually and practically, the decay, ugliness, and inhumanity that it exploited and concealed. The attempt proved as impotent, finally, as Wordsworth's anachronistic celebration of the Lakes, but Ruskin's life and work remain an articulate, impassioned, and aesthetic critique of the values that defined the age.

---

[23] On this point, see Landow, *The Aesthetic and Critical Theories of John Ruskin*, 28ff., 110 passim.

After 1860, following a crisis of faith and a religious "unconversion" during a church service in Turin, Ruskin turned increasingly to pressing social and political issues of the day, composing lectures and journal articles that made him, if not a radical in the mold of Hazlitt, certainly a powerful voice for social reform, especially in the area of education where he met with modest success.[24] At the same time, Ruskin grew increasingly isolated, geographically through his move to Brantwood House on Coniston Water in the Lake District in 1872, intellectually in the increasingly mystical and obscure tenor of his writing, and psychologically as his bouts of mental illness worsened, culminating in a final breakdown while on his last trip to the Continent and two years before his death. Ruskin was laid to rest in the graveyard of Coniston village, across the vales southeast from Cockermouth, birthplace of Wordsworth and only six miles from St. Oswald's Churchyard in Grasmere where the great poet was buried in 1850. There is poetry and pathos in this fact, that the first and last great figures of British Romanticism ended their days and took their final rest in the same small corner of England, amidst the dramatic scenery that inspired and moved them both.

Beauty and Ruskin's Theophantic Naturalism

It has been suggested that Ruskin's aesthetics underwent a major shift over the course of his writing. In *The Poetry of Architecture* (1837–8) and *Modern Painters* I (1843), the suggestion runs, Ruskin assumed "beauty" and its various manifestations sufficient to account for the entire range of aesthetic experience, but later realized this position untenable and so, from *Modern Painters* II (1846) onward, adopted the more traditional division between beauty, on the one hand, and sublimity, on the other.[25] There are certainly distinct periods in Ruskin's thinking, and, as we shall see, a definite change in "tone" between the second and third volumes of *Modern Painters* signaling (as one commentator puts it) that he became "less moved by the beauty of art and nature than by the waste, mystery, and terror of life."[26] Conceptually, however, Ruskin's work

---

[24] Ruskin was closely associated with the Working Man's College in London and Wennington School in Chesire. For a recent study on this aspect of Ruskin's thinking, see Sara Atwood, *Ruskin's Educational Ideals* (Farnham, UK: Ashgate, 2011). The most comprehensive, and sympathetic, treatment of Ruskin's often-troubled life (including the unhappy and unconsummated marriage to Effie Gray) is Tim Hilton, *John Ruskin: The Early Years 1819–1859* and *John Ruskin: The Later Years* (New Haven, CT: Yale University Press, 1985 and 2000). Somewhat different emphases are to be found in John L. Bradley, *An Introduction to Ruskin* (Boston: Houghton Mifflin, 1971), and W. G. Collingwood, *The Life of John Ruskin*, 2 vols. (Boston: Houghton Mifflin, 1893). Collingwood (1854–1932), it might be noted, was an artist in his own right (he was later Professor of Fine Art at the University of Reading), and after meeting Ruskin at Oxford became his protégé, assistant, and traveling companion. His son, R. G. Collingwood, was destined to become a famous philosopher and historian in his own right, and to make an important contribution to the aesthetic tradition (see ch. 7).
[25] This line is pursued by Landow, *The Aesthetic and Critical Theories of John Ruskin*.
[26] Rosenberg, *The Darkening Glass*, 22.

displays a remarkable unity, and what might look like changes of direction are really stages in a natural process of maturation and growth. Early, in *The Poetry of Architecture*, written while an undergraduate at Oxford,[27] Ruskin employs terms capriciously, but with time and reflection he imposes a more definite structure on his ideas and greater precision to their mode of expression. Thus, in *The Poetry of Architecture*, he distinguishes beauty from the sublime – the former "astonishes" and requires a "tinge of melancholy," while the latter "impresses" and requires a "sense of danger" (PA 16 and 19) – predicates "grandeur" and "picturesque" of the same landscape (PA 150–1), and defines picturesque "blue country" in terms of qualities as diverse as "grace," the undulation and variety of line, "mystery," given by "sublimity of distance," and "sensuality," expressed in line, color, and "luxuriance of life" (PA 148–90). Ruskin also identifies beauty with what is "useful" (PA 21), and equates it presumptuously with moral value: Christian virtues of cleanliness, softness, and purity go hand in hand with "pastoral life" and the English cottage (PA 37), along with the activity, resolution, and industry of its wholesome inhabitants. Among the Swiss, similar virtues combine with bucolic images of happy peasants with full milk pails, content at the end of a summer day spent in Alpine pastures, a scene Ruskin describes as "beautifully national" (PA 38).

Modern Painters I brings order to these disparate elements, though the occasion is not a search for clarity per se but a defense of Turner against the criticism that his impressionistic canvases strayed too far from nature. The aim of art in general, Ruskin argues by way of response, and with loud echoes of Reynolds, is not to produce a copy at all, but to embody "great" or "noble ideas" (MP I, 91), whether these express powers of mind and body, the effect of imitation and relation, or, as in the case of beauty, the sensed qualities of objects viewed. Moreover, that art is "greatest," he insists,

which conveys to the mind of the spectator, by any means whatsoever, the greatest number of the greatest ideas; and I call an idea great in proportion as it is received by a higher faculty of the mind, and as it more fully occupies, and in occupying, exercises and exalts, the faculty by which it is received. (MP I, 91–2)

The most important ideas for Ruskin, then, are not those that express beauty – the product of sensibility and thus tied to the real presence of some material object – but those that are "true" and convey a single attribute – a passion, emotion, or thought – grasped by intellect. Great artists make a "faithful statement, either to the mind or senses, of any fact of nature" (MP I, 104), he acknowledges, but, like Hume's poet who disdains the chitchat of the dinner table and ignores Achilles tying his shoelaces, they do not capture a likeness: the more realistic a Dutch still life, a landscape *à la* Poussin, or a Canaletto view

---

[27] Ruskin originally wrote *The Poetry of Architecture* as a series of papers for J. C. Loudon's *Architectural Magazine* in 1837–8. The first single volume of the papers as *The Poetry of Architecture* appeared in 1873 as a pirated American version; the first edition in England was published in 1893.

of Venice (an artist Ruskin despised above all others), the more occupied is the mind with the merely novel fact that "what has been suggested to it is not what it appears to be" (MP I, 108). A great artist, by contrast, focuses the mind's attention "upon its own conception of the fact, or form, or feeling stated" (MP I, 108), and this is achieved by *re*-presentation that – as in the drama of Turner's seascapes – does *not look like nature at all*. "Ideas of truth," then – found in tone, color, chiaroscuro, space, skies, clouds, earth, and water, each of which Ruskin considers in turn – are the real "foundation" of art, while those that focus on imitation and beauty are its "destruction" (MP I, 108).

In *Modern Painters* I, then, Ruskin clearly connects beauty with the lowly province of sense, and makes mind and its activities the source of highest aesthetic value. Even here, however, beauty bears the marks destined to make it center stage three years later in *Modern Painters* II (1846). First, like Hutcheson more than a century earlier, Ruskin exploits the analogy with external sense: beauty is an idea or "emotion" (MP I, 48), he urges, the effect of qualities that excite ideas and produce a corresponding pleasure "without any definite exertion of the intellect," but rather "instinctively and necessarily" by virtue of one of the "ultimate instincts" or "primary principles" of human nature formed by the Deity and illustrative of His attributes (MP I, 109). Unlike Hutcheson, though, Ruskin refuses to posit an internal sense as such, but insists instead on a capacity he calls "moral perception," which he takes to arise (in the spirit of Shaftesbury) from "simple contemplation" (MP I, 109). This means, second, that the idea or emotion of beauty is the result of apprehending some real objective feature of God's Creation. Beauty is real and everything in nature is beautiful, albeit relative to a species and manifest perfectly within each class as the "ideal of the object" (MP I, 111). Third, for Ruskin, it is also axiomatic that experiencing the beauty of nature is equivalent to apprehending the moral value of the universe as ordained by the Creator. Pleasure, on this view, becomes an element of the "natural laws of aversion and desire," and the extent of one's sensibility becomes an indication of "constant obedience" and proximity to the original intention of God; "taste" is transformed into a moral imperative, no longer the function of "judgment" – a "definite action of the intellect" with respect to any "kind of subject which can be submitted to it" – but the "instinctive and instant preferring of one material object to another without any obvious reason, except that it is proper to human nature in its perfection do to so." "Perfect taste" is then the "faculty of receiving the greatest possible pleasure from those material sources which are attractive to our moral nature in its purity and perfection. He who receives little pleasure from these sources wants taste," Ruskin can conclude with confidence, "he who receives pleasure from any other sources, has false or bad taste" (MP I, 110).

In *Modern Painters* II Ruskin elaborates these basic principles in the most developed expression of what we can call his "theophantic naturalism," the view that all aesthetic value is objective because it relates directly to the Divine and the way God appears to human beings in nature, which presupposes in turn two faculties on the part of the subject – the "theoretic" and "imaginative" – themselves of divine origin. Ruskin's "imaginative faculty" is borrowed largely from Locke and Hume. It denotes what the "mind exercises in a certain mode of regarding or combining the ideas it has received from external nature, and the operations of which become in their turn objects of the theoretic faculty to other minds" (MP II, 36; see also 223); the faculty, moreover, is incapable of producing anything entirely new, creativity being the province of God alone (MP II, 236–7, 253), and does not trade in falsehoods ("exhibit things as they are *not*"), which would be an attempt to "mend the works of God" (MP II, 37), which are already perfect. Ruskin distinguishes further among three "forms" corresponding to different functions or powers of imagination: its "Combining" or "Associative" function isolates imperfect elements that it unifies subsequently into a perfect whole; through its "Analytic" or "Penetrative" power it grasps the essence of its object, the "heart and inner nature" (MP II, 253) beyond merely surface qualities, and its "Regardant" or "Contemplative" function forges images into groups, rendering them consistent in terms of some single element. Under (one assumes) the influence of Coleridge, Ruskin also identifies three corresponding forms of "fancy" that are "subordinate to" but shadow the same power manifest at a higher level in the imagination. The "Associative Fancy" calls up "images apposite and resembling ... quickly and in multitudes" (MP II, 232); the "Penetrative Fancy" "sees the outside" and collects details (MP II, 253), and the "Contemplative Fancy" forges groups according to some element, though one nonessential, which leads the mind away from the true nature of the object.[28]

If Ruskin's concept of imagination is largely derivative, his "theoretical faculty" is both original and provides required conceptual support for the nonrepresentational nature of art advanced in *Modern Painters* I. He achieves this by effectively unifying what was previously divided into "ideas of truth" and "ideas of beauty": beauty and truth become one in a single act of "moral perception" (MP II, 35). Ruskin names the faculty responsible for this act after Aristotle, finding in "theoria" a way of emphasizing that impressions of beauty are "neither sensual nor intellectual, but moral" (MP II, 42), apprehended rather than perceived, and experienced as pleasure taken in "external creation" (MP II, 223). All of this is obscured by the term *aesthetic*, Ruskin insists, which (with a distinctly Coleridgean/Kantian ring) he associates with the "mere operation of sense ... or custom" (MP II, 35–6). The "mere animal consciousness of the pleasantness of it [beauty] I call Æsthesis," he writes accordingly, "but the exulting, reverent, and grateful perception of it I call Theoria. For this, and only this, is the full comprehension and contemplation of the Beautiful as a gift of God" (MP

---

[28] It is not clear that these conceptual distinctions do much work for Ruskin, and revising *Modern Painters* II in the 1880s he later dismissed the whole attempt as "insignificant," there being no meaningful division, he concedes in retrospect, among "imagined," "fancied," and "invented" (MP II, 219–20).

II, 47). Beauty is "the record of conscience, written in things external," he writes later, " ... a symbolizing of Divine attributes in matter, ... the felicity of living things, or the perfect fulfillment of their duties and functions" (MP II, 210).

"Beauty," Ruskin then explains, is either "Typical" or "Vital," all other meanings being "either false or metaphorical." "Typical Beauty" denotes "qualities," "properties" or "characteristics" of "*mere* matter," which is agreeable due to an "instinctive sense" (MP II, 211) and moves the passions because the *material* qualities "convey the idea of *immaterial* ones" (MP II, 76n, emphasis added), that is, the Divine attributes with which they are "typical" or "absolutely identical" (MP II, 64). There are six "palpable and powerful modes" in which these Divine attributes are manifest and through them "every division of creation" appears, whether in "stones, mountains, waves, clouds, and all organic bodies ... from the mollusk to man," as the "necessary perfection of God's working, and the inevitable stamp of His image on what He creates" (MP II, 142–3). Ruskin enumerates these as infinity ("divine incomprehensibility"), unity ("divine comprehensiveness"), repose ("divine permanence"), symmetry ("divine justice"), purity ("divine energy"), and moderation ("government by law").

Unlike typical beauty, its "vital" counterpart refers to the "felicitous fulfillment of function in living things, more especially ... the joyful and right exertion of perfect life in man" (MP II, 64), which Ruskin divides into two "perfections." The first, "relative vital beauty," arises from our tendency to associate what is lovely with happiness (MP II, 147) and the fact that we possess a "kindness and unselfish fullness of heart, which receives the utmost amount of pleasure from the happiness of all things" (MP II, 148).[29] Beauty is then excited through sympathy, which, in a clear echo of Hazlitt, Ruskin understands as the capacity to share in the "happiness" or well-being of all living things, a pleasure felt "in proportion" to a viewed organism's "appearance of healthy vital energy." When we look upon a plant with withered leaves, for example, we "feel it to be painful ... because it seems to hurt the plant, and conveys to us an idea of pain and disease and failure in the life in *it*" (MP II, 151): a flourishing organism is beautiful and elicits a corresponding feeling of pleasure, whereas a failing one is ugly and arouses pain. The second "perfection" – "generic vital beauty" – depends on the ability to compare and judge the perfection of other creatures on the basis of the standard of moral perfection by which human beings test themselves. Beauty here involves grasping the "perfect idea of the form and condition in which all the properties of the species are fully developed, ... the Ideal of the species," or "all that can be expected" of some specimen given the circumstances of its occurrence in nature (MP II, 165). In the case of human beings, the Ideal is found in the physical effects of virtue on the human body, and, on the face in particular, as signs of beatitude. Beyond this lies what Ruskin

---

[29] Ruskin sees this exemplified – not surprisingly – in the poetry of Wordsworth (especially the "White Doe of Rylston" and "Hartleap Well") and Coleridge ("The Song of the Ancient Mariner").

calls (obscurely) "soul-culture," which cultivates the immortal part of human nature in an "ideal glory of a ... purer and higher range" than can be captured even in perfect physical form (MP II 182). Ironically, a good deal of Ruskin's discussion is less about generic vital beauty than about ugliness, because vice and misery prevail over virtue and happiness, and human beings more often carry "signs of evil" (pride, sensuality, fear, and ferocity) that crease, line, and emaciate the human body.[30]

The Sublime

Given, as noted earlier, Ruskin's remarks in *The Poetry of Architecture* to the effect that sublimity and beauty should be held apart – one requires a "sense of danger" (PA 19), the other "melancholy" – it is surprising in *Modern Painters* I to find a categorical declaration that the "sublime is not distinct from what is beautiful," but a "mode or manifestation" of the other sources of ideas, namely, power, imitation, relation, beauty, and truth (MP I, 130). "The fact is," Ruskin writes in a chapter only three pages in length and clearly designed to put the matter to rest,

that sublimity is not a specific term, – not a term descriptive of the effect of a particular class of ideas. Anything which elevates the mind is sublime, and elevation of mind is produced by the contemplation of greatness of any kind, but chiefly, of course, by the greatness of noble things. Sublimity is, therefore, only another word for the effect of greatness upon the feelings; – greatness, whether of matter, space, power, virtue, or beauty: and there is perhaps no desirable quality of a work of art, which, in its perfection, is not, in some way or degree, sublime. (MP I, 128)

Apart from this statement, much of the space Ruskin allots to the subject is an attempted refutation of Burke's claim that the sublime arises from fear and self-preservation, when the real feeling of sublimity, Ruskin asserts cheerfully, concerns the "contemplation of death ... [and] the deliberate measurement of the doom" involved (MP I, 129).

By *Modern Painters* II, Ruskin has changed his mind or, more accurately, adopted self-consciously the more traditional albeit unstated position he assumed in *The Poetry of Architecture*. Perhaps ruing and slightly embarrassed by his earlier confidence, Ruskin marks the reversion by quietly dropping the matter altogether: the published version of *Modern Painters* II contains no treatment of the sublime at all, not even acknowledging it as a mode of the beautiful. An earlier draft, however, contains material intended for a projected section "Of the Sublime," and some of it is well developed.[31] There, Ruskin reiterates and expands the earlier definition of sublimity, emphasizing features familiar from Addison onward, with the same emphasis on sympathy and repose found in Wordsworth. The sublime is that "attribute of any object by

---

[30] See Landow, *The Aesthetic and Critical Theories of John Ruskin*, 166–7.
[31] This material is included by Cook and Wedderburn in an appendix to *Modern Painters* II, *Works* 4, 368–81.

which it expands or raises the feelings, so as to prevent them from dwelling on subjects little or momentary," he writes,

– the effect, in short, upon the mind of anything above it. Anything which disposes us to the contemplation of things great or generalized, of large effects of fate and spaces of time, – anything which banishes paltry interests and agitations, and gives the feeling a repose in which they are at liberty to look far and broadly and calmly into or over the great laws and masses of being – anything which being itself great makes us great by the sympathy we have with it is sublime. (*Works* 4, 369)

Ruskin thus associates sublimity with some fairly familiar qualities – breadth, size, energy, mystery, awe – with an emphasis on the "supernatural unity of God" to which the mind is led when it experiences sublime forms of sound and color, as in the wind, darkness, and power of a storm. Ruskin adds the proviso that the effect of greatness is comparative, because scale begins with "*human* power or size" (emphasis added). Something that is ordinarily small – a butterfly or a lizard, for example – would not be sublime even if made spectacularly large (it would be merely "monstrous"), whereas a crocodile or a megalosaurus, being actually large, is sublime because it surpasses the standard of human strength. Of particular interest are Ruskin's remarks on "awe," a term he reserves for the particular "apprehension of power superior to our own, and of the great perpetual operations of death and pain in the system of the universe" (*Works* 4, 374). It is the mark of a great mind, moreover, to feel this and other manifestations of sublimity, and take pleasure in the terrible scenes that excite it.

A notable feature of the material for the projected section is that Ruskin there embraces what he had acknowledged in *The Poetry of Architecture* and explicitly denied in *Modern Painters* I, namely, that beauty and sublimity are "distinct," although he maintains at the same time that they also have "something in common." "It will readily, I believe, be admitted that many things are sublime in the highest degree," Ruskin writes,

which are not in the highest degree beautiful, and *vice versa*; *i.e.* that the two ideas are distinct, and one is not merely a particular form or state of the other. It will also, I believe, be admitted on reflection that nothing can be perfectly sublime without being in some degree or way beautiful, and nothing perfectly beautiful, without being in some degree sublime; *i.e.* that the two ideas, though distinct, have yet something in common, and are not altogether separable. (*Works* 4, 369)

This attempted clarification of the proposed admixture of beauty and sublimity is hardly illuminating, and Ruskin fails to elaborate the "something" that makes them "not altogether separable," reasons perhaps for the material remaining unpublished. A clue to what he might have in mind can be gleaned from *The Seven Lamps of Architecture* (1849), however, which is Ruskin's attempt to enumerate the laws that explain why various architectural forms excite emotions of different kinds (the motif of the "lamp" is biblical, borrowed from Proverbs and Psalms). Employing the same language used in "Of the Sublime," Ruskin there argues that beauty arises from imitating nature whereas sublimity is the expression of human power. The "lamp of beauty" and "lamp of power" denote two distinct classes of architecture, "the one characterized by an exceeding preciousness and delicacy, to which we recur with a sense of affectionate admiration; and the other by a severe, and, in many cases, mysterious awe, like that felt at the presence and operation of some great Spiritual Power" (SLA 100). Ruskin emphasizes that the difference between the two orders is "not merely that which there is in nature between things beautiful and sublime [but] also, the difference between what is derivative and original in man's work" (SLA 101); or, as he expresses it in his religious idiom, they differ in showing human beings either as "gathering or governing," the "one consisting in a just and humble veneration for the works of God upon the earth, and the other in an understanding of the dominion over those works which has been vested in man" (SLA 102). Beauty is derived because buildings that possess it do so in virtue of imitating and adapting lines commonly found in natural forms (cylindrical columns imitate the trunks of trees, pointed arches the shapes of leaves, and so forth), while sublimity is original because buildings with "nobility," "dignity," "honor," "majesty," or "grandeur" express directly the power of the human mind responsible for arranging the materials that compose them. Importantly, because beauty depends on qualities that originate elsewhere it is a reflection of something external, whereas the qualities that constitute sublimity are inherent in the object. As Ruskin readily admits, the features responsible for the effect of sublimity – magnitude, totality, height, expanse of surface area, mass, and areas of shadow – are also features of naturally occurring objects, so that sublime architecture is ultimately in sympathy "with what is most sublime in natural things" (SLA 102), although not derivative in the way that gives objects of beauty their value.

Ruskin's Moral Picturesque

In *The Seven Lamps of Architecture*, then, Ruskin provides a clear way in which beauty and sublimity are "distinct," though he leaves unspecified what they might have "in common." One way to understand the connection is through the category of the picturesque, which Ruskin treats as an amalgamation of or meeting point for beauty and sublimity much in line, initially at least, with Price's claim in *An Essay on the Picturesque* that it falls "between beauty and sublimity" while remaining "perfectly distinct from either" (E 68), or that the picturesque "fills up a vacancy between the sublime and the beautiful, and accounts for the pleasure we receive from many objects, on principles distinct from them both" (E 114).[32] The comparison ends there, for in Ruskin's hands

---

[32] See the discussion of Price in ch. 4, and Landow, *The Aesthetic and Critical Theories of John Ruskin*, 239–40, who makes a similar comparison between Ruskin and Price. Ruskin's mature view also bears comparison with Knight's account of perceptual experience in the *Analytic*

the picturesque undergoes a radical transformation: it ceases to be the purely aesthetic category of Gilpin, Price, and Knight, and becomes one with primarily moral content. Ruskin pushes the "picturesque" to its conceptual limits, and in doing so marks the end of the tradition it forms. As with beauty and sublimity, it is tempting to think of Ruskin as having two distinct views of the picturesque corresponding to *The Poetry of Architecture*, on the one hand, and *The Seven Lamps of Architecture* and *Modern Painters* IV (1856), on the other. In fact, Ruskin really has a single concept, but emphasizes different modes it can take depending on one's view: the shift in emphasis on Ruskin's part is what explains his rejection of the "surface" picturesque – the aesthetic articulated in the tradition from Gilpin through to Wordsworth – to its "higher" or "Turnerian" counterpart.

Officially, *The Poetry of Architecture* is Ruskin's attempt to account for good taste and right judgment in architecture by appeal to the ideal unity that exists in the relationship between nature and the people who dwell in her. Architecture should conform to nature's dress, and, whether in lowly cottage or splendid villa, succeeds when it "bestow[s] animation" on a scene without "disturbing repose" (PA 11 and 17 passim). Ruskin's immediate inspiration for the work was the tour he took with his parents through the north of England in the summer of 1837, but, as his adopted pseudonym announces – "Kata Phusin" ("according to nature") – Ruskin's perspective was shaped by the Romantic lens of Wordsworth and, by extension, the picturesque literature going back to Gilpin.[33] In language, imagery, and tone, *The Poetry of Architecture* often recalls *A Guide through the District of the Lakes* (in its sixth edition by 1835) and throughout Ruskin indulges in a Wordsworthian myth of a rural idyll lost, ruined by the "horrors of improvement" (PA 49), ills engendered by mechanization, and effects of tourism, all of which in his mind had despoiled, aesthetically and morally, the perfection of God's creation. "Merry England," with its forests, demesne, iconic tree-lined avenues, he remarks at one point, is "a name which, in this age of steam and iron, it will have some difficulty keeping" (PA 120; see SLA 66–9). Such antimodern nostalgia is most evident in Ruskin's praise of the Lake District inhabitants for their gentleness, simplicity, and capacity to experience the "calmer flow of human felicity, the stillness of domestic peace, and the pleasures of the humble hearth, consisting

---

Inquiry. Because Ruskin never read either Price or Knight, it seems that he attained by empirical observation the same conclusion they had reached earlier through the more abstract methods of philosophical inquiry.

[33] Ruskin appears to have had no direct knowledge of the philosophical literature on the picturesque (except in the diffuse form of Wordsworth's poetry and perhaps the *Guide*), although he does refer *en passant* later to the "frequent" and "prolonged" disputes over the term *picturesque* (SLA 235). Landow, *The Aesthetic and Critical Theories of John Ruskin*, 226ff., suggests Ruskin's drawing master J. D. Harding as a source for some of the ideas, and notes the work of the picturesque artist Samuel Prout as a profound influence on his early picturesque sketches.

in every-day duties performed, and every-day mercies received" (PA 50), good Christian virtues expressed spontaneously in the humble cottages in which they live, the buildings "adopted and cherished" by the mountains that surround them (PA 44). There is also a specific echo of Wordsworth's Preface (and of the Romantic poets more generally) in Ruskin's insistence that the body of knowledge contained in *The Poetry of Architecture* is "poetic" because "a science of feeling more than of rule, a ministry to mind, more than to the eye," available not to the man of science armed with "rule and compass," but only to the "metaphysician" (PA 5), the man of feeling – like Ruskin – who can read poetic truth directly from the book of nature itself.

Given its form and content, it is not surprising that *The Poetry of Architecture* should contain a picturesque aesthetic that is rich, like that of Wordsworth, in the imagery of Gilpin, but at once confident that nature – *la belle Nature* – has value inherently, free of artifice and the meddling hands of the landscape gardener. "Every fragment of rock is finished in its effect," Ruskin writes in a typical passage, "tinted with thousands of pale lichens and fresh mosses; every pine trunk is warm with the life of various vegetation; every grassy bank glowing with mellowed colour, and waving with delicate leafage" (PA 36). Characteristically, Ruskin cannot help projecting his favorite prejudice or handy half-truth onto scenes he describes – the English are a picture of propriety (PA 12), the French dirty and indolent (PA 23), the Swiss "have no character" (PA 40) – but otherwise his imagery is conventional: the picturesque is defined by the age, decay, and decrepitude of structures, an accompanying mood of nonchalance, darkness, and despair, and corresponds generally to his category of "blue" landscape consisting of foothills broken by crag and dingle, and marked by mystery, sensuality, and variety of line.[34] Swiss cottages gathered together in a village are "picturesque in the extreme" (PA 38), Ruskin observes, especially when the buildings are a "little rotten" (PA 38); the cottage of the French (whose eye, for some reason, he thinks "accustomed to the picturesque" [PA 16]) is a model of "neglected beauty, and obliterated ornament" exhibited in its disorder, worn whitewash, creeping moss, and wandering lichens, all dramatized by the comfortless position of the structure on the public road (PA 13). The pleasure afforded by the Italian cottage and its resident "aristocracy" (PA 21), by contrast, lies in its elevated character and the mixture of grandeur and desolation that stands as a living testament to faded glory and departed pride. The cottage of Westmoreland, finally, affects the viewer through the "trouble and wrath of life" it expresses, "its sorrow and its mystery" reflected in the "depth or diffusion of gloom, by the frown upon its front, and the shadow of its recess" (PA 116–17).

As these various examples show, like the French cottage that exemplifies it, Ruskin's early picturesque is a disordered affair, an admixture of qualities from

---

34 Ruskin's other categories are the "green" and woody landscape that conveys a feeling of reverence for age, the "grey" of the swept moorland with the sense of wildness, and the "brown" of hills that excites humility before nature.

which a more systematic writer would extract a subset, leaving the remainder to beauty and sublimity; as we have seen, Ruskin even makes the picturesque the *sine qua non* of beauty, which requires that "tinge of melancholy" for its effects. In *The Seven Lamps of Architecture* and *Modern Painters* IV, by contrast, Ruskin devotes significant space to a more careful and self-consciously theoretical adumbration of the concept from which it emerges as a point on a scale between "pure beauty," which "is not picturesque at all" (SLA 236), and "true" sublimity, which arises from real qualities inherent in objects. Ruskin acknowledges the etymological roots of the term and its correspondent meaning – "fit to become the subject of a picture" – but emphasizes (as did Price) how that definition hardly distinguishes it from beauty and the sublime, both of which are also subjects fit for artistic representation. Instead, he insists, more forcefully even than Wordsworth before him, that the picturesque should be understood as a mode of the sublime, resulting from introducing "characters" evocative of the latter into scenes otherwise beautiful: delicacy, health, vigor, and clarity are transformed aesthetically by what is rugged, ruined, weary, and confused, effects achieved by artists through angular and broken lines, dramatic oppositions of light and shadow, and boldly contrasting color, all of which become more powerful when "by resemblance or association, they remind us of objects on which a true and essential sublimity exists, as of rocks or mountains, or stormy clouds or waves" (SLA 237; see MP IV, 15). The picturesque can never be true sublimity, Ruskin reminds his readers, because it is "not inherent in the nature of the thing, [but] caused by something external to it; as the ruggedness of a cottage roof possesses something of a mountain aspect, not belonging to the cottage as such" (MP IV, 10). The picturesque, in this sense, is closer to beauty, derived because the features that compose it imitate and adapt lines commonly found in external nature; the picturesque is a reflection or shadow of the true sublime and therefore what Ruskin calls "parasitical" or "engrafted," a "sublimity dependent on the accidents, or on the least essential characters, of the objects to which it belongs" (SLA 236).

This species of picturesque effect is manifest in the "Material Form" of "the Gothic," the general "nature" or "Gothicness" of which Ruskin celebrates in *The Stones of Venice* II (1853). The architectural features of gabled roof, pointed apertures, and foliated ornamentation that typify the style resemble and remind us of truly sublime objects, that is, they reflect natural shapes external to them (mountains, leaves, and so forth) and therefore produce a picturesque effect parasitic upon true sublimity. The other, more profound, part of the Gothic, however, is its "Mental Power or Expression," the characteristics or "moral elements" that Gothic builders loved or "instinctively" expressed in their work (SV II, 183). Understood as features belonging to the building, Ruskin enumerates these in descending order of importance as savageness, variety, naturalism, grotesqueness, rigidity, and redundancy; or, understood as affective states of the builder responsible for arranging the materials, as rudeness, love of change, love of nature, disturbed imagination, obstinacy, and generosity. Unlike its formal aspect, this expressive part of the Gothic style belongs to the building itself and is original, like the true sublime with respect to nature, because it directly expresses the power of human mind. For Ruskin, the essence of the Gothic is its ethos, that it is an aesthetic that conveys a whole way of "life," not only in the lines of its architectural features, but also in the virtues of freedom, invention, humanity, peace, and repose, all light and vivacity against the darkness and enervation of industrial Britain with its blighted landscape, Satanic mills, and moral degradation.[35]

This expressive part of the Gothic, then, marks a shift in Ruskin's appreciation of the picturesque and its incipient reformulation from an aesthetic to a moral category, more implied than stated in *The Stones of Venice*, but clearly formulated three years later in *Modern Painters* IV (1856). There, the parasitical picturesque of *The Seven Lamps of Architecture* becomes the "lower," "surface," or "literal sense" picturesque, the source of a "merely outward delightfulness" (MP IV, 15) that corresponds to its reflected being and its origin in the imitation of external forms. Ruskin's characterization captures perfectly the idiom of the earlier *The Poetry of Architecture*, with its Gilpinesque language and Wordsworthian romance, that distills the "essence" of the picturesque into "delight in ruin" and celebration of "poverty-stricken rusticity" (MP IV, 10), disguised with a veneer of "gentility," contemptible "trimness," and superficial love of everything "old fashioned" (MP IV, 12–13). Ruskin finds the lower picturesque reflected artistically in the landscapes of Claude, the long-time poster child of the genre perhaps, in whom he sees in an irony unimaginable to writers and tourists only some half-century earlier, "one mass of error from beginning to end" (MP I, 167; see also MP IV, 9).

There is, however, an alternative aesthetic of the picturesque, adumbrated but never named in *The Stones of Venice*, that emerges distinctly and emphatically in *Modern Painters* IV with the title of "higher," "true," "noble," or – in the name of the artist who epitomizes it – the "Turnerian" picturesque. This mode is defined not by delight in or artistic record of the external qualities of a scene, but lies in grasping or, as an artist, capturing, the "real nature of a thing," its "inner character," which the surface obscures. A dilapidated windmill, the old tower of Calais church, the aged laborer with "grey hair, ... withered arms, and sunburnt breast" (MP IV, 15) – these are Ruskin's iconic images – might be "charming" or "delightful" when viewed with the literally yet superficial picturesque eye, but are truly picturesque only when grasped through the theoretical faculty as the "unconscious confession of the facts of distress and decay" where "no pity [is] asked for, nor contempt feared" (MP IV, 15). The

---

[35] The fact that the Middle Ages and Gothic architecture were associated both historically and in the popular mind with Catholicism (and not his own Protestant faith that was also the official religion of his country) was a source of some difficulty for Ruskin, and he was at great pains to emphasize the merely contingent nature of the relationship between the two. See Rosenberg, *The Darkening Glass*, 55ff.

picturesque is "higher" from the same "mental power" that gives the Gothic style its moral content, articulating life as the stoic expression of *"suffering, of poverty,* or *decay,* nobly endured by unpretending strength of heart" (MP IV, 15–16). Ruskin, it should be emphasized, does not descry the lover of the lower picturesque as a monster, and even finds in such depraved taste potential opportunity for cultivating "feeling" and realizing a "truer sympathy with the poor," lack of which he saw in the avarice and greed that raised profit above beauty and demolished great monuments in the name of "improvement." Lovers of the lower picturesque are still selfish, however, "heartless" in their ability to find joy in disorder, ruin, poverty, decrepitude, "ragged misery," and "wasting age" (MP IV, 19), all of which take on through an ideal of artistic representation an illusory aspect that mitigates real suffering and prevents it from entering their consciousness or (if artists) their pictures.

This dramatic shift in the meaning of "picturesque," a conceptual shift from the surface to inner, lower to higher, aesthetic to moral, cannot, moreover, be separated from the profound personal change that took place in Ruskin as the man of conscience supplanted the disinterested critic. In a footnote to *Modern Painters* IV Ruskin reproduces (in slightly altered form) a diary entry from May 1854 that records his surreal vision and moment of insight when the picturesque idiom from Gilpin through Wordsworth was revealed to him as a lie, a superficial delight premised on willful ignorance of the pain endured by some for the sake of pleasure enjoyed by others. Ruskin reports having taken a "happy walk here this afternoon down among the branching currents of the Somme," but then, as if the Claude Glass had been removed to reveal Being in-itself, Ruskin finds himself confronted with a scene of poverty and degradation: waterways "narrow and foul ... running beneath clusters of fearful houses, reeling masses of rotten timber ... an old flamboyant Gothic church, whose richly traceried buttresses sloped into the filthy stream; – all exquisitely picturesque, and no less miserable." We might delight in such scenes, Ruskin reflects,

but as I looked to-day at the unhealthy face and melancholy mien of the man in the boat pushing his load of peats along the ditch, and of the people, men as well as women, who at spinning gloomily at the cottage doors, I could not help feeling how many suffering persons must pay for my picturesque subject and happy walk. (MP IV, 20n)

Ruskin articulates what Gilpin had suspected but repressed more than half a century earlier, and Wordsworth had later ignored for his convenience: that whether one identifies the picturesque with the painterly eye or pristine nature, it remains at bottom a magical glass, which transforms and embellishes objects under its gaze, and turns the real world into a fiction. Even Gilpin, to recall the earlier discussion, had difficulty accommodating into his sketches the sorry souls amid the ruins of Tintern Abbey, and Wordsworth wrote his lines conveniently "a few miles above" the same structure twenty years later; even the resources of his poetical imagination were tested when put in service of purifying rural life of the barbarity and destitution that, as Hazlitt so inconveniently pointed out, were the real elements of its composition.

What was but unpleasant at the Somme was to become the stuff of nightmares, populated by scenes of horror that Ruskin describes with a surreal quality most famously in "The Mountain Gloom." Amidst the undeniable majesty of the Swiss Alps, he is conscious not of the "glory" the mountains hold, but the corruption of existence they portray, the "gloomy foulness," torpor, anguish, and "darkness of calm enduring" (MP IV, 388). In language that brings to mind Hazlitt's unforgiving castigation of country life, Ruskin describes in hallucinatory terms life in a mountain village that could, with only a slight reorientation, apply to the worker of the Lancashire mill. "For them, there is neither hope nor passion of spirit; for them neither advance nor exultation," Ruskin writes. "Black bread, rude roof, dark night, laborious day, weary arm at sunset; and life ebbs away. No books, no thoughts, no attainments, no rest; except only sometimes a little sitting in the sun under the church wall, as the bell tolls thin and far in the mountain air" (MP IV, 388-9). This final vision is apocalyptic, a revelation about earthly life and the presence of evil in God's Creation. In the history of aesthetics it is the grand finale of the picturesque – that fascinating aesthetic run its course – and although it will receive passing mention in the early decades of the twentieth century, and endures today in glossy holiday brochure and picture postcard, history has shown it to be profoundly of its time and place and destined never, in its first and valiant form, to return.

WALTER PATER

The criticism of Walter Pater (1839–94) is a subtle, complex, and fitting dénouement to the British aesthetic tradition as we have traced it from Shaftesbury to Ruskin, captured succinctly and brilliantly in the influential and controversial *Studies in the History of the Renaissance*.[36] The work appeared in 1873, consisting of a preface, eight essays (five of them written previously and already published in periodicals between 1867–71), and the scandalous "Conclusion" with its dictum of "the love of art for art's sake"[37] – championed famously by

---

[36] Walter Pater, *Studies in the History of the Renaissance*, in *The Works of Walter Pater*, 10 vols. (London: Macmillan, 1901), vol. 10. All references are to page numbers of the critical edition: *The Renaissance; Studies in Art and Poetry: The 1893 Text*, ed. Donald L. Hill (Berkeley: University of California Press, 1980).

[37] In the fourth edition, Pater changed this to read "the love of art for its own sake." The phrase had already been used by Algemon Charles Swinburne (1837–1909) in *William Blake: A Critical Essay* (London: John Camden Hotten, 1868), and the idea it captures is generally held to have its source in the dictum of Pierre Jules Théophile Gautier (1811–72) that "everything that is useful is ugly, for it is the expression of some need, and the needs of men are ignoble and disgusting, like his infirm nature." See the preface to his novel, *Mademoiselle de Maupin*, trans. Helen Constantine (London: Penguin, 2005 [1835]), 23. Cf. T. S. Eliot, "The Place of Pater," in *The Eighteen-Eighties: Essays by Fellows of the Royal Society of Literature*, ed. Walter de la Mare (Cambridge: Cambridge University Press, 1930), 93–106, who claims

Oscar Wilde and the Aesthetic Movement – and, as contemporary celebrants and detractors read it at least, a defense of decadence and call to overturn traditional standards of moral behavior: it was denounced from the pulpit by the Bishop of Oxford and legend tells of students at the university chanting passages of the book in unison in hall and quad.[38] Pater retracted the "Conclusion" for the second edition, which bore the revised title of *The Renaissance; Studies in Art and Poetry* (1877) – reviewers had pointed out that its claim to be "history" was at best misleading – but subsequently reinserted it in the third (1888) with an explanatory footnote; by that stage the issue was largely moot, because, as Pater points out, he had subsequently dealt "more fully ... with the thoughts suggested by it" in his novel, *Marius the Epicurean* (1885).[39] For the second edition Pater also expanded and renamed the first essay on medieval French poetry ("Aucassin and Nicolette" became "Two Early French Stories"), and in the third edition added an essay, "The School of Giorgione," which had appeared in the *Fortnightly Review* in 1877. A fourth and final edition corrected by Pater was published in 1893, shortly before his death.

Throughout, notwithstanding revisions and alterations – including those to appease sensitive Victorian souls – *The Renaissance* remained, among much else, a full-throated celebration of sensuality (the homoerotic variety included) and unapologetic valorization of Hellenic culture and the "ideal of Greek art": the unified product of self-reflection, but one in which thought does not "outstrip ... its sensible embodiment" and become, as in medievalism, inward, brooding, and sunk into the "depths of religious mysticism" (165). Precisely in this latter element, ironically, one discerns the presence and powerful influence of Pater's immediate, albeit unnamed, adversary, Ruskin. Pater read Ruskin's writings as a young man and, in almost every way possible, appears to contradict and reject everything he found there: in Pater the Renaissance supplants the Gothic; pagan values outshine the Christian; reason and truth are undermined by irrationality and relativism; and, with beauty uncoupled from

that Pater is a "moralist." Eliot writes, dissmisively, of *The Renaissance*: "I do not believe that Pater, in this book, has influenced a single first-rate mind of a later generation. His view of art, as expressed in *The Renaissance*, impressed itself upon a number of writers in the nineties, and propagated some confusion between life and art which is not wholly irresponsible for some untidy lives. The theory (if it can be called a theory) of 'art for art's sake' is still valid in so far as it can be taken as an exhortation to the artist to stick to his job; it never was and never can be valid for the spectator, reader or auditor" (105).

[38] Revelations about Pater's personal life only fueled controversy over the text. On this topic and reception of *The Renaissance*, see Gerald Monsman, *Walter Pater* (Boston: Twayne, 1977), ch. 2. A discussion and summary of reviews and responses is also to be found in Hill's critical and explanatory notes (284ff.).

[39] "This brief 'Conclusion,'" Pater writes, "was omitted in the second edition of this book, as I conceived it might possibly mislead some of those young men into whose hands it might fall. On the whole, I have thought it best to reprint here, with some slight changes which bring it closer to my original meaning. I have dealt more fully in *Marius the Epicurean* with the thoughts suggested by it" (186n1).

morality, the hopeful vision of the engaged critic succumbs not only to political indifferentism, but also slides into decadence and dandyism.[40] All of this is true, but the story is more interesting, for Pater does not simply reject Ruskin, but subverts and sublimates him, an act only possible because he absorbs and follows certain clear strains in Ruskin's thinking: first, that there is a single superior system of values that expresses and completes the perfection of human beings, and, second, that discovering and articulating them involves rejecting the abstract, universalizing tendency of philosophy in favor of what Pater calls "aesthetic criticism." The fundamental difference between the two thinkers lies in the diametrically opposed elements that constitute their respective systems of value, yet it is Pater who successfully uncouples criticism from theoretical thought, a promise that Ruskin made, but was unable to keep.

The Renaissance is suffused with the idea of what Ruskin called "power," "life," and "spirit," the latter being Pater's favorite term and one he captures and employs in his concept of "the Renaissance." Pater accepts fifteenth-century Italy as the height and perfection of its manifestation, but does not use the term as a simple historical marker; in fact, his essays expand the temporal stretch of the period usually associated with the Renaissance backward into late twelfth-century France – "a Renaissance within the limits of the middle age itself" (1) – and forward into the eighteenth-century scholarship of Joachim Winckelmann (1717–68), a singular and late genius in "sympathy with the humanists of a previous century [and] ... the last fruit of the Renaissance" (xxv). For Pater, the term delineates more fundamentally a mode of valuation behind which he finds a set of passions and drives that, when allowed expression, circumscribe the conditions for a full and flourishing human life. The Renaissance is a "spirit going abroad" (4), as Pater describes it,

the name of a many-sided but yet united movement, in which the love of things of the intellect and the imagination for their own sake, the desire for a more liberal and comely way of conceiving life, make themselves felt, urging those who experience this desire to search out first one and then another means of intellectual or imaginative enjoyment, and directing them not only to the discovery of old and forgotten sources of enjoyment, but to the divination of fresh sources thereof – new experiences, new subjects of poetry, new forms of art. (1–2)

---

[40] At one point Pater takes Leonardo de Vinci's "political indifferentism" as a mark of his strength (100). As commentators have emphasized, in this respect Pater very much follows Matthew Arnold (1822–88) and his notion of seeing the "object as in itself it really is," expressed first in *On Translating Homer: Three Lectures Given at Oxford* (London: Longman, Green, Longman, and Roberts, 1861), and again in the opening paragraph of "The Function of Criticism at the Present Time," in *Essays in Criticism* (London: Macmillan and Co., 1865), 1–41. Wilde, characteristically, plays ironically on the idea in suggesting that the "aim of the critic is to see the object as in itself it really is not." See "The Critic as Artist – Part I," in *Oscar Wilde: The Major Works*, ed. Isobel Murray (Oxford: Oxford University Press, 1989), 241–66, p. 264.

Pater takes the term *enlightenment* in its literal sense of "revival," but expands it beyond the antiquarian notion of rediscovering a body of art and literature, to invoke the idea of a promise renewed, the reemergence and expression of an "instinct" crushed by the "dark age" (2). Pater also rejects as superficial the view of the Renaissance as a break between two worlds, the ancient and modern, when it is actually the point at which they meet and fuse into continuity, symbolized by one of its iconic images, *La Gioconda*, "The Mona Lisa," "the joyful one," whose famous smile gives outward form to all the "thoughts and experience of the world ... the animalism of Greece, the lust of Rome, the mysticism of the middle age with its spiritual ambition and imaginative loves, the return of the Pagan world, the sins of the Borgias" (98–9). The import of the Renaissance for Pater, is really existential and cultural; its significance that of a revolutionary "movement in which ... the human mind wins for itself a new kingdom of feeling and sensation and thought" (5), reaches in "revolt against the moral and religious ideas of the time" (18), and moves outside prescribed limits to "modes of ideal living" beyond (6).

The "spirit" Pater finds displayed in this movement of rebellion and renewal is quite at odds with the "life" celebrated by Ruskin. Pater acknowledges and even admires the "curious strength" of the Middle Ages, one of its "resources" (11) displayed in the genius of Michelangelo, and the story of Amis and Amile, the latter murdering his own children so that his friend may be cured of leprosy by their blood, only to find their lives restored by faith. Otherwise, the Gothic is antilife, darkness, and constraint, its art the spiritualization of death, captured by Pater in a vocabulary to match: shadow, solidity, heaviness, somberness, and repression, all cast with the pall of medieval religion, which tends to "depreciate man's nature, to sacrifice this or that element in it, to make it ashamed of itself, to keep degrading or painful accidents of its always in view" (31). The Renaissance comes into this medieval gloom as light into dark, health after a long illness, and freedom after centuries of captivity, expressed by Pater in a language of life and flourishing: all is pleasure, passion, energy, curiosity, creativity, intensity, and exultation; intimacy, sympathy, rebellion, variety, joy, harmony, and elevation; and completeness, refreshment, lightness, grace, elegance, worship of the body, the "liberty of the heart" and "free play" of intelligence and affection (3 and 7). Everything is diffused, moreover, by deliciousness, loveliness, tenderness, and – the *sine qua non* of the Greek spirit and its rebirth – *sweetness*, a term with an echo of Kames and his "common character" of beauty, that appears repeatedly and with various qualifications ("perfect," "touch of," "languid," "excess," "grave and temperate") repeatedly over the course of Pater's essays. Even the landscapes and cities in which the spirit of the Renaissance resides are in a perpetual early summer of light, warmth, and deep color, the air infused with the sweet scent of flowers and grass, the "fulness of the world" made manifest (60).

In addition to following and subverting Ruskin's "spirit," Pater also adopts his decisive rejection of philosophy as a mode of investigation that seeks for universality and abstract definition. Although Ruskin might be an immediate foil in this respect, Pater's target is much wider and encompasses a broad sweep of the tradition we have traced. Identifying this focus is not to deny the presence of theoretical influences in Pater's work: he was a long admirer of the British Romantics (his first publication was "Coleridge's Writings," which appeared anonymously in the *Westminster Review* in 1866), and he is indebted to Plato (his *Plato and Platonism* appeared in 1893) for the idea that there is "real, direct, aesthetic charm in the thing itself" (15). There are also plain and perhaps unconscious echoes of the British tradition in Pater's writing: in the empiricist language of pain and pleasure, and qualities and excitation; in the division among sense, reason, and imagination; and in his decisive identification of the Greeks with a permanent element of genius in art; the "standard of taste ... was fixed in Greece," he writes, "at a definite historical period" (159). At the same time, it is notable that Pater's intellectual peers are not philosophers from the Age of Taste at all, but, for the first time since Coleridge, their German contemporaries and the Romantically inclined ones, in particular: not only Kant and Hegel, but also Gotthold Ephraim Lessing (1729–81), Georg Philipp Friedrich Freiherr von Hardenberg (better known as Novalis) (1772–1801), Johann Wolfgang von Goethe (1749–1832), Schiller, and Winckelmann who, in Pater's telling, is the standard bearer of the Renaissance spirit into modernity. Throughout all these elements, however, the centerpiece of Pater's aesthetics is the thought that criticism, like the Renaissance itself, is a celebration of *physis* – it delights in the sensuous surface of things – while philosophy is a labor of the intellect that penetrates into the same gloomy place reached in Ruskin's Gothic. The real challenge, as Friedrich Nietzsche put it around the same time, is to remain superficial.[41]

In Ruskin, as we have seen, protestations about the limits of abstract thought belie the sturdy philosophical frame on which his aesthetics hang, and without which it would be a much flabbier affair. Pater, by contrast, follows through on the same insight but actually severs the critic from the philosopher by making explicit what is contained already in the nature of aesthetic experience as the Romantics understood it. "Many attempts have been made by writers on art and poetry to define beauty in the abstract," he writes in the opening lines of the preface, "to express it in the most general terms, to find some universal formula for it." Such efforts aid little in enjoying good art and poetry, Pater observes, and, more importantly, misunderstand the nature and phenomenology of "beauty," which

like all other qualities presented to human experience, is relative; and the definition of it becomes unmeaning and useless in proportion to is abstractness. To define

---

[41] There are bold intimations of Nietzsche in Pater's thinking, though no evidence he ever read him. For some consideration of the parallels, see Patrick Bridgwater, *Nietzsche in Anglosaxony: A Study of Nietzsche's Impact on English and American Literature* (Leicester, UK: Leicester University Press, 1972), 21–9.

beauty, not in the most abstract but in the most concrete terms possible, to find, not its universal formula, but the formula which expresses most adequately this or that special manifestation of it, is the aim of the true student of aesthetics. (xix)

The meaning of beauty really lies in the concrete experience of an object, the impressions a work of art or nature makes on and "relative" to the subject; one always asks, what does it mean "to *me*"?, and in the face of doing so all "metaphysical questions" about the nature of beauty "in itself," or the relationship it bears to "truth" are not so much rendered "unanswerable" as simply drop away (xx). To be persuaded intellectually that something is beautiful is not the same as being moved passionally by a beautiful object. In Pater's estimation of beauty the Romantic subject thus becomes aestheticized – the aesthete and decadent personified famously by Wilde – because all value is reduced to internal passion and degrees of the creative intensity described by Mill as "feeling confessing itself to itself in moments of solitude." Pater refines this even further by tracing feeling to its expression as pleasure, and gives to the subject both the honesty to enjoy it and the strength of character to do so amidst the slings and arrows of moralizers and ideologues.

From concretized beauty and an aestheticized subject emerges a particular view of the "critic," a person with a "certain kind of temperament, the power of being deeply moved by the presence of beautiful objects" (xxi); critics regard all works of art and nature "as powers or forces producing pleasurable sensation, each of a more or less peculiar or unique kind" (xx), and understand the beginning of their craft to lie in recognizing "that the sensuous material of each art brings with it a special phase or quality of beauty, untranslatable into the forms of any other, an order of impressions distinct in kind" (102). The "chief question" for the critic confronting an artist, Pater insists, is always "What is the peculiar sensation, what is the peculiar quality of pleasure, which his work has the property of exciting in us, and which we cannot get elsewhere?" (39). At the same time, criticism cannot be a mere recording of personal impressions, but involves a process of drawing from them conclusions with general validity and real content. Drawing on the terminology of the previous century, Pater's critic transcends the agreeable to show what constitutes taste or the "virtue" of the art or artist in question. The critic is disinterested because he aims to

distinguish, to analyse, and separate from its adjuncts, the virtue by which a picture, a landscape, a fair personality in life or in a book, produces this special impression of beauty or pleasure, to indicate what the source of that impression is, and under what conditions it is experienced. His end is reached when he has disengaged that virtue, and noted it, as a chemist notes some natural element, for himself and others. (xx–xxi)

"Take, for instance, the writings of Wordsworth," Pater writes by way of example,

... we trace the action of his unique, incommunicable faculty, that strange, mystical sense of a life in natural things, and of man's life as part of nature, drawing strength and colour and character from local influences, from the hills and streams, and from natural sights and sounds ... that is the virtue, the active principle in Wordsworth's poetry;

and then the function of the critic of Wordsworth is to follow up that active principle, to disengage it, to mark the degree in which it penetrates his verse. (xxi–xxii)

Even in the greatest writers, imagination has "fused and transformed" only a part of their work, but there will be there something "individual, unique, the impress ... of the writer's own temper and personality" (137). It is the work of the critic to identify this element and extract from the debris in which they are hidden the shiny nuggets forged by the heat of artistic creativity.

These two moments – the nature of aesthetic experience and the work of the critic derived from it – come together in the distinct aesthetics of *The Renaissance*, which reflects an attempt by a man of refined temperament to discover concretely the peculiar sentiments that mark the distinctive genius of the age. The essays that compose the book do not, as Pater emphasizes, seek to define the period or extract its essence – as if there were a *Renaissanceness* as counterpart to Ruskin's *Gothicness* – but are intended to "touch on ... chief points" and isolate the virtues, which, if they do not compose a unity exactly, form a set that captures on a broad and lively canvas the complexity of that many-sided movement. In the medieval French poetry of Provence, then, Pater discerns a celebration of earthly passion; in philosopher Pico della Morandola an attempt to reconcile pagan Greek thought with Christianity; and in Sandro Botticello's paintings the visions of a poetical painter combined with the force of realism. Similarly, the sculpture of Luca della Robbia is singular in its expressiveness of inward soul, the poetry of Michelangelo in its strength and strangeness, and Leonardo's work is shot throughout with the enigma and sorcery captured in the smile of *La Giaconda*. In the Venetian School of Giorgione, Ruskin finds the perfect coincidence of artistic activity with color and design; in the sixteenth-century French poetry of Joachim du Bellay, an effort to transform French culture and language through the rediscovered classical culture; and, finally, in Winckelmann, the Greek mind incarnate, wholeness, unity with self, intellectual integrity, and intensity.

There are consequences that follow upon this brand of aesthetic criticism, including the parody, play, and self-referential tropes that have led some to celebrate *The Renaissance*, albeit anachronistically, as a Modernist text, or an attempt to repair the damage done when lying – as Wilde was to express it famously – "decays": the "true liar," as Wilde quips, is hardly interested in anything as low as proof, discussion, and argument, and in disdaining these moves beyond the sphere of mere "misrepresentation": his temper is marked by "his frank fearless statements, his superb irresponsibility, his healthy, natural disdain of proof of any kind!" The "fine lie" is "simply that which is its own evidence."[42] The result is a different kind of criticism – what we might call the Pateresque – which Wilde sums up admirably in his idea of the "critic as artist." Criticism of the "highest kind," he writes,

---

[42] Oscar Wilde, "The Decay of Lying: An Observation," in *Oscar Wilde*, 215–39, p. 216.

treats the work of art simply as a starting-point for a new creation. It does not confine itself ... to discovering the real intention of the artist and accepting that as final. And in this it is right, for the meaning of any beautiful created thing is, at least, as much in the soul of him who looks at it, as it was in his soul who wrought it.

No one really "cares" whether Ruskin's views on Turner are "sound" or whether Pater puts into the Mona Lisa "something that Lionardo never dreamed of," for they are works of art in their own right and thus not beholden to the "truth" of their subject.[43] In this sense, Pater's book is deliberately and self-consciously dishonest, although his various ploys are obvious and on display openly for anybody to see. The last two essays of the book, on Winckelmann (1867) and the "Conclusion," for example, were actually written first, the latter being an edited version of a review Pater wrote of William Morris's poems for the *Westminster Review* (1868). The essays as a whole, moreover, are clearly arranged with a particular plan in mind, and, as one editor points out, the book becomes quite different if the essays are read in order of composition. Pater also seems deliberately to parody accepted practices of good scholarship, falsifying facts (the drawing by Michelangelo supposedly in a collection at Oxford), embracing spurious texts (poems attributed to Michelangelo), misattributing works (Leonardo's drawings are not by him at all), and willfully altering the content of his sources (Abelard does not die "like Tannhäuser"), all, one assumes, for purposes of crafting a singular narrative in which all Pater's characters look remarkably similar.[44]

For the serious-minded philosopher this sort of play is reckless, the first dreamy moment in the deep sleep of reason that produces the monsters of irrationality and relativism, threatening the line between fact and fiction, truth and falsehood, presentation and representation that, whatever their predilection, thinkers from Shaftesbury through Ruskin embraced, defended, and sought to preserve. Whether or not Pater saw himself to be working in this manner, he can surely be read that way. At the same time, it is important to situate the Pateresque rebellion in the context of the aesthetic tradition of which it is a late growth, and like "the Renaissance," a point of continuity between two worlds. In one direction, from the perspective of the aestheticized subject, Pater looks back to Romanticism and, by extension, writers from the Age of Taste who set the scene and coined the language of philosophical aesthetics. In the other direction, from the vantage point of the critic, Pater looks forward to a brave new world of philosophy that takes to heart the idea that philosophical thought is a barrier to its own development. The aesthetics of the Age of Analysis are not Pater's, but they are at least in part a legacy of the antiphilosophical spirit in which he worked.

---

[43] Wilde, "The Critic as Artist – Part I," in *Oscar Wilde*, 241–66, see pp. 262–3.

[44] For discussion of these and related points, see editor's introduction in *Walter Pater, The Renaissance; Studies in Art and Poetry*, ed. Adam Philips (Oxford: Oxford University Press, 1986).

PART III

THE AGE OF ANALYSIS

7

Theories of Expression

As in other areas of philosophy, *analysis* and *analytic* – terms that best describe the developmental sweep of aesthetics in the twentieth century – can hardly be described as uncontested terrain, the meaning they convey and the figures and themes to which they refer being due in no small part to a matter of emphasis, itself sometimes a function of ideologically inspired posturing rather than the disinterested pursuit of truth. At a general level, "analysis" is synonymous with clarity, the idea that, approached with lucidity of expression and precision of argument, any philosophical problem can be solved by reducing what is complex to its most simple constituents; certain strains of Continental philosophy notwithstanding, these are virtues to which any philosopher would aspire, irrespective of peculiar interest or methodological proclivity. As one narrows the focus of the term, however, these generally desirable desiderata start to blend with normative claims about the proper issues with which the real philosopher should deal – language, formal logic, and the methods of natural science loom large – elements that combine to yield not only an identifiable approach to philosophy but also a favorite source for what practitioners see as the central "problems" for philosophical investigation.

More specifically still, "analytic philosophy" has acquired a temporal dimension and settled comfortably into its place as a discrete and identifiable episode in the history of the discipline. Its origins are traced to the advances in logic made by Gottlob Frege (1848–1925), which inspired members of the "logical positivist" circles of Vienna and Berlin – including, most famously perhaps, Otto Neurath (1882–1945) and Rudolf Carnap (1891–1970) – and the generation of philosophers at Cambridge headed by G. E. Moore (1873–1958), Bertrand Russell (1872–1970), and his precocious student Ludwig Wittgenstein (1889–1951). Those who followed in their stead were gathered subsequently under the heading of "Oxford Philosophy," a phrase that conjures a style and common interest in "conceptual analysis" as a way of approaching issues primarily in moral philosophy, epistemology, metaphysics, and philosophy of mind. Analytic philosophy as a movement in this narrower sense "ended" – if one can speak in such terms – in 1951 when Willard Van Orman Quine (1908–2000) attacked the concept of "analyticity" in his celebrated and now famous paper "Two Dogmas of Empiricism."[1] To speak of an end here is hyperbole; Quine was an analytic philosopher par excellence, and the general approach and familiar explananda in the ascendancy from Frege onward are entrenched to the point of official recognition, and although they are not always clear in their own minds of what they mean by the epithet, the overwhelming majority of philosophers in departments of philosophy in the English-speaking world (and, increasingly, beyond) identify themselves as "analytic philosophers" in the "analytic tradition."

Given the variety and shades of meaning that beset (or enrich) the analytic approach, it is not surprising to find philosophical aesthetics woven into its fabric in diverse and complex ways. At one extreme, under the influence of logical positivism, philosophers simply dismissed the subject as nonsense, its objects beyond experience and therefore as "metaphysical" as "God" or the "thing in itself." At best, such people thought the subject "dreary" or simply denied the possibility of its very existence.[2] Such statements are difficult to reconcile with the state of the discipline both past and present, especially given the work being published at the very time that these naysayers penned their views. For, as we shall see in Part 3, by mid-century, aesthetics had produced its "formalists" and "expressivists" (the subject of the current chapter) and witnessed the birth of a distinct sort of "criticism" in the form of Wittgenstein's later philosophy, which inspired in turn significant contributions to the field in the 1950s and 1960s (Chapter 8) and made possible the prominent views that defined the discipline toward century's end and continue to inform current debate. We begin with what can be characterized collectively as "theories of expression."

THEORIES OF EXPRESSION

One mark of the views developed by writers whom we are to consider under the "theories of expression" is that they all look back, in some way, shape, or form, to Romanticism, both the earlier variety of Wordsworth, Coleridge, Shelley, and Keats, and the later one of Pater and especially Ruskin, whose body of work towers like an immovable Gothic cathedral, no easier to ignore for those of the new century than was Burke's *Enquiry* (1757) for those writing after

---

[1] Willard Van Orman Quine, "Main Trends in Recent Philosophy: Two Dogmas of Empiricism," *Philosophical Review* 60, 1 (1951): 20–43; reprinted (with minor revisions) in *From a Logical Point of View: Nine Logical-Philosophical Essays*, 2nd rev. ed. (Cambridge, MA: Harvard University Press, 1980 [1953]), 20–46.

[2] See, respectively, J. A. Passmore, "The Dreariness of Aesthetics," in *Aesthetics and Language*, ed. William Elton (Oxford: Blackwell, 1959), 36–55, and Stuart Hampshire, "Logic and Appreciation," in ibid., 161–9. Cf. Peter Kivy, "Introduction: Aesthetics Today," in *The Blackwell Guide to Aesthetics*, ed. Peter Kivy (Oxford: Blackwell, 2004), 1–11.

the middle of the eighteenth century. The period is now associated with two schools of thought. The first, "expressivism," holds that the principle aim of art is to express the ideas or emotions of the artist that are subsequently embodied in the artistic object and thereby communicated to an audience. In the English-speaking world, the view is associated primarily with John Dewey's *Art as Experience* (1934), R. G. Collingwood's *The Principles of Art* (1938), and, more tangentially, with George Santayana's *The Sense of Beauty* (1896), a work that occupies an awkward and anachronistic place in the tradition. The origins of expressivism are much older, however. The doctrine is contained clearly, as we have seen, in Reid's *Lectures on the Fine Arts* (delivered in the 1760s) and "On Taste" (1785); taken up by Alison in the 1790s; and developed in the last decade of the nineteenth century by Leo Tolstoy (1828–1910) in his widely read "What is Art?" (1896; English trans. 1899). Its most systematic development prior to Dewey and Collingwood was in the philosophy of Italian philosopher Benedetto Croce (1860–1952); his *L'Estetica come scienza dell'espressione e linguistica generale* (1902) was translated and published in English as *Aesthetic as Science of Expression and General Linguistic* in 1909, and his thought prescribed the philosophical parameters for a generation of lesser-known British and American philosophers concerned with aesthetics and the arts.[3]

The second school of the period is "formalism," an approach to aesthetics born of a more specific focus on the relationship among the perceptual elements of an artwork, finding aesthetic value in the formal features (predominantly line and color) that compose it irrespective of utility or any meaning that might accrue from external referents. The philosophical origins of this view and the concomitant idea of disinterested contemplation on which it depends originated in Plato; are given voice by Shaftesbury; adumbrated in the writings of Reynolds, Alison, Shelley, and Keats; and also treated in a protean way by Santayana. Its most important single philosophical precursor, however, is surely Kant and especially §13–16 of the *Critique of the Power of Judgment*. Because "pure" judgments of taste exclude charm and emotion, he argues there, art is beautiful not by virtue of ornament or color ("adherent beauty"), but due to lines and shapes that compose and constitute its form ("free beauty"): "designs *à la greque*, foliage for borders or on wallpaper [that] signify nothing themselves ... [and] do not represent anything" (CJ 5:229). In the nineteenth century, Austrian critic Eduard Hanslick's treatment of musical structure in *Vom Musikalisch-Schönen* (*On the Musically Beautiful*) (1854)

---

[3] These include, most importantly, E[dgar] F[rederick] Carritt (1876–1964) in *The Theory of Beauty*, 5th ed. (London: Methuen, 1949 [1914]); Louis Arnauld Reid (1895–1986) in *A Study of Aesthetics* (Allen and Unwin, 1931); and the Australian-born Samuel Alexander (1859–1938), primarily in *Beauty and Other Forms of Value* (London: Macmillan, 1933). The details of these views fall beyond the scope of the current study, but for a discussion of these and other writers of the generation after Croce, see Guyer, *A History of Aesthetics*, vol. 3.

is sometimes cited as an early work of formalism,[4] and the import of Kant's distinction for visual art was stated succinctly some decades later by French painter Maurice Denis (1870–1943), who, in an oft-quoted passage from "Definition du néo-traditionnisme" (1890), wrote that a "picture, before it is a warhorse, a naked woman, or some anecdote, is essentially a flat surface covered with colors assembled in a certain order" (1890).[5] Still, credit for the first clear and systematic statement of formalism as a distinct aesthetic theory must go to Roger Fry and the essays on art and art theory he wrote in the first two decades of the twentieth century. The most important of these philosophically is "An Essay in Aesthetics" (1909), though its originality and importance are often overlooked in light of the more forceful, formulaic, and digestible presentation of Fry's views by Clive Bell in his widely read *Art* (1914) with its central notion of "significant form," which has become largely synonymous with formalism and the aesthetic theory it promotes.[6]

Although the forces of professionalization have distinguished these two schools, and the influence of Croce notwithstanding, there is really a single movement of aesthetic thought discernible in the wake of Ruskin and Pater, united from a complication of common elements and, for that reason, appropriately gathered under a single head. First, there is an enthusiastic, even bacchanalic, celebration of the subject and its affective states ("emotion" being the favored term) as the *locus primus* of all aesthetic value. This is accompanied, second, in the wake of Charles Darwin (1809–82) and developments in the burgeoning field of psychology, by a heightened awareness of the physical nature of the human organism and the place of its "vital" functioning in aesthetic experience, which leads, third, to a sharpened focus on the phenomenology of that experience and the specifically "aesthetic attitude" it involves. Along with this, finally, comes a new appreciation for the complex relations that obtain among artists, between them and their audience, and the role of both in creating and appreciating works of art. These are common themes even though, as we shall see, they are articulated in various ways and with different degrees of emphasis.

---

[4] Eduard Hanslick, *Vom Musikalisch-Schönen: Ein Beitrag zur Revision der Ästhetik in der Tonkunst* (Leipzig, Germany: Weigel, 1854).

[5] Maurice Denis, "Definition du néo-traditionnisme," *Art et critique* (August 1890); reprinted in *Théories, 1890–1910*, 4th ed. (Paris: Rouart et Watelin, 1920), 1–13. Denis was also author of a critical appreciation of Cézanne – "Cézanne-I," *L'Occident* 12 (September 1907) – that Fry translated and published in *The Burlington Magazine for Connoisseurs* 16, 82 (January 1910): 207–19, along with an introductory note.

[6] It also bears comparison with views developed by Rudolf Arnheim (1904–2007), who draws on German *Gestalt* psychology to argue that all art is "symbolic," that is, a representation of reality, but as an expression of the inherent features or pattern of objects that an artist communicates to an audience. See Rudolf Aruheim, *Art and Visual Perception: A Pyschology of the Creative Eye, The New Version* (Berkeley: University of Californian Press, 1974 [1954]), esp. ch. 10.

GEORGE SANTAYANA

Despite being born in Madrid and living more than half his life in Europe, Jorge Agustín Nicolás Ruiz de Santayana y Borrás (1863–1952) – "George," on the insistence of his half-sister – is claimed by the United States as one of its own and celebrated, if no longer widely read, as poet, novelist, critic and, above all, philosopher of prodigious output and stylish English prose. Santayana made his contribution to aesthetics early, when, after receiving his PhD from Harvard in 1889, at the urging of colleagues that for professional reasons he find a "specialty," he developed and offered the first course in "Aesthetics." Santayana lectured on the subject between 1892–5 and the content of what he later described as his "sham course in 'aesthetics'" became his "little book," *The Sense of Beauty*, published after multiple rejections and with the help of a colleague, in 1896.[7] Santayana acknowledged that the book's only claim to originality lay in its "attempt to put together the scattered commonplaces of criticism into a system, under the inspiration of a naturalistic psychology" (3); he later dismissed it (anecdotally) as a "wretched potboiler," and was critical (in print) of its methodology and oversubjectivist leanings.[8] He largely abandoned the study of aesthetics as a separate field and incorporated it into his wider philosophical system developed in his five-volume *The Life of Reason: Or, The Phases of Human Progress* (1905–6), volume four of which he entitled *Reason in Art*. Whatever his reservations, *The Sense of Beauty* has been heralded by many as a major contribution to the field. It also had the desired effect at the time of securing Santayana successive reappointments at Harvard and a seat on the faculty that he held until 1912 when, at the age of forty-eight, he left both the university and the United States for good.

The title of the work – *The Sense of Beauty* – clearly (and deliberately one assumes) recalls the tradition of Shaftesbury, Hutcheson, and Reid and the thesis that human beings are endowed with an inner sense for beauty comparable or analogous to the external ones that perceive their objects in the form of sight, hearing, and touch. Santayana also reserves a special place for the "process of association," emphasizing, like his eighteenth-century forebears, how something might also acquire aesthetic value, or acquire more value, because it is colored by other ideas connected to it. It is difficult, however, to glean whether and to what extent these or any other writers from the tradition inform

---

[7] George Santayana, *The Sense of Beauty: Being the Outlines of Aesthetic Theory*, ed. William G. Holzberger and Herman J. Saatkamp Jr., *The Critical Edition of the Works of George Santayana*, vol. 2. (Cambridge, MA: MIT Press, 1988 [1896]). Unless otherwise indicated, all references are to the pagination of this text. For the origin of the lectures and the book, see George Santayana, *Persons and Places: Fragments of Autobiography*, ed. William G. Holzberger and Herman J. Saatkamp Jr., *The Critical Edition of the Works of George Santayana*, vol. 1 (Cambridge, MA: MIT Press, 1986 [1944–53]), 389ff. (PP).

[8] The anecdote is supplied by Arthur Danto in his introduction to *The Sense of Beauty*, xvi.

Santayana's thinking directly, because, with the exception of a passing reference to Burke (80n), he neither cites nor mentions any, pleading in the preface
that his "influences" are "too general and pervasive to admit specification" and
that references are omitted both to avoid controversy and allow the reader "to
compare what is said more directly with the reality of his own experience" (3).
These caveats ring hollow, not only because the first renders the second irrelevant – if his influences cannot be specified in the first place, they could hardly
be omitted – but also due to the observations the reader soon meets in the first
few pages of the introduction: Santayana claims that the subject of the book
has "received so little attention from the world" (5) and that there has been
an "absence [and] ... failure of aesthetic speculation" (6); he also betrays but
a vague idea both of the history of the term *aesthetics* and the meaning it had
acquired by the latter part of the century, associating it exclusively, it seems,
with what he judged to be the scientific tenor of the age (14). These are hardly
claims likely forthcoming from somebody who had acquainted himself with the
literary and scholarly output in Britain since Addison, not to mention Germany
where the great systems of nineteenth-century aesthetics were being built right
under Santayana's nose. Nor is there anything in Santayana's autobiography,
Persons and Places, to suggest any serious contact with the tradition, the only
relevant name on the British side being Ruskin, whose *Stones of Venice* he came
across as a teenager through the influence of his sister (PP 86). Kant's third
Critique certainly appears to be lurking under Santayana's mellifluous prose,
sometimes as ally (aesthetic judgments differ from their moral counterparts)
and other times as whipping boy (they are neither disinterested nor universal), and the influence of Plato is discernible throughout, specifically the strange
version developed by Arthur Schopenhauer (1788–1860) in *Die Welt als Wille
und Vorstellung* (*The World as Will and Representation*) (1818). Santayana read
the work sometime in the 1880s and, it is generally assumed, borrowed from it
the concept of "objectification," the main piece of metaphysics in *The Sense of
Beauty* and one that anchors the central thesis of the book.[9] He could not have
failed to notice, in addition, Schopenhauer's emphasis on the intense, contemplative nature of aesthetic experience as a specific attitude all of its own, an idea
destined to have a similar impact on the young Wittgenstein.

Whatever Santayana read or failed to read for his lectures and book, *The
Sense of Beauty* feels like a work of the nineteenth century and, like a good

---

[9] See Arthur Schopenhauer, *The World as Will and Representation*, trans. E. F. J. Payne, 2 vols.
(New York: Dover, 1969), 2 §25–6 passim. Santayana also spent time in Germany – primarily
in Göttingen, Dresden, Berlin, and Hamburg – and reports attending various lectures there
(none on aesthetics) (PP 253–65). Hegel was also a major influence on Santayana's thought,
whom he read both as a graduate student at Harvard under Josiah Royce (1855–1916) and
later (less fruitfully apparently) with J. M. E. MacTaggart (1866–1925) at Cambridge (see PP,
389–90 and 444–5). "Hegel's *Pheanomenologie*," Santayana later wrote, " ... set me planning
my *Life of Reason*" (PP, 389).

deal of the intellectual content that characterizes the Romantic period, also looks back further to the philosophical output of the eighteenth century. Most striking is the use of the words *sense* and *beauty* in the title, which is fitting, because, despite a gap of two centuries, only the idiom really separates the work from its eighteenth-century predecessors: Hutcheson's "powers" are effectively the same processes Santayana finds in "naturalistic psychology"; "senses" are equivalent to the perceptual apparatus of the human organism; and "qualities" of objects are explicable as the material, formal, and associative elements of consciousness through which, Santayana urges, pleasure is excited and the "idea" of beauty is raised in the subject immediately and without intervention of conscious reflection. The feeling of pleasure is then transferred – "objectified" in Santayana's language – onto the object in question in which, much as Locke and Hume had described the same process, it is then taken to inhere. Like them, Santayana also speaks easily of beauty being "inherent" in a thing, though never as a quality in itself, but always as a value conferred by consciousness through perception of material and form, or from the association of that act with further mental processes. Beauty is thus "value positive, intrinsic, and objectified. ... in less technical language, ... pleasure regarded as the quality of a thing" (33), Santayana writes, and "sense" appropriately describes the capacities that underline and facilitate the process that gives rise to it.[10]

Santayana reaches this definition by first dispatching various differentia he takes to be attached erroneously to "aesthetics." First, it has no interest in "matter of fact or relation" and cannot therefore be a science or other creature of the intellect, both of which are anathema of creativity and an enemy of aesthetic sensibility (16–17); nor should it be passed into the sphere of morals, because its judgments are positive (of good rather than evil) and lack interest in utility. Second, aesthetic judgments are not disinterested, whether one means by that "unselfish" or, more in line with Shaftesbury and Kant, indicative of an awareness not to "mix up the satisfactions of vanity and proprietorship with the delight of contemplation." The former speaks only to the "intensity and delicacy" of aesthetic enjoyment rather than its "nature," which reflects the desire of ownership or access to rare things (26–7); besides, "contemplation" is hardly a desideratum unique to aesthetic judgment, being an aspect of "all pursuits and enjoyments" (27). Third, and finally, Santayana denies that aesthetic judgments involve "universality," if taken to mean (in a roughly Kantian sense) that a "thing is beautiful in itself," that "it should seem so to everybody,"

---

[10] Cf. Danto's remark in his introduction: "Against this powerful tradition [of Shaftesbury et al.], Santayana's use of the term 'sense' in the title of his book must be satiric, since it is the burden of his argument that, if there *is* a sense of beauty, it does not, for all the features it may share with the standard senses, *function* like them at all" (xxi). Danto relies (xix–xx) on Kivy's view of Hutcheson as a realist, which makes it easier for him both to downplay Santayana's conceptual ties to the eighteenth century and, concomitantly, overstate the originality of his view.

or that the perception of beauty is an intellectual judgment "rather than a sensation" (28). Any claims to universality are undermined by empirical evidence of disagreement in aesthetic judgment and the obviously diverse conditions under which people make them; it also absurd, Santayana maintains, to speak of "ought" in matters of beauty, because (though the same might be said for moral judgments) one cannot impose an obligation on somebody to see what to him is invisible. Santayana considers the appeal to universality as really an expression of our desire that others be like us: we others *would* judge as we do if only their training and disposition were what was demanded by our idea of what ought to be case.

Santayana takes this propensity of desire to generalize from personal opinion to universal validity as a fundamental psychological phenomenon, and finds in it a principle to explain the origin of beauty: through the "transformation of an element of sensation into the quality of a thing," beauty is taken to be in the object no less than color, proportion, and size (30). The "ideational" faculty of understanding thus objectifies perceptions of sense, and when the human organism also receives pleasure, from material elements (vital functions, lower senses, or natural instincts for love and society), formal elements (the symmetry, unity, uniformity, and variety of line and shape), or expression (the transformation of some thing when it takes on value from associated ideas), it is "merged" with the ideas to imbue the object of our attention with a peculiar quality: pleasure objectified "lends to the world that mysterious and subtle charm which we call beauty" (38).

These elements that make up *The Sense of Beauty* are certainly familiar, but there are also aspects of note, especially given the direction philosophical aesthetics was destined to take over the coming decades. First, Santayana gives a central place to the formal elements of beauty, though unlike Fry and Bell later he insists that pleasure of form is greatest only when combined with material elements (51). He emphasizes how lines have an "intrinsic quality" due to "their emotional tinge or specific value" (57) that makes symmetry charming, a circle balanced, a straight line dry and stiff, and curves flowing or graceful. In the spirit of Burke and Knight before him, Santayana traces these effects to physiological principles: tensions in the eye bring the point of vision to the center and relates all other points to it in what we experience as the web of visual experience. On this basis Santayana identifies the pleasure of the picturesque – the eye running over objects spaced at equal intervals shocked when interrupted by an interesting object (61) – and explains feelings of exultation – Kant's famous starry sky above and moral law within – as "sensations or physical tension" rather than the play of imagination, understanding, and reason (68–9).

Second, tracing objective value exclusively to the subject and psychological process of objectification leaves a good deal of room for Santayana to account for what he sees as the considerable variation in individual taste. There is no "single standard of beauty," he insists, but degrees that obtain due to diverse habits and capacities, age, health, education, genius and the apperceptive reaction of individuals to things perceived. Because the "essence" of beauty lies in its subjective character it is misleading to speak of equality and degrees at all. "All things are not equally beautiful," he writes, "because the subjective bias that discriminates between them is the cause of their being beautiful at all" (83). A good deal of this variation falls under what Santayana calls "expression," a term he uses not in its more commonsense connection to emotion (as in Fry, Dewey, and Collingwood), but to mean something close to the associationist approach of the late eighteenth century; it is reminiscent, in particular, of Alison's "trains of emotions." He captures much the same view by distinguishing two terms, the "expressive thing" and the "thing expressed." The former is the object presented, be it word or image, and the latter the "further thought, emotion, or image evoked" (123). Or stated otherwise, "expressiveness" is the capacity an object has to arouse associations, and "expression" denotes the point at which these acquire aesthetic value, namely, when they are "incorporated" into the original object (124). As Santayana points out, not only does this account for the diversity of taste and rule out the possibility of a standard, but also explains how objects "themselves indifferent" (i.e., not otherwise beautiful as objectified pleasure) can be made beautiful "by suggestion" or, if already so valued, will have their beauty enhanced (122).

If Santayana looks back to the Age of Taste, it is also worth emphasizing how his subjectivism leads strikingly to conclusions that become central to the formalist aesthetics that takes root in the first decades of the twentieth century. He emphasizes that aesthetic experience is hampered by visual directives to guide the spectator's response – the lonely figure or blasted oak of the picturesque landscape, for example – because human beings actually seek "mastery of the formless" (87) and the imagination glories in the vague and indeterminate, what Fry later calls "unfinished art." "It is the free exercise of the activity of apperception," Santayana writes, "that gives so peculiar an interest to indeterminate objects, to the vague, the incoherent, the suggestive, the variously interpretable," and it is a mark of a great mind that it can "enjoy the opportunity of reverie and construction given by the stimulus of indeterminate objects" (84), as in a landscape that requires fancy to give it unity (85–6).[11] This leads Santayana to observe that the "appreciation of beauty and its embodiment in the arts are activities which belong to our holiday life, when we are redeemed for the moment from the shadow of evil and slavery of fear, and are following the bent of our nature where it chooses to lead us" (19). They satisfy a "demand for entertainment" and stimulate the affective faculties where "truth enters ... only as it subserves these ends" (17). As Fry emphasizes later, transposing it into the idea of "imaginative life," this is quite literally the case,

---

[11] It is worth noting that unlike Fry, Santayana does not extend the same to the artist: to "float in the region of the indeterminate" is a mark of "too many irrepressible talents and too little skill" (84).

because only when we are freed from the necessities and cares of the workaday world are our minds able spontaneously to take notice of details that are otherwise invisible, an aspect of aesthetic life properly called "play," a eulogistic term Santayana rescues from the disparaging overtones of frivolity and uselessness (20–1).

Related to this idea of vagueness and holiday life, Santayana also observes what Fry and Bell later identify as the end and culmination of representative art in the form of French Impressionism: after that point, they argue, art turns away from content – representations of landscapes, people, bowls of fruit, and so on – to explore form, a revolution the formalists identify with the "Post-Impressionist" movement exemplified by Cézanne. Some two decades before Fry, Santayana observes that this had already come about. "Not very long ago," he writes,

it was usual for painters of landscapes to introduce figures, buildings, or ruins to add some human association to the beauty of the place. Or, if wildness and desolation were to be pictured, at least one weary wayfarer must be seen sitting upon a broken column. ... The indeterminateness of the suggestions of an unhumanised scene was then felt as a defect; now we feel it rather as an exaltation. (86)

This exaltation comes with a statement of what the picturesque tradition finally recognized as well, the important truth that there really is no such thing as a landscape to represent, or more precisely – as revealed to Ruskin amid the stink and poverty of the Somme – nothing but a representation: only "different scraps and glimpses given in succession" (86), Santayana writes, and gathered by the artist; once this creative act has taken place, the whole is surveyed by the spectator as a representation of a "real" landscape. Here lies the genius of Impressionism for it captures a momentary view of a landscape, not as the representation of some putatively real object, but in order to present the beholder with a striking "aspect" that imbues the picture with "an extraordinary force and emotional value" (86). This is the point, as Fry was to emphasize later, beyond which art could not develop unless it abandoned the assumption it had long held dear: art was *not* representation. Form had come of age and Roger Fry was its spokesman and champion.

ROGER FRY AND CLIVE BELL

The names of Roger Eliot Fry (1866–1934) and Arthur Clive Heward Bell (1881–1964) – known as Clive Bell – are linked inextricably, their lives intertwined intellectually, as members of the collection of artists, writers, and thinkers known as the Bloomsbury Group; personally, in the entanglements into which their private lives led them; and, more pertinent in the present context, philosophically, through the doctrine of aesthetic formalism to which their names are inexorably attached.[12] They were both influenced, moreover, by

[12] Fry married fellow art student Helen Coombe (1864–1937) in 1896, with whom he had two children; she had mental health problems and was finally committed to an asylum in 1910

Moore's view of intrinsic value and especially his claims in the final chapter of *Principia Ethica* – "The Ideal" – that "the appreciation of what is beautiful in Art or Nature" is good in itself, and (following Henry Sidgwick) that value is derived less from the "mere existence of what is beautiful" than from "that which attaches to the *consciousness* of beauty" (6.113).[13] It then follows, Moore argues, that such "aesthetic enjoyments" or "aesthetic appreciation" involves not only cognition of those qualities, but "some kind of feeling or emotion" as well (6.114). This idea that art has independent value and elicits an "appropriate emotion" is central to the thought of Fry and, albeit it with less subtlety, Bell in particular.

Fry took a first in natural science at Cambridge, but had by then become absorbed in art and art history, study of which he continued as a postgraduate fellow in France and Italy. He was also a painter in his own right, specializing primarily in landscape, though he also painted portraits (including Bell and other members of the Bloomsbury Group), and continued to produce work throughout his life. He began to make his name as a critic, however, with articles on early Italian art, notably the popular monograph *Giovanni Bellini* (1899, in its third edition by 1901) and "Giotto," published in the *Monthly Review* (1901), though he later distanced himself from the essay when it was republished in *Vision and Design* (1920) as being "at variance" with "more recent expressions" of his views.[14] From 1904–10, Fry was curator of European painting at the Metropolitan Museum of Art in New York, during which time he met Matthew Prichard, then curator of classical antiquities at the Boston Museum of Fine Art, who introduced him to the work of modern French artists. Fry's passion for this new school of painting led him to organize in November 1910 an exhibition at the Grafton Galleries, *Manet and the Post-Impressionists*, what proved to be an enduring title coined apparently at the last minute to cover the diverse range of artists on display including not only Manet, but Cézanne, Van Gogh, Gauguin, Matisse, and Picasso, as well. Both this exhibition and its

from which she never emerged. In 1907 Bell met and married Vanessa Stephen (1879–1961), painter and sister of Virginia Woolf; the marriage was over by the onset of World War I, though the two never formally divorced and remained friends for the rest of their lives. Fry met the Bells in the same year that his wife was committed and in the next year started an affair with Vanessa that lasted for two years (1911–13) (and was briefly rekindled again later in 1821), before she developed what proved to be a lifelong relationship with Scottish painter Duncan Grant (who had been openly gay and counted Lytton Strachey and John Maynard Keynes among his lovers). Shortly before the war she and Grant moved to Charleston House near Lewes in Sussex, which became the country meeting place for the group, including Bell and Fry who were frequent visitors. In 1925 Fry met Helen Maitland Anrep (1885–1965) who left her husband and family to live with Fry, and the couple remained together until his death.

[13] See G. E. Moore, *Principia Ethica*, rev. ed. (Cambridge: Cambridge University Press, 1993 [1903]). References are to chapter and paragraph number.
[14] Roger Fry, "Giotto" (1901), in *Vision and Design* (London: Chatto and Windus, 1920), 87–116, p. 87n.

successor of 1912 were highly controversial, and both Fry and the works on display roundly condemned. They also proved to be a watershed in the history of British taste that led Kenneth Clark to claim, in a now-famous assessment, that "In so far as taste can be changed by one man, it was changed by Roger Fry."[15]

Art and "Imaginative Life"

Fry considered his aesthetics less the result of sustained philosophical investigation than the outgrowth of his personal relationship with and critical appreciation of works of visual art, the fruit of which ripened in the many critical essays and lectures that make up the body of his work. In a later essay (1926), Fry describes his method as "experimental" as opposed to "*a priori*," beginning not with some theoretical principle of how pictures ought to work, but considering various examples and then seeing "what happens."[16] "An Essay on Aesthetics" does not contradict this principle per se, but is notable as a rare occasion on which Fry develops his views in a deliberately theoretical manner.[17] Bell praised it later as "the most useful contribution to the science [of aesthetics] ... since the days of Kant,"[18] an exaggeration no doubt, due as much to the considerable debt Bell owed its author as to the intrinsic merit he saw in the work itself. Philosophically, there is good reason to consider the "Essay" as an elaboration and development of Pater's "Conclusion" to *The Renaissance* and, specifically, as Clark again notes, the cry taken up by Wilde and the Aesthetic Movement of "art for art's sake."[19] Fry read Pater sometime in the 1890s while living in Italy, and must have found in him a good basis for the principled wedge he was to drive subsequently between art and ordinary life. This position was no doubt affirmed later by his study of the Impressionists who, as he writes in a later essay (1917), upheld the "complete detachment of the artistic vision from the values imposed on vision by everyday life," and claimed, "as did Whistler in his '10 o'clock,' to be pure artists."[20] While in the United States, Fry

---

[15] Kenneth Clark, introduction to *Last Lectures by Roger Fry* (New York: MacMillan, 1939), ix.

[16] See "Some Questions in Esthetics" (1920), in *Transformations: Critical and Speculative Essays on Art* (London: Chatto and Windus, 1926), 1–43, p. 15. The specific question under discussion is framed by Fry's response to criticisms of his view raised by A. I. Richards in *Principles of Criticism* (London: Routledge and Kegan Paul, 1924), and concerns the proper relation between the representational or plastic elements of a picture and its psychological impact. Richards argues that these two elements can occur in the same work, thus undermining the formalists' idea of a specifically aesthetic emotion; Fry employs his experimental method to show that this is rarely the case, and even where both appear in the same picture, the viewer is obliged to consider each separately and move alternately from one to the other.

[17] Roger Fry, "An Essay on Aesthetics," *New Quarterly* (1909), reprinted in *Vision and Design*, 11–25. Unless otherwise noted, all references in the text are to this work.

[18] Clive Bell, *Art* (London: Chatto and Windus, 1914), 8. All references to Bell are this text.

[19] This point is emphasized by Clark, *Last Lectures by Roger Fry*, xv.

[20] See "Art and Life" (1917), in *Vision and Design*, 1–10, pp. 6–7. For Whistler's expression of the same idea, see *Mr Whistler's "Ten O'Clock,"* in *Whistler on Art: Selected Letters and Writings*

was also introduced to Santayana's *The Sense of Beauty* – perhaps by Denman Ross of Harvard who had developed a theory of color, form, and perception in his own right, published later as *Theory of Pure Design* (1907) and mentioned conspicuously by Fry in the "Essay" (21).[21] There is no similar reference to Santayana, although Fry does acknowledge him briefly in the preface to the edition of Reynolds's *Discourses* he edited, notated, and published in 1905: he writes there of having "also derived assistance from Mr G. Santayana's admirable study of aesthetics, 'The Sense of Beauty.'"[22] Santayana seems an unlikely resource for reflection on Reynolds, and absent more details one assumes the "assistance" was of a general rather than specific sort. However, Fry could hardly have failed to find in *The Sense of Beauty* themes that were to become prominent in his own writing: the physiological basis of aesthetic experience in organic function, a clear division and treatment of the relationship between material and form, the observation that aesthetic appreciation is a "holiday life" set apart from the ordinary, the insight that impressionistic art is the end and fulfillment of representation, and the conviction that the best and most profound art is vague because it enables the spectator to engage in the free play of imagination that allows him to "finish" it for himself.

A more explicit and acknowledged source of inspiration was Tolstoy's "What is Art?," a work Fry describes as "marvelously original and yet perverse and even exasperating" (18) and, as he put it in 1920, in the course of reviewing his own intellectual development, the "beginning of fruitful speculation in aesthetic."[23] Tolstoy, Fry observes, manages to discern that art is essentially a means of communication among human beings, even though he proceeds to restrict "art" to what is morally desirable, a view that inevitably leads him to "condemn the whole of Michelangelo, Raphael and Titian, and most of Beethoven, not to mention nearly everything he himself has written, as bad or false art" (19). If this is the perverse and exasperating, Tolstoy's originality lies in showing, albeit inadvertently, that objects earn the status of art not through meeting standards that govern everyday life, but by satisfying criteria internal to art and artistic activity itself, a fact all but acknowledged by Tolstoy when he admits that works he *allows* as "art" are of inferior quality. The general mistake here, as Fry argues more forcefully elsewhere, is to think that art and life affect one another, a myth exploded easily by even a cursory survey of the history of art: "if we consider this spiritual activity of art we find it no doubt open at times to influences from life," Fry writes, "but in the main self-contained – we find the rhythmic sequences of change determined much more by its own internal forces – and by the readjustment within it, of its own elements – than

1849–1903 of James McNeill Whistler, ed. Nigel Thorp (Manchester, UK: Carcanet Press, 1994), 79–95.

[21] See Frances Spalding, *Roger Fry: Art and Life* (Berkeley: University of California Press, 1980), 85–6.

[22] Preface to *Discourses Delivered to the Students of the Royal Academy*, v.

[23] "Retrospect" (1920), in *Vision and Design*, 188–99, p. 193.

by external forces."[24] "Morality," as Fry puts it succinctly in the "Essay," " ... appreciates emotion by the standard of resultant action. Art appreciates emotion in and for itself" (18).

Fry reaches this conclusion by observing, first, that human beings share with other species an animal life that includes "instinctive reactions to sensible objects, and their accompanying emotions" – fear and flight, for instance, at the sight of a bull – but also possess the capacity to "call up" such events again "in imagination." The result is a "double life": one "actual," the sphere of action guided and constrained by ethical considerations, the other "imaginative," the province of mind, which is free to roam its domains without the practical constraints imposed in and by the real world. This "imaginative life" also involves a shift of perspective that enables consciousness to consider the "perceptive and emotional aspects of ... experience" (12) otherwise hidden or obscured, likened by Fry to the way a disinterested viewer observes details of a scene that would be invisible were he part of the action portrayed. For in actual life, energies are directed to what is necessary – a "specialization of vision," Fry calls it felicitously – as if people read only the labels of things without seeing the contents, fitting everything with a "cap of invisibility" (16). When, by contrast, an object exists in one's life for no other reason than to be looked at, it is seen anew and encountered through an "aesthetic" or "artistic attitude of pure vision abstracted from necessity" (16–17). Only in this attitude is it possible to see what things "really" look like, and it is an irony, Fry emphasizes, that people dismiss nonrepresentational art for not being "true to nature" when an unbiased walk in the woods would show them that she really looks like a Monet or Seurat and thus how "true" to nature is the work they produce (17).

Elsewhere, Fry expresses the same idea in terms of the distinction between the biological function of *seeing* and the aesthetic attitude of *looking* that yields different kinds of "vision" among which one might move as between gears in a car. "Biologically speaking," Fry observes, "art is a blasphemy," and the profanity it utters is increasingly profound the further one moves away from the appearances of everyday life and the "practical" vision that governs it marked by an instinctive concern for utility at the expense of everything else.[25] Children still possess a "disinterested vision," which continues piecemeal into adulthood where certain peculiarities of appearance – "curios" – catch the eye: precious stones, fossils, and incrustations furnished by nature, and the pleasing ornaments supplied by art. "Aesthetic vision" – the mode of criticism in which one apprehends a work of art – is then a sustained version of this way of looking, but is distinct from mere curiosity in being "more detached" from actual life, and unconditioned by "considerations of space or time," with those who indulge it "entirely absorbed in apprehending the relation of forms and colour to one another, as they cohere within the object"

[24] "Art and Life," 6.
[25] "The Artist's Vision" (1919), in *Vision and Design*, 31–5, p. 31 (AV).

(AV, 32–3). At the extremes of this attitude, finally, lies the "creative vision" of the artist, which involves "complete detachment from any of the meanings and implications of appearances" (AV, 33). The artist apprehends objects "passionately" and the world is rearranged by him, fused into a whole formed by the relation of color to color and line to line. In this state, everything is aestheticized – the greatest work is no more significant than "any casual piece of matter" (AV, 34) – and for the artist, aesthetic value disappears, consumed in the heat and passion of creativity.

Fry's notion of imaginative life and its corresponding attitude or vision is reminiscent of the "conversion" thesis Hume defends to explain the unaccountable pleasure of tragedy, the eloquence with which a scene is represented converting the melancholy passions into pleasure. Fry, too, emphasizes that emotions felt in imagination are weaker, and argues that they are transformed and enlivened when represented aesthetically. He also insists – in a departure from Hume's position – that the distance achieved when released from moral demands of actual life enables one to confront those emotions directly, for which reason they are "pure," perceived, that is, with greater clarity because the spectator knows that the images of events are different in kind from correspondingly real ones in everyday life: we feel pain and horror at a depiction of an accident, but know we will not be called upon to assist in any way. Imaginative life is a mirror, as Fry describes it, into which we look as spectators on a scene abstracted and freed from the details that would otherwise detain and distract us: in the mirror image of a street scene we no longer wonder, as we would in actual life, why an acquaintance looks unhappy, or take notice of a new fashion in hats. We focus instead simply on *what is expressed*, and in this way, the "frame of the mirror makes its surface into a very rudimentary work of art" (13).

There are disturbing or, depending on one's view, liberating consequences of separating art from life in this way, a veritable "suspension of the ethical" (to borrow a phrase from Søren Kierkegaard) of the sort that led the Bishop of Oxford to denounce Pater from the pulpit while undergraduates were chanting passages from *The Renaissance* in their college quads. There is not even a question for Fry of "justifying" art, a call that would only elicit one of two equally otiose responses: either (*à la* Tolstoy) to denounce its supreme achievements as immoral, or engage (like Ruskin) in special pleading on behalf of imagination to reconcile its doings with morality. Besides, there is no reason prima facie why the life of imagination should be viewed from the perspective of actual life when the former holds the promise of full and free expression and might, for that reason, be given priority over its infinitely duller counterpart. As Fry points out, moral progress does not even track the richness of imaginative life: in the thirteenth century, the state of humanity was incomparably lower compared to advances in the wake of Victorian social and political reform, but imaginative life at the beginning of the twentieth century was (and is arguably to this day) "sheer barbarity and squalor" compared to the artistic achievements of the Middle Ages. Both the moral and aesthetic parts of human nature are "worthy of exercise" (15), and who is to say which one is more worthy than the other?

"Emotional Elements of Design"

On the upside, the pleasures of decadence and threat of moral turpitude bring with them the reward of formalist aesthetics. When art is understood as a function of imagination rather than actual life, two "qualities" are revealed as the *sine qua non* of an artistic object. The first falls on the side of the aesthetic attitude where the object must be adapted to the "disinterested intensity of contemplation" and "heightened power of perception" that result from leaving actual life behind. The second falls on the side of sensations, which should exhibit "order" and "variety," Fry maintains, without which they are "troubled and perplexed" and will not be "fully stimulated" (19). Together these provide for the unity of the artistic object, both as expression on the side of the artist and restful contemplation on that of the audience. If a work lacks unity or that unity is dissipated by the distractions of representation, one is obliged to move outside the object in order to complete it, and the aesthetic effect decreases. Fry concedes that these qualities also exist in nature, and the beauty of its objects may inspire the spectator to the same disinterested contemplation as a work of art.

On the whole, however, nature does not excite the appropriate emotion because it lacks precisely what aesthetic judgment demands: purpose and feeling on the side of artist and audience. Artists embody emotions aroused in them by natural forms, but deliberately presents them so as to appeal to the "fundamental necessities" of the spectator's "physical and physiological nature" (24–5). In a remnant of the picturesque, Fry holds that the natural world requires perfecting at the hands of the artist whose job is "to arrange the sensuous presentment of objects that the emotional elements are elicited with an order and appropriateness altogether beyond what Nature herself provided" (24). For its part, the audience has consciousness of the fact that the object was created "to be regarded and enjoyed" (24), which excites a sympathy with the artist who made it "to arouse precisely the sensations ... experienced [by the spectator]." There is then a "special tie" (20) between artist and audience that grows stronger the greater the artwork in question and the deeper the emotions it arouses.

Fry's emphasis on disinterestedness and contemplation also results in a view of beauty that recalls both the neo-Platonism of Shaftesbury, with its valorization of mind and corresponding denigration of the senses, and Kant's distinction between inherent and adherent beauty; it is also reminiscent of the emphasis placed by Gerard and Alison on the freedom of the imagination as a precondition for aesthetic experience. For Fry, aesthetic value is in and of the subject, but the beauty excited is "supersensual," concerned with the "appropriateness and intensity of the emotions aroused" rather than with "sensuous charm" (20), a species of "beauty" perhaps, but one that involves only the perceptual aspect of imaginative life. Sensations are the medium through which supersensual beauty is attained, and the spectator delights in them only because they "possess purposeful order and variety" in relation to those emotions that constitute the higher aesthetic experience (20). When considered in terms of sensuous beauty a great work of art can be "ugly" because it lacks charm (Fry mentions Rembrandt and Degas in this connection), but still be beautiful supersensually because other features arouse emotion as an end in itself.

These other features Fry calls the "emotional elements of design," which embody the feelings of the artist and purposefully inspire the same in the audience, and can be manipulated and emphasized in various ways to convey the emotion in question. Thus lines are gestures that achieve a rhythm through being modified by the artist's emotion, which is then conveyed formally to the spectator. In a similar way, the representation of mass can be managed to convey inertia, power, and the movement of one object against another; space plays with size and shape, as light and shade produces "totally different" emotions depending on whether an object is strongly illuminated against a black background or darkness against a light one. Colors, finally, are a powerful conveyer of feeling, their "direct emotional effect," Fry observes, evident from ordinary language where they are attached to evaluative terms such as "gay, dull, melancholy" (22). With all these elements, Fry insists, one automatically abandons any thoughts of "likeness to Nature, of correctness or incorrectness as a test," the important point being "only whether the emotional elements inherent in natural form are adequately discovered" (25).

Bell and "Significant Form"

Fry's popularity and reputation was such that Chatto and Windus invited him to present his views more systematically and at greater length in the form of a book. He turned the invitation down and suggested Bell instead, and the result was *Art*. Fry reviewed the work for *The Nation* (March 1914) shortly after its publication, observing, perhaps wistfully, that although he had never claimed (like Bell) to have "stated a complete theory of art," he noted that his own "various essays towards that end have by very slow steps been approaching more and more in that direction which Mr. Bell has here indicated with an assurance denied to me."[26] Bell, for his part, acknowledged a debt to Fry, for friendship, intellectual camaraderie, and, as noted already, "An Essay on Aesthetics" to which his own statement of formalism differs only in emphasis, terminology, detail, and (as Fry indicated in his subtle way) tone. It is also regrettable that

---

[26] Fry, "A New Theory of Art," *The Nation*, March 7, 1914, 937–9, in *A Roger Fry Reader*, ed. Christopher Reed (Chicago: University of Chicago Press, 1996), 158–62, p. 158 (NTA).

formalism in aesthetic theory is now synonymous not with Fry's original exposition but with Bell's considerably less subtle version of the theory, making it
an easy target for analysts in mid-century who trotted it out every time they
needed an example of the failure of aesthetic "theory."

This eventuality notwithstanding, Fry's observations about Bell were right
on the mark, for *Art* is the work of an assured and at times rude and arrogant
man (in keeping with his reputation among the Bloomsbury set), so much so
that in the preface to the revised edition of 1948, Bell lets the "exaggerations,
childish simplifications and injustices stand" (10) while freely acknowledging
the book's "too confident" and "aggressive" tone; its youthful impertinencies
and overgeneralizations; and the too brief, simplistic, and sometimes false history of Christian art that occupies Part 3 in which Bell moves at breakneck
speed from sixth-century Byzantium to nineteenth-century Britain where,
with art at its nadir, Cézanne and the Post-Impressionists appear providentially
to urge a return to the "first commandment of art – Thou shalt create form"
(38). The retractions (or apologies) are all weaknesses of the book, it might be
noted, that Fry had highlighted in his review more than three decades earlier,
capturing the iconoclasm and slight clownishness of the author with an image
as memorable then, no doubt, as it is now: "Mr Bell walks into the holy of holies
of culture in knickerbockers with a big walking-stick in his hand," Fry writes,
"and just knocks one head off after another with a dexterous back-hander that
leaves us gasping" (NTA 161).

One head that certainly flies is Pater's, whose beloved Renaissance Bell
regards with something of the same distaste expressed by Ruskin, whom he
regards, albeit grudgingly, as a fellow pugilist who also "shook his fist at the
old order to some purpose" (138). For Bell, however, it is not the loss of religion or the resulting moral turpitude intimated in the oversophistication of
Renaissance architecture that repels him, but the canker of modern commerce
that begins to eat away at art with the twin "diseases" of "rarity-hunting" and a
new breed of "experts" spawned consequently to advise would-be collectors on
their purchases. Somewhere between 1350 and 1600, moreover, Bell maintains,
the visual arts lost decisively that "quality" (17) (like Fry he speaks easily the
language of Locke and the empiricists) that makes them "art": painting moves
toward pure representation – imitation of the sort denigrated by writers from
Addison onward – and artists degraded to mere functionaries slogging away in
their drab copy shops. That Bell has something in common with Ruskin does
not mean he is enthralled by Turner, though, whose head rolls very messily
and with a great deal of abuse from the walking stick. "There they hang," Bell
writes of the Claudes in the National Gallery, in a passage worth quoting if for
no other reason than to reveal the character of its author,

besides the Turners that all the world may see the difference between a great artist
and an after-dinner poet. Turner was so much excited by his observations and his sentiments that he set them all down without even trying to co-ordinate them in a work
of art: clearly he could not have done so in any case. That was a cheap and spiteful

thought that prompted the clause wherein it is decreed that his picture shall hang for ever beside those of Claude. He wishes to call attention to a difference and he has succeeded beyond his expectations: curses, like hens, come home to roost. (119)

Dismissing Turner does not mean that Bell is seduced exactly by the idea of the Gothic (Northern or otherwise) as the high point of civilization (he is very nasty about Gothic cathedrals), and actually finds reason to speak kindly of Ruskin's nemesis, Whistler, a "lonely artist," still hanging onto the defunct concept of "beauty," but "standing up and hitting below the belt for art" nevertheless (129–30). In general, Bell is far from approving the mass of blurry images he discerns through Ruskin's "cloudy rhetoric" (130).

Officially at least, *Art* does take a decisive turn toward Ruskin and away from Pater, ironic given that Bell's "aesthetic hypothesis" and the candidate "quality" it proposes are founded on a view of the subject straight from the pages of *The Renaissance*. No system of aesthetics can be based on "some objective truth," he insists, because the only way of recognizing a work of art *as art* lies in "our feeling for it" (18). Like Pater, Bell emphasizes how critics can point to elements that ought to arouse one's passion – that after all is the "function of criticism" – but one can only call it art when one is moved in a certain way. Because "all systems of aesthetics must be based on personal experience – that is to say, they must be subjective," Bell insists (18), the "starting-point for all systems of aesthetics must be the personal experience of a peculiar emotion. The objects that provoke this emotion we call works of art" (16–17). This is not to assert, as Bell makes clear, that every work provokes precisely the same emotion, but when they do arise the emotions are "recognisably the same in kind." One is thus justified in isolating a "particular kind of emotion provoked by works of visual art, and that this emotion is provoked by every kind of visual art, by pictures, sculptures, buildings, pots, carvings, textiles, &c., &c., is not disputed, I think, by anyone capable of feeling it. This emotion is called the *aesthetic emotion*," Bell continues,

and if we can discover some quality common and peculiar to all the objects that provoke it, we shall have solved what I take to be the central problem of aesthetics. We shall have discovered the essential quality in a work of art, the quality that distinguishes works of art from all other classes of objects. (17, emphasis added)

Unlike Fry, who spoke generally of "emotions" in the plural, not to mention Moore who allowed "different emotions … *appropriate* to different kinds of beauty" (6.114), Bell is willing to pick out a particular "emotion" in the singular (though he is not always consistent), disregarding warnings given by Ruskin, Pater, and others of the folly endemic to seeking some universal feature to encompass otherwise diverse artistic objects: the Sta. Sophia, the windows of Chartres, Mexican sculpture, Chinese carpets, and the canvases of Cézanne, are in many respects different, but share relations and combinations of lines and colors that universally "stir our aesthetic emotion" (17–18) and constitute "Significant Form."

As Fry notes in his review, Bell seems to be moving in a circle here, since prompted to ask "What is aesthetic emotion? Mr Bell will reply, the emotion aroused by significant form." Fry defends Bell by pointing out that he at least shows what aesthetic emotions are *not*: because "emotions of pity, love, tenderness, and what not" occur when we look at a Persian bowl but do not when we look at the Sta. Sophia, we can conclude that these are not good candidates for the universal quality being sought (NTA, 159). This might be faint praise, but it is an accurate summary of Bell's conclusion. Bell's aesthetic hypothesis, moreover, is, in its essentials, remarkably atavistic, tracing as it does outlines of the model formed in the Age of Taste: there is a quality in objects (formal features of line, color, and their combinations) that excite a particular feeling (the aesthetic emotion) in a subject (as taste and experience) fitted to receive it. This lends *Art* a certain naïve philosophical charm, and, as Fry puts it in his characteristically understated way, makes the book "as simple and suggestive as its title" (NTA 158).

It is not surprising given its eighteenth-century ring that *Art* should also hit upon a number of other related and familiar themes. First, Bell revives the eighteenth-century debate over "standards," poked at by Ruskin and prodded by Santayana, but pretty much put to rest by the Romantics whose faith in the power and efficacy of their own subjective states was so firm that the question was rendered moot. Bell is less assured in this respect at least, and feels obliged to emphasize that equating aesthetics with personal taste does not rob his theory of "general validity": he assures readers that it is possible to disagree whether particular works of art have the quality in question, but that is quite consistent with holding that there is a quality that makes any object art. Bell emphasizes, second, that significant form includes not only lines, but also color, a feature Kant denied as a formal element of art, Fry accepted as the same, and Santayana classed as material. Bell, in fact, asserts exactly what Santayana denied, namely, that color and form are really inseparable, there being no such thing as colorless lines or space, or colors without form (19–20). The departure from Kant is only apparent, however, because Bell counts black and white as colors, and if Kant had done the same then the lines of his wallpaper and designs *à la greque* would be colored and color would by definition be a formal element.

Third, Bell rejects explicitly the stock in trade of theories up to and including Pater and Fry that found value in calling what moves us in the realm of art by the name "beauty." Fry, to recall, reserved this term for the effect of contemplating the supersensual elements of design and was willing to admit nature as sometimes the object of this attitude and always containing the forms that move the artist and provide material for manipulation and arrangement. Bell, by contrast, not only severs art decisively from nature and confines his "aesthetic emotion" to the former alone, but also rejects the notion of beauty as a confusion and red herring. With more than a hint of Collingwood and even Wittgenstein's conceptual analysis to come, Bell insists that as a general rule "beauty" is used either to refer to natural objects – butterflies and flowers are his example – or to indicate other emotional states, such as sexual desire, as when one speaks of a "beautiful woman" (20–1). "Beauty" is thus used commonly in a "non-aesthetic sense," he insists, which is to say that objects of which it is predicated do not excite the peculiar emotion provoked by significant form that makes objects works of art. One can still speak meaningfully of "natural beauty," with the important proviso that it is not concerned with "aesthetic emotion," but a "beautiful painting" or a "beautiful sonata" denotes a separate state entirely, and to use the term for both is to court "confusions" and "misunderstandings" (22–3).

Fourth, and finally, Bell reiterates the empiricist contention that there is a difference in kind between the phenomenology of experience and its causes, the former being the proper purview of aesthetic theory and the latter an investigation of a different sort, depending on the candidate explanation in question: *why* significant form moves a spectator has nothing to do with what that quality is, because all that matters, Bell contends, is the object and the emotion it arouses. Like Burke, however, Bell cannot resist the temptation of going further, although unlike the physiological explanation to be met with in Part 4 of the *Enquiry*, the "metaphysical hypothesis" he proposes as a counterpart to the aesthetic does not leave the body of the theory untouched. One possible reason for setting Bell off in search of some *ens realissimum* is that having proposed the existence of a phenomenon called "aesthetic emotion," there is some obligation on his part to explain in what that emotion consists. He is admittedly vague on both counts, willing to admit the emotion "mysterious" in character and "uncertain" in origin, and his speculations come down to a lot of philosophical hand waving or, if one prefers, running up against the limit of his prosaic powers to express something to which, as Wordsworth and Keats recognized, only poetry is adequate: through the relationship between artist and audience, Bell writes at one point, "we become aware of its [art's] essential reality, of the God in everything, of the universal in the particular, of the all-pervading rhythm ... that which is behind appearance of all things – that which gives to all things their individual significance, the thing in itself, the ultimate reality" (54).

Although speculation of this sort is not, in itself, illuminating exactly, the details of the creative and appreciative process Bell enumerates are of considerable interest, not least because they contain the germ of ideas that become prominent in Collingwood ("collaboration" of artists with various aspects of the community) and Dewey ("doing and undergoing"). Bell does not specify the *content* of "aesthetic emotion," but he does an admirable job of building on Fry and outlining its *form*: emotion is excited in the artist, he proposes, as a result of contemplating the significant form (combinations of lines and colors) of some thing – a scene witnessed, a natural object viewed, an experience remembered – though never as means to an end, but always as an end in itself independent of any practical application or use to which it might be put. This emotion is transmitted subsequently through the work the artist creates, the significant form of which (end in itself, not means to end) is contemplated by an audience. An artist can be said to get it "right" when he accomplishes a "complete realisation of a conception" in which case the object "expresses his emotion for reality or is capable of provoking aesthetic emotion in others" (52), and it is "right" for the audience when they experience aesthetic satisfaction from contemplating the artwork in question. Bell also observes, perspicuously, that for this reason artists do not vaguely direct their energies to some unspecified activity of "creating," but direct and "canalise" them toward particular artistic "problems" – realizing *this* figure in *that* marble, *that* landscape on *this* canvas – which imposes intellectual and material limits on the process, focusing creative power on one spot and simultaneously increasing the likelihood of getting it "right" (51–2).

Bell's concept of significant form also goes to the heart of the problem of representation, not only by devaluing art that mimics or copies – Ruskin and Fry had done that decisively already – but also by ruling out at a single blow a whole class of artistic works that fall under the general title of "Descriptive Painting." Bell considers a strength of his view to be that it allows easy discrimination between works that are objects of emotion and others that are simply a "means of *suggesting* emotion or *conveying* information" (22, emphasis added). Even technique is nugatory (Reynolds, too, receives blows from the walking stick [120]) as the question is not "how it [a picture] was painted, but whether it provokes aesthetic emotion" (39). Like butterflies and flowers presumably, these might move the viewer in various ways, but not *aesthetically*, and once this fact is realized the descriptive painter will be replaced by the photojournalist whose techniques can achieve verisimilitude that the painter-cum-copier can only dream of. Bell does not deny that representation might have a place – it is "indifferent" but not "bad in itself" (26n1/27) – although its presence always denotes an inability to excite aesthetic emotion, which obliges one so impoverished to provoke feelings of everyday life instead (29). On the other side of the process, it is also a sign of weak sensibility on the part of the viewer, who, incapable of being moved by forms themselves, treats art as a photograph and traces its elements back to familiar, practical details of their ordinary existence. Such people recall a picture through its subject matter rather than the formal features that should have produced an aesthetic emotion. Bell concedes that even a perfect imitation does not necessarily mean sacrificing significant form, although there is always the tendency for it to become lost in the "preoccupation with exact representation and ostentatious cunning"; the problem is less that it might cause harm, but simply that "it is irrelevant" (26–7).

This view of aesthetic experience recalls much of the Romantics' approach to poetry, where art occupies a separate and self-enclosed realm, and the artist, to recall Mill's phrase, is "ignorant of life." Bell, too, is drawn by the metaphysical promises of neo-Platonism, though in his hands it sounds tired and worn.

The "rapt philosopher," Bell writes, drawing an appropriate if familiar comparison, "and he who contemplates a work of art, inhabit a world with an intense and peculiar significance of its own; that significance is unrelated to the significance of life. In this world the emotions of life find no place. It is a world with emotion of its own" (28). Great art, moreover, has an appeal that is "universal and eternal" (33), Bell emphasizes, "pure" because it lifts its gaze above the mere content of life – institutions, customs, fashions, and prejudices that define an age – in search of the general form that conveys real value. The artist is from a rare breed that does not merely perceive physical objects – that makes but a shallow impression on the wax tablet – but has the capacity to see emotionally (61–2). In this sense, art is comparable to religion, also "an expression of the individual's sense of the emotional significance of the universe" (62), because for both mystic and artist the physical universe is a means to that state of mind called "ecstasy" (68).

This view of art and the artist adds another dimension to what is "significant" about form, namely, that it denotes a world unto itself at the threshold of which the dreary details of life, knowledge of its affairs, and familiarity with its emotions should be abandoned. Art takes one *from* the everyday world life *to* another world of exultation where, with the addition of knowing a "little bit" about three-dimensional space, one requires only "sense" of or "feeling" for the formal aspects of objects (28). Bell even flirts with the idea that the required quality is grasped through intellect as the mathematician sees the relation between numbers so that, in a nod to Moore, creating works of art is a direct means to good, and to pronounce anything a work of art is akin to "momentous moral judgment" (84).

R. G. COLLINGWOOD

Robin George Collingwood (1889–1943) was Waynflete Professor of Metaphysics at Oxford from 1935 until his early and untimely death, and despite the relative shortness of his career he left behind an extensive body of work in philosophy, history, and archaeology that made him a leading intellectual of his day, and, in the assessment of many, one of the most influential philosophers of the twentieth century. He is less widely read today, but still remembered for two major works published in his lifetime – *An Essay on Philosophical Method* (1933) and *An Essay on Metaphysics* (1940) – and, most famously perhaps, for the posthumous *The Idea of History* (1946), which played a central role in debates over the logic and methods of the natural and human sciences, providing much fuel in particular for those opposed to Carl Hempel and his "covering law of explanation." In addition to work in epistemology and metaphysics, Collingwood also published a major and widely read book on aesthetics – *The Principles of Art* (1938) – now the standard bearer of the expressive theory of art and, as such, generally distinguished from the formalism propounded by Fry and Bell.[27] As already noted, credit for the theory cannot go to Collingwood, though given his protestations against the nonsense of "plagiarism," he would not have much cared. The single and *en passant* reference to him (46n) notwithstanding, the most direct and important source was Croce, whose work from the first decades of the century Collingwood read and translated. There are points of contrast between the two – Collingwood focuses specifically on emotions, devotes much energy to distinguishing art from craft, and considers the relation between artist and audience in a way that Croce does not – but his debt is widely acknowledged and so well established that the result of their combined efforts has long been referred to as the "Croce-Collingwood theory."[28]

More interesting in the present context than Collingwood's debt to Croce or anybody else is the figure he cuts as a point of transition from the Age of Criticism to the Age of Analysis. Other writers such as Santayana or Fry might well be considered in the same vain, but none have a foot in each century, biographically, culturally, and philosophically, quite like Collingwood. He was the son of W. G. Collingwood (1854–1932), Professor of Fine Art at the University of Reading and before that, student, protégé, traveling companion, secretary, and finally biographer of Ruskin. As a result of this connection, the Collingwood family was based in the Lake District where Collingwood senior could attend his illustrious and by now failing employee, first on the shore of Lake Windermere (where Collingwood junior was born), and after 1891 in Lanehead on Coniston Water, closer to Ruskin's house at Brantwood. When Collingwood died he was buried, as if looking back to the century of his birth, in the same Coniston graveyard as Ruskin, with the great art critic on one side and his parents on the other. Philosophically, and in a parallel of perfect symmetry, Collingwood's aesthetics straddles the two intellectual movements that dominate the nineteenth and twentieth centuries respectively: the culmination and end of Romanticism, and the emergence of the philosophical focus on language and analysis, the latter already well advanced in Collingwood's lifetime and destined to become the official and often-featureless face of Anglo-American philosophy.

This makes *The Principles of Art* an interesting blend. On the one hand, Collingwood adopts (albeit with important addenda) the picture of the Romantic subject bequeathed by Ruskin and Pater, rejecting categorically the

[27] R. G. Collingwood, *The Principles of Art* (Oxford: Clarendon Press, 1938). All references are to this text. Collingwood also published *Outlines of a Philosophy of Art* (Oxford: Clarendon Press, 1925), which *The Principles* was designed to replace and supersede. I follow the standard procedure and concentrate on the later work as the definitive statement of Collingwood's view.

[28] It is also worth noting that the central doctrines of *The Principles of Art* bear comparison to Collingwood's view of history as the "re-enactment of past experience." See R. G. Collingwood, *The Idea of History* (Oxford: Clarendon Press, 1946), 282ff.

idea that there are any such things as objective aesthetic qualities, favoring instead a view of art as exclusively the purview of mind in the form of the creative imagination of the artist. On the other hand, Collingwood advertises the book as a work of conceptual analysis, its purpose and guiding methodological thread being "to clarify and systematize ideas we already possess" by coming to see how we ordinarily do and thus should philosophically "apply" and "use" the word *art* and its conceptual relata (1–2). Proceeding in this fashion, Collingwood contends, ensures that one will arrive at the "proper meaning" or "sense" of the word *art* free of other obsolete, analogical, or courtesy meanings with which it has become mixed and confused. The result is a "theory of art in general," substantively Romantic in content, but analytic in method and tone.[29]

Collingwood's aesthetics still has admirers, but generally speaking it has become something of an historical curio, due largely to the rather strange and counterintuitive conclusions that follow from its central claim that artists express emotion and that the work of art is an "ideal" or "imagined object." The conclusions are all the stranger given Collingwood's claim to be rescuing the ordinary meaning of "art" from the obfuscation accrued by tradition, muddle-headed philosophers, and the unreflective masses, most of whom he takes disparagingly to be quite satisfied with vulgar "amusement." Notably, Collingwood's view eviscerates the differences between genres – tragedy and comedy in literature, for example – and denies that a writer can actually "set out to write a comedy, a tragedy, an elegy, or the like" (116), because to do so presupposes that he knows which emotion he will express before he expresses it; that Shakespeare sat down with the intention of writing a tragedy called *Hamlet* seems perfectly reasonable, but Collingwood, armed with a particular metaphysics of mind, finds the idea incoherent. The corollary of this view is that the primary component of art is not its realization in some material form – again a perfectly sensible thing to believe – but is contained in the act of mind that constitutes its generation. Collingwood also rejects any meaningful distinction between artist and audience, and although, as we shall see, this has far-reaching, even radical, implications for the place of the artist in society at large, it effectively denies to the spectator a central component of aesthetic experience, namely, that a work of art stands to be interpreted and might even contain features that had nothing to do directly with the consciousness of its creator. Collingwood insists, however, that both ideas do not belong to "art

---

[29] For a recent and spirited defense of Collingwood, see Gary Kemp, "The Croce-Collingwood Theory as Theory," *Journal of Aesthetics and Art Criticism*, 61, 2 (2003): 171–93. Kemp insists, evidence to the contrary notwithstanding, that Collingwood's self-advertisement as a conceptual analyst should be ignored because it belies the "substantive" theory his work contains. His praise for *The Principles of Art*, moreover, as "probably the most important aesthetic treatise" between Burke and the 1960s deserves the same respect as Bell's assessment of Fry's "Essay" as the most useful treatise since Kant. See also J. Grant, "On Reading Collingwood's Principles of Art," *Journal of Aesthetics and Art Criticism*, 46, 2 (1987): 239–48.

proper," but to "art falsely called," especially the pernicious and widespread "technical theory," which Collingwood pursues with a monomania to rival Ahab's pursuit of the Whale.

"Art Falsely Called"

Collingwood devotes the first part of *The Principles of Art* to dismantling the four erroneous "meanings" of "art" and the respective theories that support them: art as craft, art as representation, art as magic, and art as amusement. In practice, it becomes clear that the first of these – art as craft or the "technical theory of art" – is the master category under which the others are reducible as species to genus. The last two, moreover, seem obvious nonstarters for a general theory of art, though Collingwood considers them widespread enough (at the time at least) to devote considerable space to their refutation. (Santayana had emphasized stimulation and entertainment as the two great needs that art seeks to satisfy.) Conceived as magic, art is the ritualized representation of some emotion for its practical value – an admirable feature requisite for any healthy society – as in a war dance designed to instill courage in a warrior and fear in his enemy. Collingwood does not deny that art can have this effect, but urges, noncontroversially it seems, that a work of art might be magical in this sense, but that is not what makes it art. Equally noncontentious is his rejection of the view that art is simply a matter of amusement, that artistic objects are designed solely to simulate emotion through make-believe and provide cathartic discharge simply for the sake of pleasure; again, an object might well perform such a function, but that is independent of its status as art.

It is also worth noting that Collingwood, no doubt influenced by the effects of mass culture in 1930s Germany, expresses a good deal of contempt for a whole range of "modern" activities from thrillers through cinema to jazz, which, in a flood of nostalgia worthy of Wordsworth and a fit of moralizing to rival Ruskin, he associates with the decline of a genuine rural culture marked by the magic art of songs, dances, feasts, and pageants "organically connected with agricultural work" (101), all swept aside by the brutishness of industrialization. The result, Collingwood laments, is a class of *nouveaux riche* northerners with an excess of poor taste and a dearth of community attachment that had checked the apparent superiority of their feudal forebears, along with the unwashed mass of "entertainment mad" working poor, pathetically addicted to a diet of soccer, novels about sex, and magazines full of "cattishness" regaling readers with sordid details about the lives of the rich and famous (84ff.). Collingwood identifies here a threat to "practical life" – hedonism encroaches on "stores of energy" required for the "ordinary course of living" (95) – that, in the creeping shadow of Ruskin's mountain gloom, portends the death of civilization hard won through centuries of toil. "Civilizations die," Collingwood writes under the shadow of Hitler certainly but with unselfconscious melodrama nevertheless, "not with waving of flags or the noise of machine-guns in the streets, but in the dark, in a stillness, when no one is aware of it" (104).

The political context not withstanding, Collingwood's self-righteousness surely gets the upper hand in these protestations, and he indiscriminately lumps together and dismisses so many forms of art that it is hard to read it as much more than a vulgar declaration of his own taste. There are, thankfully, also philosophical grounds upon which his own prejudices stand, and these are to be found in his treatment of the other two theories of art, that of representation and, because of its long history and pervasive character, the more fundamental "technical theory." Collingwood coins this latter phrase from the theory's origins in the Ancient concept of *technê* – meaning craft or specialized form of skill – the category in which the Greeks put both ordinary activities such as raising animals or baking bread, as well as what since the eighteenth century have come under the heading "fine arts," namely, poetry, sculpture, painting, and architecture. The technical view equates art with craft in this sense and although its origin is old, Collingwood emphasizes, it is "actually the way in which most people nowadays think of art" (19).

As soon as one considers the features that define this sort of activity, however, it becomes clear how inadequate it is as a way of understanding art. Crafts, Collingwood urges, display six distinct features: they involve 1) a relation of means and ends, and 2) planning and execution, where 3) ends precede means (planning) or means precede ends (execution); they use 4) raw materials that are distinguished from the finished product that 5) can be articulated through the distinction between form and matter. Crafts also stand 6) in three sorts of hierarchy to each other: (a) the raw material of one craft is the finished product of another, (b) one craft has as its end product the tools employed as means in another, and (c) some trades work in concert to bring about the finished product. Combining these various elements, one might imagine a carpenter, who cuts wood in order to make a table; assembles the parts according to a plan; in the process he turns raw material into a finished product; and does so by imposing a form (tableness) on the matter of the material (wood). The carpenter also uses as raw stuff the finished products of the woodcutter and sawyer, supplies his own finished product for use as means for the draftsman to draw up designs, and works in concert with the varnish manufacturer who provides the finish for the wood.

The problem, Collingwood urges, is that none of these features apply to what we call "art," and if it did, a good deal of "art" would no longer enjoy that status. At the same time, Collingwood does not deny that artistic activity and the objects created might sometimes display one or more of these features, but that would be quite irrelevant to the status of the activity as artistic and the object as art. We can see immediately how the technical theory of art is a master theory that shows magic and amusement to be crafts, because both involve a relation of means to an end, which Collingwood takes as the "central and primary characteristic of craft" (107–8): magic brings about an emotional response, amusement stimulates and discharges emotion. The same is true of Collingwood's third "false theory," art as representation. For if "representation is a matter of skill, a craft of a special

kind," and art is not a craft, it follows that art cannot be a matter of representation (42).

Independent of the power of *modus tollens*, Collingwood finds other
grounds for attacking representative art, and these are considerably more
interesting given the place of representation in the history of aesthetics; at one
point, it is worth noting, Collingwood claims that "most of what was written
and said about art in the nineteenth century was written and said, not about
art proper, but about representation; with the assumption, of course, that it was
for that reason about art" (42). Collingwood's view of representation deviates
little from the way it was understood by Addison, Hutcheson, and others who
followed, especially as they distinguished it from mere copy or "imitation." "A
work of art is imitative in virtue of its relation to another work of art which
affords it a model of artistic excellence," Collingwood writes in this spirit, but
"it is representative in virtue of its relation to something in 'nature,' that is,
something not a work of art" (42). The primary sense of representation is thus
the relation a portrait bears to the sitter, though Collingwood insists that its
"true definition" is "not that the artifact resembles an original ... but that the
feeling evoked by the artifact resembles the feeling evoked by the original."
The former is a "literal" representation – a presentation or mere copy – and
the latter an "emotional representation" (53), and in order to produce this, the
artist creates an "emotionally correct likeness," a re-presentation of the original for particular purposes and a specific audience. Collingwood subsequently
specifies three degrees of representation each of which aims at emotional
effect: "naïve or almost non-selective representation" that attempts a literal
likeness (as in Egyptian portrait-sculpture); "bold selection of important or
characteristic features" (the pattern or shape formed by people dancing, for
example), or abandoning literal representation altogether in which case it
might bear no resemblance to the origin at all (a Turner seascape would be a
good illustration). All three – even the highly impressionistic and abstract case
of Turner – are examples of craft rather than art, because the central aim is to
bring about emotional effect.

Collingwood, one assumes, draws on Reynolds here, although in doing so
he effectively denies that Reynolds was actually talking about art. Abandoning
the technical theory of art means that Collingwood at once rejects a good deal
of what thinkers from the eighteenth century onward took to be commonplaces or at least uncontroversial features of art and artistic practice. First,
Collingwood's approach casts considerable doubt on the importance attributed to technique, the "specialized form of skill" putatively required of all artists, however great their native talents and powers. Nobody would deny that
poetry, for example, displays ingenious patterns of rhyme, rhythm, meter, and
alliteration as painting does brushstrokes, washes, and principles of perspective; we might even say that the poet and painter "employ" these techniques
in a certain way. The problem, Collingwood insists, is that this theory of artistic

technique misdescribes art by reducing it to a relation between means and ends: it invents the falsehood of an unrealized work of art (end) that exists prior to its expression through technical skill (means). This picture is clearly true of the carpenter designing his table – and is true of art in which art is a craft – but denies an essential element of artistic practice, namely, that an object is produced in and through the act of production: "the poet extemporizing his verses, the sculptor playing with his clay, and so forth," cases where the "artist has no idea what the experience is which demands expression until he has expressed it" (29).

This same thought extends, second, to a view that Collingwood attributes to a "large school of modern psychologists," and traces to Book X of Plato's *Republic*, Aristotle's *Poetics*, and Horace's *Ars Poaletica* (it is also an accurate description of Hume, although he goes unnamed in this regard). On this view, the "entire work of art … [is] an artifact, designed … as means to the realization of an end beyond it, namely, the state of mind in the artist's audience" (30). There are occasions where "artists" do deliberately set out to excite an audience in this manner, but they are really crafts, "pseudo-arts," or, Collingwood emphasizes, psychological reactions that amount to "various kinds of use to which art may be put" (33), namely, to arouse an emotion for its own sake (amusement) or some practical purpose (magic); to stimulate the intellectual faculties for exercise (puzzle) or to gain knowledge (instruction); or to stimulate some practical activity as expedient (propaganda) or right (exhortation).

Third, abandoning the technical theory of art also involves abandoning a "certain terminology" associated with the "fine arts." Collingwood thinks this is all to the good, because the concept embodies the technical theory itself reflected in the idea that art is essentially the activity of producing artifacts, which are either "fine" or "useful" depending on the qualities they are supposed to possess, and implies erroneously that making the "bodily or perceptible thing" is the *sine qua non* of artistic activity when it is but secondary to the internal experience of the artist. Further, and this flies in the face of everything in the tradition since Locke, "fine art" implies that the "bodily or perceptible work of art has a peculiarity distinguishing it from the products of useful art, viz. beauty" (37). Collingwood's denial that there is any such thing – that "beauty" is a philosopher's "name for something non-existent" (40) – does not much separate him from the empiricists of the eighteenth century, but he draws from it conclusions that they would have had difficulty accepting: that "aesthetic experience is an autonomous activity" (40), and that words like *beauty* and *beautiful* (and, one assumes, *sublime* and *picturesque*, although he does not address these) "have no aesthetic implication" but really mean "admirable or excellent" (38) or in some way desirable. There are clear hints of Reid in this view, though the implications Collingwood draws from it take him in a different and, to many, untenable direction.

"Art Proper"

Having dispatched the technical theory and the various false theories that depend on it, Collingwood turns in the second part of *The Principles of Art* to the positive part of his doctrine that art "proper" expresses emotion. Collingwood rejects categorically the idea embraced by Bell that there can be any such thing as a specifically "aesthetic emotion" (though we can speak of having "successfully expressed ourselves") (117), insisting that the artist is in the same boat as anybody else who is said to "express emotion," which has three central components. First, one becomes aware or "conscious" of the emotion in the course of expressing it, which means one does not know in advance what the emotion is, though one is aware that there is an emotion – a "perturbation or excitement" – of some kind (109). Becoming conscious of the emotion in this way involves, second, becoming conscious of and expressing "all its particularities," thus "individualizing," clarifying, and distinguishing the emotion from others of the same sort; it does not involve labeling emotions as "instances of this or that general kind" (113). Third, as for the Romantics, it is an "exploration" (111) of one's own emotions and addressed primarily to oneself; it is not an attempt to arouse feelings in others to whom it is only addressed secondarily and only if they can understand it. As Collingwood then emphasizes, none of these are applicable to craft, which involves plan and execution and thus a relation of means to ends; produces this or that object as an instance of a general type; and tries to arouse emotion in others. They are, however, features that characterize "art proper."

The question that follows is then quite naturally, what is a "work of art?" to which Collingwood answers: it is a kind of "comprehensive awareness" (304), a "total imaginative experience," or an "imaginative experience of total activity" (148 passim). What this means depends in turn on Collingwood's "general theory of imagination," which owes a good deal to Hume and Kant and the elucidation of which takes up Book II of *The Principles of Art*. Collingwood is anxious to get away from what he regards as the confused notion that imagination is identical to make-believe – that leads to the mistake of seeing the artist (as did Hume) as a "kind of liar" (286) – when it is a bona fide faculty of mind. He calls the immediate objects of experience "impressions" (sense data), which involves both "sensation and emotion" and constitutes the "psychic level" or "feeling" in its raw, "sheer or crude" state. Feelings of this sort are never experienced as such, but are transformed or "domesticated" into "ideas of imagination." The imagination effectively transforms the flux of impressions into a unified perception, which presupposes, following Kant, apperception or self-consciousness.

We can think of Collingwood's view of mind as working back from the ordinary observation that "what we get out of a work of art" is not contained in actually seeing or hearing the formal features of an object or even patterns among its elements (impressions), but on what is seen imaginatively: the imagination transforms sensed objects into objects of experience. This can work "positively," as when expressions on the masks of a Greek chorus "change," or a series of parallel lines in a drawing are "shadows" on a wall, or "negatively," when the faculty works to "disimagine" (143) or filter out what is aesthetically irrelevant: the noise of shuffling neighbors at a concert, for example, or the light reflected from the varnished surface of a painting. When Collingwood speaks of a total imaginative experience he has in mind the move from the first (sensation) to the second part (imagination) of this process: a man could be seeing all the shapes and colors of a picture or hearing all the notes of a symphony, but he would "not on that account be enjoying an aesthetic experience. To do that he must use his imagination," Collingwood insists, "and so proceed from the first part of the experience, which is given in sensation, to the second part, which is imaginatively constructed" (149).

A "work of art," it follows on this view, is a kind of "making" on the part of the artist that we call "creation," though not in the sense of "transforming a given raw material" into some object – that is the mark of craft – but in an act of mind called imagination. This leads Collingwood to his distinctive, and for some, distinctly odd proposal that a "poem or a painting or any other work of art" is properly described as an "imaginary object" (139) and its corollary that a "work of art may be completely created when it has been created as a thing whose only place is in the artist's mind" (130). Collingwood thinks this is shown in our ordinary conception of what it means to "listen." An audience does not for a moment think that a piece of music – the work of art – consists of the noises being played by the musicians on stage, nor do they consider it somehow contained in the printed score. The work of art remains the "tune in the composer's head" (139) and that is to be accessed only through the audience "understanding" what the artist "records" in the work; the aesthetic experience is the act of imagination given in and through the activity of listening – not simply hearing the sounds – where members of the audience "reproduce" or "reconstruct" in their own minds the composer's creative activity and the emotion being expressed through it. Thus, the total act of imagination takes part on the side of the artist who creates an imaginary object, and on the side of the audience whose members are recreating the same for themselves by doing something, that is, "having" an aesthetic experience.

The "Cult of 'Genius'"

This view of the experience of the audience leads Collingwood to reject a central conception dominant (Reynolds notwithstanding) in the tradition from Gerard's *Essay*, through the Romantics' conception of the poet, to the various "virtues" Pater discovers as the spirit of the Renaissance, namely, the "cult of 'genius'" (312) with its underlying thought that the "artist" is distinguished from the "ordinary man" by being a "special kind" of person (117). Collingwood sees this tradition sedimented and crystallized in the notion of "aesthetic individualism," the widespread and laudatory treatment of the artist "as if he were a God, a self-contained and self-sufficient creative power whose only task is to be himself and to exhibit his nature in whatever works are appropriate to it" (316). It is easy to see how this view of the artist might be generated and sustained by the technical theory: if art were a specialized form of skill then only those in possession of it could produce art, and only others with at least some knowledge of the same could properly be said to understand it. Art proper, however, is given in the expression of emotion – and not any special kind of "aesthetic emotion" at that (116) – and the only criterion for understanding art is that the audience is capable of experiencing that emotion as well. At the same time, the reader might expect that with his endorsement of highbrow literature (T. S. Eliot is the model) and categorical rejection of almost everything else as mere amusement (see 325ff.), Collingwood would find some notion of the artistic genius appealing. He admits that it is a short step from the view he has propounded to regarding the artist as a "kind of transcendent genius whose meaning is always too profound for his audience of humble mortals to grasp in a more than fragmentary way" (311); the audience is largely irrelevant, "inessential," and, in an image that would have the Romantics nodding in general approval, seems "to consist at best of persons whom the artist permits to overhear him as he speaks" (300).

Collingwood, however, takes a firm stand in the very opposite direction, and argues that while art proper is an activity of consciousness, it requires both public expression and depends on a high degree of "collaboration" with members of the wider community. As with clarifying the concept of "art," he considers his task no more than making explicit what artists have done all along, the details of which have been obscured by the cult of genius and its expression in the assumption of aesthetic individualism. First, there is collaboration among artists, and although there is much value placed on "originality," the idea that an artist's work is "purely his own" is a myth given credence and respectability by the development of a "code of artistic morality" in the nineteenth century. In practice, Collingwood insists, any artist "grafts his own work upon that of another" (319), and to wrap art in the legal garb of property and ownership in the name of protection and creative endeavor is actually to deprive it of the very soil that has produced the likes of Shakespeare, Beethoven, and Turner. "Let painters and writers and musicians steal with both hands whatever they can find," Collingwood declares. "And if any one objects to having his own precious ideas borrowed by others, the remedy is easy. He can keep them to himself by not publishing; and the public will probably have cause to thank him" (320).

Second, art involves collaboration between author and performer. Works do not, as aesthetic individualism would have it, issue complete and finished from a writer's pen, but stand as a "rough outline" of directions for how a symphony or play is to be performed. Artists actually insist that the performer does not simply execute the work, but collaborates intelligently as a "co-author the work he performs" (321). Third, and perhaps most important, there is collaboration between artist and audience. Not only does the audience understand the work of art only when attempting to reconstruct for itself the imaginative experience of the artist, but also this activity is projected in the mind of the artist and forms an "integral part" of the creative act: the artist takes his audience into account in producing the work so that their "limitations" in comprehending it are transformed into "conditions determining the subject-matter or meaning of the work itself." In so doing, the artist is not so much expressing his own emotions as expressing those he shares with the audience for whom he is "spokesman" (311–12). Recalling Collingwood's view of aesthetic activity, one might see why he regards the live performance as the *sine qua non* of art: only where author, performers, and audience are "in touch," fused into a living present, can sensuous experience be transformed through consciousness into imagination. For this reason, all art that depends on mechanical reproduction – recorded music or voice, film, and printed word – is inferior, amusements of one sort or another, because they deaden the "lively reality" of aesthetic experience and open an insurmountable breach between artist and audience; the latter, to recall Mill again, is then no longer collaborating but simply "overhearing" and that, in a profound departure from the Romantics, heralds if not quite the death of art then certainly a recipe for its impoverishment.

JOHN DEWEY

As noted earlier, John Dewey (1859–1952) published his principal work in aesthetics, *Art and Experience* (1934), four years before Collingwood's *The Principles of Art*. The work began life even earlier, in the winter and spring of 1931, when as the inaugural speaker of the William James Lectureship, Dewey delivered ten lectures on "the Philosophy of Art" to the Department of Philosophy and Psychology at Harvard University.[30] Like Collingwood, Dewey too was a man with a foot in two centuries, though his world was not that of Ruskin, the Lakes, and the quads of Oxford, but rural Vermont (he was born in Burlington), the universities of the American Midwest (he held appointments at Michigan, Minnesota, and Chicago before going to Columbia in 1904), and an intellectual climate dominated by Charles Sanders Peirce (1839–1914) and William James (1842–1910); the influence of these thinkers was so profound as to associate his name inexorably with the school of American pragmatism they founded. Despite difference of place and intellectual lineage, Dewey and Collingwood do have important sources in common, notably the poetry and prose writings of the Romantics and Croce: Dewey is much taken with Pater, Coleridge, Wordsworth, Shelley, and especially Keats of the letters

---

[30] John Dewey, *Art as Experience*, in *John Dewey: The Later Works, Volume 10: 1934*, ed. Jo Ann Boydston and Harriet Furst Simon (Carbondale: Southern Illinois University Press, 1987). All references are to the pagination of this edition.

(36ff.), and absorbed enough from his Italian forebear that he was all but accused by him of plagiarism (a charge Croce did not, one might note, bring against Collingwood), and, what may have been worse, claimed by him as a fellow Hegelian, albeit one in denial. The latter is reasonable and was raised as a criticism by fellow pragmatists as well, a fact Croce reports (twice) with obvious pleasure. The former charge, however, is tenuous at best: not only are the outlines of the position Dewey develops clearly visible in Fry and Bell through the Romantics and the British tradition that preceded them, but a glimpse at the list of works referenced in *Art as Experience* (see 423–30) – including his own *Experience and Nature* (1925) – shows how eclectic Dewey's sources and long held his views were. Croce reveals a certain sneakiness and dishonesty himself in exploiting Dewey's confession (one he probably regretted) of feeling embarrassed at being unable to acknowledge specific debts to "other writers on the subject" and recognizing "obligations to a number of writers much greater than might be gathered from allusions to them in the volume itself" (7). Unlike Santayana, however, Dewey does mention and cite many of the sources on which he draws.[31]

The nature of the specific debt to Croce and others notwithstanding, the pertinent point of interest in the present context lies in the aspects of philosophical heritage shared by Collingwood and Dewey, reflected in the overlapping points visible in the respective positions they develop: both give central place to expression and emotion; focus on the practical component of aesthetic experience; find (with qualification on Dewey's side) the essence of art in its ideal status; and identify language with art, which they agree, at bottom, to be expressive. They also emphasize the dynamic relation between artist and audience, with Collingwood's notion of "collaboration" captured by Dewey in "doing and undergoing" – active production and receptive surrender – on both sides. One also finds a good deal of convergence in their respective philosophies of mind, and though Dewey speaks the language of Darwin and contemporary psychology rather than the philosophical one of Hume and Kant, the mental landscape they sketch is of a piece: where art for Collingwood is consciousness transmuting sensation into ideas of imagination, for Dewey it is born of the human capacity for "restoring consciously, and thus on the plane of meaning, the union of sense, need, impulse, and action, characteristic of the live creature" (31).

---

[31] See Benedetto Croce, "On the Aesthetics of John Dewey," *Journal of Aesthetics and Art Criticism*, 6, 1 (1948): 203–7, and Dewey's reply, "A Comment on the Foregoing Criticisms," in ibid., 207–9. Croce, clearly unsatisfied and unwilling to let sleeping dogs lie, tried to make his case again four years later in "Dewey's Aesthetics and Theory of Knowledge," *Journal of Aesthetics and Art Criticism*, 11, 1 (1952): 1–6. The exchange inspired a defense of Croce by an admirer and protégé, one Frederic S. Simoni, in "Benedetto Croce: A Case of International Misunderstanding," *Journal of Aesthetics and Art Criticism* 11, 1 (1952): 7–14. For the criticism of Dewey's Hegelianism from fellow pragmatists, see Stephen Pepper, "Some Questions on Dewey's Aesthetics," in *The Philosophy of John Dewey*, ed. Paul A. Schilpp (Evanston, IL: Northwestern University Press, 1939), 369–90.

Emphasizing these similarities is not to deny differences, although, on balance, these reflect the presence of alternative methodologies and matters of emphasis rather than any fundamental disagreement. The main point of contrast, in fact, lies in the conclusions that follow upon the positions they develop: Collingwood's conceptual analysis and near obsession with refuting the technical theory guides him to rein in the scope of "aesthetic experience" and narrow the definition of "art," while Dewey's naturalistic approach to "experience" leads to a broader conception of both such that "aesthetic" describes (at least potentially) human activity in general, and "art" becomes one instance of it. In so doing, Dewey effectively reclaims something of the original Greek – *aisthetikos*, sensuous perception – even if, ironically, it leaves him open to the mirror image of the charge raised against Collingwood: if the latter can be faulted for ruling out activities to which few would deny the status of art, Dewey can surely be criticized for ruling in a good many that do not deserve that epithet at all.

The Museum Conception of Art and the Task of Aesthetics

Art as Experience is a long, sprawling, and repetitive work, and despite providing discrete headings to indicate the main focus of each of its fourteen chapters, Dewey routinely circles back to issues considered in earlier chapters. It is also remarkably eclectic, although the main interest for the aesthetician lies in its organizing thought that – as the title indicates – art is to be approached in terms of "experience," understood in a specific sense. Dewey begins by bemoaning the prevailing and dominant conception that only objects placed in the detached space of museum and gallery can and should count as art. This banishing of artistic objects to the interiors of specially designated buildings might seem a natural state of affairs, he observes, but such an attitude is only possible after those objects have been separated from the conditions that gave rise to them. Once incarcerated, their special status as "art" is perpetuated, because, remote from everyday life, they appear to the mass of the population as anemic, the province of a cultivated minority, and it is hardly surprising, Dewey observes, that most people react by satisfying their "esthetic hunger" through consuming "cheap and vulgar" alternatives instead (12).

The impression created and perpetuated by the museum model, moreover, hides the fact that a good number of the objects that fill glass cabinets and cover gallery walls, not to mention churches, palaces, and other buildings considered art (Dewey's example is the Parthenon), have their origin in practical activities of one sort or another; this history is obscured, however, by turning them into dead artifacts and severing them from the culture and context in and through which they were created. "Domestic utensils, furnishings of tent and house, rugs, mats, jars, pots, bows, spears," Dewey points out,

were wrought with such delighted care that today we hunt them out and give them places of honor in our art museums. Yet in their own time and place, such things were enhancements of the processes of everyday life. Instead of being elevated to a niche apart, they belonged to display of prowess, the manifestation of group and clan membership, worship of gods, feasting and fasting, fighting, hunting, and the rhythmic crises that punctuate the stream of living. (12)

Dewey identifies certain sociological and historical factors to account for this phenomenon: the politics of nationhood and the conspicuous consumption of capitalism transform art objects into commodities to express one's social standing and exhibit one's higher taste, and the pleasures of ownership, display, and collecting become confused with aesthetic enjoyment. The separation of art from its origins in everyday life also has its corollary in the rise of the same aesthetic individualism attacked by Collingwood, although Dewey considers it a particular manifestation of a general pattern in modern life to valorize what is "spiritual" or "ideal" and simultaneously denigrate the "material" or "matter" – Ruskin being a case in point – as "something to be explained away or apologized for" (12 passim). Placing art in museums, tracing creativity to some genius of the artist, and reducing enjoyment of artistic objects to intellectual appreciation alone each reflects this tendency. The unintended result of thus extracting the pure element from the course stuff in which it occurs is to remove from art the very element – *experience* – that gives it life and vitality.

The museum conception, then, is not only a diagnosis of the place of art in modern life, but also suggests the kind of therapy the aesthetician should undertake, namely, to "restore continuity between the refined and intensified forms of experience that are works of art and the everyday events, doings, and sufferings that are universally recognized to constitute experience" (9). One should proceed like a botanist, Dewey urges, who studies specimens in their natural settings, which, translated into a philosophical idiom, means seeing man as a "live creature in its environment" (34). Understanding the "meaning of artistic products" thus requires an *epochê*, bracketing artistic objects in order to reveal the conditions for their possibility: "we have to forget them for a time," Dewey writes, "to turn aside from them and have recourse to the ordinary forces and conditions of experience that we do not usually regard as esthetic" (10). Dewey proceeds in this endeavor by exposing, first, the general prejudice against practice and its concomitant faculty of imagination, of lowly stature in comparison to its ethereal counterpart of theory and intellect. The ostensibly sharp distinction between these realms is but a function of thought itself and the imposition of categories upon what is, in reality, a single process and flow, of interaction between organism and environment, of doing and undergoing that gives rise to the phenomenological whole that we call "experience": the "interaction of live creature and environing conditions" that constitute the "process of living" (42) and makes experience as a whole aesthetic, and thus experience itself "appreciative, perceiving, and enjoying" (53).

A qualification is immediately in order, however. All experience might be continuous, but that does not confer the unity required to make it properly aesthetic. Experience is more often disrupted and disordered. At one extreme, the elements that compose it are connected only mechanically, which gives rise to a sense of arrest and constriction, a yielding to external pressure over which one has no control. At the other extreme, parts lack any discernible connection at all, but are dispersed, loose, and interrupted; the mind is distracted and the flow broken by barriers, interruptions, and cessation that produces frustration and restlessness. Like a man at the plow, to use Dewey's example, we put our hands to it and turn back, "we start and then stop," not because the task has ended but "because of extraneous interruptions or of inner lethargy" (42). At either extreme, Dewey observes, the mechanical at one pole and looseness at the other, experience becomes "non-esthetic" or "anesthetic" (47), because there is nothing to unify the elements of interaction between organism and environment into a recognizable and coherent whole.

This is quite different from "*an* experience," Dewey emphasizes, in which, whether practical or intellectual, the activity "runs its course to fulfillment" (42) and each element is integrated into a unified totality where the quality of the part recapitulates and pervades the whole. This is not the mindless connection of parts in a machine, nor is it the aimlessness of the man at the plow, but like the free flow of a river moving to culmination and consummation in the sea, it involves continuity without seam or break, complete identity with itself. As Dewey points out, we have all had such experiences – good and bad – and they are remembered for the quality – pleasurable or painful – that "pervades the entire experience in spite of the variation of its constituent parts": "*that* meal, that storm, that rupture of friendship" (44). These experiences are aesthetic through and through, and convey a richness and depth that make them stand out as details against the unvariegated background of experience in general.

Art as Experience

Art, in Dewey's view, should be understood precisely as an experience of this sort, and one manifestation of the "clarified and intensified development of traits that belong to every normally complete experience" (53). All art, he remarks at one point, is "prefigured in the process of living. A bird builds its nest and a beaver its dam when internal organic pressures cooperate with external materials so that the former are fulfilled and the latter are transformed in a satisfying culmination. We may hesitate to apply the word 'art,' since we doubt the presence of direct intent, but all deliberation, all conscious intent, grows out of things once performed organically through the interplay of natural energies" (30). One potential problem with this approach is that one immediately runs into the ambiguity of "art" and "aesthetic," and the suggestion that there is a clear division between "the doing" of artistic production on one side and "the undergoing" of aesthetic enjoyment on the other. This is reflected, as we have seen, more or less self-consciously by various writers in the tradition stretching back to Addison, especially the imagination theorists of the eighteenth century who saw in that faculty both a source of artistic creativity and the capacity for aesthetic reception. The distinction, Dewey urges, prevalent as it might be, is artificial; the terms clearly distinguish an appropriate emphasis on different sorts of activity, but they should not be pushed to "become a separation" (54) because both elements are present for artist and audience. Art must be understood as the relation between production and undergoing in terms of having an experience, but where "art," Dewey insists, "in its form, unites the very same relation of doing and undergoing, outgoing and incoming energy, that makes an experience to be an experience" (55).

On one side stands the artist, set apart from others, in an obvious holdover of Romanticism, by enlarged "powers of execution" and "unusual sensitivity to the qualities of things" (56). The doing of the artist is found in manipulating the physical medium where the activity achieves unity because the "perceived result is of such a nature that *its* qualities *as perceived* have controlled the question of production." The activity also involves undergoing for an artist who imagines the effect of the work on the viewer, reader, or listener, and in the course of the experience molds the object creatively with this give and take in mind; the artist thus "embodies in himself the attitude of the perceiver while he works" (55). As Dewey points out, this gives added importance to the "prior period of gestation in which doings and perceptions projected in imagination interact and mutually modify one another" (58). Dewey does not go as far as Collingwood in equating "art proper" with the ideal or imagined object; that is impossible given his emphasis on the continuity of theory and practice, thought and action, which means that "without external embodiment, an experience remains incomplete" (57–8). The artist, moreover, requires some "medium" without which expression would remain a mere "impulse" (69–70), and there would be nothing to "represent" the artist's experience (93ff.). At the same time, Dewey is close kin to Collingwood in downgrading the activity of embodiment, for when an "author puts on paper ideas that are already clearly conceived and consistently ordered," he remarks, "the real work has been previously done. ... The mere act of transcription is esthetically irrelevant save as it enters integrally into the formation of an experience moving to completeness" (57). For this reason, the artist can retrace the productive experience, modify to some degree, and even start afresh, although this depends upon the art and the medium in question. This is most obvious in the case of architecture, where, Dewey acknowledges, the building is designed and built at a rapid pace with little or no chance to reflect on the degree to which the idea is embodied in the object; in architectural traditions where buildings developed over the course of centuries, however – the great Gothic cathedral, for example – even the nature of stone on stone was not an insurmountable barrier to alternations that could arise as a result of the going and undergoing in the course of construction.

Although doing and undergoing on the part of the artist is relatively easy to appreciate, it is more difficult to see it in the case of the audience because, as Dewey notes, there is a general supposition that the perceiver is wholly passive and "merely takes in what is there in finished form" (58). There is obviously an undergoing – the audience is affected by the object in question – but on closer examination it becomes clear that appreciation is not simply "bare" passive recognition and the mind not a Lockean cabinet to be furnished with ideas emanating from the artist; this is but the beginning and arrest of perception where, more often than not, the spectator falls back on some stereotype or preconceived scheme to make the object comprehensible. Being an audience in a fuller and more meaningful sense involves receptivity, as when one really "takes in" a person for the first time, looking deeper than the characteristics previously considered adequate. Aesthetic appreciation is similar in kind, a "process consisting of a series of responsive acts that accumulate toward objective fulfillment" (58), and this is an "act of reconstructive doing, and consciousness becomes fresh and alive" (59).

Finally, this raises for Dewey the same problem faced by Collingwood, namely, how an audience can ever know whether it has accurately "reconstructed" what the artist had in mind; for, as Dewey puts it, the beholder "must *create* his own experience" and that "creation must include relations comparable to those which the original producer underwent." They cannot be "the same in any literal sense," Dewey admits, but there is no reason why, with the proper attention, work, and period of apprenticeship, the beholder cannot recapitulate the experience of the artist: order the elements that compose the whole and, like the creator, select, simplify, clarify, abridge, and condense according to "his own point of view and interest." Without this act of "recreation," the perceived object is quite simply "not perceived as a work of art" (60).

8

Wittgenstein and After

While anyone familiar with the literature would not hesitate to acknowledge the influence of Ludwig Wittgenstein in the development of twentieth-century aesthetics, fewer perhaps would regard him as having made a substantive contribution to the tradition in his own right. On a personal level, Wittgenstein was engaged intensely with matters artistic and aesthetic, especially music, references to which occur throughout his writings. His father Karl was a prominent patron of the arts, and as a member of a prominent family the young Ludwig grew up at the heart of Viennese cultural life, the world of Gustav Klimt (who painted the wedding portrait of Wittgenstein's sister, Margaret), Johannes Brahms, and Gustav Mahler (both of whom regularly gave concerts in the music rooms of the Palais Wittgenstein); Maurice Ravel, famously, composed the *Piano Concerto for the Left Hand* for Wittgenstein's older brother Paul, who became a concert pianist despite losing an arm in World War I.[1] The thought that Wittgenstein's cultural biography might not have translated into a decipherable philosophical aesthetics is due to the fact that his influence in the field is felt not primarily from anything he said about aesthetic matters per se, but through central concepts drawn by others from his philosophy of language more generally: as we shall see in the latter part of this chapter, his view of "rule following" and the concepts of "seeing as," "language games," and "family resemblances" inspired major, even landmark contributions to the field.

That the official influence of Wittgenstein should have taken this form is hardly surprising given that the only work he dedicated explicitly to the subject, although in limited circulation before, was not widely available until its publication in 1967: the eponymous "Lectures on Aesthetics," transcriptions of notes taken by students in a small private seminar Wittgenstein gave at

---

[1] For details of Wittgenstein's life and intellectual development, see Ray Monk, *Wittgenstein: The Duty of Genius* (London: Free Press, 1990). For a glimpse into the intellectual world in which he grew up and lived, the best account remains Alan Janik and Stephen Toulmin, *Wittgenstein's Vienna* (New York: Simon and Shuster, 1973).

Cambridge in the summer of 1938. As a result, aestheticians working in the spirit of Wittgenstein's philosophy looked to insights developed in the course of pursuing extraaesthetic matters, and this is reflected in the work that was done in his name. Thus, in his early essay, "Aesthetic Problems of Modern Philosophy," for example, Stanley Cavell refers to Wittgenstein's application of his methods to aesthetics only through Moore's 1955 report of Wittgenstein's lectures and not from the "Lectures" themselves.[2] The delayed availability of this work, however, should not obscure its content, and even if its direct influence on the discipline was marginal, it should still be appreciated retrospectively for the distinct and independent contribution it represents. There is warrant, then, as we shall see in the first part of the chapter, to speak of "Wittgenstein's aesthetics" or more appropriately "Wittgensteinian criticism," because, although philosophically distinct, it bears many marks of the tradition stretching back to Shaftesbury and Hutcheson of which it is an integral part.

LUDWIG WITTGENSTEIN

Many consider Ludwig Josef Johann Wittgenstein (1889–1951) the greatest philosopher of the twentieth century, and if greatness is measured by influence the assessment is hard to resist. One might even say, adapting Clark's comment on Fry, that insofar as philosophy can be changed by one man, it was changed by Ludwig Wittgenstein. If one follows common wisdom and divides his thinking into two distinct periods, he changed philosophy not once but twice, first in the spirit of logical positivism and then as philosopher of language. The "early" Wittgenstein is found in the *Tractatus Logic-Philosophicus*, first published in the German periodical *Annalen der Naturphilosophie* as *Logisch-Philosophische Abhandlung* (1921; English trans. 1922), composed during World War I (which Wittgenstein spent serving with the Austrian army and then as a prisoner), and the outcome of his study of logic and mathematics, including two seminal years (1911–13) spent under Bertrand Russell at Cambridge. The "later" Wittgenstein, by contrast, dates from the 1930s and 1940s, and is contained in many posthumously published writings, both transitional ones from what is sometimes called his "middle" period – notably *Philosophical Grammar* and *The Blue and the Brown Books* – and the celebrated *Philosophical Investigations* in which they culminated. Wittgenstein finished the first part of the work in 1945, the second by 1949, and they were published together as a single work in 1953, two years after his death.

---

[2] See Stanley Cavell, "Aesthetic Problems of Modern Aesthetics," in *Philosophy in America*, ed. Max Black (Ithaca, NY: Cornell University Press, 1965), 74–97; reprinted in Stanley Cavell, *Must We Mean What We Say: A Book of Essays* (Cambridge: Cambridge University Press, 2002 [1969]), 1–43. See G. E. Moore, "Wittgenstein's Lectures in 1930–33," *Mind* 64, 253 (1955): 1–27, reprinted (with revisions) in his *Philosophical Papers* (London: Allen and Unwin, 1959), 252–324.

There is a good deal of scholarly debate over points of contrast and conti-nuity between the early and later philosophy, and while some commentators have identified common themes, there is general agreement on the undeniable and, in many ways, radical shift from the *logical analysis* of the former period to the *conceptual analysis* of the latter. In the *Tractatus*, Wittgenstein devel-ops a metaphysics in which thoughts represent or "picture" the "facts" that comprise the "world," and do so as propositions that are meaningful in virtue of their logical form, a feature they also share with thoughts and the facts of the world they represent. What cannot be pictured by thought and expressed propositionally is nonsense, that is, either (depending on one's interpretation) without meaning or mystical insofar as they constitute a transcendental realm about which nothing can be said. On this view, philosophical problems are to be approached by analyzing the logical form of linguistic propositions, and Wittgenstein claimed famously that in the *Tractatus* he had effectively solved all the problems of philosophy. In the *Investigations* and other later writings, however, he rejects the method and retracts the claim, proposing instead that language is an activity, and the role of the philosopher is to study the use of the words that constitute it. This is captured famously in Wittgenstein's metaphor of language as a toolbox, words being so many instruments with which speak-ers do various things or, in another conception, "play" a complicated array of "language games." Philosophical problems are not now *solved* through separating propositions into sense and nonsense, but *dissolved* by showing that words are governed by a "grammar," which, if not properly appreciated, leads philosophers astray. The revolutionary impact of Wittgenstein's thought, then – and the reason for its deep and enduring influence – is that it provides a method, which can be applied to a whole range of traditional "problems," to show, through a process of philosophical therapy, that and how they are really conceptual confusions of one sort or another. The aim of philosophy, as Wittgenstein expresses it in one memorable image, is to "show the fly the way out of the fly-bottle" (PI 308).[3]

---

[3] In what follows, I concentrate on the "Lectures on Aesthetics," in Ludwig Wittgenstein, *Lectures and Conversations on Aesthetics, Pyschology, and Religious Belief. Compiled from Notes taken by Yorrick Smythies, Rush Rhees and James Taylor*, ed. Cyril Barrett (Berkeley: University of California Press, 1967); all references are to lecture number (there are four in all) and paragraph. All other references to Wittgenstein's works are given according to the following abbreviations and refer to paragraph (§) or page number: *Notebooks 1914–1916*, trans. G. E. M. Anscombe (Oxford: Basil Blackwell, 1961) (NB); *Tractatus Logico-Philosophicus*, trans. D. F. Pears and B. F. McGuinness (London: Routledge and Kegan Paul, 1974 [1961]) (T); "A Lecture on Ethics," *Philosophical Review* 74, 1 (1965): 3–12 (LE); *The Blue and Brown Books: Preliminary Studies for the Philosophical Investigations* (Oxford: Basil Blackwell, 1958) (BBB); *Philosophische Untersuchungen/Philosophical Investigations*, trans. G. E. M. Anscombe (Oxford: Basil Blackwell, 1958 [1953]) (PI); and *Vermischte Bermerkungen/Culture and Value*, trans. Peter Winch, ed. G. H. von Wright (Oxford: Basil Blackwell, 1977) (CV).

The "Early" Aesthetics

Before considering the "Lectures" and Wittgenstein's mature views on aesthetics that they contain, it is worth paying some attention to remarks, few as they may be, dating from the earlier writings; these are valuable in their own right, but also informative for certain elements that persist into the later period. The *Tractatus* contains only one direct reference to "aesthetics," although the context in which it appears reveals a good deal about Wittgenstein's views on the matter. He writes:

> It is clear that ethics cannot be put into words [*nicht aussprechen lässt*].
>
> Ethics is transcendental.
>
> (Ethics and aesthetics are one and the same [*sind Eins*]). (T 6.421)

Or, as he expresses the same thought in an entry in the earlier *Notebooks 1914–16* (dated July 24, 1916):

> ... Life is the world.
>
> Ethics does not treat of [*handelt nicht von*] the world. Ethics must be a condition of the world, like logic.
>
> Ethics and aesthetics are one [*sind Eins*]. (NB 77e)

Wittgenstein does not expand on the comparison, but some light can be shed on it through a similar likeness he draws in "A Lecture on Ethics."[4] The lecture (the only public one he ever gave) was composed and delivered a good number of years after the *Tractatus* (the editors date it to sometime between September 1929 and December 1930), and, while hinting at the later work to come, is still indebted to the metaphysics of the *Tractatus*. Wittgenstein begins with Moore's definition of *ethics* from the *Principia Ethica* as "the general enquiry into what is good,"[5] but quickly widens the sense of the term to mean "enquiry into what is valuable, or into what is really important ... into the meaning of life, or into what makes life worth living, or into the right way of living" (LE 4); this wider sense "*includes* ... the most essential part of what is generally called Aesthetics" (LE 4, emphasis added). As in the *Tractatus*, then, Wittgenstein takes what he says about ethics and ethical judgments to hold *pari passu* for aesthetics and aesthetic judgment as well.

What one notices straightaway about moral judgments, Wittgenstein observes, is that they function in two quite different ways, one "trivial or relative," the other "ethical or absolute" (LE 5). Judgments of the former type are not about ethics, but are really *statements of fact* made in accord with some

---

[4] For the connection between this lecture and Wittgenstein's early views on aesthetics, I am indebted to Diané Collinson, "Ethics and Aesthetics Are One," *British Journal of Aesthetics*, 23, 3 (1985): 266–72.

[5] See Moore, *Principia Ethica*, 1.2.

predetermined standard, and can, for that reason, be reformulated so as not to express value at all: "he is a good pianist" means "the man can play difficult pieces with skill and dexterity," as "that is a good chair" means "the piece of furniture in question serves its intended purpose." Absolute judgments, by contrast, are imperatives – they carry the "ought" of obligation – and express intrinsic value independent of any use or purpose; as a result, unlike their relative counterparts, they can never be translated into nor derived from statements of fact. Employing the terminology of the *Tractatus*, judgments of relative value state facts, picture the world, and thus convey (as the "Lecture" has it) "*natural* meaning and sense" (LE 7). Judgments of absolute value, by contrast, are not about facts and picture nothing, but refer instead to phenomena beyond experience – the "transcendental" or (in the language of the "Lecture") the "supernatural" (LE 7) – and attempt to articulate what "cannot be put into words."

What emerges from all this, Wittgenstein urges, is an unsettling paradox in which relative judgments concerning matters of fact seem to be the source or somehow give rise to absolute judgments about the transcendental. We encounter this absurdity *phenomenologically*, because our absolute judgments take the form of or at least involve an experience of pleasure, itself a matter of fact, as well as *philosophically*, when upon reflection it becomes clear that ethical judgments are nonsense, the results of trying to say something that cannot be said. Tempting as the suggestion might be, the paradox cannot be dispelled by pointing to an inadequate logical analysis of ethical expressions – as if an adequate version might one day come to light – because "their nonsensicality ... [is] their very essence" and in uttering them we are forced "*to go beyond* the world and that is to say beyond significant language" (LE 11). We seem here to "run against the boundaries of language," Wittgenstein concludes, "... against the walls of our cage" (LE 12).

In the rattling of bars, moreover, one hears (in an auditory premonition of the later philosophy to come) a fundamental confusion and "misuse" of language, the outcome of supposing that we can make absolute judgments about matter of fact. This is not to say that absolute judgments of value are meaningless – although they are, strictly speaking, nonsense – because they express the profound human "desire" or "tendency" to say something about the "ultimate meaning of life" or the "absolute good." The only problem is that they are about no thing, that is, nothing: in attempting to speak of what lies beyond possible experience we resort to simile or allegory, but suppose mistakenly that we refer to some matter of fact; when the simile is removed, however, there is nothing left. If we take Wittgenstein at his word – that ethics and aesthetics "are one" – then everything he says about the former can be transferred to the latter: aesthetic judgments are not descriptions of matter of fact, but expressions of absolute value that attempt to say what is unsayable about something transcendental. As a result, traditional aesthetic language – "beauty," "sublimity," "picturesqueness," and so forth – works through simile and allegory, behind which is nothing; we misuse these terms mistakenly, however, assuming that it is possible to make absolute judgments about matter of fact, and take them to refer to an object or quality, or on the side of the subject to correspond to some emotion or feeling.

Needless to say, this conclusion leaves little room for "philosophical aesthetics" of the sort familiar from the early eighteenth century onward, although, as we shall see, the conceptual analysis pursued in the "Lectures" yields far more positive results. Before considering these, it is worth emphasizing one notable aspect of the earlier view. As Diané Collinson emphasizes, drawing on a remark from the *Notebooks*, in the early philosophy Wittgenstein regards ethics and aesthetics to involve a common "way of seeing"[6] or a discernible "attitude" (a word Wittgenstein uses later), to comprise a view that puts him very much in the company of Santayana and Fry. Wittgenstein writes (dated October 7, 1916):

> The work of art is the object seen *sub specie aeternitatis*; and the good life is the world seen *sub specie aeternitatis*. This is the connexion between art and ethics.
>
> The usual [*gewöhnliche*] way of looking at things [*Betrachtungsweise*] sees objects as it were from the midst of them, the view *sub specie aeternitatis* from the outside.
>
> In such a way that they have the whole world as background. (NB 83e)

Wittgenstein was much indebted to Schopenhauer and through him to Spinoza for this idea of "seeing," which, absorbed into the body of the *Tractatus*, becomes one with the transcendental realm that cannot be described in significant language. Through it Wittgenstein clearly identifies a double life in the manner of Fry, one of the world and matter of fact, the other of logical space and ideas. Aesthetics and art fall into the latter as ideal objects of contemplation articulated through the language of eternity, reminiscent of the way Schopenhauer describes how, in the experience of art, perceiver and percept form a unity, and the object of attention becomes one's entire world.[7] The language of Fry and Schopenhauer/Wittgenstein might be different, but the import for aesthetics is the same: the artistic object occupies a sphere outside of space and time, and involves an attitude distinct from the one that defines everyday life; the result is an experience of a particular and singular sort.

The "Later" Aesthetics

By the summer of 1938 when he gave his informal seminar to the small group of students at Cambridge, Wittgenstein had apparently shifted from the pure *Tractatus* view of aesthetics being either meaningless or supernatural, to embracing fully the insight adumbrated in the "Lecture on Ethics" that it might involve a misuse of language.[8] He still considers the subject of great importance

---

[6] See Collinson, "Ethics and Aesthetics Are One," 267–8.
[7] Schopenhauer develops what he calls the "aesthetic way of knowing" in *World as Will and Representation* 1, Bk. 3, esp. §38ff.
[8] Cf. Roger Shiner, "Wittgenstein on the Beautiful, the Good and the Tremendous," *British Journal of Aesthetics* 14,3 (1974): 258–71, who finds the "Lectures" "confused and inconsistent"

(it is "very big") and to involve similes in the way we describe aesthetic experience; the subject is no longer transcendental, however, but a "new field" with its own language games that surprise and trick ordinary speaker and philosopher alike (I.4). It is for these reasons, one assumes, that Wittgenstein considers it a subject "entirely misunderstood" (I.1). Initially, some insight into the source of the misunderstandings can be gleaned by refining aesthetic language to its most "primitive" form, not unlike the way Wittgenstein later imagines a simple "slab" language at the beginning of the *Investigations* (PI §4). This is clearly not the language spoken by adults, he emphasizes, but the simpler version has the methodological virtue of showing that words such as *beautiful*, *fine*, *good*, and *lovely* are initially taught and learned "roughly as interjections" and "expressions of approval" (I.5); children first apply many value terms to food, often accompanied by facial expressions, gestures, or tones of voice for which the word comes to substitute (I.5). Were we to find ourselves in a foreign culture, Wittgenstein observes, we would learn the value terms of the natives by observing such behavior: seeing what makes them smile, noting the gestures they use when playing with toys, and listening to the vocabulary they associate with food. In some imagined place where the inhabitants were not of human form, but spheres with sticks pointing out, such behavior could not be observed and it would be impossible to discover the aesthetic words they use (I.5).

This primitive use of aesthetic terms as interjections to express approval is more difficult to discern once they become a part of the fully formed language, where, to employ a metaphor from the *Investigations*, they are but one section of streets and houses amidst a large and complex city (PI §18). Like other words, those that make up our aesthetic vocabulary are ordered (to employ another image from the same work) by the "surface grammar" or syntactical structure of the sentences in which they appear, obscuring the "depth grammar" discernible only in the uses to which words are put (PI §664). Wittgenstein considers aesthetic terms more likely to confuse than others because they are adjectival and appear in locutions of the form "This is beautiful" that seem to name some extant property, subjective or objective, that stands outside them: we are inclined to say: "This has a certain quality, that of being beautiful" (I.1). We also assume that aesthetic words have their proper home in critical discourse where they invariably express approval or disapproval (as the primitive language suggests they might), but on closer examination neither of these things is unequivocally the case. Aesthetic words "play hardly any role at all" (I.8) in these contexts, Wittgenstein observes; use of them is at best uninformative – "This is a beautiful picture" tells us very little about the work or what the speaker really thinks of it – and often shows a decided lack of critical acumen (CV 52e). The words we actually use in these contexts are akin to "right"

---

because Wittgenstein unwittingly mixes remarks on the affective aspect of aesthetics judgment ("Subjective Strand") with others that concern justification ("Objective Strand"). He traces this in part to the "residual influence exercised by the *Tractatus* aesthetics" (258–9).

and "correct" (or their antonyms), and this is what is conveyed in praising the transition in a piece of music, say, the precision of images employed by a poet, or coherence in a passage of prose writing. Even so-called aesthetic judgments through which value is supposedly expressed are "entirely uncharacteristic" of locutions speakers actually use, and reveal only the logical relation between "subject and predicate ('This is beautiful')" (I.5). We do sometimes employ that formal construction with an "aesthetic" term when we say of a piece of music, for example, that it is "lovely," as we might say of a suit of clothes that it is "good." Or the meaning of the term is revealed by the context in question as when Blaise Pascal speaks of the "beauty" of mathematics: "Within *that* way of looking at the world these demonstrations did have *beauty*," Wittgenstein observes in a remark dating to 1949,

– not what superficial people call beauty. Again, a crystal is not beautiful in just any "setting" – though perhaps it always looks *attractive*. – Strange that whole epochs can't free themselves from the grip of certain concepts – the concept of "beautiful" and "beauty" for example. (CV 79e)

Even where terms are given meaning by their context of use, Wittgenstein is inclined to think, they function largely as a way of attributing a character or a "face" to the object in question – a mathematical proof, a precious stone, a work of art – a practice more obvious perhaps with terms such as *stately*, *pompous*, or *melancholy*, which give things an inside. In the critical appreciation of art, however – as when directing the tailor fitting us for a suit – our vocabulary is quite different.

Perhaps the most significant issue Wittgenstein raises about the surface grammar of aesthetic language, or certainly one to which he devotes a good deal of time, is the erroneous model of explanation that philosophers adopt to account for the connection between an object and the effect it excites in a spectator.[9] There are a number of ways in which this is manifest, but each reflects the almost irresistible desire to reduce otherwise complex and subtle phenomena to something simple, yielding explanations of the sort "This is really only this" (III.22) or "This is *really* this" (III.34). The first manifestation of this desire is to reduce aesthetic experience to a single phenomenon. The tradition from Addison through Fry is replete with examples – pleasures of imagination, uniformity amidst variety, the line of beauty, significant form, and so on – but Wittgenstein mentions two, the "aesthetic attitude" and the role of "associations." Wittgenstein comes close to committing a philosophical faux pas with the first of these in his early philosophy, where he equates aesthetics with a way of seeing and a peculiar quality of the experience that attends it. In the "Lectures," he continues to emphasize the importance of the attitude people

---

[9] For a critical appreciation of this part of the view Wittgenstein develops in the "Lectures," see Frank Cioffi, "Aesthetic Explanation and Aesthetic Perplexity," in *Essays on Wittgenstein in Honour of G. H. von Wright, Acta Philosophica Fennica*, 28 (1976), 417–49.

take to works of art, comparing, by way of example, the difference between a monk and an atheist looking at a picture of the vision of the Virgin Mary; the former will respond with reverence, the latter perhaps with an amused smile. Unlike the *Tractatus*, however, there is no single "aesthetic attitude" that covers all cases, but rather different attitudes that color one's experience, and to acknowledge this fact is not the same as asserting that aesthetics is "all" a matter of attitude (IV.10). Associations are significant in a similar way, and "change the picture ever so slightly" even to the point that "you won't want to look at it any more." Again, acknowledging the importance of association as one element of aesthetic life is a far cry from raising association to the level of a theory and assuming that it is "all that matters" (IV.12).

Second, and again typical of many approaches we have considered, there is a temptation to regard aesthetics as a "science" capable of showing us what is beautiful (a suggestion "almost too ridiculous for words" [II.2]) or at least proceeding on the assumption that it can isolate the mechanism that connects affective states in people to some trigger in the world (the "fit" of eighteenth-century writers); translated into the language of psychology, it becomes a search for a "mechanics of the soul" (IV.1). At times, that aesthetics is a science appears to be supported by the apparent "click" of an aesthetic experience, as if something has fallen into place – we say things like "Ah!" or "That's it!" – as when two pointers come together opposite one another (III.5). On reflection, however, this language of cause and mechanism turns out to be quite inappropriate. To speak of a "click" is to use a simile behind which there is nothing, and to isolate an event or object in the mind through experimentation, statistical regularity, or introspection is as strange as thinking that identifying what is "at the back of one's mind" is to have isolated some mental item in space and time. Not only are there different uses to which the word *cause* is put (II.12), but also that language rarely if ever enters our critical discourse – "That picture caused me to feel discomfort" is an odd locution indeed.

One manifestation of this mechanist model – worthy of particular note given the discussion of previous chapters – is the separation of works of art from their "effects"; the latter take the form of ideas, feelings, images, and emotions, which are separated from the artistic object and turned into a medium for conveying the "intention" of the artist who brings them about deliberately. Wittgenstein takes the example of music:

> It has sometimes been said that what music conveys to us are feelings of joyfulness, melancholy, triumph, etc., etc. and what repels us in this account is that it seems to say that music is an instrument for producing in us sequences of feelings. And from this one might gather that any other means of producing such feelings would do for us instead of music – To such an account we are tempted to reply "Music conveys to us *itself*!" (BBB 178)

The confusion here stems from the grammar of certain locutions that leads us to conclude that meaning is connected to the effect of a work of art. Thus the phrase "the sense of a proposition," Wittgenstein observes, leads to the "idea that a sentence has a relation to an object, such that, whatever has this effect is the *sense* of the sentence." The utterance "an appreciation of art" has exactly the same form, and inclines us to think that the affective state of the spectator ("effect") is the meaning of the aesthetic object ("cause") (IV.2). Once exposed, this might seem like an obvious error, but under the guise of "expressivist" theories of art, it has done a good deal of mischief.

Finally, and a variant on the appealing picture of a causal mechanism, Wittgenstein points to the seductive idea that aesthetic experience involves the secret workings of unconscious or subconscious motives. This is an appealing picture, there being a "charm" to the image of the mind as an underworld populated by strange creatures or a secret cellar full of mysterious objects (III.26); it is absurd nevertheless, like explaining the quality of a scent by listing its chemical components, or reducing somebody to ashes and then declaring that this is all the person was (III.21). It is, on reflection, odd that people are willing to reduce complex experiential phenomena to other ones that are simple and obviously different, but it is odder still that such explanations are regarded as correct despite evidence in their favor being thin and, strikingly, that they denude the explanandum – aesthetic experience – of the pleasure and value that comprise and characterize it (III.32): that the heady scent is really chemicals or that a human being is just ashes takes a good deal away from the experience of fine perfume or a long life richly lived. Wittgenstein cites an example in which Sigmund Freud robs a patient's dream of all its beauty, reducing the flowers and trees that composed it to nothing but expressions of the unconscious desire for bawdy sex. Philosophers and those persuaded of their arguments might not follow Freud exactly, but they are very often willing to explain aesthetic experience in similarly reductive terms.

"Wittgensteinian Criticism"

In the "Lectures," then, Wittgenstein expends a good deal of energy showing what aesthetics is not: it is not a "science" of the beautiful in either a normative or explanatory sense; it is not identical with "judgments," analysis of which yields only formal relations between predicate and subject terms; and it has very little if anything to do with words like *beauty*, whether in the locutions that make up critical discourse, "qualities" to which they putatively refer, or the various "theories" philosophers have constructed to account for their origin and effects. This negative effort obviously sidelines much traditional aesthetic theory, although, if one accepts Wittgenstein's method and embraces his conclusions, this change in our "style of thinking" (III.40–1) also yields a new and potentially rewarding species of "criticism." In "Wittgensteinian criticism" – as we might call it – the problems of aesthetics reappear as "puzzles about the effects that the arts have on us" (IV.1), the discomfort, discontent, or distaste (and their opposites), which form the "aesthetic reactions" or "impressions" that works of art excite. Solving these puzzles, and thus dissolving the philosophical problems they pose, is really a matter of understanding what it is to "appreciate" works of art. As Wittgenstein points out, it is "impossible" to say exactly in what appreciation consists, because an "extraordinary number of cases" fall under the concept's purview (I.21), and an exhaustive account of any would involve describing the "whole environment" within which the activity takes place (I.20). "Appreciation," moreover, denotes that specifically critical mode through which we confront works of art, and therefore excludes other aesthetic reactions; we do not, for example, "appreciate" the *tremendous* things in Art" – a Beethoven symphony, say – which moves, overwhelms, or strikes us with awe, reactions that (while Wittgenstein does not use the term) are sublime, and suspend the cool, reflective activity of criticism.

With these caveats in mind, however, one can get a good sense from the "Lectures" of what aesthetics so conceived might look like. Wittgenstein makes some familiar observations about the good critic or, to invoke Hume's phrase, the true judge, including the idea that appreciation involves "knowing a lot" about a given area (I.21) and being able to employ a more or less technical or informed vocabulary to talk about it: a man who can only say "Ah!" or "marvelous" when he hears a piece of music is no more musical than a dog wagging its tail at the same (I.17). We might also characterize this in terms of the way a critic employs the rules that govern a given activity. One can simply learn them, as one is drilled in principles of harmony or counterpoint, or like a tailor trying to master the cutting of cloth. We know them by rote or automatically, and they stand as "crystallized" expression of desire: the rules of harmony express the way people want chords to follow and while composers change the rules slightly each time, the old rules remain (we still listen to Beethoven despite atonal music) (I.16). While critics require the knowledge embedded in rules of this sort to make, correct, and refine their judgments, aesthetic judgment consists in the way these rules are used in what the eighteenth century called connoisseurship or taste: appreciation, that is, involves "interpreting" the rules or developing a "feeling" for them (I.15).

Such taste is not contained simply in using so-called aesthetic terms, which, as we have seen, rarely enter into critical discourse, nor is it revealed in the relation between subject and predicate that give judgments their syntactical shape; appreciation, rather, is shown in what the critic does, just as the tailor's skill is displayed in the way he cuts the cloth. The same is true of inferences we make about approval or disapproval. It is tempting to posit some affective state of pleasure or discomfort "behind" the judgment and then seek the psychological or physical mechanism to connect it to some putative quality in the object: hence the pleasurable "click" of parts falling into place or the discomfort of them failing to do so. The correct analogy, Wittgenstein urges, is with jurisprudence: in a court of law one should be able to say why one did something (motive), but there is no expectation that one knows the laws (causes) that govern mind and body (III.12). Thus "There is a 'Why?' to aesthetic comfort" (or discomfort), Wittgenstein points out, but "not a 'cause' to it"; the answer to the why-question is given in the praise or censure conferred on objects in critical discourse (II.19), and "justification" or "explanation" is a matter of recognizing that something is right or correct – playing music with "crescendo here, a diminuendo there, a caesura in this place, etc." rather than doing something else (BBB, 166).

What makes something "right" and thus constitutes praise or censure will depend, moreover, on the practice in question – literature, music, architecture, and so on, as well as distinct genres of each – and only by comparison, "grouping together of certain cases" (IV.2), can one see what is correct or incorrect in particular instances: why words in this poem work while these in another do not fit at all, how changing chords here or adding syncopation there makes for a perfect musical composition; why a door is "too low" in a Gothic cathedral though it might be just right in a building of a different style. We might extend this insight further and note that there are different kinds of appreciation, which means – to recall the debate of the eighteenth century – standards of judgment are internal to a culture. This occurs most obviously between cultures in which a native's "appreciation" for an artistic tradition might be radically different than for an outsider; we might have no sense at all what appreciation means for the indigenous member: an African's appreciation of African art as opposed to a European's, for example (I.28). There is also a good deal of variation within the same culture, from the well-traveled, educated individual who can speak fluently about many paintings to somebody who has seen only a few works but looks intensely at each and receives from them a deep impression: one is "broad, neither deep nor wide" and the other "very narrow, concentrated and circumscribed." Both may be "called 'appreciation,'" Wittgenstein remarks, but of "different kinds" (I.30). There is often a temporal dimension to standards and the meaning of terms as well, so that in "order to get clear about aesthetic words you have to describe ways of living" (I.35), without which the "art of the Middle Ages" or "high German culture" would be vacuous (I.22). Even appreciating something as apparently straightforward as the coronation robe of Edward II would involve knowing a good deal about early fourteenth-century clothes and the attitudes, practices, and vocabulary surrounding them (I.31).

AFTER WITTGENSTEIN

The "Lectures" might not have been published until 1967, but by that point the influence of Wittgenstein and ordinary language philosophy had already been felt, and the collection of articles published as *Aesthetics and Language* in 1954 can be taken as a landmark in the newly acquired but not yet familiar analytic face of aesthetics: "to diagnose and clarify some aesthetic confusions … mainly linguistic in origin," as William Elton characterizes the common theme of the volume in his editorial introduction.[10] The general feeling regarded this as a positive development, aesthetics having lagged behind what had already borne fruit in other areas of philosophy.[11] The central theme of these and a number of influential papers that followed was summed up succinctly by Maurice Mandelbaum in the course of a valiant albeit doomed effort to stem the tide: "one finds the conviction," he writes, "… that it is a mistake to offer generalizations concerning the arts, or, to put the matter in a more provocative manner, that it is a mistake to attempt to discuss what art, or beauty, or the aesthetic, or a poem, *essentially* is."[12] This line of inquiry was hardly new, the same having been canvassed and developed – as we saw in Part I – by Kames, Reid, Knight, and, most notably Stewart, who exploited the concept of transitivity to argue that the meaning of "beauty" and "sublimity" arises not from some common quality, but due to the transference of the term through a series of objects that share some other quite different feature. Otherwise, Stewart asks, how is it possible for such diverse things as governments and flowers to be accorded the same aesthetic value? For Stewart and other associationists, this was but one arrow in the philosophical quiver and not, as it became in the mid-twentieth century, the *condicio sine qua non* of aesthetics, and prescribed like so much snake oil for a discipline variously diagnosed by self-professed experts far and wide as dreary, dull, confused, or simply a waste of time.[13] Certainly nobody in the eighteenth century could have written on poetry, as Charles Stevenson managed to do, without mentioning a single poem, the reason being that (as he all but admits in the closing paragraph), he is not concerned with poetry at all but with various "meanings" of the phrase "What is a poem?"[14]

Not all work of the period was as dismissive or narrow, although even constructive attempts share this prevailing notion that aesthetics was in need of rescue or resuscitation, an attitude difficult to reconcile with the body of work spanning more than two centuries. The problem was less the dreariness of aesthetics, than the dreariness of philosophers writing on aesthetics, and surely only ideological commitments or ignorance, genuine or willed, can explain some of the claims made. W. E. Kennick is typical when, in the course of uncovering the "mistakes" on which the discipline "rests," he cites Croce, Santayana, and Bell as representative thinkers, and even though his argument is intended

---

[10] William Elton, "Introduction," in *Aesthetics and Language*, 1.

[11] See Jerome Stolnitz, "Notes on Analytic Philosophy and Aesthetics," *British Journal of Aesthetics* 3, 3 (1961): 210–22, and Joseph Margolis, "Recent Work in Aesthetics," *American Philosophical Quarterly* 2, 3 (1965): 182–92.

[12] Maurice Mandelbaum, "Family Resemblances and Generalization Concerning the Arts," *American Philosophical Quarterly* 2, 3 (1965): 219–28.

[13] In addition to the papers in *Aesthetics and Language*, see W. E. Kennick, "Does Traditional Aesthetics Rest on a Mistake?," *Mind, New Series* 67 (1958): 317–34.

[14] Charles L. Stevenson, "On 'What is a Poem?,'" *Philosophical Review* 66, 3 (1957): 329–62.

to undermine the entire discipline, Kennick discusses only the attempt to define art, as if undermining this project were tantamount to undermining the whole. The logical faux pas is amusing enough, but is compounded in the irony that the issue was tangential to what was termed dismissively as "traditional" aesthetics until pushed to center stage by the very analytic forces in whose ranks Kennick himself stands. It is a sad episode in the story that in the Age of Analysis the elegant aesthetic systems of the eighteenth century, the epic character of nineteenth-century criticism, and even the subtle message of Wittgenstein's "Lectures," succumb to an enervated narrowness and want of imagination that, at its lowest points, is deflationary to the point of carping. Even at this low ebb, however, there are patches of bright water, and in the remainder of the chapter and the book I want to trace three important directions that stand out and deserve consideration as influential and substantive contributions to the tradition: Frank Sibley's work on "aesthetic concepts"; Kendall Walton's extension of Wittgenstein's remarks on "seeing as"; and the debate on defining the arts inspired by Morris Weitz's application of Wittgenstein's notion of "family resemblances."

Frank Sibley and a "Feeling" for the Rules

In "Aesthetic Concepts,"[15] Frank Sibley (1923–96) develops Wittgenstein's observation that explanation in aesthetics is distinct, so that to ask why a picture is "balanced" or a musical composition "dramatic" is to raise a certain kind of question and demand a particular sort of answer. Sibley emphasizes that our acquisition and use of aesthetic language is not mysterious or esoteric; we learn it and mastery develops with time and practice, and in conversation people typically move between nonaesthetic and aesthetic terms in a natural and spontaneous way. We come to engage in critical discourse by focusing on specific features of phenomena – sunsets, woods, flowers, and so forth – and we learn to apply terms to them, terms Sibley calls "*aesthetic* concepts or *taste* concepts," distinguishable from the rest of ordinary language because they involve the "exercise of taste, perceptiveness, or sensitivity, ... discrimination or appreciation" (1). It is one thing simply to *describe* the characters and setting of a novel, say, or the palette and subject of a painting, and anybody with "normal eyes, ears, and intelligence" can do so (1). It is quite a different matter, however, to speak of the same works in aesthetic terms: to grasp the *unity* of plot, see the *balance* of composition, hear the *frenzy* of the music, or feel the *power* of a novel. This is a singular species of judgment because it presupposes

15 Frank Sibley, "Aesthetic Concepts," *Philosophical Review* 68, 4 (1959): 421–50; reprinted with minor revisions in *Philosophy Looks at the Arts*, ed. J. Margolis (New York: Scribners, 1962) and subsequently reproduced in Frank Sibley, *Approach to Aesthetics*, ed. John Benson, Betty Redfern, and Jeremy Roxbee Cox (Oxford: Clarendon Press, 2001), 1–23. Unless indicated otherwise, all references are to this paper as it appears in the latter book.

the "ability to notice or see or tell that things have certain qualities" (3) – what Sibley elsewhere calls "aesthetic perception" – and requires command over an appropriate critical vocabulary; this, at least in part, is what it means to have that capacity called "taste."[16]

When this class of concepts is made the object of philosophical investigation, a number of interesting features emerge. First, it appears that the class is surprisingly eclectic. Some of its members, such as *unified, balanced, integrated, lifeless, somber*, and *powerful*, function as aesthetic terms within critical discourse, but also have uses unconnected with taste when employed elsewhere, and others, like *lovely, pretty, beautiful, dainty, graceful*, and *elegant*, work only or predominantly as aesthetic terms whether in critical discourse or not; many terms are seldom or never used as aesthetic terms at all: *red, noisy, brackish, clammy, square*, and so on. Like Wittgenstein, Sibley emphasizes that in employing aesthetic concepts "we are often making and using metaphors," and some words "*have come* to be aesthetic through metaphorical transference" – *dynamic, melancholy, balanced*, and *tightly knit*, for example – although because they are not "standard vocabulary" in critical discourse it might be more accurate to call them "quasimetaphorical." Many other terms, by contrast, are not metaphorical at all because their only or primary use is aesthetic and they lack any nonaesthetic sense to which a metaphorical use could have been transferred.

Second, and more fundamentally, Sibley observes that although some judgments employ aesthetic terms that refer to other such terms – a work "graceful in the smooth flow of its lines," for instance – more often that not they are employed without any further reference to taste, as in "delicate because of its pastel shades and curving lines." In practice, it is sometimes difficult to locate the nonaesthetic feature to which the aesthetic term refers, and the taste of a fine critic is often required to recognize it. In principle, however, it is always possible to find such a feature and thus explain the use of aesthetic terms by reference to something nonaesthetic and from which they are "emergent" or "dependent," or in respect to which they form a "*Gestalt*."[17] For

aesthetic terms always ultimately apply because of, and aesthetic qualities always ultimately depend upon, the presence of features which, like curving or angular lines, colour contrasts, placing of masses, or speed of movement, are visible, audible, or otherwise discernible without any exercise of taste or sensibility. (3)

What comes as a surprise, however, is that although aesthetic qualities always refer to nonaesthetic features, it does not follow that nonaesthetic features serve as "conditions" for the application of aesthetic terms. "Aesthetic or taste concepts," Sibley urges, "are not in this respect condition-governed at all" (4). We expect to be able to state the necessary and sufficient conditions of

---

[16] See Frank Sibley, "Aesthetic and Non-Aesthetic" (1965), in *Approach to Aesthetics*, 33–51, pp. 34–5.
[17] See Sibley, "Aesthetic and Non-Aesthetic," 35–7.

"square" (four equal sides and four right angles), and even with terms such as *intelligent* it is possible to list features, if not exhaustively, then at least sufficient "to ensure or warrant the application of that term" (4): the ability to grasp and follow instructions, master facts and weigh evidence, solve mathematical problems, and so forth. It is thus tempting to think the same of aesthetic concepts, and although it is often possible to specify features that *exclude* the use of a term – a painting of gray and pale blue lines can hardly be "gaudy" – or even state characteristics typical of an object described in aesthetic terms – a "delicate" vase will tend to be slim, light, and lack intense color – it is impossible to state the nonaesthetic features that *rule a term in*. For "things may be described to us in non-aesthetic terms as fully as we please," Sibley writes, "but we are not thereby put in a position of having to admit (or being able to deny) that they are delicate or graceful or garish or exquisitely balanced" (5).

Sibley, then, makes much the same point as Wittgenstein when he distinguishes the automatic application of rules learned by rote from their critical interpretation and employment in the course of aesthetic judgment. Wittgenstein, to recall, speaks in this context of having a "feeling" for the rules, which, in Sibley's vocabulary, is equivalent to the aesthetic perception that enables an individual to use aesthetic concepts with taste or discrimination, an activity quite different from simply applying or following rules. In addition, Sibley raises a further question that Wittgenstein passes over, namely, "if we are not following rules and there are no conditions to appeal to, how are we to know when they [aesthetic concepts] are applicable?" (13). One possibility is to look back to Hutcheson and, considering taste as an internal sense, compare its exercise with that of the external senses: we "look and see" that something is delicate in much the same way we "look and see" that the book is red. There are obvious differences in the case of taste that preclude this answer however, because, as Sibley points out, it is possible to *see* aesthetic features of an object but fail to *discern* and thus appreciate them. There is, moreover, a difference in the way judgments that employ aesthetic concepts are supported; the critic justifies his judgment by using various tropes in order to "mention" and "point out" (15) the aesthetic and nonaesthetic qualities of the object and relation between them: similes and metaphors, for instance; contrasts, comparisons, and repetition; tone of voice, expressions, nods, looks, and gestures (18ff.). This might sound like a woolly alternative to the clean application of rules, but, Sibley urges, this simply is the way in which aesthetic concepts are acquired and used, and how the activity of "criticism" proceeds.

Kendall Walton and "Seeing As"

In his widely anthologized article "Categories of Art,"[18] Kendall Walton (1939–) takes up Sibley's distinction between aesthetic and nonaesthetic concepts, but

---

[18] Kendall Walton, "Categories of Art," *Philosophical Review* 79, 3 (1970): 334–67. All references in the text are to this article.

in order to reject one of the conclusions that follows from it, namely, that criticism should focus on works of art and purge itself of excursions into extraneous matters "outside" – to use the language of Fry and Bell – the work. Walton takes the burden of his argument to show that far from being extraneous, some facts about the origins of works have an "*essential* role in criticism" because "aesthetic judgments rest on them in an absolutely fundamental way" (337). This is because the "correct" perception of the aesthetic properties a work of art displays is determined at least in part by "historical facts about the artist's intention and/or his society"; thus, even the most thorough examination of a given work will not in itself reveal the properties that make it art (363–4). Walton supports this contention by following Sibley's proposal that aesthetic properties emerge from their nonaesthetic counterparts, but argues further that what constitute the aesthetic properties of a work depends not on nonaesthetic properties per se, but on which of them are "standard," "variable," or "contra-standard." A property is "standard," Walton explains, when it identifies the work of art as belonging to a particular category and thus tells us what kind of work it is; a property is "variable" when it is irrelevant to all the categories in which the work is perceived and thus determines what the work represents; a property, finally, is "contra-standard" when it disqualifies the work as belonging to the categories under which it is perceived.

In order for this division to make sense, Walton relies on Wittgenstein's treatment of "seeing as," found primarily in the second part of the *Investigations*. The important component for Sibley's purposes is the insight that a given object can undergo a "change of aspect," a *Gestalt* shift, through which a different pattern emerges. The most dramatic example, which Wittgenstein borrows from the Polish psychologist Joseph Jastrow, is the now-famous image of the "Duck/Rabbit" (see Fig. 6).[19] Seeing this "picture object" (as Wittgenstein calls it) either "as a duck" or "as a rabbit" is not simply a matter of recognizing some property in it – that would be a "momentary occurrence," as Walton points out – but of perceiving some quality in a "continuous state which may last for a short or long time" (341). This is precisely what we do when looking at art, Walton contends, effectively categorizing a different work according to some recognized pattern: a painting looks to be in style of Impressionism, or a composition sounds Brahmsian. Some ways of seeing necessarily exclude others – one cannot simultaneously see the duck-rabbit as a duck *and* a rabbit or a

---

[19] As the line accompanying Jastrow's acknowledgment makes clear, he models his Duck/Rabbit figure on a cartoon originally published in *Harper's Weekly* (November 19, 1892, 1114), which was based in turn on one that had appeared earlier the same year in *Fliegende Blätter* (October 23, 1892, 147), a German humor magazine published in Munich. Wittgenstein's citation (PI, 194) is to Jastrow's *Fact and Fable in Psychology* (Boston: Houghton Mifflin, 1900). For a catalogue of the published variants of the figure, see Peter Brugger, "One Hundred Years of an Ambiguous Figure: Happy Birthday, Duck/Rabbit!" *Perceptual and Motor Skills* 89 (1999): 973–7.

Fɪɢ. 20.—Do you see a duck or a rabbit, or either? (From Harper's Weekly, originally in Fliegende Blätter.)

FIGURE 6. "Duck/Rabbit," from Joseph Jastrow, "The Mind's Eye," *Popular Science Monthly* 54 (1899): 299–312. Image courtesy of Special Collections Research Center, Earl Gregg Swem Library, College of William & Mary.

photograph as a still *and* part of a film – and precisely how it is seen depends on extraneous and often contingent factors: familiarity with genres, the opinions of others with which one happens to be acquainted, the particular setting in which the work is viewed, and so on. On the face of it, Walton makes these properties sound like features of the object, even if only in the weak sense of Gerard and Alison's associationism, but if the division among standard, variable, and contrastandard has merit, it lies on the side of the subject and the "psychological thesis" that what a work of art "is" depends on which features belong to a perceptually distinguishable category *"for a particular person on a particular occasion"* (340).

The fruits of Walton's labor are illustrated most obviously in the case of representation where works of art "look like" things: people, buildings, flowers, bowls of fruit, fish stalls, and the like. There must be *some* resemblance between the copy and the object – though it need not be perfect – but even when slight, there are clearly elements the viewer brackets out and ignores: a portrait that "looks like" the sitter ignores the obvious fact that the former is a flat canvas with paint and the latter a living human being. The viewer still "sees" a resemblance, however – as one "sees" a duck or a rabbit – precisely because the experience is tied to categories under which the art is perceived. This is because, in Walton's terminology, its properties as a painting are standard and being taken for granted they do not count for or against the degree of resemblance between the portrait and the sitter. Other qualities, by contrast, are variable – the colors and shapes on the surface, say – and although irrelevant to it being a painting, they are crucial to it being a good portrait and, as we say, catching a likeness. The same thought can be applied to other works of art as well: a statue of marble, whitish in color, motionless, and consisting only of a head and shoulders; a figure with a square head in a cubist painting, or drawings in black and white. All these features are standard for the genres in question and thus overlooked aesthetically, while the shape of the marble or the color of the paint are variable and therefore relevant to the issue of resemblance. More dramatically, we might compare a still photograph of a high jumper who is frozen in midair as a standard feature of static images, but "seen as" being in motion precisely because the lack of motion is standard and therefore perceptually irrelevant.

In addition to providing a rich description of aesthetic experience in this way, Walton shows how his division might enlighten other issues close to the aesthetician's heart. The distinction between standard and variable features explains, for example, the different effects a work of art has on an audience. Walton imagines a society with a style of art called "guernicas," like relief maps of mountainous terrain or three-dimensional versions in the style of Picasso's *Guernica* (Fig. 7), commissioned by the Republican government of Spain to bring attention to the bombing of the city in April 1937 by German and Italian warplanes at the behest of Nationalist forces. The flatness of the work for us is a standard feature of it being a "painting," and as is fitting to the scene depicted, it strikes the audience as shocking, violent, and dynamic due to the dramatic way Picasso portrays the figures, a variable feature of the painting to which its flatness is irrelevant. In the imagined society, by contrast, that same feature is variable, and "guernicas" being a class of art, the flatness of the work would make *Guernica* cold, serene, and bland precisely because being in bas-relief is standard and the dramatic effect of the figures would be lost. Being flat and thus two-dimensional, *Guernica* would not qualify as a "guernica" at all.

In addition, Walton's class of contrastandard features has the interesting result of explaining why works might shock or upset an audience. Features that do not belong to a category under which a work falls stand out and even obscure the variable properties that are the source of the work's value.[20] A statue that moves, for example, invariably elicits screams from the viewer – a fact long-exploited by street performers – as a three-dimensional object protruding from a canvas tends to strike the unprepared spectator as being out of place. Similarly, monochromatic canvases are disturbing because we see them as paintings while they contravene standard features of that genre; that

[20] Paul Ziff makes much the same point earlier in "The Task of Defining a Work of Art," *Philosophical Review* 62, 1 (1953): 58–78, p. 63–4.

FIGURE 7. Pablo Picasso, *Guernica*, 1967, oil on canvas, 137½ × 305½ in. Madrid: Museo Reina Sofia. Image: The Art Archive at Art Resource, New York. © 2012 Estate of Pablo Picasso Artists Rights Society (ARS), New York.

reaction is not generated by the same color on the wall of one's bedroom, where monochrome colors are the norm. The boundaries between genres can shift – a category can expand in order to accommodate innovations – or the spectator can simply switch categories to appreciate the aesthetic value of what is otherwise confusing: a statue becomes a "kinetic sculpture," a three-dimensional painting a "collage." As Walton notes, however, the most disturbing objects are those that display only slight contrastandard features and prevent viewers from moving easily to another category, forcing them instead to regard the change in terms of expectations circumscribed by the original category: a statue with a twitching ear is more disturbing than one with all its limbs in motion. For this reason, a Wagner opera is more shocking than the radical atonality of Debussy or Schoenberg because the latter demands the listener perceive the music as a new genre entirely with its own standard and variable features, while the former is sufficiently tonal to remain classical and the challenge becomes to hear its contrastandard features against the background of Beethoven and Brahms.

One question that does arise for Walton – as it did for Sibley – is precisely how a spectator can ever determine which properties a given work really displays and thus be sure that the "correct" category is operative. An obvious solution is to say that all judgments are category relative and, apparent differences notwithstanding, ultimately compatible; incompatibility would then be simply a matter of miscategorization. As Walton points out, however, this conforms neither to critical practice nor to peoples' intuitions about art. To recall Hume, mountains and molehills are quite different and some judgments better than others. In some, or many cases, it is correct to perceive a work in one category but incorrect to perceive it in another. To say that "Beethoven's *Pathétique* is percussive, or that a Roman bust looks like a unicolored, immobile man

severed at the chest, is simply wrong" (356). As with Sibley's suggestion that
we learn aesthetic categories through the expressions, nods, and gestures of
the qualified critic, and very much in the spirit of Wittgenstein's "Lectures,"
Walton, too, emphasizes that no clear procedure exists for solving the problem
entirely, although there are various circumstances that "count toward" correct categorization: a large number of certain standard features will move a
work into one category rather than another, for instance; one category might
make the work more interesting or enjoyable; the artist's intention might be
given weight; and that a category is well established and recognized as such
in a given society will raise it above others. These too might seem vague, but
some criteria are required to know what aesthetic properties a work contains
and – as Walton concludes – they are not simply aids to aesthetic appreciation,
but play a central role and without them we would not be able to see a work as
the work it is. As thinkers of the Age of Taste emphasized long before, we must
learn to see correctly, not only by immersing ourselves in the work, but also by
actively training ourselves to see what was there all along. Besides, attempting
to specify criteria more strictly would be to "legislate gratuitously," Walton
observes, which would be to clean up unduly a process that is inherently messy:
the "intuitions and precedents we have to go on are highly variable and often
confused," he writes, and works are "fascinating precisely because of shifts
between equally permissible ways of perceiving them" (362).

"Family Resemblances" and Defining the Arts

Whether criteria can be specified for correctly "applying" aesthetic concepts
or "perceiving" aesthetic properties is a question that arises for Sibley and
Walton at the conclusion of the views they develop; in another form the same
question sets the terms of a debate, that continues to this day, namely, whether
"art" or the "arts" can be defined. Philosophical investigation into the nature
and origin of the arts is not peculiar to the Age of Analysis, though for earlier writers it arose either as one part of their more general inquiry into aesthetic matters, or with respect to specific genres: the nature of painting in
Hogarth and Reynolds, for example, or poetry for the Romantics. The debate
that ensued in the latter half of the mid-twentieth century differs, however, in
focusing primarily on the concept of "art" and attempting to discover (or deny
the existence of) its "true definition." The issue is raised in its most influential
form by Morris Weitz (1916–81) in "The Role of Theory in Aesthetics," a first
sally in what proved a long and protracted war over whether one might discover a set of necessary and sufficient conditions or properties to distinguish
art "from everything else."[21] In the spirit of Wittgenstein, Weitz responds with

---

[21] Morris Weitz, "The Role of Theory in Aesthetics," *Journal of Aesthetics and Art Criticism* 15, 1
(1956): 27–35. All references in the text are to this article. See also Ziff, "The Task of Defining
a Work of Art."

a resounding no, for "theory" in the "requisite classical sense" is *"never* forth-coming in aesthetics" (27). Consider the formalism of Fry and Bell, he urges, where the "essence of painting, they maintain," is to be found in the

plastic elements in relation. Its defining property is significant form, i.e., certain combinations of lines, colors, shapes, volumes ... which evoke a unique response to such combinations. ... The nature of art, what it *really* is, so there theory goes, is a unique combination of certain elements (the specifiable plastic ones) in their relations. Anything which is art is an instance of significant form; and anything which is not art has no such form. (28)

One might be hard-pressed to find quite this presentation of formalism in either Fry or even Bell, and in general Weitz rather oversimplifies matters in suggesting that many movements in aesthetics are really engaged in no other business than defining the properties of art or saying what art "really is." Nevertheless, his contention is clear: that the history of aesthetics can be plausibly read, as Ruskin had urged earlier in his summary dismissal of theories of beauty (MP II, 66–75), in terms of competing, conflicting, and even contradictory views, each claiming completion but haphazardly omitting what others incorporate, rendering them a collection of "circular, incomplete, untestable, pseudo-factual, disguised proposals to change the meanings of concepts" (30). This failure is due not to the complicated nature of the explanandum, but arises from a fundamental misconception of "art" and, specifically, the false assumption that it is logically permissible to define the concept in terms of necessary and sufficient conditions. Weitz claims not to be rejecting "theory" per se, although he finally delegates it the lowly task of recognizing or praising an object, the sole possible meaning of "work of art"and the only realistic outcome if one follows his recommendation to reject the question "what is art?" in favor of asking what "sort of concept" "art" might be (30).

As we have seen, Wittgenstein had already achieved a good deal from moving in that direction, although without the "Lectures" Weitz could hardly have been aware of this fact, and he looks instead to those sections of the *Investigations* (§65–75) where Wittgenstein explores the metaphor of "games" to emphasize that language is composed of various interconnected activities or ways of using words. Crucial for Weitz's purposes is the idea that these activities "do not have one thing common which makes us use the same word for all, – but that they are *related* to one another in many different ways" in virtue of which "we call them language" (PI §65). "Consider for example the proceedings we call 'games,'" Wittgenstein writes,

I mean board-games, card-games, ball-games, Olympic games, and so on. What is common to them all? – Don't say: "There *must* be something common, or they would not be called 'games'" – but *look and see* whether there is anything common to all. – For if you look at them you will not see something that is common to *all*, but similarities, relationships, and a whole series of them at that. And the result of this examination is: we see a complicated network of similarities overlapping and criss-crossing: sometimes overall similarities, sometimes similarities of detail. (PI §66)

There is no "better expression to characterize these similarities," Wittgenstein observes, than "'family resemblances'; for the various resemblances between members of a family: build, features, colour of eyes, gait, temperament, etc. etc. overlap and criss-cross in the same way. – And I shall say: 'games' form a family" (PI §67). Or, as Weitz expresses the idea, with the exception of logic and mathematics where concepts are "closed" because "constructed and completely defined," the otherwise "empirically-descriptive and normative concepts" of natural language are "open," that is, their "conditions of application are emendable and corrigible": consider how the meaning of *gay*, *marriage*, and *Pluto* have changed. Some parties, of course, are motivated by extralinguistic interests and attempt to close such terms by defining them in pursuit of their own ends, but change would be impossible were they closed artificially and arbitrarily by stipulating what they "really" mean.

The denial that concepts change is just the error at the heart of "aesthetic theory," Weitz contends, which attempts to close "art" when the concept is an open one. Like games, there is no single feature that all art has in common and while aestheticians lay down conditions that purport to show that one manifestation is "similar" to another, they routinely fail to specify the "necessary and sufficient conditions of application of the concept" (32). The same is true of particular "subconcepts" that fall under "art." Weitz acknowledges that some subconcepts are closed: "Greek tragedy," "painting of the Quattrocentro," or "the Gothic novel" are circumscribed and historically specific, and while one can produce a work in the style of these genres, it is impossible to produce a work that could be properly classified as falling under them. This is not true of "tragedy," "painting," or "the novel." To take the latter as an example, whether some work such as Virginia Woolf's *To the Lighthouse* or James Joyce's *Finnegan's Wake* count as novels when they appear is not decided by checking them against a definition, but involves that one "*look and see*" what they have in common with their predecessors and thus extend "the novel" – as was in fact done – to cover the new cases. The transition need not be smooth, and the question of extension is often disputed territory with attempts to defend the old concept by extracting conditions drawn from extant and accepted examples. This rarely works, however, not least because if successful it would effectively end the process of creativity that is at the root of all art.

Weitz's argument might elicit a variety of critical responses,[22] but the most provocative and philosophically astute one is probably that of Mandelbaum, who takes issue explicitly with Weitz's central thesis against *aesthetic theory*. In "Family Resemblances and Generalization Concerning the Arts" (1965), Mandelbaum observes that although Weitz relies heavily on the notion of family resemblances, he fails to define the concept adequately. The idea seems plausible when illustrated with concrete examples (as does Wittgenstein at

---

[22] See Joseph Margolis, "Mr. Weitz and the Definition of Art," *Philosophical Studies* 9, 5/6 (1958): 88–95.

PI §66 quoted earlier), but in Weitz's appropriation of the doctrine it fails to show "why a common name, such as 'game,' is in all cases applied or withheld" (220). Fortune-telling, for example, resembles solitaire (cards are shuffled, arranged in piles face-up and face-down) and fighting looks a great deal like wrestling (both consist of an angry struggle with one party seeking submission from the other), but neither fortune-telling nor fighting are "games" in the requisite sense of the term. Designating an activity as a game, then, Mandelbaum concludes, is "not merely a matter of noting a number of specific resemblances between it and other activities which we denote as games, but involves something further" (220).

This "something further" becomes clear if we distinguish the literal meaning of "family resemblance" – on which Wittgenstein and Weitz focus – from its metaphorical counterpart, in which case it becomes evident that families do have an "essential" feature, namely, a common ancestry, a "nonexhibited feature" they share with one another. Weitz, at least (Mandelbaum finds in the original German evidence that Wittgenstein had recognized and presupposed the fact), simply assumes that resemblances must be manifest and visible, but on the analogy of ancestry, games can also been seen to have a shared "genetic" component, a nonvisible "relational attribute" to be sure, but a likely candidate for the elusive "essence," the existence of which Weitz denies: the activities or intentions of the artist, for example; being a mode of communication or, as Sigmund Freud argues, a species of "wish-fulfillment."[23] Mandelbaum concludes by suggesting that Weitz's distinction between open and closed concepts is nugatory because it only has explanatory power in extreme cases: the work of Woolf and Joyce stood at the very limits of "the novel," but the vast majority of new work falls under the category of what Weitz calls "paradigm" or "normal" cases – a term borrowed felicitously from Thomas Kuhn's not unrelated observations on the history of science – and absorbed easily into the genre without any extension of the concept.[24] It is also possible to define features of an art form without closing the concept and thus excluding work that apparently deviates from it, as long as one focuses on the appropriate relational attribute. Photography, for example, a partly mechanical operation that seems to contravene many features traditionally associated with "art," can be readily brought under that classification because it arises from the similar interests and is evaluated in the same ways as other arts.[25]

---

[23] See Sigmund Freud, *Introductory Lectures on Psychoanalysis: The Standard Edition* (delivered 1915–17), trans. James Strachey (New York: W. W. Norton, 1989 [1966]), Lectures XIV and XXIII.

[24] See Thomas Kuhn, *The Structure of Scientific Revolutions* (Chicago: University of Chicago Press, 1962).

[25] See also George Dickie, *Art and the Aesthetic: An Institutional Analysis* (Ithaca, NY: Cornell University Press, 1974), who questions whether the open/closed distinction can be sustained (Dickie calls it the "generalization argument") given that species (subconcepts of "art") can remain open while the genus "art" is closed. "Tragedies," for example, Dickie contends, "may

Although he does not address himself explicitly to the question of defining "art," Arthur Danto takes up the related theme of how the concept of art is extended to reflect change and accommodate new artistic practices.[26] Rather than Weitz, however, who speaks genteelly of "enlarging" the set of conditions for applying the concept to a new case, Danto speaks more violently the language of revolution and, in the wake of Kuhn, compares such radical change to episodes of scientific change. "One might," he writes in "The Artworld,"

... compare certain episodes in the history of art as not dissimilar to certain episodes in the history of science, where conceptual revolution is being effected and where refusal to countenance certain facts, while in part due to prejudice, inertia, and self-interest, is due also to the fact that a well-established, or at least widely credited theory is being threatened in such a way that all coherence goes. (573)

The particular episode on which Danto concentrates is that heralded by the advent of "Post-Impressionism," the term, to recall, coined by Fry in 1910 to characterize the likes of Cézanne, Gaugin, and Van Gogh, who turned in their work from the "truth" of perceptual impressions to the emotional significance of objects in themselves; they aimed, in Fry's words, "not at illusion but reality" (574). The revolution they effected, as Danto characterizes Fry's insight about the art these painters produced, amounts to a "victory in ontology," that is, effectively severing art from the constraints of representation (mimesis) on one side and pure fiction (idealism) on the other, to occupy a "freshly opened area between real objects and real facsimiles of real objects" (574). A picture such as Van Gogh's *Potato Eaters*, for example, is then neither a copy nor mere fantasy – too distorted for the former, too realistic for the latter – but at once a "nonfacsimile" of real-life potato eaters. The picture is real, however, and has every right to be called and seen as "art."

Danto's insight is not that there is change in the history of art or that new work always has to be enfranchised, but that the specific revolution effected by Post-Impressionism is of a different order. On the one hand, it ushers in a new theory of art. "Mimetic theory," reaching from the Ancients to the Impressionists, is replaced by a "reality theory" in which art is no longer regarded as a less-real copy of the world it imitates, but seen as bringing something new and substantial into existence. On the other hand, art is not restricted to arousing pleasure

not have any characteristics in common which would distinguish them from, say, comedies within the domain of art, but it may be that there are common characteristics that works of art have which distinguish them as nonart" (22).

[26] The core of his argument is contained in Arthur C. Danto, "The Artworld," *Journal of Philosophy* 61, 19 (1964): 571–84, expanded later in *The Transfiguration of the Commonplace: A Philosophy of Art* (Cambridge, MA: Harvard University Press, 1981) (TCP). Unless indicated (TC) all references are to "The Artworld." It might be noted that while Danto does not propose a "definition" of "art" as such, he accepts the idea that all objects of art have something in common even though, *á la* Mandelbaum, not in terms of features available through perception.

FIGURE 8. Claude Monet, *Haystacks (Effect of Snow and Sun)*, 1891, oil on canvas, 25¾ × 36¼ in. H. O. Havemeyer Collection, Bequest of Mrs. H. O. Havemeyer, 1929 (29.11.109). The Metropolitan Museum of Art, New York. Image © The Metropolitan Museum of Art. Image: Art Resource, New York.

due to some fit (however complex the mechanism) between a subject and the object viewed, but is appreciated intellectually, for which, concomitantly, the spectator requires knowledge of some theory; this is what takes an object "up into the world of art, and keeps it from collapsing into the real object which it is" (581). These "theories of art" compose what Danto calls the "artworld" and without it "modern" art would be impossible. For in its representational mode, art always depicts objects that look like something, and whether images on canvas or tangible elements of a landscaped estate, they are instantly recognizable as phenomena reconstructed out of elements drawn from the world: the limits of art coincide with Locke's characterization of mind as capable of creating an almost infinite variety of new ideas by repeating, comparing, and combining the materials already derived from experience. *Haystacks (Effect of Snow and Sun)* (Fig. 8), for example, one of Claude Monet's Haystack series, unnatural though it looks, remains a representation of some recognizable thing, albeit refracted through the effects of light and color. Robert Rauschenberg's *Bed* (Fig. 9), by contrast, is not a representation at all, but irrefutably a work of art.

The question Danto raises, then, is why Rauschenberg's *Bed* or any other similarly iconic work of modern art – Andy Warhol's *Brillo Box*, or Marcel Duchamp's *Fountain* – is a work of art that properly hangs on a wall or stands

FIGURE 9. Robert Rauschenberg, *Bed*, 1955, combine painting: oil and pencil on pillow, quilt and sheet on wood supports, 6 ft. 3¼ in. × 31½ × 8 in. Gift of Leo Castelli in honor of Alfred H. Barr Jr. The Museum of Modern Art, New York. Image © The Museum of Modern Art/Licensed by SCALA Art Resource, New York. © VAGA, New York.

on some museum floor. After all, it is an actual bed (fabricated as such) and a real object (rather than a representation), and yet a work of art (created as such with the addition of paint and pencil). How, then, can we see it as art when it falls outside the familiar mode of imitation and fails to meet criteria of skill and creativity that are otherwise visible in works of "art" (surely anyone, as people are want to say, could have made it)? Or in the parlance of post-Wittgensteinian philosophy, what sort of language game do we have to recognize and master? Danto's answer is to make explicit what is involved logically in the reality theory of art and show to what one is committed conceptually when one says "Rauschenberg's *Bed* is a work of art," as opposed to saying "Rauschenberg's *Bed* is a bed." Statements of the first sort involve a special use of the copula "is," not the "is" of identity ("This is me"), predication ("That is red"), existence ("I am," that is, "I exist"), or identity ("That man is English"), but the "*is of artistic identification*": when we use the copula in this sense in statements of the form "a is b," Danto explains, the "*a* stands for some property of, or physical part of, an object; and ... it is a necessary condition for something to be an artwork that some part or property of it be designable by the subject of a sentence that employs this special is" (577). Mastering this game involves grasping what constitutes the object as art, and failing to do so leaves a viewer bemused and in the presence of a "bed with streaks of housepaint on it." Consider, by way of example, Danto urges, two indiscernible works of art, each consisting of a black, horizontal line on a white background, equally large in each dimension and element.

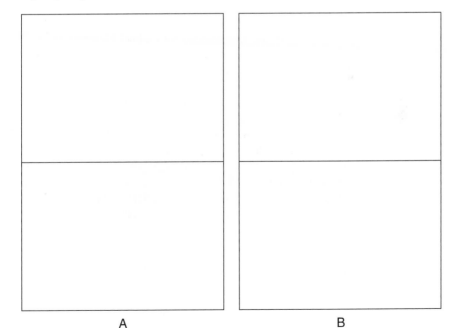

A   B

"A" is titled *Newton's First Law* and "B" *Newton's Third Law*, and as such, they are identified artistically in very different ways, because they occupy alternative and mutually exclusive artworlds that allow or oblige the viewer to see them as one thing rather than another. Within these identifications there are alternative ways to "see" the picture as art. In the first, the middle line is an edge, so the top and bottom part become two masses butting up against each other or alternatively one mass jutting up or down into empty space. In the second case, by contrast, the line moves through space, so that there are not masses at all and the line can be seen to go beyond the edges of the picture. We could add to the gallery a third identical picture called simply "No. 7," and when the artist is called upon to explain it he says that it is simply black and white paint. It would be a mistake, however, to think that the artist is in the same position as the viewer who takes Rauschenberg's *Bed* as "a bed with streaks of housepaint on it." In fact, the artist has "returned to the physicality of paint through an atmosphere compounded of artistic theories and history of recent and remote painting, elements of which he is trying to refine out of his own work; and as a consequence," Danto concludes, "his work belongs in the atmosphere and is part of this history" (579). His work, that is, and his and the viewer's understanding of that work, requires an artworld.

In the preface to *The Transfiguration of the Common Place*, Danto recognizes Dickie (along with Richard Sclafani) for having honored his article "The Artworld" (misunderstood, he claims, at the time) a "modest fame," saving it from otherwise slumbering "in a back number issue of the sepulchral *Journal of Philosophy*." He also acknowledges those who had used his ideas to "erect something called the Institutional Theory of Art," although he is careful to emphasize how that "theory itself is quite alien to anything I believe" (TC, vii). This theory is now associated primarily with Dickie, developed in a number of papers in the 1960s and 1970s and worked up into a whole to compose the first chapter of *Art and The Aesthetic: An Institutional Analysis*.[27] Dickie presents this theory as an alternative to the "psychologistic" view of those who argue that a particular "state of mind" is required for the aesthetic features of an object to become accessible, his own theory concentrating attention "on the practices and conventions used in presenting certain aspects of works of art to their audiences and argues that the presentational conventions locate or isolate the aesthetic objects (features) of works of art" (12). The institutional theory is independent of Dickie's critique of the "aesthetic attitude" – that "distance" and "disinterested" do not name any particular state of mind and amount to synonyms for "being attentive"[28] – and depends more on combining

[27] In Dickie, *Art and the Aesthetic*, 19–52. Unless noted otherwise, all references in what follows are to this book.
[28] George Dickie, "The Myth of the Aesthetic Attitude," *American Philosophical Quarterly* 1, 1 (1964): 56–65. This and other papers on the same theme are incorporated into *Art and the Aesthetic*, chs. 4 and 5.

Mandelbaum's claim that objects are art in virtue of nonexhibited features with Danto's idea that some context – the artworld – is required for an object to be enfranchised as art. In Dickie's hands, these become the "relational properties" of "artifactuality" and the "institutional nature of art," respectively.

Dickie argues for the first of these properties by taking issue with what he identifies as the second of Weitz's two arguments (the other being "the generalization argument"), "the classification argument" and, specifically, the rather startling conclusion that Weitz draws from it to the effect that a work of art need not be an artifact in order to be so called. Because there are no necessary and sufficient conditions definitive of something being classified "art" – it is, after all, an open concept – it is quite conceivable that any one of a range of criteria (which, according to Weitz is very large) is dispensable, "even the one which has traditionally been taken to be basic," namely, that it is the result of "human skill, ingenuity, and imagination, which embodies in its sensuous, public medium – stone, wood, sounds, words, etc. – certain distinguishable elements and relations." One might say, then, "This piece of driftwood is a lovely piece of sculpture," which, being a perfectly intelligible utterance, seems to show that certain nonartifacts can be works of art, in this case "sculpture."[29] Dickie does not disagree with Weitz's distinction between the evaluative and descriptive meanings of "work of art," but, drawing on an argument and terminology developed by Sclafani,[30] proposes a third meaning of this phrase that makes explicit the fact that even calling driftwood a sculpture presupposes a paradigm case with which the nonartifact shares certain features: *Driftwood Sculpture* (Fig. 10) *resembles* Constantin Brancusi's *Bird in Space* (Fig. 11) and only in virtue of that relationship could it be categorized as art.

"Work of art," then, can have a classificatory or primary sense as in "Bird in Space is a work of art (and is an artifact)"; a derivative or secondary sense as in "This piece of driftwood is art (even though there is no artifactuality involved)"; or an evaluative sense, as when we use it as an honorific in "Sally's cake is a work of art." We speak often in this latter way to express the view that some object has valuable qualities, and sometimes combine the evaluative with the classificatory – "This Rembrandt is a work of art" – though the latter (evaluative) meaning is redundant. The crucial case, however, and one that establishes the point of artifactuality being a necessary and sufficient condition for something to be "art," is that when we say "This piece of driftwood is a lovely piece of sculpture" we are using *sculpture* in a derivative or secondary sense, and the epithet "work of art" is only applied because it resembles some

---

[29] Weitz, "The Role of Theory in Aesthetics," 33. As Sclafani observes (see n. 30), Ziff had already made a similar point using Poussin's *Rape of the Sabine Women* and a rock naturally shaped like a reclining woman. See "The Task of Defining a Work of Art," 65–6.

[30] Richard Sclafani, "'Art' and Artifactuality," *Southwestern Journal of Philosophy* I (1970): 103–10. Sclafani (108–9) actually traces the "primary" sense of the term *sculpture* to a passage in Dewey's *Art and Experience*.

FIGURE 10. Timothy M. Costelloe and Amy E. Gernon, *Driftwood Sculpture*. Photo: Timothy M. Costelloe.

paradigm that is an artifact, and therefore "art" in the classificatory or primary sense.

The second "relational property" is derived from Danto, who, although he "does not attempt to formulate a definition," as Dickie acknowledges, still

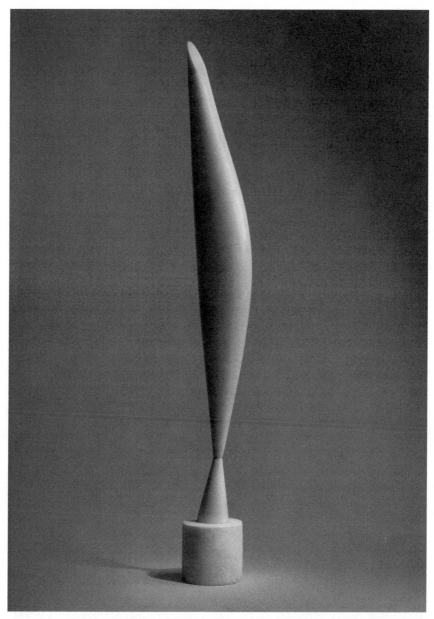

FIGURE 11. Constantin Brancusi, *Bird in Space*, 1923. Marble, (with base) H. 56¾ D. 6½ in. Bequest of Florence M. Schoenborn, 1995 (1996.403.7ab). The Metropolitan Museum of Art, New York. Image © The Metropolitan Museum of Art. Image: Art Resource, New York. © 2012 Artists Rights Society (ARS), New York, ADAGP, Paris.

points the "direction that must be taken by an attempt to define 'art'" (28; see
29n9). Dickie follows Danto by using "artworld" as content to fill Mandelbaum's "nonexhibited feature" with a "rich structure in which particular works
of art are embedded: ... *the institutional nature of art*" (29). Danto's "artworld,"
to recall, indicates the collection of theories under which art is produced,
knowledge of which the viewer requires to appreciate that Rauschenberg's
Bed and Warhol's *Brillo Boxes* are in fact *art*. Though he is reluctant to provide
what he calls a "definition," Dickie explicitly expands the scope of the term to
include the "broad social institution in which works of art have their place"
(31), or that "bundle of systems" that constitute the world of theater, painting,
sculpture, literature, and music (33). Even more specifically, Dickie conceives
the artworld as a set of established practices and social arrangements organized in a more or less formal way. "The core of personnel of the artworld," he
explains,

is a loosely organized, but nevertheless related, set of persons including artists
(understood to refer to painters, writers, composers), producers, museum directors,
museum-goers, theater-goers, reporters for newspapers, critics for publications of all
sorts, art historians, art theorists, philosophers of art, and others. These are the people who keep the artworld working and thereby provide for its continuing existence.
(35–6)

Like many institutions, the artworld and the practices it contains are largely
invisible – it is, after all, a nonexhibited feature – and the various personnel
that occupy and constitute its institutional space are largely taken for granted.
Only when limit cases are presented – painted beds, cans of soup, urinals, and
the like – which subvert and call into question the very idea of art, does its
"institutional essence" become visible, namely, of conferring the status of "art"
on otherwise nonart objects. This is a social process through which any object
must pass, analogous in Dickie's mind to the way legal status is conferred on an
object by setting it within a complex of legal practices and systems of law. An
object must first be raised to "candidacy," a status conferred by an individual or
set of individuals, a "presentation group" with requisite status and power. The
candidate object must then be appreciated, have its qualities seen as valuable
by "goers." This is quite independent, it might be noted, of whether the object
is "good" or "bad," which is beside the point for it becoming and being "art,"
a status obtained from being placed in art galleries, reviewed in art magazines,
sold for large sums of money, and so on.

    The appeal of Dickie's theory lies in the way it explains how otherwise mun-
dane objects produced without any apparent skill or ingenuity can be as highly
regarded (in some circles at least) as other artifacts that are obviously beautiful and technically complex. It is also explains why it is that Duchamp could
exhibit a urinal as art, while the plumbing supplies salesman who "spreads his
wares before us" could not:

"Placing before" and "conferring the status for appreciation" are very different notions, and this difference can be brought out by comparing the salesman's action with the superficially similar act of Duchamp in entering a urinal which he christened Fountain. ... The difference is that Duchamp's action took place with the institutional setting of the artworld and the plumbing salesman's action took place outside of it. (38)

Dickie's theory is an innovative extension of Mandelbaum and Danto to explain in largely sociological terms much about modern art that many casual observers find otherwise perplexing. Its major drawback, however, is effectively to ignore all those complex philosophical questions that the appeal to institutions leaves untouched. It might account for the presence of urinals in museums of art, but is less satisfying when it comes to a painting by Rembrandt, where we find ourselves in the presence of something of a different order with qualities that distinguish it from all others: in such cases, the conferring of status would seem to be a forgone conclusion and marginal at best to its status as art. Perhaps, as Wittgenstein suggested in his characteristically subtle way, attempts to define "art" are asking the wrong question, and that is why pursuing it as far as Dickie does terminates in a theory that works at such a level of generality as to explain only a few extreme cases. One is left with the nagging thought that, as the eighteenth-century founders of aesthetics urged, there might really be something about certain objects that affects us in unusual and unique ways, and for want of better terms, we might call that "beauty" "sublimity," or "the picturesque."

Bibliography

Abrams, Meyer H. *The Mirror and the Lamp: Romantic Theory and Critical Theory* (Oxford: Oxford University Press, 1953).

Addison, Joseph, and Richard Steele. *The Spectator*, ed. Donald F. Bond, 5 vols. (Oxford: Clarendon Press, 1965).

Akenside, Mark. *The Pleasures of the Imagination*. In *The Poetical Works of Mark Akenside*, ed. Robin Dix (Cranbury, NJ: Associated University Presses, 1996).

Alexander, Samuel. *Beauty and Other Forms of Value* (London: Macmillan, 1933).

Alison, Archibald. *Essays on the Nature and Principles of Taste* (Dublin: Byrne, Moore, Grueber, McAllister, Jones, and White, 1790).

Andrews, Malcolm. *The Search for the Picturesque: Landscape Aesthetics and Tourism in Britain, 1760–1800* (Stanford, CA: Stanford University Press, 1989).

Ariosto, Lodovico. *Orlando Furioso: Translated from the Italian of Lodovico Ariosto; with notes by John Hoole*, 2nd ed., 5 vols. (London: George Nicol, 1785 [1783]).

Orlando Furioso, trans. William Stewart Rose (London: J. Murray, 1823–31).

Aristotle. *Poetics*. In *The Complete Works of Aristotle*, ed. Jonathan Barnes, vol. 2 (Princeton, NJ: Princeton University Press, 1984).

Arnheim, Rudolf. *Art and Visual Perception: A Psychology of the Creative Eye, The New Version* (Berkeley: University of California Press, 1974 [1954]).

Arnold, Matthew. *On Translating Homer: Three Lectures Given at Oxford* (London: Longman, Green, Longman, and Roberts, 1861).

"The Function of Criticism at the Present Time." In *Essays in Criticism* (London: Macmillan and Co., 1865), 1–41.

Ashfield, Andrew, and Peter de Bolla, eds. *The Sublime: A Reader in Eighteenth-Century Aesthetic Theory* (Cambridge: Cambridge University Press, 1996).

Atwood, Sara. *Ruskin's Educational Ideals* (Farnham, UK: Ashgate, 2011).

Austen, Jane. *Mansfield Park*, ed. John Wiltshire (Cambridge: Cambridge University Press, 2005 [1814]).

Northanger Abbey, ed. Barbara M. Benedict and Deirdre Le Faye (Cambridge: Cambridge University Press, 2006 [1817]).

Pride and Prejudice, ed. Pat Rogers (Cambridge: Cambridge University Press, 2006 [1813]).

Bacon, Francis. *Bacon's Essays*, ed. W. Aldis Wright (London: Macmillan, 1881 [1625]).

Baumgarten, Alexander Gottlieb. *Reflections on Poetry: Alexander Gottlieb Baumgarten's Meditationes philosophicae de nonnullis ad poema pertinentibus*, trans. Karl Aschenbrenner and William B. Holther (Berkeley: University of California Press, 1954 [1735]).

Aesthetica/Ästhetik, Latin text edited with facing German translation by Dagmar Mirbach, 2 vols. (Hamburg: Felix Meiner Verlag, 2007 [1750/1758]).

Beardsley, Monroe. *Aesthetics: Problems in the Philosophy of Criticism* (New York: Harcourt Brace, 1958).

Beattie, James. *Dissertations: Moral and Critical* (London: W. Strahan and T. Cadell; Edinburgh: W. Creech, 1783).

Bell, Clive. *Art* (London: Chatto and Windus, 1914).

Blackburn, Simon. "Hume on the Mezzanine Level." *Hume Studies* 19, 2 (1993): 273–88.

Blake, William. "Annotations to the Works of Sir Joshua Reynolds." In *The Complete Poetry and Prose of William Blake*, ed. David V. Erdman (Garden City, NY: Anchor/Doubleday, 1982), 635–62.

Bosanquet, Bernard. *Three Lectures on Aesthetic* (London: Macmillan, 1915).

Bradley, John L. *An Introduction to Ruskin* (Boston: Houghton Mifflin, 1971).

Bridgwater, Patrick. *Nietzsche in Anglosaxony: A Study of Nietzsche's Impact on English and American Literature* (Leicester, UK: Leicester University Press, 1972).

Bromwich, David. *Hazlitt: The Mind of a Critic* (New Haven, CT: Yale University Press, 1999 [1983]).

Brugger, Peter. "One Hundred Years of an Ambiguous Figure: Happy Birthday, Duck/Rabbit!" *Perceptual and Motor Skills* 89 (1999): 973–7.

Bullough, Edward. "Psychical Distance." *British Journal of Psychology* 5 (1912): 87–117.

Burke, Edmund. *A Philosophical Enquiry into the Sublime and Beautiful*, ed. James T. Boulton (London: Routledge and Kegan Paul, 1958 [1757]).

Carey, Daniel. *Locke, Shaftesbury, and Hutcheson: Contesting Diversity in the Enlightenment and Beyond* (Cambridge: Cambridge University Press, 2006).

Carritt, E. F. *The Theory of Beauty*, 5th ed. (London: Methuen, 1949 [1914]).

Cavell, Stanley. "Aesthetic Problems of Modern Aesthetics." In *Philosophy in America*, ed. Max Black (Ithaca, NY: Cornell University Press, 1965), 74–97. Reprinted in Stanley Cavell, *Must We Mean What We Say? A Book of Essays* (Cambridge: Cambridge University Press, 2002 [1969]), 1–43.

Cioffi, Frank. "Aesthetic Explanation and Aesthetic Perplexity." In *Essays on Wittgenstein in Honour of G. H. von Wright, Acta Philosophica Fennica* 28 (1976): 417–49.

Cohen, Ted. "The Possibility of Art: Remarks on a Proposal by Dickie." *Philosophical Review* 82, 1 (1973): 69–82.

Coleridge, Samuel Taylor. *The Collected Works of Samuel Taylor Coleridge*, 16 vols. (Princeton, NJ: Princeton University Press, 1983).

Collected Letters of Samuel Taylor Coleridge, ed. Earl Leslie Griggs, 6 vols. (Oxford: Clarendon Press, 2000 [c. 1956–71]).

Collingwood, W. G. *The Life of John Ruskin*, 2 vols. (Boston: Houghton Mifflin, 1893).

Collingwood, R. G. *Outlines of a Philosophy of Art* (Oxford: Clarendon Press, 1925).

The Principles of Art (Oxford: Clarendon Press, 1938).

The Idea of History (Oxford: Clarendon Press, 1946).

Collinson, Diané. "Ethics and Aesthetics Are One." *British Journal of Aesthetics* 23, 3 (1985): 266–72.

Cooper, Anthony Ashley, third Earl of Shaftesbury. *Characteristicks of Men, Manners, Opinions, Times*, 3 vols. (Indianapolis, IN: Liberty Fund, 2001 [1711]).

Costelloe, Timothy M. "Hume's Aesthetics: The Literature and Directions for Future Research." *Hume Studies* 30, 1 (2004): 87–126.

Aesthetics and Morals in the Philosophy of David Hume (New York: Routledge, 2007).

ed. *The Sublime: From Antiquity to the Present* (Cambridge: Cambridge University Press, 2012).

Croce, Benedetto. *L'Estetica come scienza dell'espressione e linguistica generale* (Florence, Italy: Sandron, 1902); *Aesthetic: As science of expression and general linguistic*, rev. ed., trans. Douglas Ainslie (London: Macmillan, 1922 [1909]).

"On the Aesthetics of John Dewey." *Journal of Aesthetics and Art Criticism* 6, 1 (1948): 203–7.

"Dewey's Aesthetics and Theory of Knowledge." *Journal of Aesthetics and Art Criticism* 11, 1 (1952): 1–6.

Dadlez, Eva. "Ideal Presence: How Kames Solved the Problem of Fiction and Emotion." *Journal of Scottish Philosophy* 9, 1 (2011): 115–33.

Damrosch, Leopold. *Fictions of Reality in the Age of Johnson and Hume* (Madison: University of Wisconsin Press, 1989).

Daniels, Stephen. *Humphry Repton: Landscape Gardening and the Geography of Georgian England* (New Haven, CT: Yale University Press, 1999).

Danto, Arthur C. "The Artworld." *Journal of Philosophy* 61, 19 (1964): 571–84.

The Transfiguration of the Commonplace: A Philosophy of Art (Cambridge, MA: Harvard University Press, 1981).

de Bolla, Peter. *The Education of the Eye: Painting, Landscape, and Architecture in Eighteenth Century Britain* (Stanford, CA: Stanford University Press, 2003).

Denis, Maurice. "Définition du néo-traditionnisme." *Art et critique* (August 1890); reprinted in *Théories, 1890–1910*, 4th ed. (Paris: Rouart et Watelin, 1920), 1–13.

Denis, Maurice, and Roger Fry. "Cézanne-I by Maurice Denis, translated by Roger E. Fry." *The Burlington Magazine for Connoisseurs* 16, 82 (January 1910): 207–19.

Dennis, John. *The Critical Works of John Dennis*, ed. Edward Niles Hooker, 2 vols. (Baltimore, MD: Johns Hopkins University Press, 1939).

Descartes, René. *Meditations on First Philosophy*. In *The Philosophical Writings of Descartes*, vol. 2, trans. John Cottingham, Robert Stoothoff, and Dugald Murdoch (Cambridge: Cambridge University Press, 1984).

Dewey, John. "A Comment on the Foregoing Criticisms." *Journal of Aesthetics and Art Criticism* 6, 1 (1948): 207–9.

Art as Experience. In *John Dewey: The Later Works, Volume 10: 1934*, ed. Jo Ann Boydston and Harriet Furst Simon (Carbondale: Southern Illinois University Press, 1987 [1934]).

Dickie, George. *Art and the Aesthetic: An Institutional Analysis* (Ithaca, NY: Cornell University Press, 1974).

The Century of Taste: The Philosophical Odyssey of Taste in the Eighteenth Century (Oxford: Oxford University Press, 1996).

Duff, William. *An Essay on Original Genius; and its Various Modes of Exertion in Philosophy and the Fine Arts, particularly in Poetry* (London: Edward and Charles Dilly, 1767).

Eagleton, Terry. *The Ideology of the Aesthetic* (Oxford: Blackwell, 1990).

Eliot, T. S. "The Place of Pater." In *The Eighteen-Eighties: Essays by Fellows of the Royal Society of Literature*, ed. Walter de la Mare (Cambridge: Cambridge University Press, 1930), 93–106.

Elton, William, ed. *Aesthetics and Language* (Oxford: Basil Blackwell, 1959).

Engell, James. *The Creative Imagination: Enlightenment to Romanticism* (Cambridge, MA: Harvard University Press, 1981).

Ferry, Luc. *Homo Aestheticus: The Invention of Taste in the Democratic Age*, trans. Robert de Loaizia (Chicago: Chicago University Press, 1993).

Freud, Sigmund. *Introductory Lectures on Psychoanalysis. The Standard Edition* (delivered 1915–17), trans. James Strachey (New York: W. W. Norton, 1989 [1966]).

Fry, Roger E. *Vision and Design* (London: Chatto and Windus, 1920).

Transformations: Critical and Speculative Essays on Art (London: Chatto and Windus, 1926).

Reflections on British Paintings (New York: Macmillan, 1934).

Last Lectures by Roger Fry (New York: MacMillan, 1939).

"A New Theory of Art," *The Nation*, March 7, 1914, 937–9. Reprinted in *A Roger Fry Reader*, ed. Christopher Reed (Chicago: University of Chicago Press, 1996), 158–62.

Furniss, Tom. *Edmund Burke's Aesthetic Ideology. Language, Gender, and Political Economy in Revolution* (Cambridge: Cambridge University Press, 1993).

Gautier, Pierre Jules Théophile. *Mademoiselle de Maupin*, trans. Helen Constantine (London: Penguin, 2005 [1835]).

Gerard, Alexander. *An Essay on Genius* (London: W. Strahan; Edinburgh: W. Creech, 1774).

An Essay on Taste with Three Dissertations on the same subject by Mr. De Voltaire, Mr. D' Alembert, F.R.S. Mr. Montesquieu (London: A. Millar; Edinburgh: A. Kincaid and J. Bell, 1759).

An Essay on Taste. To Which Is Now Added Part Fourth, Of the Standard of Taste; with Observations Concerning the Imitative Nature of Poetry, 3rd ed. (Edinburgh: J. Bell and W. Creech; London: T. Cadell, 1780).

An Essay on Genius, ed. Bernhard Fabian (Munich: Wilhelm Fink, 1966 [1774]).

Gilpin, William. *Observations, relative chiefly to Picturesque Beauty, Made in the Year 1772, On Several Parts of England; particularly the Mountains, and Lakes of Cumberland, and Westmoreland*, 2 vols. (London: R. Blamire, 1786).

Remarks on Forest Scenery, and Other Woodland Views, Relative Chiefly to Picturesque Beauty Illustrated by the Scenes of New Forest in Hampshire. In Three Books (London: R. Blamire, 1791).

Three Essays: On Picturesque Beauty; On Picturesque Travel; and On Sketching Landscape to which is added a poem, On Landscape Painting, 2nd ed. (London: R. Blamire, 1794 [1792]).

Observations on the River Wye and Several Part of South Wales Relative Chiefly to Picturesque Beauty made in the summer of the year 1770, 5ᵗʰ ed. (London: A. Strahan, 1800 [1782]).

Gracyk, Theodore A. "Rethinking Hume's Standard of Taste." *Journal of Aesthetics and Art Criticism* 52, 2 (1994): 169–82.

Grant, J. "On Reading Collingwood's Principles of Art." *Journal of Aesthetics and Art Criticism* 46, 2 (1987): 239–48.

Grayling, A. C. *The Quarrel of the Age: The Life and Times of William Hazlitt* (London: Weidenfeld and Nicolson, 2000).

Guyer, Paul. "The Origins of Modern Aesthetics: 1711–35." In *The Blackwell Guide to Aesthetics*, ed. Peter Kivy (Oxford: Blackwell, 2004). Reprinted in Paul Guyer, *Values of Beauty. Historical Essays in Aesthetics* (Cambridge: Cambridge University Press, 2005), 3–36.

A History of Aesthetics, 3 vols. (Cambridge: Cambridge University Press, forthcoming).

Halberstadt, William H. "A Problem in Hume's Aesthetics." *Journal of Aesthetics and Art Criticism* 30, 2 (1971): 209–11.

Halliwell, Stephen. *The Poetics of Aristotle: Translation and Commentary* (Chapel Hill: University of North Carolina Press, 1985).

Hamilton, Sir William. *Works of Sir William Hamilton*, ed. H. L. Mansel and John Veitch, 7 vols. (London: William Blackwood and Sons, 1828–1960).

Hammermeister, Kai. *The German Aesthetic Tradition* (Cambridge: Cambridge University Press, 2002).

Hampshire, Stuart. "Logic and Appreciation." In *Aesthetics and Language*, ed. William Elton (Oxford: Blackwell, 1959), 161–9.

Hanslick, Eduard. *Vom Musikalisch-Schönen: Ein Beitrag zur Revision der Ästhetik in der Tonkunst* (Leipzig, Germany: Weigel, 1854).

Hazlitt, William. *The Complete Works of William Hazlitt*, ed. P. P. Howe, 21 vols. (London: J. M. Dent, 1930–4).

The Selected Writings of William Hazlitt, ed. Duncan Wu, 9 vols. (London: Pickering and Chatto, 1998).

Heath, Malcolm. "Longinus and the Ancient Sublime." In *The Sublime: From Antiquity to the Present*, ed. Timothy M. Costelloe (Cambridge: Cambridge University Press, 2012), 11–23.

Hilton, Tim. *John Ruskin: The Early Years* (New Haven, CT: Yale University Press, 1985).
John Ruskin: The Later Years (New Haven, CT: Yale University Press, 2000).

Hinde, Thomas. *Capability Brown: The Story of a Master Gardener* (New York: W. W. Norton, 1986).

Hipple, Walter J., Jr. *The Beautiful, The Sublime, & The Picturesque in Eighteenth-Century British Aesthetic Theory* (Carbondale: Southern Illinois University Press, 1957).

Hogarth, William. *The Analysis of Beauty*, ed. Ronald Paulson (New Haven, CT: Yale University Press, 1997 [1753]).

Home, Henry, Lord Kames. *Elements of Criticism. The Sixth Edition. With the Author's Last Corrections and Additions*, 2 vols. (Indianapolis, IN: Liberty Fund, 2005 [1785; 1st ed. 1762]).

Essays on the Principles of Morality and Natural Religion. Corrected and Improved, in a Third Edition. Several Essays Added Concerning the Proof of a Deity (Indianapolis, IN: Liberty Fund, 2005 [1779; 1ˢᵗ ed. 1751]).

Howe, Sarah. "General and Invariable Ideas of Nature: Joshua Reynolds and His Critical Descendants." *English* 54 (2005): 1–13.

Hume, David. *The Letters of David Hume*, ed. J. Y. T. Greig, 2 vols. (Oxford: Clarendon Press, 1932).

The History of England, From the Invasion of Julius Caesar to the Revolution in 1688, with the author's last corrections and improvements, 6 vols. (Indianapolis, IN: Liberty Fund, 1983).

Essays: Moral, Political, and Literary, ed. Eugene F. Miller (Indianapolis, IN: Liberty Fund, 1985).

An Enquiry Concerning the Principles of Morals, ed. Tom Beauchamp (Oxford: Oxford University Press, 1998).

A Treatise of Human Nature, ed. David Fate Norton and Mary Norton (Oxford: Oxford University Press, 2001).

Hussey, Christopher. *The Picturesque: Studies in a Point of View* (London: Putnam, 1927; repr., Hamden, CT: Archon, 1967).

Hutcheson, Francis. *An Essay on the Nature and Conduct of the Passions and Affections, with Illustrations on the Moral Sense* (Indianapolis, IN: Liberty Fund, 2002 [1728]).

An Inquiry into the Original of Our Ideas of Beauty and Virtue in Two Treatises, 2nd ed. (Indianapolis, IN: Liberty Fund, 2004 [1726]).

Janik, Alan, and Stephen Toulmin. *Wittgenstein's Vienna* (New York: Simon and Shuster, 1973).

Jastrow, Joseph. "The Mind's Eye." *Popular Science Monthly* 54 (1899): 299–312.

Fact and Fable in Psychology (Boston: Houghton Mifflin, 1900).

Johnson, Samuel. *The Yale Edition of the Works of Samuel Johnson*, 18 vols. (New Haven, CT: Yale University Press, 1958–2004).

Jones, Peter. *Hume's Sentiments* (Edinburgh: Edinburgh University Press, 1982).

Kant, Immanuel. *Kants gesammelte Schriften*. Königlichen Preussischen (later Deutschen) Akademie der Wissenschaften, 29 vols. (Berlin: Reimer [later de Gruyter], 1900–).

Critique of Pure Reason, trans. Paul Guyer and Alan E. Wood (Cambridge: Cambridge University Press, 1999 [1781/1787]).

Critique of the Power of Judgment, ed. Paul Guyer, trans. Paul Guyer and Eric Matthews (Cambridge: Cambridge University Press, 2000 [1790]).

Notes and Fragments, ed. Paul Guyer, trans. Curtis Bowman, Paul Guyer, and Frederick Rauscher (Cambridge: Cambridge University Press, 2005).

Keats, John. *The Poetical and Other Writings of John Keats*, ed. H. Buxton Forman, rev. Maurice Buxton Forman, 8 vols. (New York: Phaeton Press, 1970).

Kelley, Theresa M. *Wordsworth's Revisionary Aesthetics* (Cambridge: Cambridge University Press, 1988).

Kemp, Gary. "The Croce-Collingwood Theory as Theory." *Journal of Aesthetics and Art Criticism* 61, 2 (2003): 171–93.

Kennick, W. E. "Does Traditional Aesthetics Rest on a Mistake?" *Mind, New Series* 67, 267 (1958): 317–34.

Kivy, Peter. "Hume's Neighbour's Wife: An Essay on the Evolution of Hume's Aesthetics." *British Journal of Aesthetics* 23, 3 (1983): 195–208.

The Seventh Sense: Francis Hutcheson and Eighteenth Century British Aesthetics, 2nd ed. (Oxford: Oxford University Press, 2003 [1976]).

"Introduction: Aesthetics Today." In *The Blackwell Guide to Aesthetics*, ed. Peter Kivy (Oxford: Blackwell, 2004), 1–11.

"Reid's Philosophy of Art." In *The Cambridge Companion to Thomas Reid*, ed. Terence Cuneo and René van Woudenberg (Cambridge: Cambridge University Press, 2004), 267–88.

Knight, Richard Payne. *The Landscape, a Didactic Poem in Three Books. Addressed to Uvedale Price, Esq.*, 2nd ed. (London: G. Nicol, 1795 [1794]).

An Analytic Inquiry into the Principles of Taste, 4th ed. (London: T. Payne and J. White, 1808 [1805]).

Kristeller, P. O. "The Modern System of the Arts: A Study in the History of Aesthetics Part I." *Journal of the History of Ideas* 12, 4 (1951): 496–527.

"The Modern System of the Arts: A Study in the History of Aesthetics Part II." *Journal of the History of Ideas* 13, 1 (1952): 17–46.

Kuhn, Thomas. *The Structure of Scientific Revolutions* (Chicago: University of Chicago Press, 1962).

Landow, George P. *The Aesthetic and Critical Theories of John Ruskin* (Princeton, NJ: Princeton University Press, 1971).

Le Trésor de la Lange français informatisé, atilf.atilf.fr/tlf.htm, accessed July 12, 2011.

Lock, F. P. *Edmund Burke. Volume I, 1730–1784* (Oxford: Clarendon Press, 1998).

Locke, John. *An Essay Concerning Human Understanding*, ed. Peter H. Nidditch (Oxford: Oxford University Press, 1975 [1689]).

Mandelbaum, Maurice. "Family Resemblances and Generalization Concerning the Arts." *American Philosophical Quarterly* 2, 3 (1965): 219–28.

Mandeville, Bernard. *The Fable of the Bees or Private Vices, Publick Benefits*, 2 vols. (Indianapolis, IN: Liberty Fund, 1988 [1732; 1st ed. 1714]).

Margolis, Joseph. "Mr. Weitz and the Definition of Art." *Philosophical Studies* 9, 5/6 (1958): 88–95.

"Recent Work in Aesthetics." *American Philosophical Quarterly* 2, 3 (1965): 182–92.

Mill, John Stuart. *Collected Works of John Stuart Mill*, ed. John M. Robson and Jack Stillinger, 33 vols. (Toronto: University of Toronto Press, 1963–).

Monk, Ray. *Wittgenstein: The Duty of Genius* (London: Free Press, 1990).

Monk, Samuel H. *The Sublime: A Study of Critical Theories in XVIII-Century England* (New York: Modern Language Association of American, 1935).

Monsman, Gerald. *Walter Pater* (Boston: Twayne, 1977).

Moore, G. E. "Wittgenstein's Lectures in 1930–33." *Mind* 64, 253 (1955): 1–27. Reprinted in G. E. Moore, *Philosophical Papers* (London: Allen and Unwin, 1959), 252–324.

Principia Ethica, rev. ed. (Cambridge: Cambridge University Press, 1993 [1903]).

Mossner, Ernest Campbell. *The Life of David Hume*, 2nd ed. (Oxford: Clarendon Press, 1980 [1954]).

Motion, Andrew. *Keats* (London: Faber and Faber, 1999).

Nabholtz, John R. "Wordsworth's *Guide to the Lakes* and the Picturesque Tradition." *Modern Philology* 61, 4 (1964): 288–97.

Neill, Alex. "Yanal and Others on Hume and Tragedy." *Journal of Aesthetics and Art Criticism* 50, 2 (1992): 151–4.

"Hume's Singular Phænomenon." *British Journal of Aesthetics* 39, 2 (1999): 112–25.

Owen, W. J. B. *Wordsworth as Critic* (Toronto: University of Toronto Press, 1969).

Oxford English Dictionary (www.oed.com).

Packer, Mark. "Dissolving the Paradox of Tragedy." *Journal of Aesthetics and Art Criticism* 47, 3 (1989): 211–19.

Passmore, J. A. "The Dreariness of Aesthetics." In *Aesthetics and Language*, ed. William Elton (Oxford: Blackwell, 1959), 36–55.

Pater, Walter. *The Renaissance; Studies in Art and Poetry. The 1893 Text*, ed. Donald L. Hill (Berkeley: University of California Press, 1980).

The Renaissance; Studies in Art and Poetry, ed. Adam Philips (Oxford: Oxford University Press, 1986 [1873]).

Paton, Margaret. "Hume on Tragedy." *British Journal of Aesthetics* 13, 2 (1973): 121–32.

Peacock, Tomas Love. *The Works of Thomas Love Peacock*, ed. H. F. B. Brett-Smith and C. E. Jones, 10 vols. (London: Constable and Co., 1934).

Pepper, Stephen. "Some Questions on Dewey's Aesthetics." In *The Philosophy of John Dewey*, ed. Paul A. Schilpp (Evanston, IL: Northwestern University Press, 1939), 369–90.

Plato. *The Republic*. In *Plato. Complete Works*, ed. John M. Cooper (Indianapolis, IN: Hackett, 1997).

Plotinus. "On Beauty." In *Plotinus*, Greek text with English translation by A. H. Armstrong, 7 vols. (Cambridge, MA: Harvard University Press; Loeb Classical Library, 1968–88), vol. 1.

Pope, Alexander. *The Twickenham Edition of the Poems of Alexander Pope*, 6 vols. (London: Methuen, 1951).

Potkay, Adam. *The Story of Joy: From the Bible to Late Romanticism* (Cambridge: Cambridge University Press, 2007).

"Wordsworth and the Ethics of Things." *Proceedings of the Modern Language Association* 123, 2 (2008): 390–404.

Wordsworth's Ethics (Baltimore, MD: Johns Hopkins University Press, 2012).

Price, Sir Uvedale. *Essays on the Picturesque, As Compared with the Sublime and the Beautiful, and On the Use of Studying Pictures, for the Purpose of Improving Real Landscape*, 3 vols. (London: J. Mawman, 1810).

Quine, Willard Van Orman. "Main Trends in Recent Philosophy: Two Dogmas of Empiricism." *Philosophical Review* 60, 1 (1951): 20–43. Reprinted in *From a Logical Point of View: Nine Logical-Philosophical Essays*, 2nd rev. ed. (Cambridge, MA: Harvard University Press, 1980 [1953]), 20–46.

Railton, Peter. "Aesthetic Value, Moral Value, and Naturalism." In *Aesthetics and Ethics: Essays at the Intersection*, ed. Jerrold Levinson (Cambridge: Cambridge University Press, 1998), 59–105.

Raphael, D. D. "The Impartial Spectator." In *Essays on Adam Smith*, ed. Andrew S. Skinner and Thomas Wilson (Oxford: Clarendon Press, 1975), 83–99.

Reid, Louis Arnauld. *A Study of Aesthetics* (Allen and Unwin, 1931).

Reid,Thomas. *Thomas Reid's Lectures on the Fine Arts:Transcribed from the Original Manuscript with an Introduction and Notes*,ed.Peter Kivy (The Hague:Martinus Nijhoff, 1973).

Essays on the Intellectual Powers of Man (University Park: Pennsylvania State University Press, 2002 [1785]).

Repton, Humphrey. *Works: The Landscape Gardening and Landscape Architecture of the Late Humphry Repton, Esq. Being His Entire Works on These Subjects. A New Edition: with an Historical and Scientific Introduction, a Systematic Analysis, a Biographical Notice, Notes, and a Copious Alphabetical Index. By J. C. Loudon, F.L.S.* (London: Longman & Co.; Edinburgh: A. & C. Black, 1840).

Reynolds, Joshua. *Discourses on Art*, ed. Robert R. Wark (New Haven, CT: Yale University Press, 1997 [1797]).

Discourses Delivered to the Students of the Royal Academy by Sir Joshua Reynolds, with Introduction and Notes by Roger Fry (London: Seely, 1905).

Richards, A. I. *Principles of Criticism* (London: Routledge and Kegan Paul, 1924).

Rosenberg, John D. *The Darkening Glass: A Portrait of Ruskin's Genius* (New York: Columbia University Press, 1986).

Ruskin, John. *The Complete Works of John Ruskin (Library Edition)*, ed. E. T. Cook and Alexander Wedderburn, 39 vols. (London: George Allen, 1903–12).

Ryan, Vanessa L. "The Physiological Sublime: Burke's Critique of Reason." *Journal of the History of Ideas* 62, 2 (2001): 265–79.

Santayana, George. *Persons and Places: Fragments of Autobiography*, ed. William G. Holzberger and Herman J. Saatkamp Jr., *The Critical Edition of the Works of George Santayana*, vol. 1 (Cambridge, MA: MIT Press, 1986 [1944–53]).

The Sense of Beauty: Being the Outlines of Aesthetic Theory, ed. William G. Holzberger and Herman J. Saatkamp Jr., *The Critical Edition of the Works of George Santayana*, vol. 2 (Cambridge, MA: MIT Press, 1988 [1896]).

Schneider, Elisabeth. *The Aesthetics of William Hazlitt: A Study of the Philosophical Basis of His Criticism* (New York: Octagon, 1969 [1933]).

Schopenhauer, Arthur. *The World as Will and Representation*, trans. E. F. J. Payne, 2 vols. (New York: Dover, 1969).

Sclafani, Richard. "'Art' and Artifactuality." *Southwestern Journal of Philosophy* 1 (1970): 103–10.

Shapiro, Gary. "The Pragmatic Picturesque: The Philosophy of Central Park." In *Gardening: Philosophy for Everyone. Cultivating Wisdom*, ed. Dan O'Brien (Oxford: Wiley-Blackwell, 2010), 148–60.

Sharpe, William. *A Dissertation upon Genius: or, an attempt to shew, that the several instances of distinction, and degrees of superiority in the human genius are not fundamentally, the result of nature, but the effect of acquisition* (London: C. Bathurst, 1755).

Shearer, Edna Astor. "Wordsworth and Coleridge Marginalia in a Copy of Richard Payne Knight's *Analytic Inquiry into the Principles of Taste*." *Huntington Library Quarterly* 1, 1 (1937): 63–99.

Shelley, James. "Hume's Double Standard of Taste." *Journal of Aesthetics and Art Criticism* 52, 4 (1994): 437–45.

"Rule and Verdict." *Journal of Aesthetics and Art Criticism* 53, 3 (1995): 319–20.

"British Aesthetics in the Eighteenth Century." *Stanford Encyclopedia of Philosophy*, ed. Edward N. Zalta, plato.stanford.edu/entries/aesthetics-18th-british (2006; rev. 2010), accessed May 15, 2007.

Shelley, Percy Bysshe. *The Complete Works of Percey Bysshe Shelley*, ed. Roger Ingpen and Walter E. Peck, 10 vols. (New York: Gordain Press, 1965).

Shelley's Poetry and Prose, ed. Donald H. Reiman and Neil Fraistat, 2nd ed. (New York: W. W. Norton, 2002).

Shiner, Roger. "Wittgenstein on the Beautiful, the Good and the Tremendous." *British Journal of Aesthetics* 14, 3 (1974): 258–71.

Sibley, Frank. *Approach to Aesthetics*, ed. John Benson, Betty Redfern, and Jeremy Roxbee Cox (Oxford: Clarendon Press, 2001).

Sidney, Sir Philip. *An Apologie for Poetry* (London: Henry Olney, 1595).

The Defense of Poesie (London: William Ponsonby, 1595).

Miscellaneous Prose of Sir Philip Sidney, ed. Katherine Duncan-Jones and Jan Van Dorsten (Oxford: Clarendon Press, 1973).

Simoni, Frederic S. "Benedetto Croce: A Case of International Misunderstanding." *Journal of Aesthetics and Art Criticism* 11, 1 (1952): 7–14.

Smith, Adam. *Essays on Philosophical Subjects, with Dugald Stewart's "Account of Adam Smith,"* ed. W. P. D. Wightman, J. C. Bryce, and I. S. Ross (Oxford: Oxford University Press, 1980). In *The Glasgow Edition of the Works and Correspondence of Adam Smith*, ed. J. C. Bryce et al., 7 vols. (Oxford: Oxford University Press, 1978–), vol. 3.

Spalding, Frances. *Roger Fry: Art and Life* (Berkeley: University of California Press, 1980).

Spenser, Herbert. *The Works of Edmund Spenser*, ed. Edwin Greenlaw et al., 9 vols. (Baltimore, MD: Johns Hopkins University Press).

Spinoza, Baruch. *Ethics*. In *The Complete Works*, ed. Michael L. Morgan, trans. Samuel Shirley (Indianapolis, IN: Hackett, 2002).

Stevenson, Charles L. "On 'What is a Poem?'" *Philosophical Review* 66, 3 (1957): 329–62.

Stewart, Dugald. *The Collected Works of Dugald Stewart*, ed. Sir William Hamilton, 11 vols. (Edinburgh: Thomas Constable and Co.; London: Hamilton, Adams and Co., 1854–60).

Stolnitz, Jerome. "Notes on Analytic Philosophy and Aesthetics." *British Journal of Aesthetics* 3, 3 (1961): 210–22.

"On the Origins of 'Aesthetic Disinterestedness.'" *Journal of Aesthetics and Art Criticism* 20, 2 (1961): 131–44.

"On the Significance of Lord Shaftesbury in Modern Aesthetic Theory." *Philosophical Quarterly* 11, 43 (1961): 97–113.

Swinburne, Algemon Charles. *William Blake: A Critical Essay* (London: John Camden Hotten, 1868).

Taylor, William. *British Synonyms Discriminated* (London: W. Pople, 1813).

Temple, Sir William. *The Works of Sir William Temple, to which is prefixed, the life and character of the author, considerably enlarged*, 4 vols. (London: F. C. and J. Rivington, 1814 [1754]).

Templeman, William D. "Sir Joshua Reynolds on the Picturesque." *Modern Language Notes* 47, 7 (1932): 446–8.

Townsend, Dabney. *Hume's Aesthetic Theory: Taste and Sentiment* (New York: Routledge, 2001).

Turner, Roger. *Capability Brown and the Eighteenth-Century English Landscape* (New York: Rizzoli International, 1985).

Valihora, Karen. *Austen's Oughts: Judgment after Locke and Shaftesbury* (Newark: University of Delaware Press, 2010).

Vico, Giambattista. *The "New Science" of Giambattista Vico, unabridged translation of the third edition (1744) with the addition of "Practic of the New Science,"* trans. Thomas Goddard Bergin and Max Harold Fisch (Ithaca, NY: Cornell University Press, 1984).

Walton, Kendall. "Categories of Art." *Philosophical Review* 79, 3 (1970): 334–67.

Wardle, R. M. *Hazlitt* (Lincoln: University of Nebraska Press, 1971).

Weiskel, Thomas. *The Romantic Sublime: Studies in the Structure and Psychology of Transcendence* (Baltimore, MD: Johns Hopkins University Press, 1976).

Weitz, Morris. "The Role of Theory in Aesthetics." *Journal of Aesthetics and Art Criticism* 15, 1 (1956): 27–35.

Wieand, Jeffrey. "Hume's Two Standards of Taste." *Philosophical Quarterly* 34, 135 (1984): 129–42.

"Hume's True Judges." *Journal of Aesthetics and Art Criticism* 53 (1995): 318–19.

Whichcote, Benjamin. *Select Sermons*, with a preface by Anthony Ashley Cooper, Third Earl of Shaftesbury (London: Awnsham and Churchill, 1698).

Whistler, James McNeill. *Whistler on Art: Selected Letters and Writings 1849–1903 of James McNeill Whistler*, ed. Nigel Thorp (Manchester, UK: Carcanet Press, 1994).

Wilde, Oscar. *Oscar Wilde: The Major Works*, ed. Isobel Murray (Oxford: Oxford University Press, 1989).

Willis, Peter. *Charles Bridgeman and the English Landscape Garden* (Newcastle-upon-Tyne, UK: Elysium Press, 2002 [1977]).

Wittgenstein, Ludwig. *Philosophische Untersuchungen/Philosophical Investigations*, trans. G. E. M. Anscombe (Oxford: Basil Blackwell, 1958 [1953]).

The Blue and Brown Books. Preliminary Studies for the Philosophical Investigations (Oxford: Basil Blackwell, 1958).

Notebooks 1914–1916, trans. G. E. M. Anscombe (Oxford: Basil Blackwell, 1961).

"A Lecture on Ethics." *Philosophical Review* 74, 1 (1965): 3–12.

Lectures and Conversations on Aesthetics, Psychology, and Religious Belief. Compiled from Notes taken by Yorrick Smythies, Rush Rhees and James Taylor, ed. Cyril Barrett (Berkeley: University of Californian Press, 1967).

Tractatus Logico-Philosophicus, trans. D. F. Pears and B. F. McGuinness (London: Routledge and Kegan Paul, 1974 [1961]).

Vermischte Bermerkungen/Culture and Value, ed. G. H. von Wright, trans. Peter Winch (Oxford: Basil Blackwell, 1977).

Woodring, Carl. "The New Sublimity in 'Tintern Abbey.'" In *The Evidence of the Imagination: Studies in the Interaction between Life and Art in English Romantic Literature*, ed. Donald H. Reiman, Michael C. Jaye, and Betty T. Bennett (New York: New York University Press, 1978). Reprinted in *Critical Essays on William Wordsworth*, ed. George H. Gilpin (Boston: G. K. Hall, 1990), 11–23.

Wordsworth, William. *The Prose Works of William Wordsworth*, ed. W. J. B. Owen and Jane Washington Smyser, 3 vols. (Oxford: Clarendon Press, 1974).

William Wordsworth, The Prelude 1799, 1805, 1850, ed. Jonathan Wordsworth, M. H. Abrams, and Stephen Hill (New York: W. W. Norton, 1979).

Bibliography

Descriptive Sketches, by William Wordsworth, ed. Eric Birdsall and Paul M. Zall (Ithaca, NY: Cornell University Press, 1984).

Lyrical Ballads and Other Poems, 1797–1800 by William Wordsworth, ed. James A. Butler and Karen Green (Ithaca, NY: Cornell University Press, 1993).

The Excursion, by William Wordsworth, ed. Sally Bushell, James A. Butler, Michael C. Jaye, and David García (Ithaca, NY: Cornell University Press, 2001), 157.

Lyrical Ballads, 2nd ed., ed. Michael Mason (London: Longman, 2007 [1992]).

Wordsworth, William, and Dorothy Wordsworth. *The Letters of William and Dorothy Wordsworth*, 8 vols. (Oxford: Clarendon Press, 1967–93).

Worrall, David. "Agrarians against the Picturesque: Ultra-radicalism and the Revolutionary Politics of Land." In *The Politics of the Picturesque*, ed. Stephen Copley and Peter Garside (Cambridge: Cambridge University Press, 1994), 240–60.

Wu, Duncan. *Wordsworth's Reading 1770–1799* (Cambridge: Cambridge University Press, 1993).

Wordsworth's Reading 1800–1815 (Cambridge: Cambridge University Press, 1993).

William Hazlitt: The First Modern Man (Oxford: Oxford University Press, 2008).

Young, Edward. *Conjectures on Original Composition. In a Letter to the Author of Sir Charles Grandison* (London: A Millar, and R. and J. Dodsley, 1759).

Zangwill, Nick. "Hume, Taste, and Teleology." *Philosophical Papers* 23, 1 (1994): 1–18.

Zerilli, Linda M. G. *Signifying Woman. Culture and Chaos in Rousseau, Burke, and Mill* (Ithaca, NY: Cornell University Press, 1994).

Ziff, Paul. "The Task of Defining a Work of Art." *Philosophical Review* 62, 1 (1953): 58–78.

Zuckert, Rachel. "The Associative Sublime: Gerard, Kames, Alison, and Stewart." In *The Sublime: From Antiquity to the Present*, ed. Timothy M. Costelloe (Cambridge: Cambridge University Press, 2012), 64–76.

Index